Research Advances in Intelligent Computing

Since the invention of computers and other similar machines, scientists and researchers have been trying very hard to enhance their capabilities to perform various tasks. As a consequence, the capabilities of computers are growing exponentially day by day in terms of diverse working domains, versatile jobs, processing speed, and reduced size. Now, we are in the race to make these machines as intelligent as human beings. Artificial intelligence (AI) came up as a way of making a computer or computer software think in a similar manner to the way that intelligent humans think. AI is inspired by the study of human brain, including how humans think, learn, decide, and act while trying to solve a problem. The outcomes of this study are the basis of developing intelligent software and systems or intelligent computing (IC). An IC system has the capabilities of reasoning, learning, problem-solving, perception, and linguistic intelligence. IC systems consist of AI techniques as well as other emerging techniques that make a system intelligent. The use of IC has been seen in almost every sub-domain of computer science such as networking, software engineering, gaming, natural language processing, computer vision, image processing, data science, robotics, expert systems, and security. Nowadays, the use of IC can also be seen for solving various complex problems in diverse domains such as for predicting disease in medical science, predicting land fertility or crop productivity in agricultural science, predicting market growth in economics, and weather forecasting. For all these reasons, this book presents the advances in AI techniques, under the umbrella of IC. In this context, the book includes recent research that has been done in the areas of machine learning, neural networks, deep learning, evolutionary algorithms, genetic algorithms, swarm intelligence, fuzzy systems, and so on. This book discusses the theoretical, algorithmic, simulation, and implementation-based recent research advancements related to IC.

Research Advances in Intelligent Computing

Edited by
Anshul Verma, Pradeepika Verma,
Kiran Kumar Pattanaik, and Lalit Garg

CRC Press
Taylor & Francis Group
Boca Raton London New York

CRC Press is an imprint of the
Taylor & Francis Group, an **informa** business

First edition published 2023
by CRC Press
6000 Broken Sound Parkway NW, Suite 300, Boca Raton, FL 33487-2742

and by CRC Press
4 Park Square, Milton Park, Abingdon, Oxon, OX14 4RN

CRC Press is an imprint of Taylor & Francis Group, LLC

Library of Congress Cataloging–in–Publication Data

Names: Verma, Anshul, editor. | Verma, Pradeepika, editor. | Pattanaik, Kiran Kumar, editor. | Garg, Lalit, 1977- editor.
Title: Research advances in intelligent computing / edited by Anshul Verma, Pradeepika Verma, Kiran Kumar Pattanaik and Lalit Garg.
Description: First edition. | Boca Raton, FL : CRC Press, 2023. | Includes bibliographical references and index.
Identifiers: LCCN 2022039584 (print) | LCCN 2022039585 (ebook) | ISBN 9781032340517 (hbk) | ISBN 9781032340524 (pbk) | ISBN 9781003320340 (ebk)
Subjects: LCSH: Expert systems (Computer science) | Artificial intelligence.
Classification: LCC QA76.76.E95 R474 2023 (print) | LCC QA76.76.E95 (ebook) | DDC 006.3/3--dc23/eng/20221114
LC record available at https://lccn.loc.gov/2022039584
LC ebook record available at https://lccn.loc.gov/2022039585

ISBN: 978-1-032-34051-7 (hbk)
ISBN: 978-1-032-34052-4 (pbk)
ISBN: 978-1-003-32034-0 (ebk)

DOI: 10.1201/9781003320340

Typeset in Times
by KnowledgeWorks Global Ltd.

Contents

Preface

OVERVIEW AND GOALS

Since the invention of computers or machines, scientists and researchers are trying very hard to enhance their capabilities to perform various tasks. As a consequence, the capabilities of computers are growing exponentially day by day in terms of diverse working domains, versatile jobs, processing speed, and reduced size. Now, we are in the race to make computers or machines as intelligent as human beings. Artificial intelligence (AI) came up as a way of making a computer or computer software think in the similar manner the intelligent humans think. AI is inspired by the study of human brain like how humans think, learn, decide, and act while trying to solve a problem. The outcomes of this study are the basis of developing intelligent software and systems or intelligent computing (IC). An IC system has the capability of reasoning, learning, problem-solving, perception, and linguistic intelligence. The IC systems consist of AI techniques as well as other emerging techniques that make a system intelligent. The use of IC has been seen in almost every sub-domain of computer science such as networking, software engineering, gaming, natural language processing, computer vision, image processing, data science, robotics, expert systems, and security. Nowadays, the use of IC can also be seen for solving various complex problems in diverse domains such as for predicting disease in medical science, predicting land fertility or crop productivity in agriculture science, predicting market growth in economics, and weather forecasting. For all these reasons, this book presents the advances in AI techniques, under the umbrella of IC. In this context, the book includes the recent research works that have been done in the areas of machine learning, neural networks, deep learning, evolutionary algorithms, genetic algorithms, swarm intelligence, fuzzy systems, and so on. This book provides theoretical, algorithmic, simulation, and implementation-based recent research advancements related to the IC.

TARGET AUDIENCE

This book will be beneficial for academicians, researchers, developers, engineers, and practitioners working in or interested in the research trends and applications of artificial and computational intelligence. This book is expected to serve as a reference book for developers and engineers working in the intelligent computing domain and for a graduate/postgraduate course in Computer Science and Engineering/Information Technology.

Acknowledgments

We are extremely thankful to the authors of the 23 chapters of this book, who have worked very hard to bring this unique resource forward for helping students, researchers, and community practitioners. We feel that it is important to mention that as the individual chapters of this book are written by different authors, the responsibility of the contents of each of the chapters lies with the concerned authors.

We would like to thank Randi Cohen, Publisher – Computer Science and IT, and Gabriella Williams, Editor, who worked with us on the project from the beginning, for their professionalism. We also thank all the team members of the publisher who tirelessly worked with us and helped us in the publication process.

This book is a part of the research work funded by "Seed Grant to Faculty Members under IoE Scheme (under Dev. Scheme No. 6031)" awarded to Anshul Verma at Banaras Hindu University, Varanasi, India.

About the Editors

Dr. Anshul Verma received M.Tech. and Ph.D. degrees in Computer Science and Engineering from ABV-Indian Institute of Information Technology and Management, Gwalior, India. He has done post-doctorate work with the Indian Institute of Technology Kharagpur, India. Currently, he is serving as an Assistant Professor in the Department of Computer Science, Institute of Science, Banaras Hindu University, Varanasi, India. He has also served as a faculty member in Computer Science and Engineering Department at Motilal Nehru National Institute of Technology (MNNIT) Allahabad and National Institute of Technology (NIT) Jamshedpur, India. His research interests include IoT, mobile ad hoc networks, distributed systems, formal verification, and mobile computing. He is serving as an Editor of the Journal of Scientific Research of the Banaras Hindu University.

Dr. Pradeepika Verma received her Ph.D. degree in Computer Science and Engineering from the Indian Institute of Technology (ISM) Dhanbad, India. She has received her M.Tech. in Computer Science and Engineering from Banasthali University, Rajasthan, India. Currently, she is working as a Faculty Fellow in the Technical Innovation Hub at the Indian Institute of Technology, Patna, India. She has worked as a Post-Doctoral Fellow in Department of Computer Science and Engineering at the Indian Institute of Technology (BHU), Varanasi, India. She has also worked as an Assistant Professor in the Department of Computer Science and Engineering at Pranveer Singh Institute of Technology, Kanpur, India, and as a Faculty member in the Department of Computer Application at Institute of Engineering and Technology, Lucknow, India. Her current research interests include IoT, natural language processing, optimisation approaches, and information retrieval.

Dr. Kiran Kumar Pattanaik holds a bachelor's degree in Electrical and Electronics Engineering followed by a master's and a doctorate in Computer Science and Engineering. He is presently working as an Associate Professor at ABV-Indian Institute of Information Technology and Management, Gwalior, India. He is enthusiastic about exploring various engineering application domains involving distributed and mobile computing, wireless sensor network protocols, IoT, and edge computing. His wireless sensor network laboratory is equipped with necessary computing facilities (simulation and hardware) and is accessible round the clock for learning. The competitive ambiance of the laboratory is instrumental for a number of public-funded research projects and high-impact-factor research publications. He is a Senior Member of IEEE, and is a reviewer for several leading journals in the areas of communication and networking.

Dr. Lalit Garg is a Senior Lecturer in Computer Information Systems at the University of Malta, Msida, Malta. He is also an honorary lecturer at the University of Liverpool, UK. He has also worked as a researcher at the Nanyang Technological University, Singapore, and the University of Ulster, UK. He is skilled in solving complex problems using machine learning and data analytics, especially from the medicine and healthcare domain. He has published over 90 technical papers in refereed high-impact journals, conferences, and books, and has over 600 citations to his publications; some of his articles have been awarded best paper awards. He has delivered more than 20 keynote speeches in different countries, organised/chaired/co-chaired 16 international conferences, and contributed as a technical committee member or a reviewer of several high-impact journals and reputed conferences. He has been awarded research studentship in Healthcare Modelling to carry out his Ph.D. research studies in the faculty of computing and engineering at the University of Ulster, UK. He completed his postgraduate in Information Technology from ABV-IIITM, Gwalior, India, and his first degree in Electronics and Communication Engineering from Barkatullah University, Bhopal, India. He has also consulted numerous public and private organisations for their information system implementations.

Contributors

Thondepu Adilakshmi
Vasavi College of Engineering
Hyderabad, India

Abhishek Aryan
Delhi Technological University
New Delhi, India

Srikanth Bethu
Gokaraju Rangaraju Institute of
    Engineering and Technology
Hyderabad, India

Sreejita Chakrabarti
Jadavpur University
Kolkata, West Bengal, India

Shanmuganathan Chandrasekaran
SRM Institute of Science and
    Technology
Ramapuram, Chennai, India

Prateek Chaturvedi
Vellore Institute of Technology
Vellore, Tamil Nadu, India

Shubham Chaudhari
Lalbhai Dalpatbhai College of
    Engineering
Ahmedabad, Gujarat, India

Bhavana Chaurasia
Banaras Hindu University
Varanasi, India

Gunjan Chhabra
Department of Computer Science
    Engineering
Graphic Era Hill University
Dehradun, Uttarakhand, India

Vishwa Dave
Lalbhai Dalpatbhai College of
    Engineering
Ahmedabad, Gujarat, India

Gerard Deepak
National Institute of Technology
Tiruchirappalli, Tamil Nadu, India

Amisha Gangwar
University of Allahabad
Prayagraj, India

Sarah Gawde
Sardar Patel Institute of
    Technology
Andheri, India

Anish Sudhir Ghiya
Vellore Institute of Technology
Vellore, Tamil Nadu, India

Arnab Ghoral
Sardar Patel Institute of Technology
Andheri, India

Nagaraja Benageri Gnaneshwara
Vidyavardhaka College of
    Engineering
Mysuru, Karnataka, India

Anurag Goel
Delhi Technological University
New Delhi, India

Thimmaraja Yadava Gopalappa
Nitte Meenakshi Institute of
    Technology
Bengaluru, Karnataka, India

Meenal Jain
Banasthali Vidyapith
Banasthali, Rajasthan, India

Haradagere Siddaramaiah Jayanna
Siddaganga Institute of Technology
Tumkur, Karnataka, India

Kavitha Kattigehalli Jayanna
GM Institute of Technology
Davangere, India

Dhananjay Kalbande
Sardar Patel Institute of Technology
Andheri, India

Subhash Kamble
University Visvesvaraya College of
    Engineering
Bengaluru, India

Vignesh Kashyap
Delhi Technological University
New Delhi, India

N. V. S. K. Vijayalakshmi Kathari
Annamalai University
Chidambaram, India

Sharmila Banu Kather
Vellore Institute of Technology
Vellore, Tamil Nadu, India

Arpit Khare
University of Allahabad
Prayagraj, India

Ajai Kumar
Center for Development of Advanced
    Computing
Pune, India

Sanjeev Kumar
Department of CSE
United University
Prayagraj, India

Machikuri Santoshi Kumari
Gokaraju Rangaraju Institute of
    Engineering and Technology
Hyderabad, India

Srinivasulu Gari Bhargavi Latha
Gokaraju Rangaraju
    Institute of Engineering
    and Technology
Hyderabad, India

Suresh Mamidisetti
Anurag University
Hyderabad, India

Department of Computer Science
    Engineering
Government Polytechnic
Hyderabad, India

Jeet Mishra
Sardar Patel Institute of
    Technology
Andheri, India

**Dhilsath Fathima Mohamed
Mohideen**
Vel Tech Rangarajan Dr. Sagunthala
    R&D Institute of Science and
    Technology
Chennai, India

Arulmozhi Varman Murugesan
SASTRA Deemed
    University
Thanjavur, Tamil Nadu, India

Sahilkumar Narola
Lalbhai Dalpatbhai College of
    Engineering
Ahmedabad, Gujarat, India

Nigam Patel
Government Engineering
    College
Gandhinagar, Gujarat, India

Pradnya Patill
K. J. Somaiya Institute of
  Engineering and Information
  Technology
Mumbai, India

Arish Pitchai
Quantum Machine Learning Lab
BosonQ Psi Pvt. Ltd.
Bhilai, India

Shiv Prakash
University of Allahabad
Prayagraj, India

Manju Bhaskara Panicker Radha
Amrita School of Arts and
  Sciences
Amritapuri Campus, India

Venugopal Kuppanna Rajuk
Bangalore University
Bengaluru, India

Sivakumar Ramachandran
College of Engineering
Trivandrum, India

Hariharan Ramamoorthy
Vel Tech Rangarajan Dr. Sagunthala
  R&D Institute of Science and
  Technology
Chennai, India

Mohan Ramasundaram
National Institute of Technology
Tiruchirappalli, India

Aditi Ranganath
Vellore Institute of Technology
Vellore, Tamil Nadu, India

Parvathy Rema
Amrita School of Arts and Sciences
Amritapuri Campus
Vallikavu, India

Yogesh R. Shahare
Mahatma Gandhi Mission's
  College of Engineering and
  Technology
Navi Mumbai, Maharashtra, India

Priestly B. Shan
Chandigarh University
Ajitgarh, Punjab, India

Rashmi Sharma
Shree Vaishnav Vidyapeeth
  Vishwavidyalaya
Shri Vaishnav Institute of Computer
  Application
Indore, Madhya Pradesh, India

Kibballi Aditya Shastry
Nitte Meenakshi Institute of
  Technology
Bengaluru, India

Arunalatha Jakkanahally Siddegowda
University Visvesvaraya College of
  Engineering
Bengaluru, India

Mukund Pratap Singh
School of Computer Science
  Engineering and Technology
Bennett University
Greater Noida, India

School of Computer Science
  Engineering and Technology
Bennett University
Greater Noida, India

Pawan Kumar Singh
Jadavpur University
Second Campus
Kolkata, West Bengal, India

Shashi Pal Singh
Center for Development of Advanced
  Computing
Pune, India

Sudhakar Singh
University of Allahabad
Prayagraj, India

Saravanan Madderi Sivalingam
Saveetha Institute of Medical and
    Technical Sciences
Chennai, India

Menaka Suman
SRM Institute of Science and Technology
Chennai, India

Mallannagari Sunitha
Vasavi College of Engineering
Hyderabad, India

Chintha Sravani
Gokaraju Rangaraju Institute of
    Engineering and Technology
Hyderabad, India

Balakrushna Tripathy
Vellore Institute of Technology
Vellore, Tamil Nadu, India

Anshul Verma
Banaras Hindu University
Varanasi, India

Pradeepika Verma
Indian Institute of Technology
Patna, India

Vaibhav Vijay
Vellore Institute of Technology
Vellore, Tamil Nadu, India

Yashfeen Zehra
Vasavi College of Engineering
Hyderabad, India

1 RNN-Based Machine Translation for Indian Languages

Shashi Pal Singh and Ajai Kumar
AAIG, Center for Development of Advanced Computing
Pune, India

Meenal Jain
Banasthali Vidyapith, Banasthali
Rajasthan, India

CONTENTS

1.1   INTRODUCTION

Machine translation (MT) is the technique used to translate between human languages. Many techniques and algorithms have been applied to develop MT models [1]. Deep learning (DL) is evolving and can be applied to train the MT model. DL allows

DOI: 10.1201/9781003320340-1

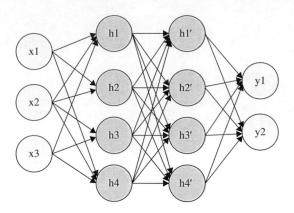

FIGURE 1.1   A deep neural network.

a machine to think and decide like a human brain with the given input and uses a neural network having two or more hidden layers consisting of several hidden units capable of capturing the semantics and syntax of the sentences in the form of features (see Figure 1.1).

Neural network-based sequence-to-sequence-based knowledge has shown remarkable success for various implementations of natural language processing (NLP) tasks, counting MT [2]. Sequence-to-sequence models essentially consist of an encoder which transforms the input sentence into a fixed-size depiction used by the decoder to produce the translation. Feedforward neural networks are unable to retain the information fed to them for a long period of time, so RNN is used to store the information using the internal memory, which is used to predict/forecast the next word in the given sentence or segment.

1.2   LITERATURE SURVEY

1.2.1   RNN Encoder-Decoder

The sequence-to-sequence networks, because of its long-distance dependency retention properties, is preferably implemented using gated RNN units (GRUs) (long short-term memory [LSTM]) and GRU, rather than vanilla RNN units.

1.2.2   Architecture

A sequence-to-sequence-based model consists of an encoder and a decoder, where the encoder maps the entire meaning of the source sentence into a final context vector, also called a thought vector [3]. This thought vector is then taken as input by the decoder, which unfolds this context vector into the target sentence (see Figure 1.2).

1.2.3   Encoder

The encoder consists of hidden layers which are made of hidden units. Using vanilla RNN may lead to vanishing gradient problem which can be solved by using LSTM

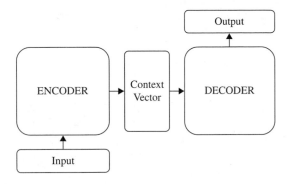

FIGURE 1.2   Architecture.

units which can retain information that has longer time spans. LSTM can retain memory using gates, namely input, forget and output gates. This increases complexity as well as the results, so a simpler version was introduced which is GRU, having only two gates, which effectively decreases the complexity of the network and increases the quality of translations.

1.2.4   DECODER

The decoder has a structure similar to the encoder, but instead of taking an empty vector as its input hidden state at time step 0, it takes the final hidden state produced by the encoder. And decoding is stopped once a special end-of-sentence marker is encountered.

1.2.5   BIDIRECTIONAL ENCODER

After feeding a sentence into a conventional RNN, the encoder learns from the previous time steps, but when the context is too far for the network to remember, the network starts to lose its efficiency.

He said, "Apple is a fruit". Here, just by looking at what he said, it is ambiguous for the machine to understand whether the Apple mentioned here is a fruit or the company Apple. So if we reverse the sentence and feed it to the encoder while keeping the target sentence intact, then this long-term dependency can be removed. But it's observed that this increases efficiency noticeably only in the case of languages following the grammatical structure subject-verb-object:

He (subject) eats (verb) Mango (object).

But in differently grammatically structured language like Hindi, it is as follows:

मैंने आम खा लिया

Here मैंने is the subject, आम is the object and खा लिया is the verb.

So, for these languages, the original encoder structure is retained, and so we feed original sentence and, in parallel, its reverse is fed to the encoder. This introduces

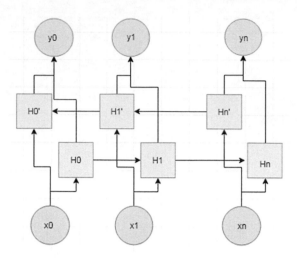

FIGURE 1.3   Bidirectional encoder.

many short-term dependencies, as during decoding, the decoder is able to see the words from both sides and understand the context more properly (see Figure 1.3).

1.2.6   ATTENTION

First introduced by Bahdanau et al. (2014) [4], the attention mechanism dynamically creates a context vector for each hidden state in the decoder, instead of summarizing the whole context in a single fixed-sized vector. The context vector c_t is represented as the prejudiced sum of the source hidden states. Bahdanau attention requires the source to be encoded with a bidirectional RNN.

1.2.7   WORD EMBEDDINGS

For the model to learn and understand the words, they need to be represented in some numerical form. An easy way to do this can be to create a vector of the size of the vocabulary where we assign each entry as zero except the position where the word is present in the vocabulary, which is assigned as one.

આ વધારે સમય સુધી રહે.

Suppose this is a sentence and the vocabulary is {આ, વધારે, સમય, સુધી, રહે,.}. Then the one hot encoding vectors for these words will be {[1, 0, 0, 0, 0, 0], [0, 1, 0, 0, 0, 0], [0, 0, 1, 0, 0, 0], [0, 0, 0, 1, 0, 0], [0, 0, 0, 0, 1, 0], [0, 0, 0, 0, 0, 1]}.

This way, each word has a unique representation, but with increasing vocabulary, the vectors become sparser and higher dimensional. To obtain better dense low-dimensional embeddings, we have several methods. Word2vec, first introduced by Mikolov et al. (2013) [5], indirectly trains a model to obtain word embeddings. In the

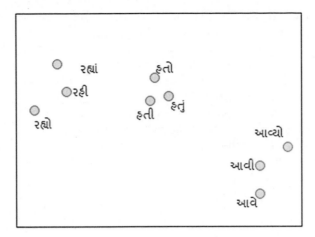

FIGURE 1.4   Similar Gujarati words are closer than their counterparts.

continuous bag-of-words (CBOW) method, the model is trained to predict the word given the neighbors as the input, whereas in the skip-gram method, the model has to predict the possible neighboring words given the word. To implement both the methods, it is important to create a context window which holds the adjacent words which convey the context of the word (see Figure 1.4).

These vectors can either be initialized randomly or be prepared by the pre-trained vectors. Vectors can be trained either using word2vec or GloVe format. Word2vec, by Mikolov et al. (2013) [5], uses CBOW method to predict word from the neighboring word or predicting neighbors from the words (skip-gram). During this process, word embeddings are created. GloVe (Pennington et al.) is a global log-bilinear model used for unsupervised learning of word representations where a co-occurrence matrix is created, which is used to train the model to obtain the word embeddings. The relationship between the words can be calculated using the co-occurrence score between the various words. These ratios encode the relationships between the words.

1.3   METHODOLOGY

1.3.1   ABOUT

There are many MT models developed for translation between foreign languages like English, French and German, but only a few models deal with Indian languages. We are developing a neural MT model to obtain translation between Indian languages like Hindi and Gujarati.

1.3.2   TOOLS USED

For implementing the machine learning algorithms and learning MT models, there are many application programming interfaces (APIs) available like OpenNMT, PyTorch, Tensorflow, Theano and Keras. We use the Tensorflow API as it is a widely used open-source software library which is written to serve the machine learning purposes like training neural networks and calculating regression and correlation. Its flexible architecture allows us to utilize graphics processing units (GPUs) and tensor processing units (TPUs) to accelerate our training. To optimize and understand the training, Tensorflow has provided us with a suite of visualization tools called TensorBoard. This can be activated during the training to see the plotted graphs between the metrics passed and also to visualize the images created.

These models can be developed in various languages like C, Python, R and Java. Python, an OOP-based, high-level, interpreted programming language, is used to develop our model. It is very popular for implementing machine learning techniques as it provides us with many special libraries like SciPy, NumPy and Pandas to process the data and is great at linear algebra.

GPUs are used for accelerating the process of training the model and Tensorflow provides drivers for NVidia GPUs, so we used Tesla and K40 to train our model.

1.3.3   SYSTEM ARCHITECTURE

The source sentence x is tokenized $(x_1, ..., x_n)$ and sent to the encoder where the tokens are converted to the word embeddings referring to the lookup table. Then for each time step, the LSTM takes in two inputs, the previous hidden state h_t and the current input x_t, to produce the current hidden state h_t, with the initial vector being a zero vector [6]. For bidirectional RNN, the final hidden state of the current output is calculated by concatenating the two hidden states h_t and h_t' obtained (see Figure 1.5).

Here, the input sentence is represented by $\{x_1, x_2, x_3\}$ and the corresponding word embeddings are represented by $\{w_1, w_2, w_3\}$. The word embeddings are fed into the network and hidden states are produced $\{e_1, e_2, e_3\}$ and the final context vector c_t is obtained. The final context vector is fed to the decoder as a hidden state and a special start of sentence w_{sos} marker is fed as an input to obtain the current hidden state [7].

$$h_0 = \text{LSTM}\left(e, w_{sos}\right)$$

We apply a function g to obtain a vector s_0 which has the same size as the embedding vector. This vector is normalized to give a vector in terms of probabilities, which will be the measure of how probable the word is in the vocabulary. We then find out the word with the highest probability using the greedy way of searching.

$$s_0 = g\left(h_0\right)$$

$$p_0 = \text{softmax}\left(s_0\right)$$

$$i_0 = \text{argmax}\left(p_0\right).$$

Now to output the second word, we take input as the first word of the target sentence and the previous hidden state, and when the end-of-sentence marker is encountered, the previous hidden state is considered to be the final hidden state of the encoder and is treated as the context vector c_t. This vector c_t is fed to the decoder at every

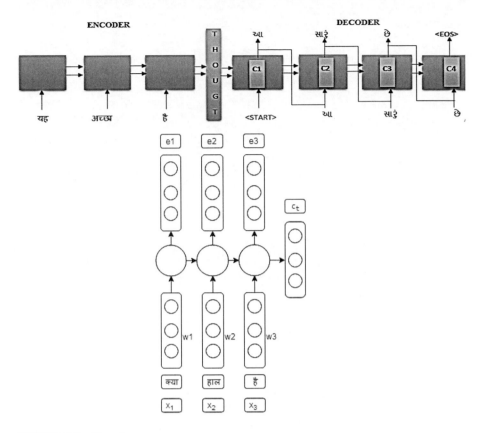

FIGURE 1.5 Encoder.

time step along with the previous output y_{t-1}, where the set of outputs is $\{y_0, \ldots, y_n\}$. Initially, y_{t-1} is not present, so instead the start of sentence marker is considered to be the input for the decoder. The fixed-sized vector c_t, however, changes in case of attention. Instead, for each time step, a fresh context vector is generated which holds the relevant context using attention. This context vector c_t at any time step can be calculated as $c_t = \sum \alpha_t' * e_t$, where α_t' is the softmax attention calculated for a time step and e_t is the corresponding encoder unit (see Figure 1.6).

$$\alpha_t = f(h_{t-1}, e_t)$$

$$\alpha_{t'} = \text{softmax}(\alpha_t)$$

where α_t is a score calculated for each hidden state e_t in the encoder over which softmax is applied to give α_t'.

After p_t vector is generated, we have to choose an output from the vocabulary matrix using the probability distribution $E \sim P(E \mid F)$. We can choose to maximize our chances of getting the best result by finding the word that best fits the probability distribution. However, this method searches only the words which best fit

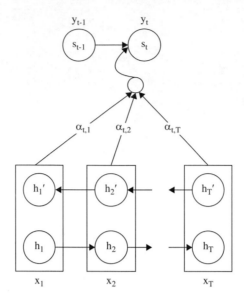

FIGURE 1.6   Bidirectional encoder with attention.

the distribution but not the best translation. So, to solve this problem, we use beam search. It is similar to greedy search but instead of considering a single best output, it searches for n best hypotheses at each time step where n is the beam width provided.

Till now, it had been the forward pass of the model, for the backward pass, we calculate and clip the gradients by the global norm. Also for optimization, a particular optimizer is chosen. Stochastic gradient descent updates the function for every sentence, which is speedy but makes the function fluctuate too much, so Adam optimizer updates the function for every batch.

1.3.4   INFERENCE

The source sentence is encoded in the same way as training, to obtain the encoder states for initializing the decoder. The decoding process starts as soon as it receives the starting symbol <s>. For each time step, the logits of the previous time step, hidden state if precious step and the current hidden state is used to calculate the logits. This process terminates when the end-of-sentence marker is encountered.

1.3.5   SEARCHING ALGORITHMS

When decoder takes in the hidden states form the encoder, it generates samples using the probability distribution $E \sim P(E \mid F)$. This can be done using the following ways:

Random sampling involves producing an output that is randomly selected from the distribution $P(E \mid F)$.

Greedy search instead produces the best output that maximizes the probability distribution chosen. For optimization of best first search, at each time step, n best

TABLE 1.1
Automatic Evaluation of BLEU and NIST

BLEU	25.226
NIST	35.260

outputs are chosen, considering the previous n best outputs, where n is the beam width in the beam search, also known as the best n search. It deals with expanding the most promising output at each time step.

1.3.6 CALCULATING LOSS

Log entropy [8] or cross-entropy is used to calculate the performance, the value of which is between 0 and 1 base on probability. The cross-entropy loss reduces as the predicted probability converges to the actual label. As predicted probability reaches 1, log loss decreases very slowly. Our aim is to train to maximize the likelihood for the model to predict the correct translation.

1.4 TEST AND EVALUATION

We used a bilingual corpus of 280000 sentences for training the model and 2000 sentences for evaluation during training. We removed the extra punctuations like parenthesis when feeding the sentence into the training [9]. We also provided the model with Hindi vocabulary of around 480000 words and Gujarati vocabulary of about the same words. We have used automatic evaluation of BiLingual Evaluation Understudy (BLEU) and National Institute of Standards and Technology (NIST), the scores were based on the statistics as observed in the above test cases, and the graphs obtained were for the Hindi to Gujarati language pair (see Tables 1.1 and 1.2 and Figure 1.7).

TABLE 1.2
Hyperparameters Used

Hyperparameters	Value
Number of units	128
Number of layers	6
Dropout	0.2
Unit type	LSTM
Batch size	500
Encoder type	bi
Search type	Beam search
Optimizer	Adam optimizer
Type of attention	Bahdanau attention
Number of training steps	10000

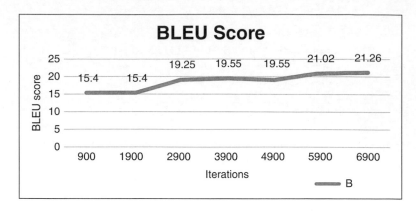

FIGURE 1.7   BLEU score.

1.5   CONCLUSION AND FUTURE WORK

The traditional sequence-to-sequence encodes the source sentence into a fixed-sized vector which captures the meaning and is used for translation. But this gets problematic for translating long sentences so bidirectional RNN architecture and attention mechanisms are introduced. The attention frees the model from the burden of capturing the whole meaning into a single vector; instead, for each time step, a new context vector is created. By feeding the sentence same and reverse helps reduce the long-range dependencies and generate more short-range dependencies. We describe in detail the techniques used, the hyperparameters used for training our model and the basis for finding the accuracy. The sequence-to-sequence model for MT can be used for training the model for other Indian language pairs. These recent advancements will find applications in tourism, for internet service providers for cross-language communication between the customers.

REFERENCES

1. Yonghui Wu, Mike Schuster, Zhifeng Chen, Quoc V Le, Mohammad Norouzi, Wolfgang Macherey, Maxim Krikun, Yuan Cao, Qin Gao, Klaus Macherey, et al. (2016). Google's neural machine translation system: Bridging the gap between human and machine translation. arXiv preprint arXiv:1609.08144.
2. Shashi Singh, Ajai Kumar, Hemant Darbari, Anshika Rastogi, Shikha Jain, and Nisheeth Joshi. (2018). Building Machine Learning System with Deep Neural Network for Text Processing. 497–504. 10.1007/978-3-319-63645-0_56.
3. Shashi Singh, Hemant Darbari, Ajai Kumar, Shikha Jain, and Anu Lohan. (2019). Overview of Neural Machine Translation for English-Hindi. 1–4. 10.1109/ICICT46931. 2019.8977715.
4. Dzmitry Bahdanau, Kyunghyun Cho, and Yoshua Bengio. (2014). Neural machine translation by jointly learning to align and translate. arXiv preprint arXiv:1409.0473.
5. Tomas Mikolov, Ilya Sutskever, Kai Chen, Greg S. Corrado, and Jeffrey Dean. (2013). Distributed Representations of Words and Phrases and their Compositionality. Advances in Neural Information Processing Systems. 26, 3111–3119.

6. Zhiwei Jin, Juan Cao, Han Guo, Yongdong Zhang, and Jiebo Luo. "Multimodal Fusion with Recurrent Neural Networks for Rumor Detection on Microblogs", MM '17: Proceedings of the 25th ACM international conference on Multimedia, October 2017, 795–816, https://doi.org/10.1145/3123266.3123454.
7. Nikolaos Arvanitis, Constantinos Constantinopoulos, and Dimitrios Kosmopoulos. "Translation of Sign Language Glosses to Text Using Sequence-to-Sequence Attention Models", 2019 15th International Conference on Signal-Image Technology & Internet-Based Systems (SITIS), 2019.
8. Jason Brownlee. (2019, January 28). Loss and Loss Functions for Training Deep Learning Neural Networks. Machine Learning Mastery. 23.
9. Jean-Francois Boucicault, and Cyrille Masson. "Data Mining Query Languages", in Maimon, Oded and Rokach, Lior (editors), Data Mining and Knowledge Discovery Handbook. 2010, Springer US, 655–664, ISBN 978-0-387-09823-4, 10.1007/978-0-387-09823-4_33.

2 Dynamic Movie Ticket Price Prediction Using Machine Learning

Kibballi Aditya Shastry
Nitte Meenakshi Institute of Technology
Bengaluru, India

CONTENTS

2.1 INTRODUCTION

Machine learning (ML) can be used in almost every field nowadays in information technology (IT). Owners of theaters must adjust to shifting consumer behavior. Otherwise, businesses risk losing contact with tomorrow's big consumer groups. The younger generation's shopping and money-spending habits are evolving. However, there are some new tendencies in terms of movie viewing preferences. With cinemas closed and film releases halted due to the shutdown, theater owners are concerned that digital platforms could soon transform the collective movie-going experience, resulting in a significant drop in footfalls when the screens reopen. Finally, competition from internet movie streaming services such as Netflix is putting traditional movie theaters out of business. Dynamic pricing has always been established to be a successful income-generating technique, and it will help cinemas maximize their revenue collections. From the customer's point of view, they can also get a fair deal. Many movie theaters are concerned about the impact of competitors' strategies on their business. The equilibrium would be thrown off by new pricing techniques. Furthermore, IT systems are frequently slow to respond to the changes that dynamic pricing necessitates. Another stumbling block is the distributors' rules and restrictions. Second, exhibitors are concerned that the market will not be prepared for advanced and complex pricing changes. Nobody likes to be the first to modify their pricing approach and take a risk. The risk of damaging the company's image and reputation is deemed too great. Finally, exhibitors are concerned that cinema is a historic sector in which new concepts are not always accepted. New flexible pricing could result in a negative customer perception and, most likely, negative press [1–10].

Keeping these points in mind, our work focused on ML techniques for forecasting movie ticket prices. This was achieved by creating a website where movie tickets are reasonably priced and pricing can fluctuate, like the airline sector, drawing more people to movie theaters. The outcome was a website that would assist both providers and customers. The website has ML algorithm running at the backend that will predict the day one price of the movie based on various factors showing the popularity of the movie among the audience and then later changing the movie ticket prices dynamically based on the time stamp and number of seats available in a particular screen of a cinema hall. The three main objectives of this work were to create a functioning website to book a ticket along with payment gateway added to it; to build a model to correctly predict day one price of the movie, and dynamically changing the ticket price.

The remained of this chapter is structured as follows. Segment 2 examines the related work. Segment 3 introduces the framework and system design. The proposed work is demonstrated in Segment 4 followed by Findings and conclusion in Segments 5 and 6 correspondingly.

2.2   RELATED WORK

One of the most often used revenue management methods is dynamic pricing. It enables businesses to increase their profits by integrating their supplies with demand, adjusting to shifting demand patterns, and achieving client segmentation. Dynamic pricing is widely employed in a variety of businesses, including the airline, entertainment, hotel, and retail industries. All three of the characteristics are present in the movie industry in a dynamic ticketing market. The region attributes were utilized to construct a hybrid dynamic pricing model for cinema tickets using data clustering and regression techniques in [11]. The categories of uncertainty targeted by the authors were: consumer arrival rate uncertainty, real number of customers arriving at different times, the highest price that buyers are willing to pay for a particular movie show, and the market's current state, which reveals how well customers are reacting to it.

In [12], authors showed that pricing policies that engage in some form of active exploration produce better results than greedy strategies that focus on short-term revenue maximization. Authors found numerous elements based on the qualities of different dynamic pricing models when compared to the movie ticketing demand pricing model as they progressed with this strategy. A two-layer stochastic model to anticipate demand price was presented based on these investigations. Authors observed that a movie with a very popular actor will have a different distribution of demand vs. price than a movie with a substantially less popular star. Clustering (or grouping) the data based on many static elements of the movie, such as "rating," "actorFameRank/Rating," "YouTube Trailer Likes," "genres," and "language," is required based on this premise. The first layer of their proposed model used K-means clustering to cluster data based on features. A regression model was used in the second layer to estimate pricing depending on demand. For examining dynamic price, the second layer used four regression analysis variants: linear regression (LR), gradient boosting regressor (GBR), random forest regressor (RFR), and neural networks regression. To train the stochastic model, a web crawler was constructed in Python using the Beautiful-Soup and App Scheduler libraries to obtain publicly available data from http://in.bookmyshow.com. After filtering, data for 45 movies and a total of 188141 data points for shows were obtained. Experiments were conducted using two-layer modeling.

The goal of the work [13] was to create a dynamic pricing mechanism for the movie ticketing industry that was based on seat demand. Based on prior ticket distribution and the number of seats left for the concert, a dependent model was employed to forecast the optimal demand price. Because the mean squared error is the minimum, authors observed that the RFR, which is based on decision trees, delivered the best results. This shows that when people buy movie tickets online, they follow a specific pattern, and the effectiveness of the dynamic pricing model is determined by how well the pattern is exploited. The next phase in this work was to collect as much information regarding movie ticket attendance and demographics as feasible. Authors were able to plot alternative pricing strategies for peak vs. off-peak dates in an ideal world. The more data gathered after using a dynamic pricing structure, the better the results will be. The employment of many models, such as recurrent neural networks and Markov models, is possible. In [14], authors have extracted the car number plate characters using several ML algorithms. In [15], the authors have performed face recognition using deep residual networks. In [16], an online prediction technique centered on incremental Support Vector Machine (SVM) was designed.

2.3 FRAMEWORK AND SYSTEM DESIGN

This section contains the fundamental theoretical information regarding every developed component and feature. It paints a picture of the webapp's software implementation. Figure 2.1 shows the design of the proposed work.

Figure 2.1 shows the page when the users open the movie ticketing site that is the movie home page where the users can see all the movies that are going on and upcoming movies. They can then select the movie and get all the information about that movie such as reviews, shows of that movie. They can also watch the trailer of that movie. In the movies page, they can click on the show time to book tickets for that show and this page redirects the user to the user login page where they must provide the email id or number. Subsequently the users will be able to select the numbers of seats and can also choose the seats they want. Then they will be redirected to the payment page where

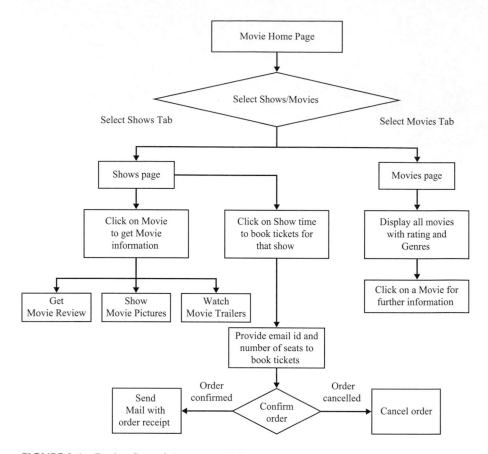

FIGURE 2.1   Design flow of the proposed ticket pricing system.

they must pay for the tickets. After that they will receive the order receipt on their email or the order cancellation message to the registered email.

In case of admin webpage, our site provides a basic user login page where normal users can login and access the features of our site like movie ticket booking and extra information about the movie. Next up, an admin access page is present where the user can login to the homepage with admin login and can access all the activity made by the user and do the approvals that are required for a basic user to do. In the admin page, admin can login and if the credentials are correct, he/she can move forward where they can select the movies they want to manage and, they will be having access to edit the movies, delete the movies, or add new movies. It also gives them access to change the timing of the movies and can edit the existing show details. And if the credentials are incorrect, then it will pop a message that login is invalid and redirect to the login page. The factors on which our complete web app will determine the price of the movie ticket are: Number of seats Available with respect to time: It is very important to change the price of ticket with respect to seat availability and the time left before the show starts; Previous days sale: Changing the price of a movie ticket with respect to previous days sale pattern, and traffic monitoring by website click: The web app click event will also play a very important role to monitor the traffic and their interest. For, e.g., a lot of customers are clicking on the movie card to check the various details of movies such as price, description but very few of them are proceeding for checkout which might mean that the customers are interested in the movie but not happy with the price of the movie or looking for a cheaper price on different websites.

2.4   PROPOSED SYSTEM

This section contains the fundamental theoretical information about each component and facet of the work that will be utilized to anticipate the movie ticket price on day one. It gives a picture of the simulation implementation and modeling, statistical analysis and calculations done. Once the day one price of the movie is predicted, it is changed dynamically based on the number of seats available for sale and considering time duration left for the movie show.

The whole procedure can be divided into two parts, training and testing. The dataset is divided to train the model and to test it. In the first part, i.e., training the training data was used to train the chosen algorithm. The results are then passed to the model. In the second part, the model is tested by predicting the value of the target variable for the test data using the results generated before, and the accuracy of the predicted target variable is evaluated. The same procedure is repeated using all algorithms under consideration, namely, ridge regression (RR), lasso (LAS), elastic net (EN), RFR, and GBR.

The dataset used for the movie price model was acquired from the "Github" repository. The dataset originally consists of 120 attributes. Attributes that were acquired from this dataset were IMDb ratings, number of ratings, genre of the movie, total runtime of the movies, and year of movie release. Some more attributes that were not present in the dataset such as YouTube likes, YouTube dislikes were added, YouTube views and price of the ticket were acquired from various sources such as from the YouTube portal and theaters nearby. The price attribute is the desired target variable, the value of which is to be predicted. It has a minimum value of Rs 75 and a maximum value of Rs 300 for a single screen movie theater. The data is split into training data and testing data. It is then trained using the algorithms RR, LAS, EN, RFR, and GBR. The accuracy of various models is evaluated, and hyper tuning is used to better fit the training data. The test data is then passed to the model and predicted data is generated. This predicted data is analyzed to find the accuracy of the model. This process represented by Figures 2.2 and 2.3 is repeated with different ML algorithms. The resulting accuracy is compared to determine the best algorithm for calculating day one price (initial price) of the movie ticket. This process is depicted in the figure using the random forest regression algorithm.

Figure 2.4 shows the detailed design of the proposed work.

The flowchart given in Figure 2.4 starts with the collection of the dataset and cleaning it. The cleaned dataset is then subject to feature selection by doing some domain research. ML algorithms predict the day 1 price of the movie ticket. The predictions are tested for accuracy. The accuracy and performance are calculated using the R-squared (R^2) score and mean squared error. Results from all models (RR, LAS,

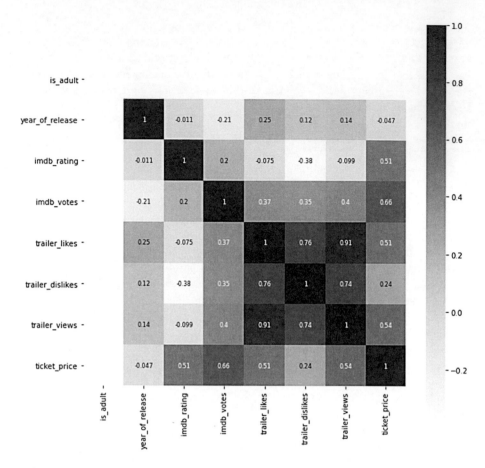

FIGURE 2.2   Heat map.

EN, RFR, and GBR) are compared to show that RFR gives the best accuracy for the given dataset. Following steps were followed in this work:

i. Dataset collection: A dataset that is applicable to the problem statement is collected from a verified source and cleaned to encourage analysis. Cleaning includes handling missing attribute values in any technique most appropriate for further processing.

ii. Feature selection: All the chosen attributes hold dissimilar degrees of significance to the problem statement. This step is to modify the dataset so that only the pivotal features on which the confirmation model depends on are selected.

iii. Exploratory data analysis: It is the process of doing preliminary studies on data to uncover patterns, detect abnormalities, test hypotheses, and verify theories using list insights and graphical representations. Figure 2.2 shows the heat map generated.

Heat map gives the correlation between the attributes of the dataset. As shown in Figure 2.2, it can be inferred how different attributes are correlated

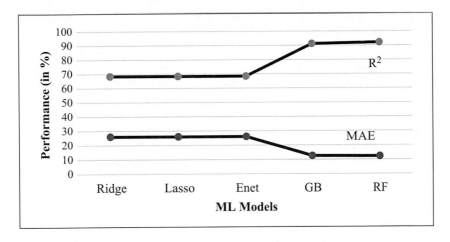

FIGURE 2.3 Comparison of ML models for ticket price prediction.

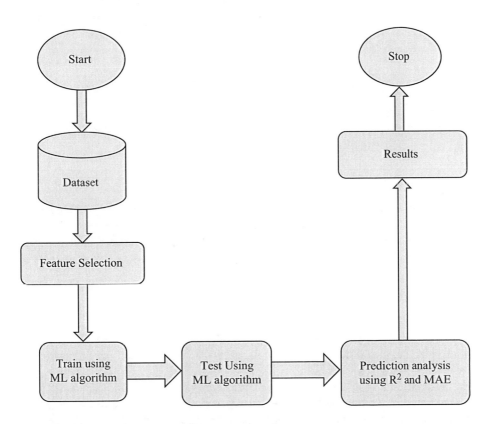

FIGURE 2.4 Detailed design of the proposed work.

to the target value, higher and positive values show that it is directly proportional and negative values depict that it is inversely proportional. The diagonal values are always 1 indicating that an attribute is highly correlated with itself. The darker shades in Figure 2.2 show that the attributes are highly correlated with each other. Lighter shades indicate less correlation between the features. For example, the attribute "imdb_votes" is negatively correlated with the attribute "is_adult" comprising a value −0.21.

iv. Training phase: A training dataset is a set of previously classified records that is used for learning to fit the attributes (e.g. IMDb rating, YouTube views) of a classifier. Most methods that are utilized to search through training data are for logical relationships and tend to overfit the data, meaning they can perceive and abuse evident relations in the training data that do not work.

v. Testing phase: A test dataset is a dataset that is independent of the training dataset; however, it follows a similar probability supply as that of the training dataset. Overfitting can happen when the ML model fits the training data well but poorly fits the test dataset. A superior fit of the training dataset rather than the test dataset typically points to overfitting. A test dataset is therefore a set of examples used uniquely to deduce the performance of a fully defined classifier.

2.4.1 RIDGE REGRESSION

By putting a penalty on the size of the coefficients, RR overcomes some of the issues with ordinary least squares. A penalized residual sum of squares is minimized using the ridge coefficients shown in Equation (2.1).

$$min_w \|X_w - y\|_2^2 + \alpha \|w\|_2^2 \tag{2.1}$$

The quantity of shrinkage is controlled by the complexity parameter $\alpha \geq 0$, the larger the value of α the greater the amount of shrinkage, and thus the coefficients become more collinearity resistant. RR, like other linear models, will take in its fit method arrays x, y and store the linear model's coefficients w in its coef member.

2.4.2 LASSO REGRESSION

The LAS is a linear model for sparse coefficient estimation. It is useful in some situations since it prefers solutions with fewer non-zero coefficients, effectively minimizing the number of features that the supplied solution is reliant on. Lasso and its variants are therefore crucial in the field of compressed sensing. It can recover the exact set of non-zero coefficients under certain conditions. It is a linear model with a regularization term added to it mathematically. The function to minimize as an objective function is given in Equation (2.2):

$$min_w \frac{1}{2n_{samples}} \|X_w - y\|_2^2 + \alpha \|w\|_1 \tag{2.2}$$

The lasso estimate solves the least-squares penalty minimization with $\alpha\|w\|1$ added, where α is a constant and $\|w\|1$ is the coefficient vector's l1-norm. To fit the coefficients, the lasso implementation uses coordinate descent as the algorithm.

2.4.3 ELASTIC NET

EN is a LR model that uses both l1 and l2-norm coefficient regularization. This combination enables for the learning of a sparse model with few non-zero weights, similar to LAS, while keeping regularization capabilities of RR model. The l1 ratio parameter is used to regulate the convex combination of l1 and l2. When there are several features that are related to one another, EN is useful. Lasso is more likely to choose one at random, but EN is more likely to choose both. Trading-off between LR and RR has the practical benefit of allowing EN to inherit some of RR rotational stability. In this situation, the objective function to reduce is given by Equation (2.3):

$$min_w \ \frac{1}{2n_{samples}} \|X_w - y\|_2^2 + \alpha\flat\|w\|_1 + \frac{\alpha(1-\flat)}{2} \|w\|_2^2 \tag{2.3}$$

2.4.4 GRADIENT BOOSTING REGRESSION

GBR supports a variety of regression loss functions, which can be provided with the loss argument; the default regression loss function is least squares ("ls"). The train and test error are plotted on the left for each iteration. The train error for each iteration is saved in the gradient boosting model's train score_ property. The staged predict method, which provides a generator that yields the predictions at each stage, can be used to get the test error at each iteration. By stopping early, plots like these can be used to find the ideal number of trees.

2.4.5 RANDOM FOREST REGRESSION

Each tree in a random forest ensemble is constructed from a sample selected with a replacement from the training set. Furthermore, the optimal split is selected from all input features or a random subset of size max features when dividing each node during tree construction. The goal of these two sources of randomness is to reduce the forest estimator's variance. Individual decision trees do, in fact, have a lot of diversity and are prone to overfitting. Forests with injected randomness produce decision trees with decoupling prediction errors. Some mistakes can be eliminated by averaging their predictions. By merging distinct trees, random forests reduce volatility, sometimes at the expense of a modest increase in bias. In practice, the variance decrease is frequently large, resulting in a superior overall model.

2.5 EXPERIMENTAL SETUP AND RESULTS

This section outlines the experimental setup and results with snapshots. The hardware used for the work was a system with processor: 64-bit 2.8 GHz 8.00 GT/s, RAM: 8 GB or higher, operating system: Windows 8 or newer, 64-bit macOS 10.13+,

TABLE 2.1

Comparison of ML Models for Movie Ticket Price Prediction

Models	R^2	MAE
RR	0.6841993898286679	26.013295130282803
LAS	0.6842018172074931	26.013198000101422
EN	0.6842220112069837	26.012389529371838
GBR	0.9125653482148449	12.549331033416916
RFR	0.9218609785932722	12.227027027027027

or Linux, including Ubuntu, RedHat, CentOS 6+, and others. The softwares used were Python 3.3, Jupyter Notebook 5.7.8, MongoDb, Node js, React, and Express.

The performance metrics R^2 and mean absolute error (MAE) were utilized to assess the ML models. R^2 is a numerical metric representing the percentage of the variation for a conditional feature that is described by an unbiased feature or attributes in a regression model. It is given by Equation (2.4) [17].

$$R^2 = 1 - \frac{Unexplained\text{-}Variation}{Total\text{-}Variation} \qquad (2.4)$$

MAE is a measure of errors among paired records conveying the similar trend [18]. It is presented in Equation (2.5) [18].

$$MAE = \frac{\Sigma_{i=1}^{r}|p_i - a_i|}{r} \qquad (2.5)$$

where "r" is the number of records, p_i is the predicted value, a_i is the actual value.

Table 2.1 shows the results of ML models for predicting the price of a movie ticket.

From Table 2.1, it can be concluded that RFR and GBR algorithms provided the best results with less MAE and a higher R^2. RFR was used for further deployment. Figure 2.3 shows the comparison of the ML models with respect to R^2 and MAE.

2.5.1 DEPLOYMENT

The model was deployed using Watson Machine Learning. International Business Machines (IBM) Watson Machine Learning, which is part of IBM Watson Studio, which lets data scientists and developers implement artificial intelligence (AI) and ML faster on IBM Cloud Pak for Data. On an open, flexible framework, AI models at scale across any cloud can be deployed. IBM user can

- Deploy models such as ML and deep learning, as well as decision optimization models.
- Dynamically retrain models with continuous learning,

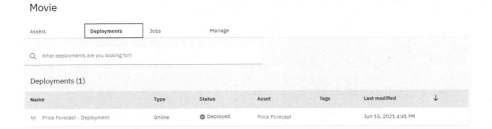

FIGURE 2.5   Deployed model for ticket price prediction.

- Deploy DevOps that can produce APIs for AI-powered applications automatically.
- Can manage and monitor all model drift, bias, and risk.
- Bring any project, including open source, third-party, and IBM tools, into production.

The deployed model is shown in Figure 2.5.

After deploying the model, the predicted price was assessed against the actual price as shown in Figure 2.6.

The last column called Scores in Figure 2.6 shows the predicted ticket price.

```
Out[87]:
```

	imdb_rating	imdb_votes	trailer_likes	trailer_dislikes	trailer_views	ticket_price	Scores
139	4.1	73	1600	241	195544	70	80.35
104	3.7	153	55000	3700	3462662	95	109.85
48	7.0	43	22000	1200	1928631	75	117.15
85	7.4	6635	59000	3100	10367956	200	201.75
40	6.1	5549	741000	81000	79085827	210	199.45
46	6.0	19	48000	1500	7293991	100	112.15
20	7.1	472	1600	38	159395	100	96.45
44	6.8	7413	756000	30000	42943241	220	210.85
94	6.8	590	30000	6800	3513804	120	135.90
80	4.1	676	251000	25000	27247399	140	143.90
62	2.2	26744	253000	68000	32271703	180	200.10
76	7.2	648	51000	791	1988384	150	136.50
108	3.8	282	21000	1300	6987629	130	109.55
2	7.9	2961	92000	2800	10970653	200	191.60
95	7.9	15499	422000	15000	31193275	250	240.05
57	5.3	1064	539000	17000	40979535	175	159.40
116	6.6	5387	408000	67000	73919127	220	205.00
103	8.3	32757	204000	9000	25765713	300	275.90

FIGURE 2.6   Performance of the deployed model.

2.6 CONCLUSION AND FUTURE SCOPE

In this work, an ML model was developed for movie-ticketing business based on various parameters that are closely related for movie ticket pricing such as trailer review, likes, dislikes on the platform where the trailer is released along with other factors. The day one price of the ticket can be predicted with the ML model built with RFR technique. For dynamically changing the price, the factors like number of seats left and time duration left for the show were considered. With our movie ticketing website, the ML model for predicting the day one is merged. The website has various features like admin login, user login, payment gateway, seat selection option. Users will get freedom of viewing the details of the movie to even book the ticket of the movie. Admin will also get various options like adding a new movie, deleting an existing movie, and updating the movie. In this work, the different ML models namely RFR, RR, LAS, EN, and GBR were evaluated using the performance metrics R^2 and MAE. The results demonstrated that RFR model performed better than others.

Lack of availability of data is the major challenge while training the model. The more the data available, the more the chances for the model to predict correctly. Dynamic pricing is the best tool for revenue generation. As the IT industry is advancing, AI, deep learning, and ML are extensively getting used. The dynamic model can be improved using AI. In future, dynamic and fair pricing of movie tickets can be a good option to increase the revenue generation of the theaters. With cinemas closed and film releases halted due to the shutdown, theater owners are concerned that digital platforms could soon transform the collective movie-going experience, resulting in a significant drop in footfalls when the screens reopen. A healthy pricing system can be a good move to save the declining movie theaters business.

REFERENCES

1. Bacham, D., Zhao, J.: Machine learning: Challenges, lessons, and opportunities in credit risk modeling. Moody's Analytics Risk Perspectives 9, 1–8 (2017).
2. Beautifulsoup. https://www.crummy.com/software/BeautifulSoup/bs4/doc/, last accessed 2020/12/02.
3. Aviv, Y., Pazgal, A.: A partially observed Markov decision process for dynamic pricing. Management Science 51, 1400–1416 (2005).
4. Caro, F., Gallien, J.: Clearance pricing optimization for a fast-fashion retailer. Operations Research 60(6), 1404–1422 (2012).
5. Carvalho, A. X., Puterman, M. L.: Learning and pricing in an internet environment with binomial demands. Journal of Revenue and Pricing Management 3(4), 320–336 (2005).
6. Erdelyi, A., Topaloglu, H.: Using decomposition methods to solve pricing problems in network revenue management. Journal of Revenue and Pricing Management 10(4), 325–343 (2011).
7. Lobo, M. S., Boyd, S.: Pricing and learning with uncertain demand. In: *INFORMS Revenue Management Conference* (2003).
8. Parlakturk, A. K.: The value of product variety when selling to strategic consumers. Manufacturing and Service Operations Management 14(3), 371–385 (2012).

9. Wang, Z., Ye, Y.: Hidden-city ticketing: The cause and impact. Transportation Science 50(1), 288–305 (2015).
10. Adrian, T., Crump, R. K., Moench, E.: Regression-based estimation of dynamic asset pricing models. Journal of Financial Economics 118(2), 211–244 (2015).
11. Bertsimas, D., Perakis, G.: Dynamic pricing: A learning approach. In: Mathematical and computational models for congestion charging, vol.101, pp. 45–79. Springer. Boston, MA (2006).
12. Chen, M., Chen, Z.-L.: Recent developments in dynamic pricing research: Multiple products, competition, and limited demand information. Production and Operations Management 24(5), 704–731 (2015).
13. Adrian, T., Crump, R. K., Moench, E.: Pricing the term structure with linear regressions. Journal of Financial Economics 110(1), 110–138 (2013).
14. Babbar, S., Kesarwani, S., Dewan, N., Shangle, K., Patel, S.: A new approach for vehicle number plate detection. In: *Eleventh International Conference on Contemporary Computing (IC3 2018)*, 2–4 August, Noida, India (2018).
15. Babbar, S., Dewan, N., Shangle, K., Kulshrestha, S., Patel, S.: Cross-age face recognition using deep residual networks In: *Fifth International Conference on Image Information Processing (ICIIP)*, 15–17 November, JUIT Waknaghat (2019).
16. Xu, D., Jiang, M., Hu, W., Li, S., Pan, R., Yen, G. G.: An online prediction approach based on incremental support vector machine for dynamic multi objective optimization. IEEE Transactions on Evolutionary Computation (2021). doi: 10.1109/TEVC.2021.3115036.
17. Chicco, D, Warrens, M. J., Jurman, G: The coefficient of determination R-squared is more informative than SMAPE, MAE, MAPE, MSE and RMSE in regression analysis evaluation. PeerJ Computer Science 7, e623 (Jul 5 2021). doi: 10.7717/peerj-cs.623. PMID: 34307865; PMCID: PMC8279135.
18. Chai, T., Draxler, R.: Root mean square error (RMSE) or mean absolute error (MAE)? Geoscientific Model Development 7 (2014). doi: 10.5194/gmdd-7-1525-2014.

3 Designing a GUI for Offline Text-Independent Writer Identification System

Sreejita Chakrabarti and Pawan Kumar Singh
Department of Information Technology, Jadavpur University
Kolkata, West Bengal, India

CONTENTS

3.1 INTRODUCTION

3.1.1 MOTIVATION

Since most electronic devices contain a digital surface which can accept a pen-based input, this advances the interactions between humans and computers. Handwriting is an important tool to be able to label humans uniquely. It is an important biometric which is similar in importance to retina and iris scans, face recognition and

DOI: 10.1201/9781003320340-3

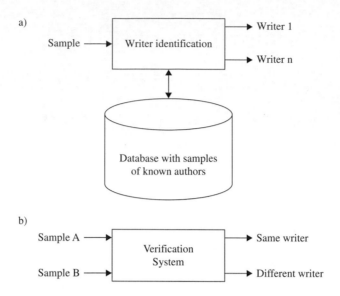

FIGURE 3.1 Schematic block diagram representing: (a) writer identification and (b) writer verification system.

fingerprints [1]. Handwriting is also a behavioral characteristic of a human which makes identification based on handwriting a very efficient strategy.

Writer identification is a procedure which determines the genuine writer from a given list of candidates. Based on the type of input, writer identification can be classified into two types: offline or online. Offline identification consists of considering a handwritten sample and then processing it to identify the writer. In case of online writer identification, handwriting samples obtained from digital surfaces using electronic devices are considered. From this method, much more detailed information can be obtained such as speed, pressure and angle [2].

Writer identification can also be implemented in two ways: text-independent or text-dependent. In text-dependent writer identification, previously written text of a writer is taken into consideration. Although this provides higher levels of accuracy, it is often not feasible because prior information is not always available. In that regard, text-independent writer identification is much more flexible since the prior text is not considered for the identification process. Therefore, this has much more real-world applications. However, for this, much more detailed information is required such as coordinates, altitude, pressure and azimuth [10–12].

There are several works that have been done on text-independent writer identification which are both offline and online [3]. This chapter intends to design a graphical user interface (GUI) system for text-independent writer identification methods. The difference between writer identification and writer verification processes is shown in Figure 3.1.

3.1.2 FOCUS OF WORK

Traditional methods of identification of a person have been identification cards (ID cards) and/or passwords. But they are unable to provide a unique identification since they can be shared among multiple users and therefore are not unique. Furthermore, the use of ID cards and passwords has several real-world problems such as forgetting to carry one's ID card or forgetting one's password so they are not at all consistent. So, a better solution for personal identification is required. Writer identification is used to determine a writer (a person) from his/her handwriting, including letters, notes and signature. This technique satisfies all four requirements of personal identification, namely, affordability, accessibility, reliability and accessibility. Although there is development of other techniques based on DNA, fingerprint, iris, etc., writer identification still is an attractive technique because of the unique behavioral and physiological characteristics of individuals and the existence of stability in everyone's handwriting.

Writer identification has its applications in several different domains, such as the management of digital rights in financial spheres, in solving expert problems by forensic experts in criminology, where the list of suspects can be narrowed down based on handwriting identification [5]. Handwriting identification can be used to regulate and monitor the access of confidential sites or data by using a combination of writer authentication and writer verification. Considering the large amount of data that is constantly being processed and managed such as notes, forms, and documents; the identification of the writer can provide additional value. It can also be used for handwriting recognition system enhancement, handheld mobile devices and also historical document analysis. Due to the recent developments in this field, it is a strong contender in the field of physiologic modalities for identification on par with DNA and fingerprint. From this, it is evident that the importance of writer identification has increased greatly in the recent years and thus warrants the involvement of several researchers in this challenging field with endless opportunities.

3.2   RELATED WORKS

Here, we analyze the various text-independent writer identification methods.

3.2.1   REPETITIVE PRIMITIVE'S ANALYSIS

Anoop Namboodiri and Sachin Gupta in [4] proposed a text-independent writer identification framework which authenticates the identity of the writer using a specified set of primitives of online handwritten data. It mainly focuses on developing a secure and automatic person identification system. This work assumes that, in most of the cases, people write uniquely and can be characterized based on the information present in their handwriting. They consider the variability in writing style as a major challenge, i.e., variability in style, shape, and size. Variability in samples of a particular writer can increase further as the writing surfaces and conditions change. This framework allows us to learn the properties of the script and the writer simultaneously and hence can be used with multiple languages or scripts.

3.2.2   TEXTURAL AND ALLOGRAPHIC FEATURES IDENTIFICATION

Marius Bulacu [13] proposed an effective technique for automatic writer identification and verification using a probability distribution function (PDF) extracted from the handwriting images to identify the genuine writer. This technique uses scanned

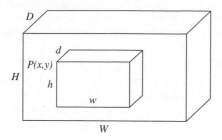

FIGURE 3.2 Fragment segmentation in a feature map space with the size: H × W × D. The fragment with the size of h × w × d is cropped on the position p(x, y).

images of handwriting samples for processing and is independent of the content of the text. This chapter distinguishes between the writer identification and writer verification operations. The system involves minimal training. This study assumes that handwriting samples are produced using a natural writing attitude. Forged or disguised handwriting is not addressed here. The two processes are shown schematically in Figure 3.1.

3.2.3 DEEP FRAGMENT NETWORKS FRAMEWORK

He and Schomaker (2020) [16] proposed that, given a set of word or text block images with writer identity, the naive way is to train a neural network on these images for writer prediction. However, as mentioned before, the neural network usually has one spotting region in the input image, which dominates the training and the information in other regions is ignored. In order to explore all writing style information contained in the whole word image, we force fragment segmentation in a feature map space with the size: H × W × D as demonstrated in Figure 3.2. The fragment with the size of h × w × d is cropped on the position p(x, y), then the neural network is trained on the fragments segmented on word images and feature maps computed from Convolutional Neural Networks (CNNs). Finally, evidences of all fragments are combined to make the final decision.

3.2.4 WHITE BOARD DATA ANALYSIS

Andreas Schlapbach et al. [23] proposed a writer identification using online handwriting captured from a white board. It is a text and language-independent online writer identification system. The system is based on the Gaussian mixture model (GMM) for the distribution of features extracted from the handwritten text. For n different writers, it creates n different GMMs. This chapter addresses the problem of identifying the author of a text written on a white board, i.e., it labels the handwriting with the writer's identity.

It includes both training and testing phases. The schematic overview of the two phases is shown in Figure 3.3. The training phase is used for the creation of one GMM for each writer. It includes the following two-step procedure. In the first step, all training data from all writers are used to train a single, writer-independent universal background model (UBM). In the second step, for each writer, a writer-specific model is

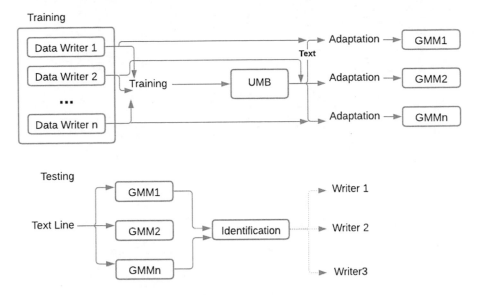

FIGURE 3.3   White board data analysis using GMM.

obtained by adaptation using the UBM and training data from that writer. As a result of the training procedure, we get a model for each writer. In the testing phase, a text of unknown identity is presented to each model. Each model returns a log-likelihood score, and these scores are sorted in descending order. Based on the resulting ranking, the text is assigned to the person whose model produces the highest log-likelihood score.

3.2.5   WRITER IDENTIFICATION USING RNN

Xu-Yao Zhang et al. [24] propose a writer identification using online handwriting captured using a pen-enabled input device. The purpose is to determine the genuine writer from a list of registered candidates according to the similarity between their handwriting, without considering the content of the text written by them. A vector named random hybrid stroke (RHS) is generated from the online handwriting information. The Recurrent Neural Network (RNN) is trained using these RHSs, which generates a particular score for each writer. The same process is repeated for another sample of handwriting during testing and an ensemble-based decision is taken to find out the writer. The system is implemented using RNN with bidirectional long short-term memory (LSTM). The training model using bidirectional LSTM is shown in Figure 3.4.

It uses RNN for both training and testing. Initially, the raw data collected is converted into a point-level representation and then a difference vector or stroke-level vector is formed by taking the difference between adjacent vectors. One stroke is the basic unit used for segmentation. Multiple strokes are combined to form an RHS vector. The RNN training is done using the RHS vectors. After training, a particular score is generated for each writer. Figure 3.5 gives an idea about the actual illustration of writer identification system using RNN. From the raw data, many RHSs are randomly sampled. After that, each RHS is fed into the RNN model individually to

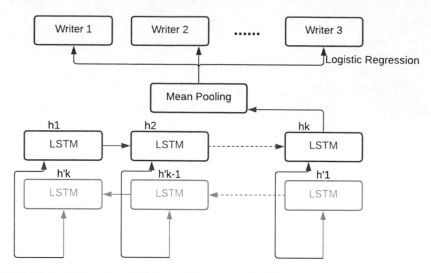

FIGURE 3.4   Bidirectional RNN model for writer identification.

produce a probability histogram. At last, all the histograms are averaged to make the ensemble-based decision.

3.3   DATABASE DETAILS

3.3.1   DATA COLLECTION

The first step for data collection is the designing of the data collection forms. In our forms, several different factors were taken into consideration, namely, age, gender, first language, dominant hand, time and date. In included variations, we collected data containing characters that are most commonly used in Bangla, Hindi and English. Unlike English, uppercase and lowercase characters are not present in

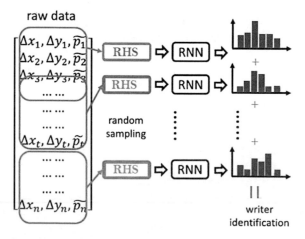

FIGURE 3.5   Illustration of writer identification using RNN.

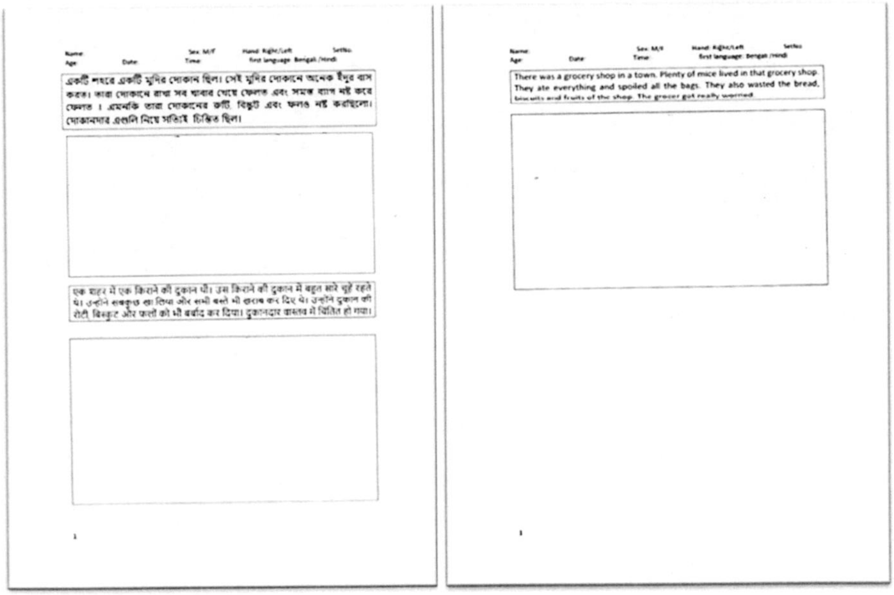

FIGURE 3.6   Illustration of blank form used for data collection.

Bangla and Hindi. However, they have some more complex and compound characters alongside the simple characters which can make the documents difficult to analyze.

Every form is designed to have three distinct zones. The header zone is used to collect information about the writer and is therefore left blank. Then the upper body contains printed text in three different languages that are meant to be copied by the writers. Finally, there are blank spaces for the writers to fill in. Figures 3.6 and 3.7 show one such blank and filled set of forms.

During data collection, writers were asked to write the sample text that was provided in the forms at their normal speed as if they were writing naturally. The writers were also given each set at different time intervals so as to be able to record some intra-writer variations along with inter-writer variations. No restrictions on writing tools such as colored pens or pencils were given to the writers. Writers of different age groups, gender, culture and educational qualifications were taken into consideration. Writers of ages 8–70 years were considered ranging from primary school students to retired personnel. Such natural variations were considered for data collection to create a realistic document database to create a robust writer identification system.

3.3.2   DATASET DETAILS

In our database, 75 writers were considered with a variable number of data per writer. Emphasis was put on acquiring variable datasets because in real-life scenarios it is not feasible to collect the same number of data from every writer. So, samples were taken in random numbers from random writers to create this variation. Figure 3.8 shows the distribution of the datasets among the writers.

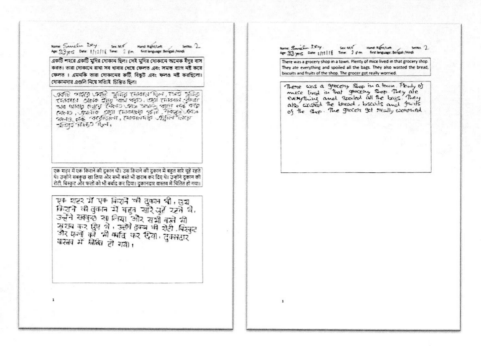

FIGURE 3.7 Sample filled-up form.

S No	Name	Age	Sex	Set No	L/R	First Language	Language	No. of Lines	Date	Time	Image File Link
1	Tarun Kumar Das	57	M	1	Right	Bengali	Bengali	6	05-12-2018	10:00	Click to open file
2	Tarun Kumar Das	57	M	1	Right	Bengali	Hindi	5	05-12-2018	10:00	Click to open file
3	Tarun Kumar Das	57	M	1	Right	Bengali	English	5	05-12-2018	10:00	Click to open file
4	Tarun Kumar Das	57	M	2	Right	Bengali	Bengali	6	05-12-2018	10:00	Click to open file
5	Tarun Kumar Das	57	M	2	Right	Bengali	Hindi	5	05-12-2018	10:00	Click to open file
6	Tarun Kumar Das	57	M	2	Right	Bengali	English	5	05-12-2018	10:00	Click to open file
7	Tarun Kumar Das	57	M	3	Right	Bengali	Bengali	6	05-12-2018	11:00	Click to open file
8	Tarun Kumar Das	57	M	3	Right	Bengali	Hindi	6	05-12-2018	11:00	Click to open file
9	Tarun Kumar Das	57	M	3	Right	Bengali	English	5	05-12-2018	11:00	Click to open file
10	Tarun Kumar Das	57	M	4	Right	Bengali	Bengali	5	05-12-2018	12:00	Click to open file
11	Tarun Kumar Das	57	M	4	Right	Bengali	Hindi	5	05-12-2018	12:00	Click to open file
12	Tarun Kumar Das	57	M	4	Right	Bengali	English	5	05-12-2018	12:00	Click to open file
13	Tarun Kumar Das	57	M	5	Right	Bengali	Bengali	6	06-12-2018	08:00	Click to open file
14	Tarun Kumar Das	57	M	5	Right	Bengali	Hindi	5	06-12-2018	08:00	Click to open file
15	Tarun Kumar Das	57	M	5	Right	Bengali	English	4	06-12-2018	08:00	Click to open file
16	Niranjan Ghosh	69	M	1	Right	Bengali	Bengali	5	29-11-2018	09:00	Click to open file
17	Niranjan Ghosh	69	M	1	Right	Bengali	Hindi	6	29-11-2018	09:00	Click to open file
18	Niranjan Ghosh	69	M	1	Right	Bengali	English	5	29-11-2018	09:00	Click to open file
19	Niranjan Ghosh	69	M	2	Right	Bengali	Bengali	6	01-12-2018	15:15	Click to open file
20	Niranjan Ghosh	69	M	2	Right	Bengali	Hindi	7	01-12-2018	15:15	Click to open file
21	Niranjan Ghosh	69	M	2	Right	Bengali	English	4	01-12-2018	15:15	Click to open file
22	Niranjan Ghosh	69	M	3	Right	Bengali	Bengali	5	01-12-2018	15:00	Click to open file

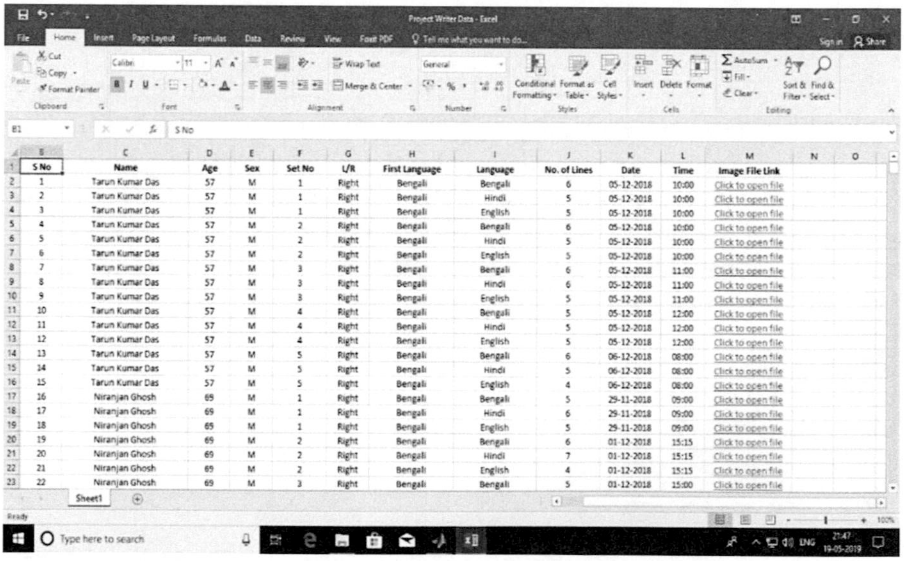

FIGURE 3.8 Text database details.

3.4 PROPOSED METHOD

Here, we have built a GUI application for identifying the author of a handwritten document. It predicts the author id of a binarized handwritten text from a set of pre-enrolled authors. Gaussian and motion blur and connected component analysis are used to segment approximate word regions [7]. Now, speeded up robust features (SURF) (scale and orientation histogram [SOH] and SURF descriptor signature [SDS]) are extracted from every word region of the images and are fed onto an extreme learning machine (ELM) classifier, which is trained with a feature database of pre-enrolled authors with known ids, for predicting the class label, i.e. the author id for the new sample. The system also provides the feature of adding a new author to the existing database and training the system with the newly updated feature database. Admin has access to the new author enroll and classifier training functionality, whereas author verification functionality can be accessed by any user.

3.4.1 OVERALL FRAMEWORK

This method is composed of five modules, which are discussed in brief in the following subsections. The overall framework is shown in Figure 3.9.

Admin login. As the name suggests this module is for Admin log in with a valid admin id and password. This module is the gateway for accessing restricted features of the system like codebook generation, enroll author and system train.

Code book generation. This module is to generate SURF codebook for future reference by the feature extraction process. Only a logged-in admin has access to this module.

Enroll author. This module allows one to enroll a new image sample in the database with the known author id. Invocation of this module needs the presence of codebook as a prerequisite. On each new enrollment, this module alters the state of the database to dirty. Only a logged-in admin has access to this module.

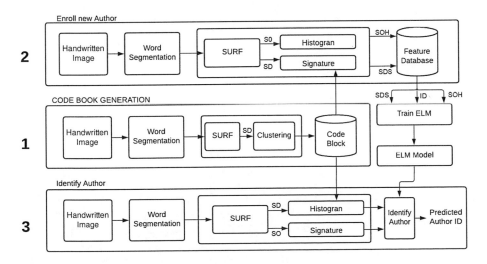

FIGURE 3.9 Overall framework of our proposed GUI system.

Train system. This module needs to be invoked after new author enrollment to alter the state of the feature database from dirty to clean. This module can only be invoked if the state of the feature database is dirty. Only a logged-in admin has access to this module.

Identify author. This is the basic module of the system and can be accessed by any user. But, this module invocation needs a codebook to be present; feature database is to be present in clean state.

3.4.2 IMPLEMENTATION

Among different core functionalities of this method, (i) word segmentation, (ii) codebook generation, (iii) feature extraction and (iv) author Id prediction are the most important ones and need in-depth discussion from an implementation point of view.

Word segmentation. This is used to cut out each word region for further processing for feature extraction. Wu et al. in [6] showed in case of offline writer identification, word-level features perform better than that of page-level or allograph-level features. This is intuitive because page-level feature extraction might produce huge redundant features to confuse the system, whereas allograph-level features might miss some key feature in a whole word [8, 9]. So, word segmentation is used here before further processing. A flowchart explaining the word segmentation process is shown in Figure 3.10.

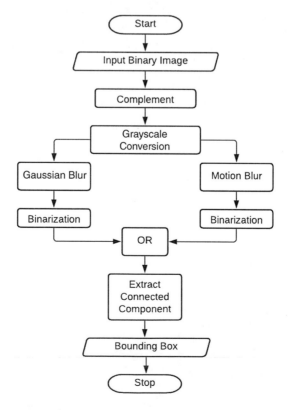

FIGURE 3.10 Flowchart of our word segmentation procedure used in the present work.

FIGURE 3.11   Word segmentation result.

Gaussian and Motion Blurs are used to connect the components in a word region. Morphological opening and closing are done to eliminate very thin connections or disjoint-ness. Finally, bounding boxes of each connected component are considered the word regions. Result of word segmentation is shown in Figure 3.11.

Codebook generation. Codebook serves the purpose of a reference for histogram-based feature extraction [17]. SURF descriptor values of all word regions of all training images were clustered into 300 categories using k-means clustering. This codebook approach makes the SURF descriptor feature length fixed [18].

Feature extraction. This method is mostly inspired by the work of Wu et al. in [6]. Similar to their approach, we have also used similar kinds of features. But, to speed up the process, we have used SURF key points [20] instead of SIFT key points [19]. The features used here are:

- SDS: This is calculated using the SURF descriptor values [20] and the codebook. For each of the 300 categories of the codebook, 300 bins are created and an SURF descriptor histogram is obtained which is called SURF descriptor signature or SDS. Detailed algorithm is explained in [6]. Though they have used SIFT descriptors, the process is the same. Figures 3.12 and 3.13 show the calculation of SURF descriptor on a sample handwritten document image at word-level and page-level, respectively.
- SOH: This is calculated by taking the orientation histogram in 24 bins of 15-degree interval at each of the SURF key points across different scales and concatenating those histograms horizontally to produce the larger histogram which is called scale and orientation histogram or SOH. Detail process is described in [6] in terms of SIFT key points [19].

Author Id prediction. Unlike Wu et al. [6], here classifier approach is used for predicting new author id. Each individual author is considered a class. A relatively new classifier ELM [21, 22] is trained with the samples with known author id and a trained ELM model is obtained. During the prediction of author id of the new sample, the feature vector and trained ELM model are passed to the prediction function. This function,

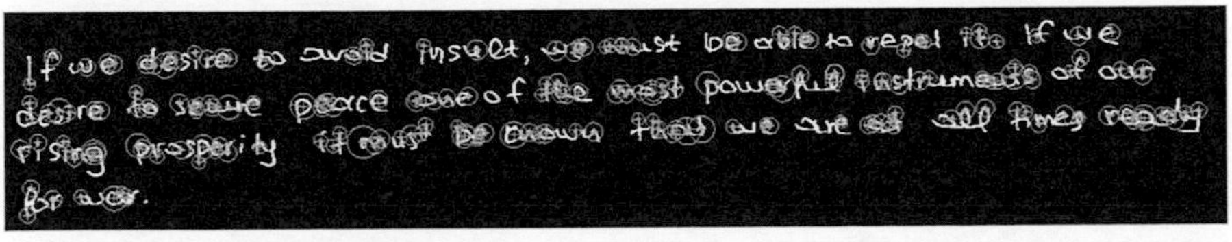

FIGURE 3.12   Word-level SURF.

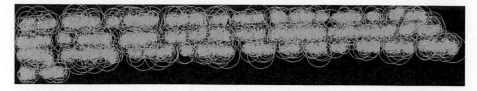

FIGURE 3.13   Too many redundant SURF at page level.

with the help of the trained model, classifies the new sample to one of the pre-registered authors and thus predicts author id.

3.5   RESULTS AND DISCUSSION

User interface is built with Matlab GUI Development Environment (GUIDE) for Method I (using SURF). It has four panels (for login, codebook generation, enroll new author and train and identify author) and one display area. Outputs are shown in the display area in Figure 3.14.

3.6   CONCLUSION AND FUTURE WORKS

Online text-independent writer identification has been receiving a considerable amount of attention and has made some great progress in the recent years. However, there is still a lot of room for improvement since the performance of the state of the art is not nearly satisfactory.

Text Independent Writer Identification by Sree   — ☐ ✕

Admin Panel

Log In

Admin Id:

Password:

Logout

Code Book

Folder Path: [Browse]

Code Book Size: 300   [Generate]

Enroll

Image Sample: C:\Users\Sreejita Chakrabarti\Desktop\Write   [Browse]

Author Id: 3   [Enroll]

Train System

User Panel

New Image Sample: C:\Users\Sreejita Chakrabarti\Desktop\Writer_Identification\Project\ImageSampl   [Browse]

Predict Author

Predicted Author id: 3

FIGURE 3.14   Window showing correct prediction.

It is generally assumed in case of writer identification that all the data accumulated will have similar acquisition conditions and that the handwriting is created by the same or similar equipment. But these assumptions are impractical and do not pertain to real-life scenarios. It is difficult to guarantee the quality of the data that might be available.

Most writer identification approaches are proposed for a particular language (Uyghur, Telugu, Oriya, French, English, Chinese, Bengali, Arabic etc.) [14, 15]. Some of these techniques claim to be effective in case of other languages as well, which poses the question of whether or not it is possible to create a language-independent writer identification system.

REFERENCES

1. Haizhou Li, Liyuan Li, and Kar-Ann Toh. *Advanced Topics in Biometrics*. World Scientific, 2012.
2. James Wayman, Anil Jain, Davide Maltoni, and Dario Maio. An introduction to biometric authentication systems. In: Wayman, J., Jain, A., Maltoni, D., Maio, D. (eds) *Biometric Systems*, 1–20, Springer, 2005. https://doi.org/10.1007/1-84628-064-8_1
3. Ameur Bensefia, Thierry Paquet, and Laurent Heutte. A writer identification and verification system. *Pattern Recognition Letters*, 26(13):2080–2092, 2005.
4. Anoop Namboodiri and Sachin Gupta. Text independent writer identification from online handwriting. In *Tenth International Workshop on Frontiers in Handwriting Recognition*. Suvisoft, 2006.
5. Rajiv Jain and David Doermann. Offline writer identification using k-adjacent segments. In *Document Analysis and Recognition (ICDAR), 2011 International Conference on*, pages 769–773. IEEE, 2011.
6. Xiangqian Wu, Youbao Tang, and Wei Bu. Offline text-independent writer identification based on scale invariant feature transform. *IEEE Transactions on Information Forensics and Security*, 9(3):526–536, 2014.
7. Diego Bertolini, Luiz S Oliveira, E Justino, and Robert Sabourin. Texture-based descriptors for writer identification and verification. *Expert Systems with Applications*, 40(6):2069–2080, 2013.
8. Zhenyu He, Xinge You, and Yuan Yan Tang. Writer identification using global wavelet-based features. *Neurocomputing*, 71(10):1832–1841, 2008.
9. Liang Du, Xinge You, Huihui Xu, Zhifan Gao, and Yuanyan Tang. Wavelet domain local binary pattern features for writer identification. In *Pattern Recognition (ICPR), 2010 20th International Conference on*, pages 3691–3694. IEEE, 2010.
10. Huwida ES Said, Tienniu N Tan, and Keith D Baker. Personal identification based on handwriting. *Pattern Recognition*, 33(1):149–160, 2000.
11. Yong Zhu, Tieniu Tan, and Yunhong Wang. Biometric personal identification based on handwriting. In *Pattern Recognition, 2000. Proceedings. 15th International Conference on*, volume 2, pages 797–800. IEEE, 2000.
12. Regiane Kowalek Hanusiak, Luiz S Oliveira, E Justino, and Robert Sabourin. Writer verification using texture-based features. *International Journal on Document Analysis and Recognition*, 15:213–226, 2012.
13. Marius Bulacu and Lambert Schomaker. Text-independent writer identification and verification using textural and allographic features. *IEEE Transactions on Pattern Analysis and Machine Intelligence*, 29(4):701–717, 2007.
14. Laurens Van Der Maaten, and Eric O Postma. Improving automatic writer identification. In *BNAIC*, pages 260–266, 2005.

15. Xin Li and Xiaoqing Ding. Writer identification of Chinese handwriting using grid microstructure feature. *Advances in Biometrics*, 5558:1230–1239, 2009.

16. Lambert Schomaker and Marius Bulacu. Automatic writer identification using connected-component contours and edge-based features of uppercase western script. *IEEE Transactions on Pattern Analysis and Machine Intelligence*, 26(6):787–798, 2004.

17. Golnaz Ghiasi and Reza Safabakhsh. Offline text-independent writer identification using codebook and efficient code extraction methods. *Image and Vision Computing*, 31(5):379–391, 2013.

18. Imran Siddiqi and Nicole Vincent. Text independent writer recognition using redundant writing patterns with contour-based orientation and curvature features. *Pattern Recognition*, 43(11):3853–3865, 2010.

19. David G Lowe. Distinctive image features from scale-invariant keypoints. *International Journal of Computer Vision*, 60(2):91–110, 2004.

20. Herbert Bay, Andreas Ess, Tinne Tuytelaars, and Luc Van Gool. Speeded-up robust features (surf). *Computer Vision and Image Understanding*, 110(3):346–359, 2008.

21. Guang-Bin Huang, Qin-Yu Zhu, and Chee-Kheong Siew. Extreme learning machine: theory and applications. *Neurocomputing*, 70(1):489–501, 2006.

22. Guang-Bin Huang, Qin-Yu Zhu, and Chee-Kheong Siew. Extreme learning machine: a new learning scheme of feedforward neural networks. In *Neural Networks, 2004. Proceedings. 2004 IEEE International Joint Conference on*, volume 2, pages 985–990. IEEE, 2004.

23. Andreas Schlapbach, Marcus Liwicki, and Horst Bunke. A writer identification system for on-line whiteboard data. *Pattern Recognition*, 41(7):2381–2397, 2008.

24. Xu-Yao Zhang, Guo-Sen Xie, Cheng-Lin Liu, and Yoshua Bengio. End-to-end online writer identification with recurrent neural network. *IEEE Transactions on Human-Machine Systems*, 47(2):285–292, 2016.

4 Soil Fertility Prediction Using a Soft Computing Approach

Yogesh R. Shahare
Department of Information Technology, MGMCET
Navi Mumbai, Maharashtra, India

Mukund Pratap Singh
School of Computer Science Engineering
and Technology, Bennett University
Greater Noida, India

Sanjeev Kumar
Department of CSE, United University
Prayagraj, India

CONTENTS

4.1 INTRODUCTION

Machine learning (ML) algorithms have provided a plethora of applications and technologies that are extremely beneficial for learning and creating training and testing models from experience repeatedly in an automated fashion. A variety of well-developed models are employed, and sophisticated algorithms are collected and employed to obtain the required outcomes. In different agricultural application techniques, ML algorithms have been employed to improve production and cultural output produced [1]. It has also been used to discourage mining and return the best crop when a specific condition has been satisfied. Agriculture soil is a critical component in the propagation of plants, since it contains both solids (mineral and organic materials) and liquids (water), as well as gases (mostly carbon dioxide and oxygen), and it contains living creatures [2]. All the elements have physical and chemical characteristics that are important for soil fertility maintenance, enhanced production, and environmental protection; they are also necessary for the appropriate nourishment of the soil [3]. Soil analytical services nutrition is extremely useful in determining the form of nutrients to be consumed. It is necessary to have a good understanding of the soil yield to be harvested and a healthy field. Controlling fertility necessitates a thorough understanding of its boundaries. The current dietary failures and improvements monitoring fertility of the soil to avoid it lack [4]. The data must be sound, and proper nutrition habits must be minimized. Managing the soil, maintaining a reasonable level of food production, and ensuring high production levels all require water, plants, and resources, as well as efficacy in many tasks at the same time [5].

The ML classification approach can be used to provide reports on a district-specific fertility index, and it should be utilized in conjunction with a decision support system (DSS) to generate fertilizer suggestion recommendations for a certain crop [6, 7]. It will be much easier to compare the state of soil fertility among different districts of soil details because of this classification and regression report, and the value of this research will be to identify the best position of soil nutrient fertility indices that are useful for crop productivity. Soil fertility with characteristics such as nitrogen (N), phosphorus (P), potassium (K), electrical conductivity (EC), organic carbon (OC), sulfur (S), zinc (Zn), Iron (Fe), copper (Cu), boron (B), manganese (Mn), and other factors such as year and month of soil fertility are considered [8–10]. It is known that Maharashtra is particularly sensitive to soil erosion and dirt leaching as well as flooding and drought. Predicting the pH of different soil types helps to minimize the overuse of chemical fertilizers in this state. Forecasting is something that people are interested in. The levels of such ML methods soil characteristics help the reduction of excessive fertilizer production expenditures and the reduction of greenhouse gas emissions. Ref. [11] conducted a health study of the soil and the nature of the climate and [5] also conducted health research of the soil and the nature of the climate. The soil fertility indices and pH in the soil are graded in this study, and the results are presented in tables. These soil parameter-based data represent the soil and projected levels for the Maharashtra area. The investigation of the soil tests the soil parameter values utilized in this study and experiment [12], which are derived from the soil parameter values [13]. The indices of reproductive potential of the results were obtained using soil nutrient levels of three different degrees, namely, high, medium, and small. If you're dealing with classification and regression difficulties, the random forest (RF) technique and decision trees (DTs) will suffice.

The primary goal of this study in terms of soil fertility is to identify field-level indicators of soil fertility using data from districts. To quickly get classification and prediction results, new meta-parameters of both the classifying and regressing methods have been created to produce a more accurate soil nutrient analysis classification model [14–17]. This section discusses the classification model as well as the tools and procedures that are used to classify things. The remaining sections of this chapter are organized as follows: Section 4.2 discusses the related works, Section 4.3 discusses the subject material and methods, the results and discussions are discussed in Section 4.4, and conclusions are described in Section 4.5.

4.2   RELATED WORK

Various applications are studied using various ML approaches in the field of soil nutrient prediction analysis over the last few years, as seen below. Ref. [18] proposed a prediction system for mustered crop yield from soil analysis. Soil data is collected from different districts of Jammu region and analysis based on nutrient deficiency for implementing the system. Five ML algorithms, including K-nearest neighbor (KNN), naive Bayes, multinomial logistic regression, artificial neural network (ANN), and RF, were employed in the experiment [19]. Using the RF algorithm, a model is proposed for estimating the performance of a crop based on historical data. Experimental data from Tamil Nadu were used for the implementation of this model based on rainfall, temperature, and RF ML algorithm. Ref. [10] proposed a model for improving the prediction accuracy from nutrient deficiency of soil analysis data using extreme learning machine (ELM) algorithm. Village wise soil nutrient data are collected and implemented by using ELM techniques and compared the accuracy based on performance. Performed a different function for calculating the prediction accuracy using ANN algorithm and to find out the better performance of ELM activation function. Ref. [2] proposed an approach for accessing two soil fertilities for evaluating paddy field cultivation. Implemented by using two methods like square root method parametric approach and fuzzy method adapt new criteria for accessing the soil fertility and computed soil fertility index. Compare both method for the cultivation of paddy field using the soil properties such as pH values, EC (ds m^{-1}), OC (%), CEC (cmol kg^{-1}), clay (%), and Ap (cm). Ref. [20] compared the study of different data mining classification techniques for predicting the sample size crop based on the availability of soil nutrient parameter. Soil nutrients datasets are taken from nine sample different districts and applied seven different ML algorithms for implementing the proposed model and compare the performance of each algorithm based on soil data parameters. Proposed model DT algorithm is given the better performance for this model. [21] performed the ML algorithm for forecasting the rice crop yield based on soil properties of nutrients pH, OC, EC, N, P, K, and S and microelements Zn, Fe, Mn, and Cu. Compare different classifiers for finding the better performance for estimating the rice crop yield based on the soil nutrients data [22, 23]. KNN, naive Bayes classifier (NBC), and DT classifier (DTC) were used for implementing to this model. A DSS for agro technology transfer-cropping system model (ATCSM) was proposed to simulate crop yield, including soil nitrogen (SN) and soil organic carbon (SOC), in a climate change environment. Four fertilizers are used for implementing to this model. The present study seeks to increase the precision rate in the Maharashtra area, fertility indices are classified as a classification of soil nutrients through DT and random ML methods of soil nutrient classification. Finally, we concentrated on the classification and regression ML principles [24]. In view of all the parameters available, ML offers a better prediction of statistical methods. This proposed ML technique is more effective than available methods for soil classification in Maharashtra. An early prediction of land status by ML algorithm [25] is very helpful in the current agricultural scenario to farmers, so that a better climate can be built for their next farm.

4.3 MATERIALS AND METHODS

4.3.1 Study Area

Maharashtra state is the third biggest state in India, covering roughly 9.4% of the country's geographical area and home to more than 52 million rural residents, or nearly 58% of the total population. The Arabian Sea region is to the west, Gujarat is to the northwest, Madhya Pradesh is to the north, Andhra Pradesh is to the southeast, and Karnataka and Goa are to the south. The state is classified into six distinct regional areas such as Konkan, Pune, Nashik, Amravati, Aurangabad, and Nagpur, these distinct regional areas contain 33 tehsils and 42778 talukas. A total of 7000 villages are considered for irrigation scheme command regions in Maharashtra state. Agriculture is critical to the state's economy since it provides employment for more than 65% of the population. Agriculture's closed relative contribution to GDP has declined in recent years, resulting in increased rural poverty and the migration of landless people from villages to towns and cities. A soil research laboratory collects soil samples from individual farms. The results of the region-by-region study, as well as the grading data for each input indication, are publicly available. Many characteristics that are directly related to plant nutrition were examined in soil samples: main nutrients (N, P, K), EC, and pH (https://soilhealth.dac.gov.in).

4.3.1.1 Classification of Soil Fertility Indices Data

Soil nutrients data is collected from Maharashtra state for predicting the efficient soil fertility. This research is helpful for farmers for cultivating the crop yield in two regions of Maharashtra state. A district wise soil data is collected for experimental setup and to find out the efficient soil fertility using ML method. Soil nutrient parameters are considered such as phosphorous (P), nitrogen (N), potassium (K), EC, and soil fertility level [3, 9, 14]. The Soil Testing Lab, Department of Agriculture, Maharashtra, provided accurate data for the research.

4.3.2 pH Classification

The acidity or alkalinity value parameter of soil pH is presented in the soil for determining the value of soil pH or soil reaction, and it is measured in pH units. Soil pH is defined as the hydrogen ion concentrations negative logarithm. pH scale consists of specified values which are assigned 7 as the neutral point while the range of others is 0–14. The soil pH content decreases thus becoming more acidic by increasing the volume of hydrogen ions in the soil. The content of soil is increasingly acidic between 7 and 0 and increasingly alkaline or simple soil between 7 and 14 pH. The range of the pH value and rating pattern is given in Table 4.1 [1, 26, 27].

TABLE 4.1

pH Values and Rating Pattern

pH Value	Rating
<04.50	For extremely acidic
04.60–05.60	For higher acidic
05.60–06.50	For moderator acidic
06.60–06.90	For slighter acidic
07.00	For neutrally
07.10–08.00	For slighter alkaline
08.10–09.00	For moderator alkaline
09.10–10.00	For stronger alkaline
10.10–11.00	For very stronger alkaline

4.3.3 PROPOSED WORK

The current study proposed a system for predicting a soil fertility index by using soil parameters of nitrogen, phosphorus, potassium, EC, which applied classification and regression ML algorithm. In Maharashtra region, district wise soil data are collected and implemented this model which is helpful for farmer for further suggestion of crop yield and cultivation of crop. Proposed work is shown in Figure 4.1. Soil datasets are collected from different districts with nutrient deficiency sample size. Each nutrient is depending on their deficiency value which is impact for growing the crops. Soil fertility is more important paramount agriculture for increasing the crop productivity. Soil fertility is computed based on the soil fertility level, i.e., low (0), medium (1), and high (2).

4.3.4 MACHINE LEARNING

4.3.4.1 Decision Tree Regression and Classification

Using DT learning, the entire sample region is divided into a smaller space, repeated which is sufficient for the formulation of a modest model. The root node's tree contains the entire sample space (first node). One way to divide sample space into smaller sub-samples is to bifurcate a root node into children nodes, with each node being divided recurrently into leaf nodes (a node cannot be further divided). The nodes are arranged in a tree, but the leaf node, split sample space, is based on a condition(s) input attribute collection, and the leaf node assigns the input attributes to the output value on the tree's root-leaf path. The aim of the sub-sample is to minimize the mixing of various output values with the DT method and to assign single output value for sub-sample space. Impurity (e.g., standard ID3 deviation; Gini index used in C4.5) and node are the divider parameters for each node (number of information present in a node). Based on the calculation of impurity criteria, a node has been created [27, 28].

4.3.4.2 Random Forest Regression and Classification

RF appears to be the most general and highly supervised ML algorithm, capable of performing regression tasks for both classifications and building several

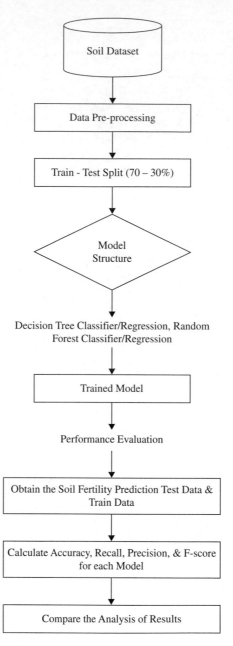

FIGURE 4.1   Flowchart of the methodology.

decision-making bodies during training, as well as the class output, which is the class mode (classification) or average prediction (regression) of the individual trees. The more trees in an RF, the better forecasting will be. An RF is a good thing three DTs that are suitable for their training [24]. Unlike algorithms for learning DT machines, the RF algorithm has the advantage of being less efficient than RFs problem. It is critical to avoid cutting. Forest random algorithms can be developed concurrently with RF ML algorithms [20, 22, 23, 28]. This chapter proposed an RF classification and regression technique for determining the achievable accuracy of training and testing data. These algorithms were used to predict the soil fertility based on the analysis of all nutrient parameters [25].

4.4 RESULTS AND DISCUSSIONS

In this research the datasets from the Maharashtra region of district wise soil fertility data tested by laboratory are collected. The datasets contain 4000 cases, each with ten input parameters representing the soil nutrient status of the Maharashtra region and one output attribute (i.e., class labels). The datasets with input features are pH (soil pH), EC, N, P, K, OC, S, Zn, Fe, B, and Mn, which represent soil nutrients, and other parameters are year, month, and district. The production attribute reflects three types of soil fertility position, which are as follows: low (0), medium (1), high (2). Total 4000 cases are collected, 2500 fall in the low class, 900 fall in the medium class, and 600 fall in the high class. For the classification and regression techniques, 80% of the data was used for training and 20% for testing. The first 15 cases of the datasets are shown in Table 4.2. Based on training and testing data, Figure 4.2 compares the results of RF classification and RF regression (RFR). For classification techniques, a classification report is used, which includes parameters such as accuracy, precision, recall, and F1-score, as well as Out of Bag (OOB) error rate (ER), area under the receiver-operating characteristic curve (AUC), and ER. For regression evaluation used a means squared error, R^2 score, and ER. Compare all parameters and find the reliable solution by using both classification and regression. Training

TABLE 4.2
First 15 Sample Data from the Soil Dataset

N	P	K	pH	EC	OC	S	Zn	Fe	Cu	Mn	B	Fertility
138	8.6	560	7.46	0.62	0.7	5.9	0.24	0.31	0.77	8.71	0.11	0
213	7.5	338	7.62	0.75	1.06	25.4	0.3	0.86	1.54	2.89	2.29	0
163	9.6	718	7.59	0.51	1.11	14.3	0.3	0.86	1.57	2.7	2.03	0
157	6.8	475	7.64	0.58	0.94	26	0.34	0.54	1.53	2.65	1.82	0
270	9.9	444	7.63	0.4	0.86	11.8	0.25	0.76	1.69	2.43	2.26	1
220	8.6	444	7.43	0.65	0.72	11.7	0.37	0.66	0.9	2.19	1.82	0
220	7.2	222	7.62	0.43	0.81	7.4	0.34	0.69	1.05	2	1.88	0
207	7	401	7.63	0.59	0.69	7.6	0.32	0.68	0.62	2.43	1.68	0
289	8.6	560	7.58	0.44	0.67	7.3	0.63	0.66	0.94	2.43	1.79	1
138	8.1	739	7.55	0.33	0.78	9	0.69	0.41	1.15	2.75	2	0
151	8.1	549	7.59	0.45	0.97	9.6	0.71	0.38	1.33	2.79	2.41	0
144	7.2	306	7.53	0.73	0.89	9.2	0.63	0.47	1.03	2.79	2.38	0
138	5.3	444	7.68	0.6	0.78	9.7	0.73	0.36	1.32	3.32	2.12	0
144	8.3	549	7.45	0.53	0.81	10.2	0.51	0.56	1.26	2.9	2.29	0
201	7.7	676	7.39	0.77	0.72	9.7	0.58	0.47	1.02	3.77	2.56	0

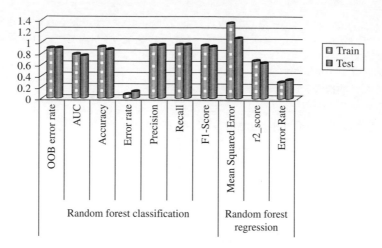

FIGURE 4.2   Random forest regression (RFR) and random forest classification (RFC).

data has an accuracy of 80%, and testing data has an accuracy of 77%. Based on training and testing data, Figure 4.3 compares the results of RF classification and DT regression. Training data have an accuracy of 80%, and testing data have an accuracy of 77%. Figure 4.4 depicts a dataset-based comparison of DT classification and RFR. Training data were 93% accurate, while testing data were 89% accurate. Figure 4.5 depicts a dataset-based comparison of DT classification and DT regression results. Training accuracy is 92%, and testing accuracy is 80%. Figure 4.6 compares train and test accuracy using RF, DT classification, and regression. When compared to other classification and regression techniques, DT classification and RFR yielded higher accuracy. This chapter proposed a model for predicting soil fertility that is suitable for decision classification and the RFR ML algorithm.

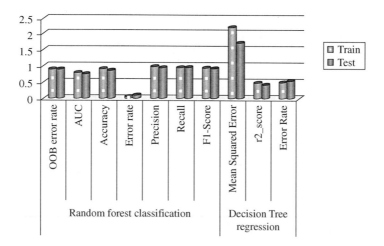

FIGURE 4.3   Random forest classification (RFC) and decision tree regression (DTR).

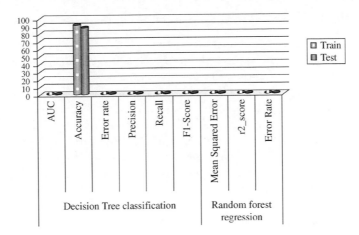

FIGURE 4.4   Random forest regression (RFR) and decision tree classifier (DTC).

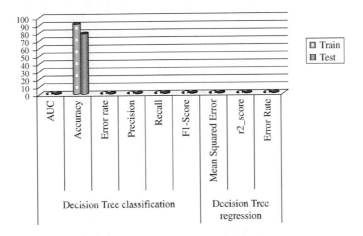

FIGURE 4.5   Classification and regression using decision trees.

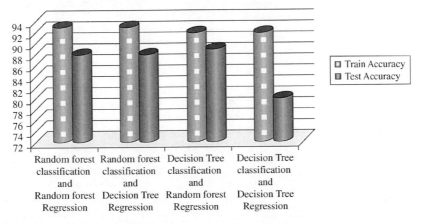

FIGURE 4.6   Using random forest and decision tree classification and regression, compare train and test accuracy.

4.5 CONCLUSION AND RECOMMENDATION

This chapter proposed an ML model for predicting soil fertility using soil nutrients deficiency data, as well as performing an ML classification algorithm and determining the most feasible algorithm for improved accuracy, F1-score, precision, and recall. District-level soil data is collected in Maharashtra to be used in this model's prediction using DT classification-regression and RF classification-regression algorithms. Compare the two algorithms to see which one is more accurate. The better algorithms used in this study are DTC and RFR, which are based on regression evaluation parameters such as mean square error (MSE), R^2 (R square), and ER. The dataset contains macro- and micronutrient parameters with specific values, which are used to calculate the soil fertility index. Future work for the model will include crop recommendations based on soil fertility properties and the addition of more ML algorithms to improve soil fertility.

REFERENCES

1. Awasthi, N., and A. Bansal. "Application of Data Mining Classification Techniques on Soil Data Using R." *International Journal of Advances in Electronics and Computer Science* 4.1 (2017): 33–37.
2. Delsouz Khaki, B., et al. "Assessment of Two Soil Fertility Indexes to Evaluate Paddy Fields for Rice Cultivation." *Sustainability* 9.8 (2017): 1299.
3. Bhuyar, V. "Comparative Analysis of Classification Techniques on Soil Data to Predict Fertility Rate for Aurangabad District." *International Journal of Emerging Trends & Technology in Computer Science* 3.2 (2014): 200–203.
4. Donges, N. A Complete Guide to the Random Forest Algorithm. Built In (2019). https://builtin.com/data-science/random-forest-algorithm
5. Djodiltachoumy, S., and E. Manjula. "A Model for Prediction of Crop Yield." *Science of the Total Environment* 6.4 (March 2017). https://soilhealth.dac.gov.in. Soil health card data.
6. Zhang, H., et al. "Prediction of Soil Organic Carbon in an Intensively Managed Reclamation Zone of Eastern China: A Comparison of Multiple Linear Regressions and the Random Forest Model." *Science of the Total Environment* 592 (2017): 704–713.
7. Gholap, J., et al. "Soil data analysis using classification techniques and soil attribute prediction." *arXiv preprint arXiv: 1206.1557* (2012).
8. Jayalakshmi, R., and M. S. Devi. "Relevance of Machine Learning Algorithms on Soil Fertility Prediction Using R." *International Journal of Computational Intelligence and Informatics* 8.4 (2019): 193–199.
9. Paul, M., S. K. Vishwakarma, and A. Verma. "Analysis of soil behaviour and prediction of crop yield using data mining approach." *2015 International Conference on Computational Intelligence and Communication Networks (CICN)*. IEEE, 2015.
10. Suchithra, M. S., and M. L. Pai. "Improving the Prediction Accuracy of Soil Nutrient Classification by Optimizing Extreme Learning Machine Parameters." *Information processing in Agriculture* 7.1 (2020): 72–82.
11. Soundarya, M., and R. Balakrishnan. "Survey on Classification Techniques in Data Mining." *International Journal of Advanced Research in Computer and Communication Engineering* 3.7 (2014): 7550–7552.
12. Datta, P., and B. Sharma. "A survey on IoT architectures, protocols, security and smart city-based applications." *2017 8th International Conference on Computing, Communication and Networking Technologies (ICCCNT)*. IEEE, 2017.

13. Koley, S., and S. Ghosh. "Machine Learning for Soil Fertility and Plant Nutrient Management." *International Journal on Recent and Innovation Trends in Computing* 2.2 (2014): 292–297.

14. Sarwar, A., V. Sharma, and V. Singh. "Analysis of Soil and Prediction of Crop Yield (Rice) Using Machine Learning Approach." *International Journal of Advanced Research in Computer Science* 8.5 (2017): 1254–1259.

15. Sirsat, M. S., E. Cernadas, M., Fernández-Delgado, and S. Barro. "Automatic Prediction of Village-Wise Soil Fertility for Several Nutrients in India Using a Wide Range of Regression Methods." *Computers and Electronics in Agriculture* 154 (2018): 120–133.

16. Sirsat, M. S., E. Cernadas, M., Fernández-Delgado, R. Khan. "Classification of Agricultural Soil Parameters in India." *Computers and Electronics in Agriculture* 135 (2017): 269–279.

17. Charles, S., S. S. Baskar, and L. Arockiam. "Applying Data Mining Techniques on Soil Fertility Prediction." *International Journal of Computer Applications Technology and Research* 2a.6 (2013): 660–662.

18. Chhabra, R., S. Verma, and C. R. Krishna. "A survey on driver behavior detection techniques for intelligent transportation systems." *2017 7th International Conference on Cloud Computing, Data Science & Engineering-Confluence.* IEEE, 2017.

19. Priya, P., U. Muthaiah, and M. Balamurugan. "Predicting Yield of the Crop Using Machine Learning Algorithm." *International Journal of Engineering Sciences and Research Technology* 7.1 (2018): 1–7.

20. Kumar, S., S. Agarwal, and Ranvijay. "Fast and Memory Efficient Approach for Mapping NGS Reads to a Reference Genome." *Journal of Bioinformatics and Computational Biology* 17.02 (2019): 1950008.

21. Koundal, D., S. Gupta, and S. Singh. "Computer Aided Thyroid Nodule Detection System Using Medical Ultrasound Images." *Biomedical Signal Processing and Control* 40 (2018): 117–130.

22. Kumar, S., and S. Agarwal. "WBMFC: Efficient and Secure Storage of Genomic Data." *Pertanika Journal of Science & Technology* 26.4 (2018): 1914–1925.

23. Recena, R., V. M. Fernández-Cabanás, and A. Delgado. "Soil Fertility Assessment by Vis-NIR Spectroscopy: Predicting Soil Functioning Rather Than Availability Indices." *Geoderma* 337 (2019): 368–374.

24. Renuka, S. T. "Evaluation of Machine Learning Algorithms for Crop Yield Prediction." *The International Journal of Engineering and Advanced Technology (IJEAT)* 8.6 (2019).

25. Sheela, P. J., and K. Sivaranjani. "A Brief Survey of Classification Techniques Applied to Soil Fertility Prediction." *International Conference on Engineering Trends and Science & Humanities* (2015): 80–83.

26. Keertanaa, E., P. S. Vijayabaskar, and R. Sreemathi "Crop prediction using predictive analytics." *International Conference on Computation of Power, Energy, Information and Communication (ICCPEIC),* 2017.

27. Singh, V., A. Sarwar, and V. Sharma. "Analysis of Soil and Prediction of Crop Yield (Rice) Using Machine Learning Approach." *International Journal of Advanced Research in Computer Science* 8.5 (2017): 1254–1259.

28. Chandrakala, M., et al. "Soil Fertility Evaluation under Different Land Use System in Tropical Humid Region of Kerala, India." *International Journal of Plant & Soil Science* (2018): 1–13.

5 Psychological Distress Detection, Classification and Assistance Using AI

Sarah Gawde, Arnab Ghorai, Jeet Mishra,
and Dhananjay Kalbande
Sardar Patel Institute of Technology
Andheri, India

CONTENTS

5.1 INTRODUCTION

According to the World Health Organization, one in four people in the world will somehow be affected by psychological distress at some point or the other in their lives [1]. If we talk about the current pandemic situation, psychological distress is one of the major issues we are facing. Daily, we come across various news articles, blogs, videos and many other talks focusing on this topic. On top of that, various connotations and social stigma are associated with it. To a great extent, most people have experienced certain forms of psychological distress directly or indirectly.

DOI: 10.1201/9781003320340-5

So, let us understand what psychological distress is and why is it important to treat it at the right time.

Basically according to biological researchers, any living organism has a steady condition, be it mental or physical, e.g. having ideal body temperature, ideal glucose level and ideal blood pressure. This state or condition is called homeostasis [2]. For humans especially, when they are going through any stressful conditions, it not only affects them mentally but also physically due to which the homeostasis is threatened. Homeostasis can be re-established by a series of different mental and behavioural adaptive responses of a person, i.e. if provided proper assistance, one can re-establish homeostasis [3].

What are these stressful conditions? We commonly use the word "depression" to refer to these stressful conditions, but we do not exactly know what it is. Depression by itself is a medical problem and it has a certain kind of diagnosis, so there are some criteria for diagnosing depression. These criteria help us to know whether a person is really suffering from any kind of psychological distress or to some extent even help us to treat these people, so there is this global consensus as to what exactly is psychological distress. The doctor has to identify and look for symptoms (both behavioural and physical) as mentioned below and also take into consideration the duration of these symptoms. Globally, it's been agreed that if a person is detected with any five of the below given symptoms for a duration of about more than two weeks, then that person is suffering from some kind of mental distress and needs immediate medical attention.

• Inability to feel pleasure/excitement	• Suicidal thoughts/ideas
• Rapid lose/gain of weight	• Fatigue
• Excessive sleeping or sleep deprived	• Sense of guilt, worthlessness
	• Mood swings
• Unable to focus and concentrate	• Decrease in pace and agility

In the mental health disorder spectrum, depression is one such disorder, but you can also have other disorders like anxiety and panic. These are other different disorders, but all of them come under a broad spectrum of psychological disorders. Moreover, psychological distress is inherently a difficult topic to talk about. Thus, psychological distress is a major problem of present era. Diagnosis of psychological distress is different from the diagnosis of other diseases. It cannot be diagnosed on the basis of physical/quantitative tests (e.g. blood tests). For many people out there, it becomes difficult to discuss these topics openly with closed ones or even strangers (like doctors).

In the last couple of decades, there has been tremendous amount of contribution in this field from the artificial intelligence (AI)/machine learning (ML) community, where they have tried to detect certain particular mental disease using various algorithms on the basis of user's voice samples, facial expressions, social media interactions and so on. With the advent of technology and increase in the rate of people suffering from distress, we thought that there is a need for a one-stop platform where people will feel comfortable and secure sharing their personal information about their feelings, by which we could give them assistance also on the same platform. **Thus, in this research, we propose a solution to detect and classify the psychological distress of users and provide assistance to the users to come out of the distress.**

5.2   LITERATURE SURVEY

Great amount of work has been done within the psychology, psychiatry and medicine fields to correlate different spectra of psychological distress with its corresponding symptoms. The diagnosis of mental disorders like depression and anxiety is carried out by finding the duration and frequency of certain symptoms. Several questionnaire-based measures indicating the level or presence of mental disorder have been proposed within these fields. Various studies have been conducted that explore the potential of statistical analysis of social media interactions of a person in order to detect any signs of mental disorder. Social media is a platform where people try to express their opinions or state of mind through posts. People react to their posts and a conversation starts. These conversations can be used to detect a person's state of mind.

5.2.1   STATISTICAL ANALYSIS OF SOCIAL MEDIA INTERACTIONS

Mandar Deshpande and Vignesh Rao [4] applied natural language processing (NLP) on feeds obtained from Twitter for detecting the presence of depression. They made their own dataset with the help of a Twitter application programming interface (API). A collection of 100 tweets was obtained by using this Twitter API with the help of a list of trigger words that depict poor mental well-being, such as "hopeless", "depressed" and "suicide". These tweets were manually labelled as neutral or negative. After some cleaning of the data, they applied preprocessing techniques like stemming, tokenisation, removal of stop words and part of speech (POS) Tagger. They formed a Bag of Words from the cleaned and preprocessed dataset. Conversion of these set of tweets along with the set of labels into a vector format was implemented and fed into a classifier. They achieved a testing accuracy of 83% and an F1 score of 83.29% with multinomial naive Bayes and accuracy of 79% and an F1 score of 79.73% with support vector machine (SVM) (see Table 5.1).

Moin Nadeem et al. [5] in the paper proposed a method that predicts whether a person is affected by major depression disorder (MDD) by using their online social interactions and personas. Here, they used a dataset created by Coppersmith et al. for the Computational Linguistics and Clinical Psychology (CLPsych) 2015 Shared Task that consisted of tweets from people that were diagnosed with depression. They proposed a "Bag of Words" approach to quantify the user's tweet, they transformed these tweets into a feature vector with 846,496 dimensions. Instead of considering all the tweets from a single user as a single class, the authors considered each tweet as a single document, thus making the approach more granular. They applied different ML algorithms such as SVM, decision trees, naive Bayes and logistic regression for the binary classification task, where the naive Bayes model gave the highest accuracy of 86% and precision score of 0.82.

De Choudhury et al. [7] used factors like the frequency of social activities, emotions, engagement, heightened thoughts and beliefs on Twitter and leveraged these features to train an SVM classifier resulting in an accuracy of 70%.

Abhilash Biradar et al. [8] proposed a system where they created a dataset by extracting tweets containing keywords like depression, sadness, tired, guilt and

TABLE 5.1
Comparison: "Statistical Analysis of Social Media Interactions"

Ref. No	Title	Methodology	Metrics
[4]	Depression detection using emotion artificial intelligence	Natural language processing on Twitter feeds for detecting the presence of depression. Multinomial naive Bayes (MNB) and SVM used.	Accuracy: 83% F1 score: 83.29% (MNB)
[5]	Identifying depression on Twitter	Prediction of Major Depression Disorder (MDD) by using online social interactions and personas. SVM, decision trees, logistic regression and naive Bayes used for binary classification task.	Accuracy: 86% Precision score: 82%
[6]	Early detection of depression: Social network analysis and random forest techniques	They proposed two different variants of classifiers one consisting of one RF and two threshold functions, whereas the other consisting of two independent RFs for the classification of depressed and non-depressed users.	Accuracy: 68%
[7]	Predicting depression via social media	Used factors like frequency of social activities, emotions, engagement, heightened thoughts and beliefs on Twitter and leveraged these features to train an SVM classifier.	Accuracy: 70%
[8]	Detecting depression in social media posts using machine learning	SentiStrength sentiment analysis for creating the training dataset, back-propagation neural network for binary classification.	Avg. Acc.: 80%
[9]	Depression detection by analysing social media posts of user	Used support vector machines and naive Bayes algorithms for classifying posts collected from social media – Facebook and Twitter.	Accuracy: 74% Precision: 100% Recall: 60%

suicide and utilized SentiStrength sentiment analysis for creating the training dataset, which is further fed to a back-propagation neural network for binary classification where the categories are depressed or not depressed.

Fidel Cacheda et al. [6] in this paper proposed a methodology that focused on the early stage detection of depression. Here, the data acquisition was done by extracting posts and comments of depressed users from Reddit. They proposed two different variants of classifiers one consisting of one random forest and two threshold functions, whereas the other consisting of two independent random forests for the classification of depressed and non-depressed users.

Nafiz Al Asad et al. [9] have used SVM and naive Bayes algorithms for classifying posts collected from social media sites Facebook and Twitter. Beautiful Soup was used to collect tweets and Facebook posts that were collected manually. Posts and tweets were cleaned using the NLTK Library. A sentiment dictionary of 8000 words containing positive and negative words was created. Using the sentiment dictionary, a percentage score was assigned to each post, and accordingly a score was assigned to each individual. Individuals with more than 55% score were considered depressed. For the evaluation of the model, a questionnaire of 10 questions was given to 50 people. Accuracy of 74%, precision of 100% and recall of 60% were obtained.

5.2.2 CONSIDERING FACIAL EXPRESSIONS

Sharifa Alghowinem et al. [10] in this paper performed the binary classification for classes – depressed and non-depressed. They extracted the eye movements feature from the video streams of the facial expressions with the help of active appearance models. This model is trained on 74 feature points that are situated in the eye region. Here, the authors have used two types of classifier – Gaussian mixture model (GMM) which comes under the generative classifier models and SVM which is under the discriminative classifier models. They achieved an accuracy of 70% by using low-level features on the hybrid of SVM and GMM classifiers. Using statistical measures, they obtained an accuracy of 75% with the help of SVM classifier over the complete course of interview.

Prajakta Bhalchandra Kulkarni et al. [11] proposed local tetra pattern (LTrP) for feature extraction from a facial image and for binary classification, i.e. depressed or non-depressed, they used Fisher vector encoding. The Fisher vector algorithm uses GMM and can also give best results using linear classifier. In this paper, the authors have used LTrP in comparison with LBP (i.e. local binary pattern). This was done because the output obtained by LTrP is in binary form, i.e. it can be either "0" or "1", but the LBP gives the output in 0, 2, 3, 4 pattern and uses the direction of the pixels. For comparison, they have also used LBP for feature extraction. Accuracy of 83.02% was achieved by using LBP, and accuracy of 87.07% was achieved by using LTrP (see Table 5.2).

5.2.3 VOICE SAMPLES

Mashrura Tasnim et al. [12] proposed an ML approach to detect depression by analysing the acoustic features of a person's voice. In this paper, four various ML algorithms were tested for both classification task and regression task, and the obtained results were then compared. The four models compared in this paper were as follows:

1. Random forest (RF) – Learning rate: 0.1 and estimator trees: 100
2. SVM – Radial basis function (RBF) kernel
3. GBT – Estimator tress: 100 for both classification task and regression task
4. Deep neural network (DNN) – No. of layers: 3, neurons in each layer 512, 256 and 512, respectively, batch size: 64, loss function: categorical cross entropy (for classification task) and mean squared error (for regression task), learning rate: 10^{-4} (for classification task) and 10^{-3} (for regression task).

Here [12], based on the results obtained – DNN gives the best results among the four models for binary classification with the highest accuracy of "80.11%" (AVEC 2017 dataset), where for the regression task, random forest gives competitive results, i.e. RMSE = 6.17 (AVEC 2017 dataset) which is the minimum RMSE value obtained as compared to all the other models.

Afef Mdhaffar et al. [13], for depressive episode detection, proposed a deep learning approach, called DL4DED (for mobile devices), which consists of CNN + LSTM architecture to extract voice features from phone calls. Two compression techniques – (1) quantisation and (2) pruning are used to compress the neural network models that are used for running the DL4DED on the end device (mobile). In the paper, the authors have

TABLE 5.2

Comparison: "Considering Facial Expressions"

Ref. No	Title	Methodology	Metrics
[10]	Eye movement analysis for depression detection	Used eye movement features extracted from face videos using active appearance models to perform binary classification task of depressed/non-depressed.	Accuracy: 70% (SVM and GMMs) Accuracy: 75% (SVM classifiers)
[11]	Clinical depression detection in adolescent by face	Used local tetra pattern (LTrP) for feature extraction from a facial image and for binary classification, i.e. depressed or non-depressed they used Fisher vector encoding.	Accuracy: 83.02% (LBP) Accuracy: 87.07% (LTrP)

also focused on the concepts of data privacy, as the voice features are extracted from the user's phone directly – DL4DED ensures data privacy. They achieved an accuracy of 52% on the original model and an accuracy of 50% for the model deployed on the end device, i.e. the accuracy of the model, which is compressed, is slightly lesser than the accuracy of the original model (see Table 5.3).

5.2.4 RESEARCH GAP IDENTIFIED

Most of the studies related to this field focus only on some particular spectrum of psychological distress and they tend to generalize or detect the broader term of the type of detected disease. For example, most of the studies only detect whether a person is suffering from depression or not. However, the term depression within itself can be classified into more specific types like MDD and bipolar disorder. Therefore, there are fewer studies that detect and classify different types of mental distress and the sub-categories within them also in depth.

For the diagnosis of mental distress, there are certain symptoms that the doctor looks for and on the basis of the duration and frequency of those symptoms, the

TABLE 5.3

Comparison: "Voice Samples"

Ref. No	Title	Methodology	Metrics
[12]	Detecting depression from voice	Machine learning approach to detect depression by analysing the acoustic features of a person's voice.	Accuracy: 80.11% (Classification – DNN) RMSE = 6.17 (Regression – RF)
[13]	Deep learning for depressive episode detection on mobile devices.	Used DL4DED consisting of CNN + LSTM architecture which extracts voice features from phone calls.	Accuracy: 52% (Original Model) Accuracy: 50% (Deployed Model)

doctor identifies the presence and type of psychological distress. These symptoms include the feeling of worthlessness, loss/gain of weight without the intent of doing so, fatigue, suicidal thoughts. If these symptoms pertain for more than a period of two weeks, the doctor diagnoses the person with mental distress. However, we have seen that most of the approaches try to predict or detect the psychological distress directly on basis of the features extracted from the person rather than detecting the symptoms first.

5.3   PROPOSED METHODOLOGY

In order to provide aid to the users suffering from psychological distress, our proposed solution consists of three modules:

- Detection module
- Classification module
- Assistance module

Here, we propose a mechanism that interacts with the user via a chat interface that predicts the probability of existence of distress and classifies predominant symptoms; this is achieved by implementing text classification algorithms on the user's text messages.

5.3.1   DATA ACQUISITION

As input to our system and for training purposes, we have prepared two different kinds of datasets: (1) distress classification dataset and (2) symptoms classification dataset. The features for both the datasets consist of posts and comments that have been scraped from different social networking sites like Reddit and Twitter. The distress classification dataset is used in the detection module, whereas the symptoms classification dataset is used in the classification module. The distress classification dataset has only two classes, where the input feature text is labelled as either "0" for non-distressed or "1" for distressed. In the case of symptoms classification dataset, it consists of total 15 classes as mentioned: *"lack of emotion", "excess of emotion", "lack of weight", "excess of weight", "lack of sleep", "excess of sleep", "lack of concentration", "suicidal thoughts", "fatigue", "sense of guilt", "worthlessness", "mood swings", "decrease in agility", "overthinking", "social awkwardness"* and *"stress"*. Multiple labels may be assigned to each instance of input feature text which is depicted by a vector of 0 and 1. The distress classification dataset comprises about 40k data points, and the symptoms classification dataset comprises about 2K data points. Both the dataset are splitted into two parts – training dataset and the test dataset in the ratio of 8:2.

5.3.2   DETECTION AND CLASSIFICATION

The detection and classification modules perform text classification tasks on their respective input dataset.

We applied different deep learning techniques like bi-directional LSTM and fine-tuned transformer-based models like Bidirectional Encoder Representations from Transformers (BERT) [14], RoBERTa [15] and Distill-BERT [16] in order to do the classification. Transformer-based models like BERT were trained on large datasets of unlabelled text and were trained in such a way that they could develop representations that are bi-directional in nature, i.e. they can extract context from both left and right sides.

There are two different variants of the BERT model: the base model and the large model. The base model consists of 12 layers of Transformer Encoder Blocks, whereas the large model comprises 24 such layers. In the base model, each encoder block comprises 12 self-attention heads, whereas in the case of large model it comprises 24 such self-attention heads. Here, in the base model encoder block has 768 hidden units, whereas in the large model there are 1024 hidden units. The base model has about 110 million parameters, whereas the large model has about 340 million parameters. We make use of the base (bertbase-uncased) model for our classification task. The pre-trained BERT model can be fine-tuned in order to create state-of-the-art models.

We have also evaluated models like RoBERTa that and Distill-BERT that are BERT-based models. RoBERTa uses dynamic masking pattern as compared to the static masking in the case of BERT model in order to optimize the results.

So in the detection module, we perform binary text classification and predict the probability of the given input text to be distressed or non-distressed. Whereas in the case of the classification module, we perform multi-label classification, i.e. each text may belong to more than one class simultaneously.

5.3.3 ASSISTANCE

RASA *(DIET Architecture)*: We are using Rasa for developing our chatbot. The architecture that Rasa uses for entity and intent detection is Dual Intent Entity Transformer (DIET). To understand DIET [17], let's take a response from a user which is sad and unhappy. This is a training example. So, we already know the intents and entities. The intent here is sad_mood, and the entities are sad, unhappy, which is a reason. The architecture first tokenizes the sentence and each token goes through a block. Each block has a pre-trained neural network which can be either GloVe [18], BERT [14] or ConveRT [19] and a feedforward layer to which the sparse features of the token is passed. The sparse features of one hot encoding of the token, n grams from 2 to 5 g. The output from the pre-trained neural network and the feedforward layer are concatenated and again passed to a feedforward layer which gives a vector of 256 floating point numbers which are then passed to the transformer layer. The architecture also has special things, a mask for calculating the mask loss, a class token for calculating the intent loss. Random tokens from the utterance are masked to make the model a general language model. The mask goes through the transformer layer and meets the token (word embedding) which had been masked where a similarity check is done which leads to a mask loss. The class token goes through the block the same as other tokens, but the key difference is that it is the summarisation of all the tokens and it goes through the transformer, and it's word embedding is compared with the intent's (which is already known) word embedding which leads to an intent loss. The tokens go through the transformer layer and to the CRF layer where they are compared with the entities that we know and this leads to an entity loss. The main goal of the algorithm is to optimize all the individual losses which in turn will optimize the total loss. The heart of this architecture is the transformer layer which is beyond the scope of this chapter.

We are providing the assistance to the user via chatbot which we have developed using Rasa. We have tried to implement some steps that are involved in cognitive behavioural theory (CBT) in our chatbot. One of the important steps is Journaling. Let's understand what Journaling is. In Journaling, we try to extract from the user his/her thoughts and moods. So when a user starts using our chatbot, the chatbot asks the user certain questions in a friendly manner that helps the chatbot in extracting the mood and the thoughts of the user. The information extracted from the user is then passed to an API where a deep learning model resides. It predicts whether the user is distressed or non-distressed. If the user is distressed, the deep learning model classifies the symptoms detected and the API returns the symptoms detected to the chatbot which in turn displays it to the user. This is the step called unravelling cognitive distortions in CBT terms. Then, the chatbot asks the user why he/she is suffering from these symptoms. What are the opinions of the user on the symptoms that have been detected. Furthermore, the chatbot tries to motivate the user to come out of the distress through motivational sentences and Graphics Interchange Format (GIF). This is the step called cognitive restructuring in CBT.

5.3.4   WORKFLOW

Once the user initializes the system, he/she can opt for monitoring mental well-being, the system displays the past interactions to the user. Based on these past interactions, the user can monitor the daily/weekly/monthly analysis of his/her behaviour. Self-monitoring of his/her behaviour will help the user to effectively overcome some of the challenges, and if any improvements are observed, then it will help them motivate for a happy and a better life.

The user interacts with the system through a simple chat interface. Here, we are using the Rasa × chat interface. Intents are being set, and stories are created on the chat interface. According to the response from the user, the intents are triggered. The flow of the conversation depends upon the responses given by the users. Each and every response of the user is fed to the detection and classification module for the accurate classification of the symptoms, if the user is distressed. The conversations are preprocessed by using NLP and sent to the detection module. The chat interface gives the user a friendly environment where he/she can express his/her thoughts (see Figure 5.1).

So, now that the responses from the users are fed to detection and classification modules as shown in Figure 5.2. Process "A" represents the workflow of these two ML modules. Firstly, the response is passed to the detection module. The output that we obtain through this module is either "1" or "0", if the probability that the person is distressed is greater than the threshold = 0.7 then the output is "1" else it is "0" indicating the person is not suffering through any psychological distress. As seen in the figure, if any kind of psychological distress is detected, the response is then fed to

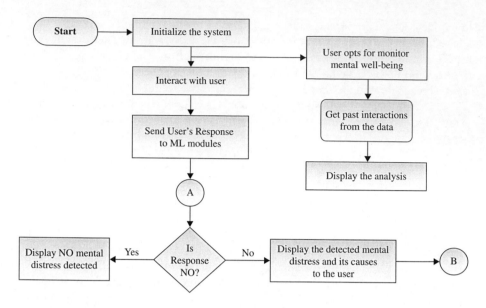

FIGURE 5.1   Process "A" and "B" – workflow diagram.

the classification module for further classification of the symptoms. Now, through this module, if the number of symptoms is greater than 5 then we confirm that the user suffers from distress and also obtain its causes. If the user wishes to see the symptoms explicitly in the middle of the conversation with the BOT, he/she can ask the BOT to show the symptoms classified.

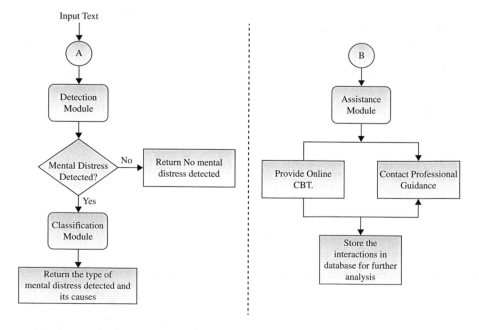

FIGURE 5.2   High-level overview of the system.

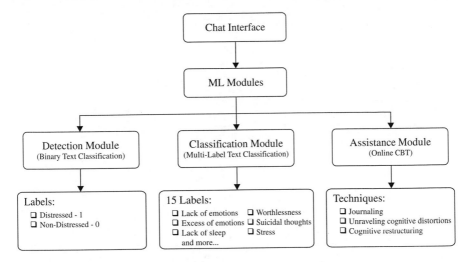

FIGURE 5.3   Entire workflow diagram.

After this process, the user now has the knowledge of his/her mental state and can then opt for the third ML module, i.e. assistance (process "B" in Figure 5.2) in this the user again has a choice, i.e. he/she can either opt for:

1. Online CBT
2. Contact professional guidance.

If the user opts for option 1, three techniques mentioned in Figure 5.3 are implemented and also as discussed the chat interface helps to provide the assistance in a user-friendly manner. As mentioned earlier, after this phase too the user can opt for the analysis of the symptoms.

5.4   RESULTS

In the detection and classification module, we have evaluated different models like bi-directional LSTM, BERT, RoBERTa and Distill-BERT on metrics like accuracy, precision, recall and F1 score for the binary classification task performed in the detection module and multi-label classification for the classification module (see Figures 5.4 and 5.5).

True Positive (TP): The correctly classified positive observations are called TP. That is, if the actual class is positive and the model also predicts it as positive, it is considered TP.

True Negative (TN): The correctly classified negative observations are called TN. That is, if the actual class is negative and the model also predicts it as negative, it is considered TN.

False Positive (FP): The incorrectly classified positive observations are called FP. That is, if the actual class is negative but the model predicts it as positive, it is considered FP.

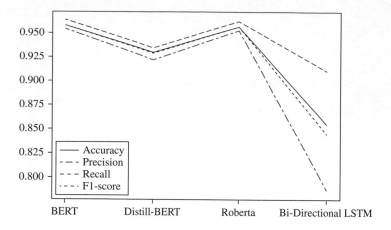

FIGURE 5.4 Detection module comparison.

False Negative (FN): These are the incorrectly predicted negative observations. That is, if the actual class is negative but the model predicts it as positive, it is considered FP.

Precision: It's defined as the ratio of TP observations to the total number of observations classified as positive by our model.

$$Precision = \frac{TP}{TP + FP}$$

Recall: It's defined as the ratio of TP observations to total actual positive observations.

$$Recall = \frac{TP}{TP + FN}$$

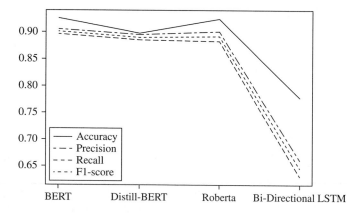

FIGURE 5.5 Classification module comparison.

Accuracy: The percentage of correctly classified observations by the model is called accuracy.

$$\text{Accuracy} = \frac{TP + TN}{TP + FP + TN + FN}$$

We performed binary text classification and multi-label text classification in the detection and classification module, respectively; we observed that transformer-based models like BERT, RoBERTa and Distill-BERT gave better results as compared to that of bi-directional LSTM for all the considered metrics.

5.4.1 DETECTION

Here in detection module, the test dataset comprised total 8k samples (20% of 40K), where distressed samples were labelled as "1" and non-distressed samples were labelled as "0". The BERT and RoBERTa model gave the highest accuracy of around 95%, whereas Distill-BERT model gave an accuracy of 92% which is slightly lower than the other transformer-based models. The confusion matrices for the different models are given below (see Figure 5.6 and Table 5.4).

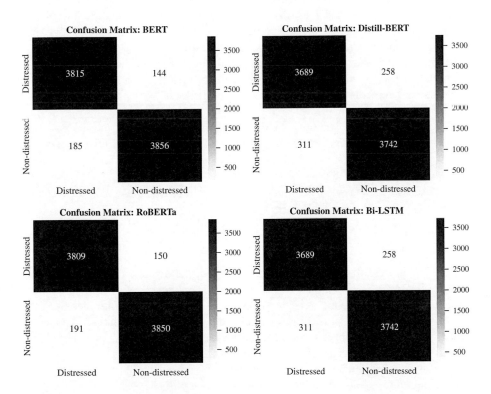

FIGURE 5.6 Confusion matrix: detection module.

TABLE 5.4

Results: Detection Module

Name	Accuracy	Precision	Recall	F1 score
BERT	0.95888	0.96362	0.95375	0.95866
Distill-BERT	0.92888	0.93463	0.92225	0.9284
RoBERTa	0.95737	0.96211	0.95225	0.95716
Bi-directional LSTM	0.85425	0.91001	0.78625	0.84362

5.4.2 CLASSIFICATION

Here in classification module, we perform multi-label classification, i.e. each sample may be associated with multiple labels/classes. Here the dataset comprised total 2k samples and each sample may be associated with one or many labels (see Figure 5.7). The labels are mentioned below: *"lack of emotion", "excess of emotion", "lack of weight", "excess of weight", "lack of sleep", "excess of sleep", "lack of concentration", "suicidal thoughts", "fatigue", "sense of guilt", "worthlessness", "mood swings", "decrease in agility", "overthinking", "social awkwardness", "stress".*

The BERT and RoBERTa model gave the highest accuracy of around 92%, whereas Distill-BERT model gave an accuracy of 89% which is slightly lower than the other transformer-based models. Whereas, in the case of bi-directional LSTM, we observed an accuracy of 77%, which is comparatively low.

Within the transformer-based models, after fine-tuning, BERT and RoBERTa gave the best results, whereas Distill-BERT gave comparable results with way fewer parameters as compared to that of RoBERTa and BERT.

Each model was trained for a total of 150 epochs. In order to avoid over-fitting, call-backs, such as early-stopping, were used. In the case of transformer-based models where we applied transfer learning on the pre-trained networks, it was noted that the model converged faster and started to give good accuracy at lesser epochs as compared to that of Bi-LSTM.

As discussed earlier, we compared the results of four ML models on the basis of the following metrics (see Table 5.5).

5.4.3 ASSISTANCE

We created an API that integrates the results from the detection and classification along with RASA'S NLU model which uses DIET architecture for intent and entity classification. The responses received from the user via the chat interface are sent to the API and the API returns the symptoms detected (if any) with their respective probabilities. The responses received from the user and the symptoms detected and all the user's interactions are stored for future analysis.

For assistance module, we implemented three aspects of online CBT, i.e. Journaling, unravelling cognitive distortions and cognitive restructuring. We have discussed each of these in detail.

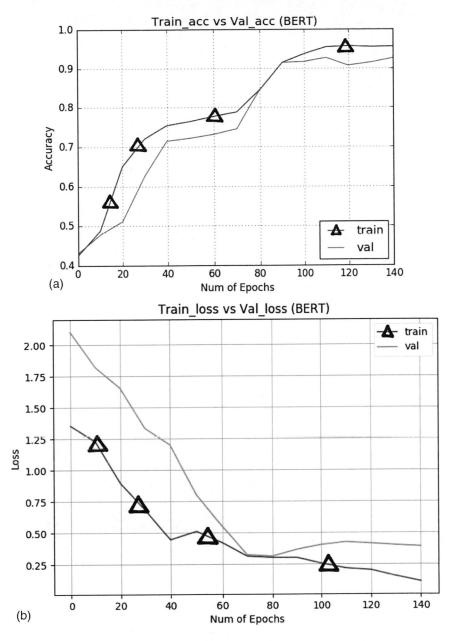

FIGURE 5.7   Accuracy and loss for BERT model: classification module. (a) Training accuracy vs. validation accuracy (BERT). (b) Training loss vs. validation loss (BERT).

Journaling: In Journaling, the person's behaviour, whether he/she is distressed or not, (detected by the detection module), the time and the intensity of each interaction are being noted and stored. So that the user can journal his daily routine by simply interacting with the chatbot (see Figure 5.8).

TABLE 5.5
Results: Multi-Label Classification

Name	Accuracy	Precision	Recall	F1-Score
BERT	0.92518	0.89521	0.90451	0.899835
Distill-BERT	0.89712	0.88475	0.89436	0.88952
RoBERTa	0.92357	0.88201	0.90021	0.89102
Bi-directional LSTM	0.77654	0.62877	0.65987	0.64394

Unravelling cognitive distortions: Here, the user is shown all the different detected symptoms (distortions) he/she is affected with. These symptoms are detected by the classification module. The end user will be able to see a chart as shown in Figure 5.9, where they will be able to analysis and introspect their symptoms they are suffering from.

Cognitive Restructuring: Our system can show the detected symptoms and the user's messages that those symptoms are associated with. Thus, the user can use these interactions and corresponding symptoms to rethink, restructure the way he/she thinks during such situations.

If the user opts to get a report of the interactions, he/she has had with the chatbot in the past. Our system can analyse their behaviour and create a time series graph representing the day-by-day analysis of the symptoms detected for given user over a month.

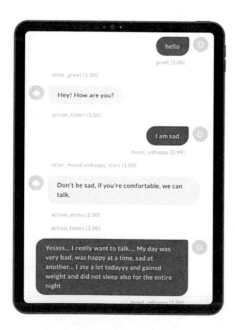 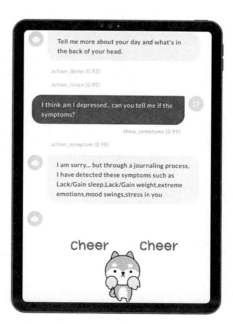

FIGURE 5.8   Implementation of ChatBot interaction – distressed person.

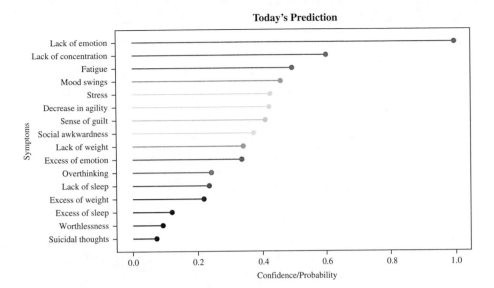

FIGURE 5.9 Detected symptoms (unravelling cognitive distortions).

5.5 CONCLUSIONS

We have seen in recent times that people are talking a lot about depression, stress and all these types of psychological distress mostly due to many notable celebrities committing suicides. Many people are not able to handle it properly since they don't even know whether they are suffering from depression/distress or not. They do even know why they are suffering and what symptoms do they have.

As we had seen in the literature survey, a lot of research in this domain had been done in only detecting whether a person has depression or not and not on finding why and from which symptoms he/she was suffering. So, the main aim of this research was to first find an effective mechanism to classify symptoms and increase the scope of the research that had been done in this domain. A lot of biological study was also required to be done which was done by us. We thank all the medical professionals for their help and also have given the due credits to them.

Different models were tried out for the classification of symptoms out of which BERT performed best on the evaluation metrics.

And then how you will tell the individual that he/she is suffering from these symptoms. For that, first you need to know what the user wants to say. And to do that a chat interface was required which was implemented by using RASA.

API was created using the BERT model. The responses received from the user were sent to the API. The API responded with the classified symptoms and their probabilities. The conversations were stored for future analysis. User had an option to see the symptoms detected through graphs on a particular day or a period of time.

In this way we tried to implement a one stop system for providing detection, classification and assistance so that they can come out of any psychological distress if they are suffering from it.

5.6   FUTURE SCOPE

As it was mentioned earlier, most of the previous research work had been done only in the detection of depression, i.e. whether a person has it or not and does not focus on why and from which symptoms he/she is suffering. Through this research, we have tried to open a new domain by identifying symptoms that a psychologically distressed person might have. We tried out different deep learning models like BERT, RoBERTa, Distill-BERT and bi-directional LSTM to classify these symptoms. We believe that, this can be taken forward for further research.

We have tried to provide detection, classification and assistance to users at a single place. However, there is a scope for improvement in the assistance module which can be achieved by collaborating with medical professionals, clinics and organisations which work in this domain.

Furthermore, the chatbot that we have developed is very simple as of now. In the future along with improvements in the chatbot, it could be integrated with different messaging platforms like WhatsApp, Telegram, Twitter, and Slack for making it available to most of the population. Also, there is a scope of making our own application consisting of these features along with some more functionalities.

REFERENCES

[1] World Health Organization: The world health report 2001: Mental disorders affect one in four people. https://www.who.int/news/item/28-09-2001-the-world-health-report-2001-mental-disorders-affect-one-in-four-people (September 2001).

[2] Sapolsky, R.M.: Robert Sapolsky: The psychology of stress. https://youtu.be/bEcdGK-4DQSg (March 2012).

[3] Chrousos, G.P.: Stress and disorders of the stress system. https://www.medscape.com/viewarticle/7059065 (October 2020).

[4] Deshpande, M., Rao, V.: Depression detection using emotion artificial intelligence. In: 2017 International Conference on Intelligent Sustainable Systems (ICISS). pp. 858–862 (2017). https://doi.org/10.1109/ISS1.2017.8389299

[5] Nadeem, M., Horn, M., Coppersmith, G., Sen, S.: Identifying depression on Twitter. https://arxiv.org/abs/1607.07384 (2016).

[6] Cacheda, F., Fernandez, D., Novoa, F.J., Carneiro, V.: Early detection of depression: Social network analysis and random forest techniques. J Med Internet Res 21(6), e12554 (Jun 2019). https://doi.org/10.2196/12554, http://www.jmir.org/2019/6/e12554/

[7] De Choudhury, M., Gamon, M., Counts, S., Horvitz, E.: Predicting depression via social media. https://ojs.aaai.org/index.php/ICWSM/article/view/14432#:~:text=We%20find%20that%20social%20media,greater%20expression%20of%20religious%20involvement (July 2013).

[8] Biradar, A., Totad, S.G.: Detecting depression in social media posts using machine learning. In: Santosh, K.C., Hegadi, R.S. (eds.) Recent Trends in Image Processing and Pattern Recognition. pp. 716–725. Springer Singapore, Singapore (2019).

[9] Asad, N.A., Mahmud Pranto, M.A., Afreen, S., Islam, M.M.: Depression detection by analyzing social media posts of user. In: 2019 IEEE International Conference on Signal Processing, Information, Communication Systems (SPICSCON). pp. 13–17 (2019). https://doi.org/10.1109/SPICSCON48833.2019.9065101

[10] Alghowinem, S., Goecke, R., Wagner, M., Parker, G., Breakspear, M.: Eye movement analysis for depression detection. In: 2013 IEEE International Conference on Image Processing. pp. 4220–4224 (2013). https://doi.org/10.1109/ICIP.2013.6738869

[11] Kulkarni, P.B., Patil, M.M.: Clinical depression detection in adolescent by face. In: 2018 International Conference on Smart City and Emerging Technology (ICSCET). pp. 1–4 (2018). https://doi.org/10.1109/ICSCET.2018.8537268

[12] Tasnim, M., Stroulia, E.: Detecting depression from voice. In: Meurs, M.J., Rudzicz, F. (eds.) Advances in Artificial Intelligence. pp. 472–478. Springer International Publishing, Cham (2019).

[13] Mdhaffar, A., Cherif, F., Kessentini, Y., Maalej, M., Thabet, J.B., Maalej, M., Jmaiel, M., Freisleben, B.: Dl4ded: Deep learning for depressive episode detection on mobile devices. In: Pagán, J., Mokhtari, M., Aloulou, H., Abdulrazak, B., Cabrera, M.F. (eds.) How AI Impacts Urban Living and Public Health. pp. 109–121. Springer International Publishing, Cham (2019).

[14] Devlin, J., Chang, M.W., Lee, K., Toutanova, K.: Bert: Pre-training of deep bi-directional transformers for language understanding. https://arxiv.org/abs/1810.04805 (2019).

[15] Liu, Y., Ott, M., Goyal, N., Du, J., Joshi, M., Chen, D., Levy, O., Lewis, M., Zettlemoyer, L., Stoyanov, V.: RoBERTa: A robustly optimized BERT pretraining approach. https://arxiv.org/abs/1907.11692 (2019).

[16] Sanh, V., Debut, L., Chaumond, J., Wolf, T.: Distill-BERT, a distilled version of BERT: Smaller, faster, cheaper and lighter. https://arxiv.org/abs/1910.01108 (2020).

[17] Rasa Research Advocate Vincent Warmerdam: Rasa algorithm whiteboard – Diet architecture 1: How it works. https://youtu.be/vWStcJDuOUk (March 2020).

[18] Pennington, J., Socher, R., Manning, C.D.: Glove: Global vectors for word representation. In: Empirical Methods in Natural Language Processing (EMNLP). pp. 1532–1543 (2014), http://www.aclweb.org/anthology/D14-1162

[19] Henderson, M., Casanueva, I., Mrkšić, N., Su, P.H., Wen, T.H., Vulić, I.: Convert: Efficient and accurate conversational representations from transformers. https://arxiv.org/abs/1911.03688 (2020).

6 Fast and Efficient Text Searching in Compressed Data Using Burrows–Wheeler Transform

Sanjeev Kumar
Department of CSE, United University
Prayagraj, India

Mukund Pratap Singh
School of Computer Science Engineering
and Technology, Bennett University
Greater Noida, India

CONTENTS

6.1   INTRODUCTION

Due to the fast rise in data size, compression has become an indispensable method of data management. Compression is significantly more beneficial when processing huge amounts of data via networks, collecting enormous amounts of text or storing massive amounts of biological data [1]. For example, archiving massive DNA sequences in preparation for future processing, in the area of computational biology, requires huge disc storage. As a result, large-scale data compression has become a need. Additionally, compression might be advantageous when searching for a pattern

DOI: 10.1201/9781003320340-6

(of any nature) in a big data collection [2]. The matching pattern is understood to be the process of identifying all instances of a pattern (of any form) within a massive body of text. It plays a key role in text mining, information retrieval, large data analysis, the detection of plagiarism computational biology and signal processing.

Pattern matching compressed (CPM) [3] is an assignment of an interior pattern in a compressed text uncompressed. The pattern here should not be compressed. CPM reduces the disc capacity, compression ratio and pattern matching time. It is more advantageous in communication networks when large amounts of data are transferred via the network, as in the case of the Internet. CPM can help reduce network traffic in this scenario.

Many authors have previously proposed the CPM solution algorithms. Amir et al. proposed the first compressed CPM on LZW (Lempel–Ziv–Welch) approach in [1]. According to this study, this is the first time a substring pattern in compressed data has been recognized. CPM should be fully compressed using LZW, as proposed by the authors in [4, 5].

In [6], authors used the LZ77 algorithm to develop CPM. The answer is better than LZW. The Ziv and Lempel compression scheme [7, 8] and the Huffman compression [8] are not suitable for large-scale text databases due to their character-oriented nature. These approaches do not function effectively when searching for a specific term within a compressed text file. Because of the extremely low compression ratio produced by Huffman-based compression techniques, they are infrequently used in natural language processing applications. The Ziv and Lempel families of compression algorithms [9], on the other contrary, provide better compression ratios but have difficulties looking for a specific word directly inside the encoded text because of their asymmetric nature.

With the introduction of the WBTC (word-based tagged code) in [10, 11], partial compression and rapid text decompression at any arbitrary location with the use of a Flag bit were made possible. It also makes use of a tagging system in order to support a compressed text pattern and identify false matches with ease. In conjunction with this [12, 13], techniques use linear search on the compressed data, and this might be quite expensive for huge text. The wavelet tree (WT) is a self-indexed data structure developed in 2003 [14]. WT is an independent index data structure that supports efficient searching operations (count, locate and occur). Khetan et al. [15] presented a novel approach for substring searching using WT and WBTC. They solve a parameterized word matching in compressed word by their algorithm. In the parameterized match [2, 16], two alphabets took the pattern: parameterized and fixed. It was intended to fragment the pattern into equal q-grams in order to identify parameterized matches, which in the actual world, particularly in the context of compression and information retrieval, is not very practical.

6.2   OVERVIEW OF RELATED LITERATURE

6.2.1   SUFFIX TREE

Weiner introduced suffix tree(ST) [1] (1973). This is a compressed data trial structure that represents all string suffixes. The first full-text indexation method for pattern search in $O(p)$ time is ST (where p is the length of substring(pattern)). The negative aspect of indexes based on ST method is that it requires memory about (20–40) times

TABLE 6.1

Construction of Suffix Array for Text "TGGCAAT$"

Suffixes		Ordered Suffixes	
Isuffixes	Ssuffixes	SA [Isuffixes]	Ssuffixes
0	TGGCAAT$	7	$
1	GGCAAT$	4	AAT$
2	GCAAT$	5	AT$
3	CAAT$	3	CAAT$
4	AAT$	2	GCAAT$
5	AT$	1	GGCAAT$
6	T$	6	T$
7	$	0	TGGCAAT$

a string size in large memory space. Indices based on ST are used in numerous applications for instance: matching pattern, multi-sequence alignment, repetitive sequence searching in genomic sequences and loss-based compression of images.

6.2.2 SUFFIX ARRAY

Manber and Myers devised the suffix array(SA) [5] as a fast, simple and memory-efficient searching technique (1989). It's a set of classified string suffixes. This is a critical data structure for a range of applications, including compressed text searching, genetic data extraction and pattern recognition. SA is an index number permutation created by sorting T string suffixes in a sorted order. The construction of the "TGGCAAT$" string is shown in Table 6.1.

6.2.3 BURROWS–WHEELER TRANSFORM

In compressed data processing, Burrows–Wheelertransform (BWT) is widely employed. The most significant aspect in BWT is to select the Burrows–Wheeler matrix (BWM) from all possible cyclic rotations of a given input string in sorted order (alphabetically) and return the final column. This final column, which contains the BWT string, is easy to compress, as it has several repeat characters. BWT provides for rapid string matching on the compressed text index of the input genome provided by the BWT algorithm. The following steps are implemented:

1. The conceptual matrix M derives, the length of which are n-cyclical changes of string T.
2. Sort the resulting matrix (M) strings called BWM lexicographically.
3. Take the final column of BWM, build the transform text T_{bwt}.
4. The resulting string T_{bwt} is also marked as L in the last column (last). This is accomplished by lexicographical sorting of the T_{bwt} alphabets to produce the very first column. The construction for BWT "ACCGTTA$" is shown in Table 6.2.

TABLE 6.2

Suffix Array of Text "AAGGCCAATA$"

Suffixes			Ordered Suffixes	
Isuffixes	Ssuffixes	I	SA [Isuffixes]	Ssuffixes
0	AAGGCCAATA$	0	10	$
1	AGGCCAATA$	1	9	A$
2	GGCCAATA$	2	0	AAGGCCAATA$
3	GCCAATA$	3	6	AATA$
4	CCAATA$	4	1	AGGCCAATA$
5	CAATA$	5	7	ATA$
6	AATA$	6	5	CAATA$
7	ATA$	7	4	CCAATA$
8	TA$	8	3	GCCAATA$
9	A$	9	2	GGCCAATA$
10	$	10	8	TA$

6.3 METHODOLOGY

The major disadvantage of the techniques outlined above is that BWT does not perform compression by default; it just organizes the text in a compressible fashion. Additional external compression strategies, such as variable length prefix coding, move-to-front encoding (MTF) and run-lengthencoding, are required in order to do this effectively [17]. All of these techniques require a significant amount of calculation overhead and the utilization of CPU peaks RAM in order to be effective. The use of BWT indexes for text data is likewise not recommended due to the huge size of the index created using BWT. In order to address the issues raised above, we propose a new searching approach called SIT, which is constructed on BWT and WT [18]. It is possible to use the WT to compress the string alone, or it may be utilized as a component of another compression technique.

Raman, Raman, and Rao (RRR) [11] is a modern library pertaining to each letter in optimum space and provides extremely fast rank/select functions used to encode the WT [19] nodes, and it responds to rank/select operations in linear time O(1). Furthermore, WT may be enhanced by altering its form (Huffman shape and its variations), as well as by employing various compression booster algorithms to achieve high levels of compression. A schematic of the building blocks of the suggested approach is presented in Figure 6.1.

SA is an indexing technique developed by Myers and Manber in 1989 [5], which is both simple and memory economical. It consists of an array of sequentially ordered suffixes for the string that was given. There are several applications for this datastructure, which involves answering a wide range of queries on compressed data, feature extraction for genetic sequence data and pattern discovery. When the suffixes of a string T are sorted, the SA is specified as a rearrangement of index numbers generated by ordering the suffixes of sequence T. Table 6.1 illustrates the process of creating a

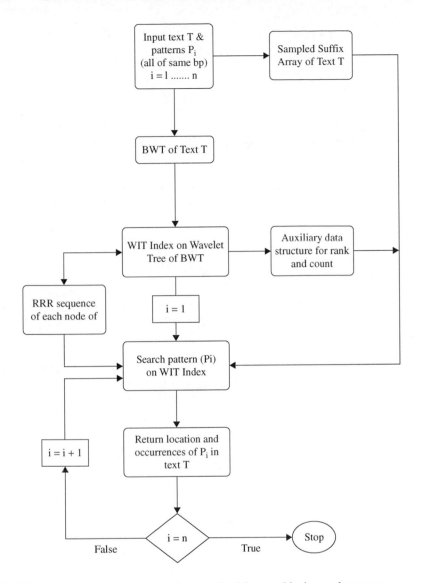

FIGURE 6.1 Proposed approach working methodology and its internal structure.

SA from the text "ACCGTTA\$". This method is intended to priorities all possible rotations of a given input text in lexicographical order using a BWM [13], and then return the final column as a result of the sorting process. A significant number of repeated letters in a single location makes it possible to easily compress the last column, which corresponds to the BWT string, in the BWT string. It is possible to index the relevant genome quickly using BWT since it enables for fast string matching on the compressed material.

The final column contains the resulting string T_{bwt}, which is also indicated as L. (last). The initial column is produced by arranging the alphabets of T_{bwt} in a

TABLE 6.3
BWT (Burrows–WheelerTransform) Construction

Index Prior to Sorting		Index after Sorting	
Index	**Cyclic Shifting**	**Index**	**Cyclic Shifting**
0	AAGGCCAATA$	0	$AAGGCCAATA
1	AGGCCAATA$A	1	A$AAGGCCAAT
2	GGCCAATA$AA	2	AAGGCCAATA$
3	GCCAATA$AAG	3	AATA$AAGGCC
4	CCAATA$AAGG	4	AGGCCAATA$A
5	CAATA$AAGGC	5	ATA$AAGGCCA
6	AATA$AAGGCC	6	CAATA$AAGGC
7	ATA$AAGGCCA	7	CCAATA$AAGG
8	TA$AAGGCCAA	8	GCCAATA$AAG
9	A$AAGGCCAAT	9	GGCCAATA$AA
10	$AAGGCCAATA	10	TA$AAGGCCAA

lexicographic manner. The creation of the BWT for the text "ACCGTTA$" is shown in Tables 6.3 and 6.4.

The text T may be searched for occurrences of the pattern P and their associated places using the techniques described above. When given a pattern P and the operation SIT-ExacttextsearchS(t, (sc, ec)) returns the suffix interval in SA of the string S = aS,

TABLE 6.4
Index of Text T="ATGGACTATCAC$"

I	Suffix#	BWT(T)	Sorted Suffixes
0	10	A	$
1	9	T	A$
2	0	$	AAGGCCAATA$
3	6	C	AATA$
4	1	A	AGGCCAATA$
5	7	A	ATA$
6	5	C	CAATA$
7	4	G	CCAATA$
8	3	G	GCCAATA$
9	2	A	GGCCAATA$
10	8	A	TA$

SIT-ExacttextsearchS(t, (sc, ec))

Let comp[t] represent the no of letters in the alphabet in S that is less than cin alphabetical order.

sc=comp[SR[i]]+pos(s-1,P[i])+1

ec=comp[SR[i]]+score(ec, SR[i])

return (sc, ec)

TABLE 6.5

The Proposed and Existing Algorithms Processing Time in Milliseconds for Query Patterns with a Length of Four and Less than Four Characters (Short)

Datasets	Text	Size(KB)	ST	SA	BruteForce	Proposed
Arabic	Quran	716.8	1007	1032	1980	985
English	Bible	3072	615	627	984	570
Italian	Orlando	737.28	1008	1037	1989	987
Chinese	Journey	1402.88	1389	1411	2108	1078
Hindi	Gita	1157.2	1256	1267	2065	994

where a represents any character, sc represents the beginning location of Text T and ec represents the end position of Text T [20]. When given any pattern P and its suffix range, it is feasible to recursively determine the suffix range of a text P inside a reference text sequence T.

6.4   RESULT ANALYSIS

Five different datasets of natural texts (Arabic, English, Italian, Chinese and Hindi) are taken for experiments [15, 21]. Searching time of proposed approach and state-of-the-art approaches (ST, SA and bruteforce approach) are compared for different patterns length. In Table 6.5,processing time of proposed approach and state-of-the-art approaches are illustrated for query pattern of length 4 and less than 4. From Table 6.5 and Figure 6.2, it is validated that the proposed strategy is outperformed w.r.t. state-of-the-art approaches. In Table 6.6, processing time of proposed approach and state of the-art approaches are illustrated for query patterns of length greater

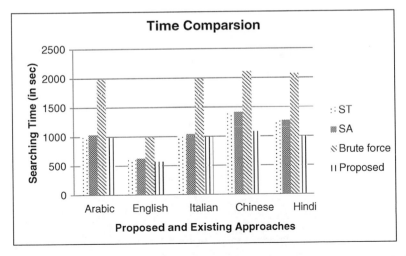

FIGURE 6.2   The proposed and existing algorithms' processing time in milliseconds for query patterns with a length of four characters and less than four characters (short).

TABLE 6.6

The Proposed and Existing Algorithms Processing Time in Milliseconds for Query Patterns with a Length Greater than Four Characters and Less than Eight Characters

Datasets	Text	Size(MB)	ST	SA	BWT	Proposed
Arabic	Quran	716.8	984	956	1234	745
English	Bible	3072	531	545	768	489
Italian	Orlando	737.28	1120	1176	1327	1038
Chinese	Journey	1402.88	1284	1293	1438	1056
Hindi	Gita	1157.2	1059	1085	1546	943

than 4 and less than 8. From Table 6.6 and Figure 6.3, it has been observed that the processing time of the proposed methodology is the least when compared to current state-of-the-art approaches.

6.5   CONCLUSION

The BWT is extended in this chapter, and a compact indexing method is provided. For pattern searching, the proposed method SIT is a straightforward and time-saving solution. Proposed method: SIT and state-of-the-art tools based on ST, SA and brute force are compared for various natural text datasets such as English, Arabic, Italian and Chinese. The results of the experiments demonstrate that the SIT-based tool produces more compression while also having a faster searching time when compared to other BWT-based methods. It has been discovered that a SIT-based technology outperforms the competition, particularly in natural text compression (Arabic, English, Italian and Chinese).

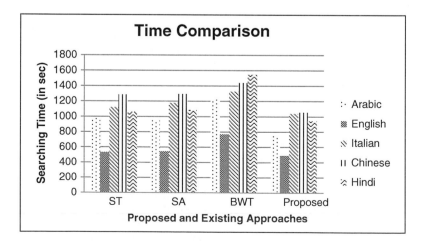

FIGURE 6.3   The proposed and existing algorithms' processing time in milliseconds for query patterns with a length greater than four characters and less than eight characters.

REFERENCES

1. D. Adjeroh, T. Bell, and A. Mukherjee, "The Burrows-Wheeler Transform: Data Compression, Suffix Arrays, and Pattern Matching", Springer, New York, 1 edition, 2008.
2. M. Burrows and D. J. Wheeler, "A block-sorting lossless data compression algorithm", Systems Research, Research R, 1(124): pp. 1–24, 1994.
3. P. Ferragina, G. Manzini, V. Makinen, and G. Navarro, "Compressed representations of sequences and full-text indexes", ACM Transactions Algorithms, 3, 2007.
4. H. Li and R. Durbin, "Fast and accurate short read alignment with burrows–wheeler transform", Bioinformatics, 25(14): pp. 1754–1760, 2009.
5. U. Manber and G. Myers, "Suffix arrays: a new method for on-line string searches", In Proceedings of the first annual ACM-SIAM symposium on Discrete algorithms, SODA '90, pp. 319–327, Philadelphia, PA, USA, 1990.
6. L.G. Asieniec and W. Rytter, "Almost optimal fully LZW-compressed pattern matching", In Proceedings of IEEE data compression conference, pp. 316–325, Snowbird, UT, USA, March 29–31, 1999.
7. M. Farach and M. Thorup, "String matching in Lempel-Ziv compressed strings", In Proceedings of annual ACM symposium on the theory of computing, pp. 703–712, Las Vegas, Nevada, USA, May 29–June 1, 1995.
8. D.A. Huffman, "A method for the construction of minimum-redundancy codes", Proceedings of the IRE, 40(9): pp. 1098–1101, 1952.
9. B. Langmead, C. Trapnell, M. Pop, and S. Salzberg, "Ultrafast and memory-efficient alignment of short DNA sequences to the human genome", Genome Biology, 10(3), Article R25: pp. 1–10, 2009.
10. H. Li and R. Durbin, "Fast and accurate long read alignment with burrows–wheeler transform", Bioinformatics, 26(5): pp. 589–595, 2010.
11. R. Raman, V. Raman, and S. Srinivasa Rao, "Succinct Indexable Dictionaries with Applications to Encoding K-ary Trees and Multi- Sets", In SODA. New York, NY, USA, pp. 233–242, 2002.
12. S. Gog, T. Beller, A. Moffat, and M. Petri, "From theory to practice: plug and play with succinct data structures", 13th International Symposium on Experimental Algorithms (SEA 2014).
13. L. Huang, V. Popic, and S. Batzoglou," Short read alignment with populations of genomes", Bioinformatics, 29: pp. i361–i370, 2013.
14. N. Homer, B. Merriman, and S. F. Nelson, "BFAST: An alignment tool for large scale genome resequencing", PLOS ONE, 4: pp. 67–77, 2009.
15. G. Navarro, "A guided tour to approximate string matching", ACM Computing Surveys (CSUR), 33(1): pp. 31–88, 2001.
16. S. Kumar and S. Agarwal, "WBMFC: Efficient and secure storage of genomic data", Pertanika Journal of Science & Technology, 26(4): pp. 1913–1925, 2018.
17. S. Kumar, S. Agarwal, and R. Vijay, "WBFQC: A new approach for compressing next-generation sequencing data splitting into homogeneous streams", Journal of Bioinformatics and Computational Biology, 16(05): pp. 1850018, 2018.
18. S. Kumar and S. Agarwal, "An efficient tool for searching maximal and super maximal repeats in large DNA/protein sequences via induced-enhanced suffix array", Recent Patents on Computer Science, 12(2): pp. 128–134, 2019.
19. R. Grossi, A. Gupta, and J. S. Vitter, "High-order entropy-compressed text indexes", In Proceedings of the fourteenth annual ACM-SIAM symposium on Discrete algorithms, SODA '03, pp. 841–850, Philadelphia, PA, USA, 2003.
20. S. Kumar, "Gene Sequence Classification Using K-mer Decomposition and Soft-Computing-Based Approach", In Soft Computing: Theories and Applications. Springer, Singapore, pp. 181–186, 2021.
21. A. Goel, et al. "Efficient parameterized matching using burrows-wheeler transform." International Arab Journal of Information Technology, 15(1): pp. 44–49, 2018.

7 A Comprehensive Exploration of Brain Tumor Segmentation Using Deep Learning Techniques

Hariharan Ramamoorthy
and Mohan Ramasundaram
Department of Computer Science and Engineering,
National Institute of Technology
Tiruchirappalli, India

Arish Pitchai
Quantum Machine Learning Lab, BosonQ Psi Pvt. Ltd.
Bhilai, India

CONTENTS

DOI: 10.1201/9781003320340-7

7.1 INTRODUCTION

Brain tumor is a fatal disease. And awareness regarding brain tumor is very important. On June 8 of every year, the world celebrates brain tumor day for creating public awareness. Mainly tumors are of two types: malignant tumors and benign tumors. As per the American Cancer Society, it is estimated that during the year 2020 there will be a possibility of occurrence of new cases which is around 1,806,590, and deaths due to brain tumors will be around 606,520. Nowadays, brain tumor cases are increasing. In the olden days, the diagnosis and detection of tumors is very difficult tasks for doctors. At present, due to improvements in advanced technologies, it will be easy for doctors. At the same time, patients need to have awareness of the diseases.

As per the statistics of the American Society of Clinical Oncology (ASCO) [1]. With an age greater than 40, the survival rate of a patient who is affected by a brain tumor will be decreased. Here, we are presenting the last five-year (2016–2021) survival rates of a brain tumor patient and the average survival rate is almost 36%. Considering the year 2006–2016, the survival rate of brain tumor patients is almost 31%. We divide the ages as per the survival rate of a patient in the last five years as shown in the form of a graph in Figure 7.1. If the patient's age is below 15 then there is a maximum chance, i.e., more than 74% chances are there for surviving. If the patient's age is between 15 and 39, the survival percentage is about 71%. If the patient's age is more than 40 then there will be fewer chances to survive, i.e., 21%. However, these percentages may vary depending upon different factors; it may include the type of brain also.

7.1.1 INTRODUCTION TO IMAGE SEGMENTATION

An image contains a number of pixels. By using image segmentation, we can group the pixels which are having the same attributes.

Need of an image segmentation method: Cancer is a dangerous disease for humans. Detection of cancer cells as early as possible can save many of our lives. For determining the status of cancer, the shape of the cell plays an important role. By using image segmentation techniques, we can get better results.

Types of image segmentation: There are several types of segmentations in image processing. Figure 7.2 shows the major classification of image segmentation.

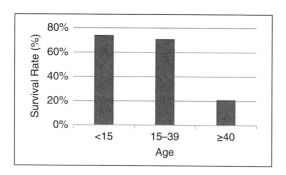

FIGURE 7.1 Survival rate as per the age of a patient.

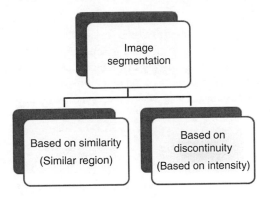

FIGURE 7.2 Classification of image segmentation.

7.1.1.1 Semantic Segmentation
Based on a single instance, this method classifies all images.

7.1.1.2 Instance Segmentation
It will identify each of the images individually.

7.1.1.3 Threshold Segmentation
An image contains a different number of pixel values. We need to set a threshold value if we found any changes between the pixel values. Depending upon above and below threshold values, we can do classification; this process is known as a threshold segmentation. It is of two types. In the first one, a global threshold, we can assign a single threshold value to divide the image into two regions. In the second one, the local threshold method we might have different backgrounds which have multiple objects, then we should set multiple threshold values.

7.1.1.4 Edge Detection Segmentation
General observation in two nearby regions with dissimilar grayscale values, we can find the edge in between them. This discontinuity can be used to detect edges and thus determine an object's boundary. This assists in the identification of multiple object shapes in a single image.

7.1.1.5 Segmentation Based on Clustering
Clustering is a method of dividing data points into several groups so that data points from the same group can be compared more easily to data points from other groups and naming clusters accordingly.

7.1.1.6 k-Means Clustering
The k-means algorithm is a popular clustering algorithm, which is used in many major applications. The major characteristic of this method is the number of clusters will represent as k.

7.1.1.7 Mask R-CNN

Mask regions with convolutional neural networks (R-CNN) is an advanced version of faster R-CNN for object identification model. In mask, R-CNN put on some branches in faster R-CNN output which is already available. Mask R-CNN includes the next branch to this which is having outputs of the object mask as well. The faster R-CNN design creates two things for each object in the image which are the bounding box coordinates and its class.

7.2 CNN ARCHITECTURES

Several types of CNN architectures are classified. Those are patch-wise CNN architecture, semantic-wise CNN architecture, and cascaded CNN architecture.

7.2.1 PATCH-WISE CNN ARCHITECTURE

It is an easy approach for the segmentation process using the CNN algorithm. From the given image we can extract an NxN patch and then these extracted are used to identify the classes. Here, Figure 7.3 shows the patch-wise CNN architecture. This architecture consists of a sequential design having a number of convolutional, pooling, and fully connected layers. Multiscale CNNs use a number of pathways for improving the performance, where each contains a different patch size around the same pixel.

7.2.2 SEMANTIC-WISE CNN ARCHITECTURE

It is similar to semantic segmentation; it includes an encoder part for extracting the features and the decoder is responsible for decoding the higher level features which get from the encoder part and merging with lower level, features an extract from the encoder part for classifying the pixels. Here, Figure 7.4 shows semantic-wise CNN architecture.

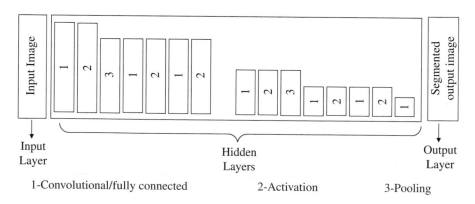

1-Convolutional/fully connected   2-Activation   3-Pooling

FIGURE 7.3 Patch-wise CNN architecture.

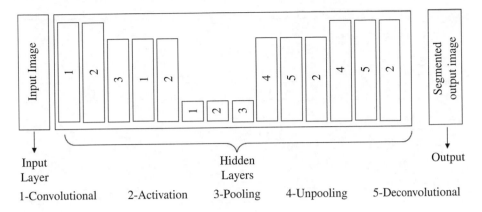

FIGURE 7.4   Semantic-wise CNN architecture.

7.2.3 CASCADED CNN ARCHITECTURE

It consists of two CNN architectures connected in a cascaded format. That is the result of the first CNN being applied as input to the next (second) CNN architecture. Here, Figure 7.5 shows the cascaded CNN architecture. Here, Figure 7.5 shows the design of cascaded CNN network (example of patch-wise CNN and fully convolutional network [FCN]) for tumor segmentation. The first CNN network part is trained for region of interest (ROI) and it will also call as rough classification and the second part of the network is for final segmentation. By using the cascaded CNN image segmentation technique, they extracted the tumor from Brats 2017 dataset [2–4] shown in Figure 7.6 [5].

7.3 LITERATURE SURVEY

This section describes various existing methods for brain tumor segmentation using deep learning. Nowadays, many applications were emerging from deep learning technology. We mainly focused on CNN-based deep learning techniques. In this survey, we go through metrics like accuracy, sensitivity, and centroid.

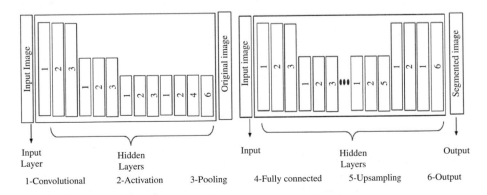

FIGURE 7.5   Cascaded CNN architecture.

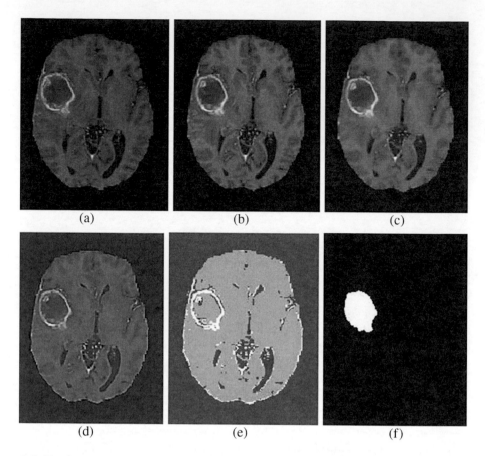

FIGURE 7.6   (a) Original image, (b) N3 corrected image, (c) output of anisotropic diffusion filtering, (d) sharpened image, (e) segmented image, and (f) tumor extracted.

Digvijay Reddy et al. proposed a new threshold approach for brain tumor segmentation [6]. The authors took a magnetic resonance imaging (MRI) image as input, and from that, they extracted tumor cells. For the removal of the noise, they used preprocessing technique. To easily identify the tumor cells, first remove the skull from the clustered image by using morphological operations. Finally, extract tumor cells by applying a threshold approach. Then evaluate performance metrics like TP (true positive), TN (true negative), FP (false positive), and FN (false negative).

Heena Hooda et al. proposed the detection of brain tumor from MRI images [7]. They used many image segmentation techniques such as fuzzy c-means (FCM) clustering k-means clustering. The authors took the images from RGCI & RC (Rajiv Gandhi Cancer Institute & Research Centre) database. First, they converted colored MRI images to grayscale images; next, they resized those images to 400×400. Next, they applied the above techniques. They removed noise by using morphological operations. Finally, the authors got the lowest error percentage value in FCM technique as compared to k-means clustering.

Eman Abdel-Maksoud et al. used a combination of k-means clustering and FCM technique for image segmentation using MRI images [8]. For getting accurate detection, they used threshold and level settings also. The authors got minimum computational time from the k-means clustering technique because it detected tumors faster than FCM technique. In this chapter, they did an experiment on four stages, like preprocessing stage, where they removed the skull. The next stage was clustering, where they performed the incorporation of FCM cluster and k-means. The third step was extraction as well as contouring, where they were used the thresholding concept. The final stage was the validation stage.

Umit Ilhan et al. used MRI images in their research. They focused mainly on one method which can distinguish cancer tissues [9]. They took images from the database of TCIA (The Cancer Imaging Archive). They used morphological operations, subtraction of the pixels, threshold-based segmentation, and some filtering techniques. Finally, they got perfect skull and tumor images as a result. They achieved a tumor with 94.28% recognition rate and a tumor without 100% recognition rate. The complete system success rate compared to others was 96%.

Sergio Pereira et al. explained gliomas as a dangerous one among all tumors, and thus, treatment will be the key to the life of any patient [10]. For evaluating tumors, the MRI image technique was widely used. But automatic segmentation requires reasonable time, so to overcome this type of problem, the automatic image segmentation method, which was based on CNN, was discovered mainly in small 3×3 kernels. With these small kernels, they designed deep architecture and also investigated the preprocessing step that they used, not only through normal CNN-based segmentation methods but also data augmentation based on MRI images. They collected images from the database of BRATS (brain tumor segmentation) 2013. By using the BRATS 2015 challenge, they got the Dice similarity coefficient metric for core 0.78, for complete 0.65, and enhanced region 0.75.

Deepthi Murthy T. S. et al. described that effective brain tumor segmentation was carried out by using thresholding and morphological operations [11]. By using the extracted features like centroid, perimeter, and area, the scanned MRI images were used as input. Image acquisition was performed with the use of Sobel filter image preprocessing, as well as with the help of histogram equalization image enhancement, and finally, the tumor was detected by thresholding and morphological operations segmentation.

Ali Işın et al. reviewed and explained that with the use of MRI images manual segmentation of the brain tumors is a difficult task and consumes a lot of time [12]. So automatic brain tumor image segmentation is needed. In their review, most of the papers proved that deep-learning-based automatic segmentation achieved good results and solved many problems than other techniques. Most of the deep learning methods used MRI-based images for tumor segmentation. Apart from others, they focused on recent deep learning methods for detecting tumors in a human brain.

Li Sun et al. used three various 3D CNN architectures for achieving robust performance [13]. They did survival prediction and extracted 4,524 radiomic features from the segmented tumor regions; a decision tree with cross-validation has been used for calculating select potent features. Finally, a random forest model has been trained for getting the overall survival rates of patients. They used the

2018 BraTS dataset and achieved 61.0% accuracy on the classification of short-, mid-, and long survivors.

Guotai Wang et al. discussed a cascade of CNNs for segmenting the brain tumors with the use of sub-regions from MRI images [5]. They introduced a 2.5D network. Along with this, they introduce test-time augmentation for achieving better accuracy. They used the BRATS 2017 dataset, and their findings revealed that their cascaded architecture with 2.5D CNN outperformed the competition. They also compared this with BraTS 2018 dataset and found that accuracy was improved.

Malathi et al. proposed fully automatic segmentation of brain tumor using a CNN [14]. They used BRATS 2015 database. Brain tumor segmentation is used with tensor flow, in which the anaconda frameworks are used to implement high-level mathematical functions. The survival rates of patients are improved; hence, the research work segments brain tumor into four classes like necrotic tumor, enhancing tumor, non-enhancing tumor, and edema.

Zahra Sobhaninia et al. observed different views of MRI images and put those into a variety of network models for segmentation [15]. The result of separate network usage for segmentation was verified and compared the result with all networks. The outcomes of the network achieved a 0.73 Dice score in a single network and 0.79 in attained for multiple networks.

Abhishta Bhandari et al. investigated the role of CNNs in the case of brain tumor segmentation by performing a literature search [16]. It is shown as an example of pipeline segmentation. They also investigated the next level of use of CNNs by exploring a unique field—radionics. From this, they extracted significant brain tumors from MRI like signal intensity, shape, and texture to find clinical outcomes.

Kavitha Angamuthu Rajasekaran discussed that MRI images were used to illustrate the causes, understanding of brain tumor segmentation, and classification [17]. They also explained about working of MRI scanning and function. It includes brain tumor classifications as well as different segmentation methodologies.

Jinping Liu et al. proposed IOUC-3DSFCNN (intersection over union [IOU] constraint 3D symmetric full CNN) model along with multimodal auto-context for the 3D brain tumor segmentation [18]. Here, the IOU constraint describes the problem of deranging foreground and background regions of tumors in MR images. Moreover, to achieve high, comprehensive, and stable 3D brain tumor profiles, the multimodal auto-context information is merged with IOUC-3DSFCNN architecture to attain end-to-end 3D brain tumor profiles and they used BRATS 2017 dataset.

Sai Meghana S et al. developed a fully automated system based on CNN for the segmentation and classification of brain tumors [19]. They used the BraTS dataset for developing this project and to test the trained models. A total of 200 patients' MRI images were present in that dataset. They used patch-wise segmentation for the MRI scans. They got 95.6% accuracy.

Guotai Wang et al. discussed a cascade of fully CNNs to segment MRI images with brain tumors by considering three hierarchical regions, such as a whole tumor, tumor core, and enhancing tumor core [20]. They segmented the entire tumor in the first phase, then used the bounding box of the result to segment the tumor center in the second. BraTS 2017 dataset has been used. From their experiment, they achieve average Dice scores of 0.7859 for enhancing tumor core, 0.9050 for the whole tumor, and 0.8378 for tumor core.

Pawel Mlynarski et al. described that many segmentation methods were based upon machine learning (ML) [21]. Moreover, automatic segmentation takes more time. By using globally labeled images, information was not clearly understood, so the proposed new method, which combined both techniques, was implemented using deep learning.

Liya Zhao et al. described that in the olden days, the detection and diagnosis of brain tumors was a difficult task [22]. They focused mainly on the automatic brain tumor segmentation method which was based on CNNs. In this technique, they considered both global features and local features, because these are important for recognition as well as classification. The tumor may be present at any place and it can comprise any size; so for detecting the tumor, they designed multiscale CNNs which detected the best three scale values of the image sizes and have considered and merged this information from various scales of the regions around that pixel. MICCAI 2013 BRATS dataset has been used. The drafting method merges multimodal features from T1, T1-enhanced, T2, and fluid-attenuated inversion recovery (FLAIR) MRI images.

Anusree P S et al. used MRI images for their research. Mainly these are used for detecting abnormal tissues like tumors or lesions [23]. Many ML-related methods were developed and used for the analysis. They proposed five ML methods. They compared results with ground image segmentation. It was done by supervised and unsupervised techniques. The drawbacks of the supervised technique are as follows: it will not check neighborhood data, it was sensitive to noise, the computational complexity was very high, and also the contrast level was very low. To overcome these drawbacks, unsupervised segmentation was performed. From the analysis finally, the authors said that FCM and watershed algorithm produced better accuracy than others.

Mobeen Ur Rehman et al. have proposed a BU-Net-modified U-Net for image segmentation [24]. Brats 2017 and 2018 dataset in high-grade glioma was taken for evaluating the model. Initially, the input image was preprocessed using N4ITK algorithm. Then the processed inputs were tested with the proposed techniques. In modified U–Net, the authors have used residual extended skip and wide context. Both of these techniques are used with customised loss function in U-Net architecture. After the training of proposed network, the output class is divided into three classes, which are tumor core, whole tumor, and enhancing core. Finally, the authors have evaluated using Dice score.

Asma Naseer et al. have proposed a CNN-based approach for detecting brain tumor [25]. The proposed model was evaluated with BR35H dataset having T1- and T2-weighted image sequence. In total, 1,775 images were used for training and testing purposes. The authors have preprocessed the images; all the images were converted to grayscale images. Then geometric data augmentation was applied where we can get different angles, rotations and all other features. Before passing to the CNN model, all the input images were resized to 256×256. CNN model was designed with 12 layers, which includes convolution, pooling dropout, and non-linearity relu where the input image is passed to train the model, but during training the network, some boundary pixel values are lost. To avoid this loss, we added the extra pixel overall the boundary value as padding. Then the model is trained and tested with other datasets also.

7.4   COMPARISON WITH VARIOUS TECHNIQUES

From the previous section of the literature survey, authors discussed various deep-learning-based models and also different metrics they calculated. We tabulated all the performance metrics as shown in Table 7.1.

In Table 7.1, we compared 21 papers with results. Even though many datasets have been taken for training and testing the model, the Brats dataset is used by most of the authors even though other datasets are used; the similarity between the datasets is that all the data are MRI images. There are many deep learning techniques that have been used to segment the tumor part. The median filter, k-means clustering, and morphological operations have been applied, which subsequently help achieve the best accuracy and precession. The combination of k-means clustering and FCM clustering region growing algorithm also gives less error value. Hybrid clustering also helps to predict the maximum accuracy. Detecting the different region is also called threshold approach. This type of approach can achieve better sensitivity but less accuracy. Patch extraction is a common method used for finding tumor; but after the extraction, the patch preprocessing will help find the level of the tumor. U-Net and SegNet are the most common models for segmentation process, but when combining SegNet with other net architectures, it helps achieve some better results. Various CNN-based architectures have been discussed in this chapter. 2D CNN and 3D CNN are important categories in authors' views. This is nothing but the representation of input dataset and various handling method of data. Feature reduction is a very important step in CNN and also various combinations will further give different results. Every article tried the different combinations of network architecture in order to do segmentation. Only the dominant feature is the patch extraction, which helps segment the tumor part and also identify the stage of tumor.

7.5   CONCLUSION

Our review on brain tumor segmentation using deep learning is successfully completed. In this survey, we reviewed 21 papers that contain a combination of both ML and deep learning techniques. We are mainly focusing on MRI images taken from different datasets like BRATS 2013, BRATS 2015, and BRATS 2017. In our survey, we discussed the merits and demerits of each technique. We can conclude that deep learning is a widely used technique that is very useful in diagnosing all image-related problems, most importantly in medicinal images, and our chapter has discussed brain tumor segmentation. We already know that we are obtaining more accuracy in image-based problems using CNN, which is based on deep learning techniques. We observed accuracy, sensitivity, Dice score value, precision, recall, and some other metrics based on the technology used. From the various observations mentioned above, a cascaded CNN performs better than a normal CNN, and other ML and deep learning techniques also have performed better, although with few snags, which are also acceptable. As per all comparisons mentioned in this chapter, we can conclude that cascaded CNN performs better.

TABLE 7.1

Comparison Table

S. No.	Corresponding Author	Database	Method	Main Modules Involved in Their Research	Result		
1.	Digvijay Reddy et al.	MRI database	Deep-learning-based image segmentation process	1. Median filter 2. k-Means clustering 3. Morphological operations	By using DS1		
					S. No.	Parameter	Value
					1	Accuracy	99.9054
					2	Precision	100
					3	Recall	99.9050
2.	Heena Hooda et al.	Large MR image dataset	Deep-learning-based performance analysis between k-means clustering, fuzzy c-means	1. k-Means clustering 2. Fuzzy c-means clustering 3. Region growing algorithm	S. No.	Technique Name	Error Percentage Value
					1	Region growing algorithm	0.04
					2	k-Means clustering	0.14
					3	Fuzzy c-means clustering	0
3.	Eman Abdel-Maksoud et al.	BRATS database	Hybrid clustering technique	Hybrid clustering technique KIFCM	By Using DS2 and DS3		
					S. No.	Parameter	Value
					1	Accuracy	100
					2	Precision	100
					3	Recall	100
4.	Umit Ilhan et al.	MRI images from TCIA	New threshold approach for brain tumor segmentation	Threshold approach	S. No.	Parameter	Value (%)
					1	Accuracy	96
					2	Sensitivity	94.28
					3	Specificity	100

(Continued)

TABLE 7.1 (Continued)
Comparison Table

S. No.	Corresponding Author	Database	Method	Main Modules Involved in Their Research	Result
5.	Sergio Pereira et al.	BRATS 2013 and BRATS 2015	Deep-learning-based CNN technique	1. Preprocessing 2. Patch extraction 3. Patch preprocessing 4. CNN	By Using Leaderboard BRATS 2013 Dataset |	DSV	PPV	Sensitivity | | Complete | 0.84 | 0.88 | 0.84 | | Core | 0.71 | 0.79 | 0.72 | | Enh. | 0.57 | 0.54 | 0.68 | By Using Challenge Brats 2013 Dataset |	DSV	PPV	Sensitivity | | Complete | 0.88 | 0.89 | 0.87 | | Core | 0.79 | 0.79 | 0.79 | | Enh. | 0.73 | 0.68 | 0.80 |
6.	Deepthi Murthy T.S. et al.	MRI database from the internet and radiologist	Brain tumor segmentation using thresholding, morphological operations	1. Sobel filter 2. Histogram equalization 3. Thresholding operation 4. Segmentation algorithm 5. tumor detection		S. No.	Parameter	Value	 | 1 | Tumor area | 896 | | 2 | Perimeter | 311.5 | | 3 | Centroid | 144.6, 160.1 |
7.	Ali Isin et al.	BRATS 2013	Review of deep-learning-based image segmentation techniques	Survey paper based on different deep learning methods	CNN having many advantages for the detection and diagnosing
8.	Li Sun et al.	BRATS 2018	Brain tumor segmentation and survival prediction using multimodal MRI scans with deep learning	1. CA-CNN 2. DFKZ Net 3. 3D U-Net 4. Ensemble model	Out of these models, ensemble model got best values as an output Mean Dice for enhancing tumor = 0.80522, whole tumor = 0.90944 Mean Hausdorff 95 (mm) for enhancing tumor = 2.77719, tumor core = 6.37318

(Continued)

TABLE 7.1 (Continued)
Comparison Table

S. No.	Corresponding Author	Database	Method	Main Modules Involved in Their Research	Result
9.	Guotai Wang et al.	BRATS 2017	Brain tumor segmentation based on cascaded convolutional neural networks	1. Segmentation pipeline and network structure 2. Augmentation for training and testing	On Validation Set of BraTS 2017 　　ET　　WT　　TC Dice 0.786 ± 0.233　0.905 ± 0.066　0.838 ± 0.158 Hausdorff (mm) 3.28 ± 3.88　3.89 ± 2.79　6.48 ± 8.26
10.	M. Malathi et al.	BRATS 2015	Brain tumor segmentation using convolutional neural network with tensor flow	1. Python-based convolutional neural network 2. Convolution 3. Classification 4. Training and validation	S. No. / Parameter Name / Value 1 Dice coefficient 0.73 2 Advancing tumor 0.7 3 Sensitivity 0.80 4 Non-advancing 0.86
11.	Zahra Sobhaninia et al.	CE-MRI image dataset	Deep-learning-based CNN technique	1. Image sorting 2. Convolutional network trained on sagittal images, coronal images, axial images 3. Segmentation	S. No. / View Name / Value 1 Coronal view 0.78 2 Sagittal view 0.79 3 Axial view 0.71
12.	Abhishta Bhandari et al.	BRATS 2017	Deep-learning-based CNN technique	Machine learning and convolutional neural networks	Deep CNN is a growing field which will help radiologists to predict with more accurate for their patients
13.	Kavitha Angamuthu Rajasekaran et al.	MRI image database	Advanced brain tumor segmentation from MRI images	1. Segmentation 2. Classification	GFSMRG with BPNN technique has been applied and sample image data given

(Continued)

TABLE 7.1 (*Continued*)
Comparison Table

S. No.	Corresponding Author	Database	Method	Main Modules Involved in Their Research	Result			
14.	Jinping Liu et al.	BRATS 2017	3D symmetric full convolution network	Multimodal auto-context fused IOUC-3DSFCNN		Whole	Core	Enh.
					Dice	0.90	0.82	0.87
					Recall	0.93	0.88	0.93
					Precision	0.88	0.78	0.83
15.	Sai Meghana S et al.	BRATS dataset	Deep-learning-based CNN technique	1. Image acquisition 2. Median filter 3. Threshold 4. Extraction of the features 5. Evaluation		Accuracy	Mean	Variance	Contrast
					Benign tumor	95.6	0.0034	0.0081	0.2433
					Malignant tumor	95.6	0.0062	0.0080	0.3012
16.	Guotai Wang et al.	BRATS 2017	Deep-learning-based CNN technique	1. Triple cascaded framework 2. Anisotropic convolutional neural networks		ET	WT	TC
					Dice	0.7831	0.8739	0.7748
					Hausdorff (mm)	15.9003	6.5528	27.0472
17.	Pawel Mlynarski et al.	BRATS 2018	Deep learning with mixed supervision for brain tumor segmentation	Mixed supervision techniques	Mixed Supervision 5 FA + 223 WA WT 78.34 (13.01) TC 50.11 (25.95) EC 60.06 (22.72)			
18.	Liya Zhao et al.	BRATS 2013	Multiscale CNNs for brain tumor segmentation and diagnosis	Multiscale three-layer neural network	Variance 0.099 versus 0.095			
19.	Anusree P S et al.	BRATS from kaggle	Machine learning	1. k-Means 2. Fuzzy c-means 3. Thresholding	Technique Name|Value	MSE	SSIM	
					k-Means	9,205.56	0.36	
					Fuzzy c-means	9,058.92	0.46	

(Continued)

TABLE 7.1 (Continued)
Comparison Table

S. No.	Corresponding Author	Database	Method	Main Modules Involved in Their Research	Result (Tumor Level)	Brats 2017 (Dice Score)	Brats 2018 (Dice Score)
20.	Mobeen Ur Rehman et al.	BRATS 2017, 2018	BU-Net	Residual extended skip and wide context	Whole	0.892	0.901
					Core	0.783	0.837
					Enhancing	0.736	0.788
21.	Asma Naseer et al.	BMI-I, BTI, BMI-II, BTS, BMI-III, BD_BT	CNN	1. Color augmentation 2. Geometric augmentation 3. Padding and stride	Dataset	Accuracy	
					BMI-I	97.08	
					BTI	85	
					BMI-II	98.91	
					BTS	100	
					BMI-III	96.49	
					BD_BT	100	

REFERENCES

1. Rebecca L. Siegel, Kimberly D. Miller, Ahmedin Jemal, Cancer Statistics, 2020. CA: *A Cancer Journal for Clinicians, American Cancer Society, 70*(1), pp. 7–30.
2. Menze, B.H., Jakab, A., Bauer, S., Kalpathy-Cramer, J., Farahani, K., Kirby, J., Burren, Y., Porz, N., Slotboom, J., Wiest, R. and Lanczi, L., 2014. The multimodal brain tumor image segmentation benchmark (BRATS). *IEEE Transactions on Medical Imaging, 34*(10), pp. 1993–2024.
3. Bakas, S., Akbari, H., Sotiras, A., Bilello, M., Rozycki, M., Kirby, J.S., Freymann, J.B., Farahani, K. and Davatzikos, C., 2017. Advancing the cancer genome atlas glioma MRI collections with expert segmentation labels and radiomic features. *Scientific Data, 4*(1), pp. 1–13.
4. Bakas, S., Reyes, M., Jakab, A., Bauer, S., Rempfler, M., Crimi, A., Shinohara, R.T., Berger, C., Ha, S.M., Rozycki, M. and Prastawa, M., 2018. Identifying the best machine learning algorithms for brain tumor segmentation, progression assessment, and overall survival prediction in the BRATS challenge. *arXiv preprint arXiv:1811.02629.*
5. Wang, G., Li, W., Ourselin, S. and Vercauteren, T., 2019. Automatic brain tumor segmentation based on cascaded convolutional neural networks with uncertainty estimation. *Frontiers in Computational Neuroscience, 13*, p. 56.
6. Reddy, D., Bhavana, V. and Krishnappa, H.K., 2018, April. Brain tumor detection using image segmentation techniques. In *2018 International Conference on Communication and Signal Processing (ICCSP)* (pp. 0018–0022). IEEE.
7. Hooda, H., Verma, O.P. and Singhal, T., 2014, May. Brain tumor segmentation: A performance analysis using k-means, fuzzy c-means and region growing algorithm. In *2014 IEEE International Conference on Advanced Communications, Control and Computing Technologies* (pp. 1621–1626). IEEE.
8. Abdel-Maksoud, E., Elmogy, M. and Al-Awadi, R., 2015. Brain tumor segmentation based on a hybrid clustering technique. *Egyptian Informatics Journal, 16*(1), pp. 71–81.
9. Ilhan, U. and Ilhan, A., 2017. Brain tumor segmentation based on a new threshold approach. *Procedia Computer Science, 120*, pp. 580–587.
10. Pereira, S., Pinto, A., Alves, V. and Silva, C.A., 2016. Brain tumor segmentation using convolutional neural networks in MRI images. *IEEE Transactions on Medical Imaging, 35*(5), pp. 1240–1251.
11. Deepthi Murthy, T.S. and Sadashivappa, G., 2014, October. Brain tumor segmentation using thresholding, morphological operations and extraction of features of tumor. In *2014 International Conference on Advances in Electronics Computers and Communications* (pp. 1–6). IEEE.
12. Işın, A., Direkoğlu, C. and Şah, M., 2016. Review of MRI-based brain tumor image segmentation using deep learning methods. *Procedia Computer Science, 102*, pp. 317–324.
13. Sun, L., Zhang, S., Chen, H. and Luo, L., 2019. Brain tumor segmentation and survival prediction using multimodal MRI scans with deep learning. *Frontiers in Neuroscience, 13*, p. 810.
14. Malathi, M. and Sinthia, P., 2019. Brain tumour segmentation using convolutional neural network with tensor flow. *Asian Pacific Journal of Cancer Prevention: APJCP, 20*(7), p. 2095.
15. Sobhaninia, Z., Rezaei, S., Noroozi, A., Ahmadi, M., Zarrabi, H., Karimi, N., Emami, A. and Samavi, S., 2018. Brain tumor segmentation using deep learning by type specific sorting of images. *arXiv preprint arXiv:1809.07786.*
16. Bhandari, A., Koppen, J. and Agzarian, M., 2020. Convolutional neural networks for brain tumour segmentation. *Insights into Imaging, 11*, pp. 1–9.
17. Rajasekaran, K.A. and Gounder, C.C., 2018. Advanced brain tumour segmentation from MRI images. In *Basic Physical Principles and Clinical Applications, High-Resolution Neuroimaging IntechOpen*, (pp. 83–108).

18. Liu, J., Liu, H., Tang, Z., Gui, W., Ma, T., Gong, S., Gao, Q., Xie, Y. and Niyoyita, J.P., 2020. IOUC-3DSFCNN: Segmentation of brain tumors via IOU constraint 3D symmetric full convolution network with multimodal auto-context. *Scientific Reports*, *10*(1), pp. 1–15.
19. Sai Meghana, S., Amulya, P., Manisha, A. and Rajarajeswari, P, 2019. A deep learning approach for brain tumor segmentation using convolution neural network. *International Journal of Scientific & Technology Research*, *8*(12), pp. 1697–1702.
20. Wang, G., Li, W., Ourselin, S. and Vercauteren, T., 2017, September. Automatic brain tumor segmentation using cascaded anisotropic convolutional neural networks. In *International MICCAI Brainlesion Workshop* (pp. 178–190). Springer, Cham.
21. Mlynarski, P., Delingette, H., Criminisi, A. and Ayache, N., 2019. Deep learning with mixed supervision for brain tumor segmentation. *Journal of Medical Imaging*, *6*(3), p. 034002.
22. Zhao, L. and Jia, K., 2016. Multiscale CNNs for brain tumor segmentation and diagnosis. *Computational and Mathematical Methods in Medicine*, *2016*, pp. 1–7.
23. Anusree, P.S., Reshma, R., Saritha, K.S. and Ani, S., 2019. MRI brain image segmentation using machine learning techniques. *International Research Journal of Engineering and Technology (IRJET)*, *06*(08), pp. 305–308. e-ISSN: 2395-0056.
24. Rehman, M.U., Cho, S., Kim, J.H. and Chong, K.T., 2020. BU-Net: Brain tumor segmentation using modified U-Net architecture. *Electronics*, *9*(12), p. 2203.
25. Naseer, A., Yasir, T., Azhar, A., Shakeel, T. and Zafar, K., 2021. Computer-aided brain tumor diagnosis: Performance evaluation of deep learner CNN using augmented brain MRI. *International Journal of Biomedical Imaging*, *2021*, pp. 1–11.

8 Hand Sign Recognition Using LeNet-like Architecture

Hariharan Ramamoorthy
Department of Information Technology, Vel Tech Rangarajan Dr. Sagunthala R&D Institute of Science and Technology
Chennai, India

Dhilsath Fathima Mohamed Mohideen
Vel Tech Rangarajan Dr. Sagunthala R&D Institute of Science and Technology
Chennai, India

Arish Pitchai
Quantum Machine Learning Lab, BosonQ Psi Pvt. Ltd.
Bhilai, India

CONTENTS

8.1   INTRODUCTION

In the current scenario, sign language is most imperative for people who are facing hearing and speaking deficiency. This is the most effective mode of communicating for such peoples for conveying their messages and this become essential for the

DOI: 10.1201/9781003320340-8

101

peoples to understand their languages. To initiate interaction and communication with deaf and hard of hearing people is essential nowadays for minimizing their isolation in the society. There are so many signs that express the complex meaning, and recognizing them is a challenging task for people who have no understanding of sign languages. Due to these communication challenges, it is a sad fact that many deaf or hard of hearing people can find it more difficult to gain employment.

Communication is a fundamental necessity in every social scale. There is a need to solve language barriers. Most research and developments focus on verbal language translation and this puts the deaf and hard of hearing community at a disadvantage. Therefore, there is a need for a sign language recognition (SLR) system, which would convert standard sign language to text, and then perhaps text to speech.

Based on our findings, there have been many related works in this field by many researchers. However, the end product that was implemented by most of them was not feasible or was a bit complicated to use for the general class of people. Therefore, we will be implementing an easy-to-use mobile application that can be used by a lot of people.

SLR and gesture-based control are the two primary applications for hand gesture recognition technology. SLR aims to interpret sign language automatically by using a computer to help the deaf communicate with non-deaf society efficiently. In the case of hand gesture, recognition is a type of sensor used and placed on the hand, when the hand performing any gesture, the data is recorded and then further analyzed.

8.1.1 OBJECTIVE

The main objective of this research is to contribute to the field of automatic SLR by creating a convolutional neural network (CNN) classifier that can recognize sign language with high accuracy, using vision-based approaches. The secondary objective is to help and facilitate people who use sign language to communicate with the outside world. And another objective is to create a platform such as a mobile application that will be accessible by almost everyone as an end product.

8.1.2 CHAPTER ORGANIZATION

The chapter starts with an abstract that addresses the sign language and the problem of identification of sign languages. This is followed by the introduction, where this problem and domain has been discussed in detail including queries like – "why this problem has been taken and the motivation behind it". There have been many people who have developed many methods to classify this sign language. A few recent and best methodologies have been discussed. Besides this, a brief introduction about the data set which we have used in our chapter has been discussed too. The detailed discussion about our proposed CNN method with results. Finally, the overall work has been concluded with results and discussion about the future plan.

8.2 RELATED WORK

Many contributions have been given by many researchers in the field of automatic SLR. Several methods have been implemented like glove-based systems (Internet of Things) and vision-based systems (Neural Network and Computer Vision).

Glove-based approaches have been more accuracy in gesture recognition but they were quite costly and inconvenient to the user, whereas vision-based methods provide more user convenience and are cost-effective. There are two dissimilar approaches to the vision-based method-Appearance-based approaches and 3D hand model-based approaches. Due to some restrictions of glove-based, most of the research works focus on appearance-based approach. The researchers are currently just focused on solving the problem with higher accuracy and not on cost or user convenience.

Ashish et al., the authors, introduced software that is presenting a system proto-type that can be able to automatically recognize sign language to help deaf and hard of hearing people to communicate more effectively with each normal individual or each other [1]. They were considering the equal like human hand shape with one thumb and four fingers, their software aims to present a real-time system for rec-ognition of hand gestures on basis of detecting of some shape-based features like orientation, center of mass centroid, fingers status, and thumb in positions of raised or folded fingers of the hand. Virender Ranga et al. suggested novel approaches of interpreting the hand signs through various methodologies such as Random Forest, Support Vector Machine (SVM), K-Nearest Neighbor (KNN) to extract features and classify various English alphabets with 95.8%, 94.3%, and 96.7% accuracy, respec-tively [2]. However, they were not able to classify the letters "z" and "j".

Wenjin Taoa et al. have demonstrated a method for ASL alphabet recognition using CNNs with multi-view augments and inference fusions, from the depth of image cap-tured by Microsoft Kinect [3]. These approaches are augmenting the original data set as a result of which the training is more effective. However, this approach is quite complex. Hyojoo Shin et al., in their paper, have demonstrated a process in which the data set was made from the video frames and these frames were given as an input to the CNN model [4]. An experiment was conducted to determine the number of con-volution layers needed. As a result, their model received an accuracy of 84.5% for ten Korean alphabets. Zhi-Jie Liang et al. have demonstrated a process of recognizing the gestures by using a data-driven system in which 3D CNNs are applying to extract-ing structural and non-linear features from video streams [5]. Also, to validate their model, they introduced a new multi-model data set captured by Kinect sensors.

Kian Ming Lim et al., in their paper, trained a custom-made CNN model using both hands. They used particle filters with the fusion of the hand motion and they called it "Hand Energy Image (HEI)" [6]. This chapter is presenting an unreachable SLR system that is comprised two main phases: hand representation and hand track-ing. In the hand representation phase, a compact hand representation is computed by averaging the segmented hand regions. In the hand tracking phase, an explained hand data set was used to extract the hand patches to pre-train CNN hand models. The hand tracking is performed by the particle filter that combines hand motion and CNN pre-trained hand models into a joint likelihood observation model.

8.3   DATA SET DESCRIPTION

Modified National Institute of Standards and Technology (MNIST) database sign language (American sign language) public available open data sets [7] were chosen to train and test our model (Figure 8.1). In MNIST, sign language data sets contain

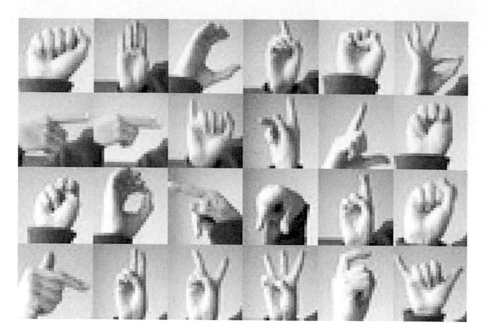

FIGURE 8.1   MNIST sign language data set sample images.

34627 images which are made as 24 classes of alphabets exclude J and Z [8]. J and Z need motion in sign language. We are experimenting only for image data set only. So, we exclude J and Z. In MNIST, sign language data set having an image size of 28*28 of 24 classes [9].

8.4   METHODOLOGY

In Section 8.2, we discussed various techniques to detect sign language with its advantages and disadvantages. This chapter implements LeNet like architecture for American SLR. Figure 8.2 represents how the system is performing the overall flow of the work. Overall implementation has been divided into five major modules. The modules will be discussed one by one in the upcoming section.

8.4.1   DATA COLLECTION

Data collection is the initial step of this method. Selection of data is also a very important task. In this model, we refer to eight countries (USA, India, Germany, Poland, Argentina, turkey, China, Arabia) sign languages different 20 data sets. Finally, we chose American sign language data set (MINST sign language data set) [10]. This chapter proposed a deep learning model for prediction. So, we analyzed among the data set which will suitable for the deep learning model and we finalize MINST sign language data set to train and test our model.

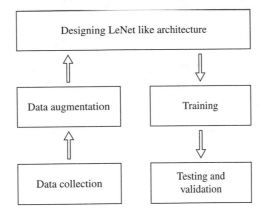

FIGURE 8.2 System working flow diagram.

8.4.2 Data Augmentation

After data selection, we need to upload our data to our model. But still, we have a problem that convolution neural network will not care about rotation of different angles. In our case, we are working in real-time data where disable people will communicate through sign language but we can't expect the same angle will show by people [11]. Even though we are having different angle images in the data set to get more accuracy, we are augmenting the image with different angles. This position augmentation will help to predict the hand sign at any angle or direction.

8.4.3 Design LeNet-like Architecture

In this section, we designed a LeNet-like architecture that contains 18 layers (Figure 8.3). Raw image with a size of 28*28 has fed into the input layer. The input data are grayscale images so we pass the channel as one. The LeNet-like architecture foundation blocks are convolution, pooling, dropout, and (dense) layers that are completely connected [12, 13]. There were 32 filters in the first convolutional layer,

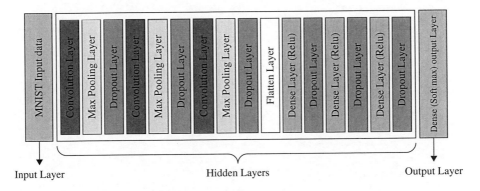

FIGURE 8.3 LeNet-like architecture layers sequence.

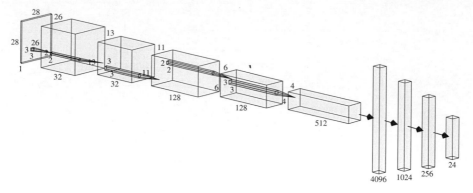

FIGURE 8.4   LeNet-like architecture.

and the filter numbers doubled as further convolutional layers were progressively introduced to form a wider network (Figure 8.4). The size of the kernel window ranged from 2 to 4, often using size 3. The convolution layers are used to enable Rectified Linear Unit (ReLU) to operate with the same padding, which ensures that the convolution layer's input and output length are the same. A max-pooling layer of size 2 was used after each convolutional layer to avoid overfitting.

With the input form of (28, 28), as the network deepens, the combination of convolutional and max-pooling layers will result in output forms of (26, 26), (13, 13), (11, 11), (6, 6), (4, 4), and (2, 2). It seems fair to speculate that, the given scale of the feature that can convey the characteristics of the landmark, symbolic features will be at levels 3, 4, and 5. The combination of convolutional, max-pooling layers was then replicated 3–5 times as a function extractor to form a deeper network [14, 15]. A dropout layer with a value of 0.2 was used after each the combination of convolutional, max-pooling layer. Finally, with Softmax activation, a completely linked layer with 24 nodes, which is the same as the total number of landmarks, is used to estimate the probabilities of each class. As a classifier, the sequence of completely linked layers functions [16]. Table 8.1 contains various parameters that are used in LeNet like architecture.

TABLE 8.1
Parameter Setting

Parameter	Value
Number of neurons in input layer	[28, 28]
Number of neurons in hidden layer	[4096, 1024, 256, 24]
Number of neurons in output layer	24
Loss function	sparse_categorical_crossentropy
Filter size	[32, 128, 512]
State activation function	ReLU
Optimizer function	Adam
Gate activation function	Softmax
Epoch's count	[25, 50, 70, 80, 100]

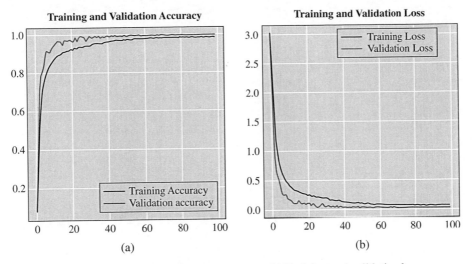

FIGURE 8.5 (a) Training and validation accuracy. (b) Training and validation loss.

8.4.4 TRAINING LENET-LIKE ARCHITECTURE

After the design of LeNet like architecture, we train our model in different epoch and continuously observing the accuracy level. We are training our model with 27455 sample images. Initially, we trained our model with 25 epochs and got an accuracy of 92%, validation loss of 0.05, and validation accuracy of 98.4%. To improve the accuracy level again increasing epoch count to 50 and observe the metrics, we got 96% accuracy, 0.01 validation loss, and validation accuracy of 99.5%. Next, we observe the changes in frequent interval in epoch count 70, 80, 90 and we got accuracy 98 .1%, 98.12%, 98.2% and validation accuracy 99.60%, 99.61%, 99.62, respectively. Finally, we achieve train accuracy 98.29 and validation accuracy 99.60 in 100th epoch. So, we are attaining maximum and constant accuracy in the interval of 70th epoch to 100th epoch. Figure 8.5(a) is a graphical representation of training and validation accuracy Figure 8.5(b) is a graphically representing training and validation loss.

8.4.5 TESTING AND VALIDATION

After training the data set, we are evaluating the testing data set which is having 7172 raw labeled images. We are achieving test accuracy of 99.59%, test loss of 0.01, and accuracy of 99.60%. Few other metrics (Table 8.2) are also evaluated and represented in Table 8.3. Random Images have been taken and verified as what is real data and what is predicted data. Some of the sample images were added to our chapter (Figure 8.6) for reference [7].

8.5 RESULT AND DISCUSSION

In Table 8.4, we compared our proposed method with the other five methods. From this table, we can conclude our method is getting the best results. Wenjin Taoa et al. have achieved 99.4% which is almost nearby our proposed method but this approach

TABLE 8.2
Comparison with Another Model

Authors(s)	Publication Year	Data Set	Model	Accuracy
Virender Ranga et al.	2018	ASL data set	Random Forest, SVM, KN	97.01
Wenjin Taoa et al.	2018	ASL alphabet data set	Convolutional neural network with multi view augmentation	99.4
Hyojoo Shin et al.	2019	Korean sign language data set	Support vector machine	84.5
Zhi-jie Liang et al.	2018	SLVM	3D CNN	89.2
Kian Ming Lim et al.	2019	Annotated hand data set	CNN	95.6
Proposed model	-	MNIST hand sign data set	LeNet like architecture	99.59

TABLE 8.3
Classification Result

Alphabet	Precision	Recall	F1 Score	Support
A	1.00	1.00	1.00	416
B	1.00	1.00	1.00	565
C	1.00	1.00	1.00	299
D	1.00	1.00	1.00	254
E	1.00	1.00	1.00	457
F	1.00	1.00	1.00	247
G	1.00	1.00	1.00	231
H	1.00	1.00	1.00	493
I	1.00	1.00	1.00	505
K	1.00	1.00	1.00	307
L	1.00	1.00	1.00	207
M	1.00	1.00	1.00	357
N	1.00	1.00	1.00	273
O	1.00	1.00	1.00	265
P	1.00	1.00	1.00	274
Q	1.00	1.00	1.00	221
R	0.99	1.00	1.00	120
S	1.00	1.00	1.00	217
T	1.00	0.95	0.98	204
U	0.99	1.00	1.00	170
V	1.00	1.00	1.00	116
W	1.00	1.00	1.00	441
X	0.96	1.00	0.98	229
Y	1.00	1.00	1.00	331
Accuracy			1.00	7172
Macro avg	1.00	1.00	1.00	7172
Weighted avg	1.00	1.00	1.00	7172

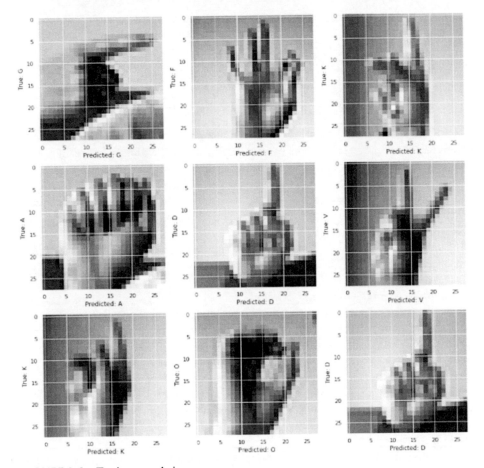

FIGURE 8.6 Testing sample images.

is quite complex. The Proposed LeNet model is easy to implement and also it gives the best result in terms of accuracy. Initially, LeNet as an architecture has designed with only convolution, max pooling, ReLU, and dense layer. When training and testing our model, we found overfitting has occurred. Training has got more accuracy 99.5% and testing we got 94% accuracy. The difference between training accuracy and the

TABLE 8.4
Various Metrics

S.No	Metrics	Description
1	Accuracy	TP+TN/TP+FP+FN+TN
2	Precision	TP/TP+FP
3	Recall	TP/TP+FN
4	F1 score	2*(Recall * Precision)/(Recall + Precision)
5	Support	Number of samples of the true response that lies in each class of target values

testing accuracy is more. So, to avoid overfitting, we add a dropout regularization layer in the proposed model. After adding the dropout layer, we train and test our LeNet like a model. Now we got greater than 99% accuracy in both training and testing accuracy.

8.6   CONCLUSION AND FUTURE WORK

In this chapter, we discussed the sign language and drawbacks of sign language. The various recent research articles have been reviewed with advantages and disadvantages. From that analysis of various models, we designed LeNet like a model with a combination of conv, max pool, dropout, and dense layer. To avoid overfitting, a dropout layer has been added in different places, which gives the best result. We trained our model with different epochs and the result has registered in our chapter. Our methodology LeNet like architecture recognizes 24 different hand signs in order to reduce the communication gap between the hearing and deaf and hard of hearing people. We trained our LeNet like a model and got an accuracy of 99.60%. The accuracy which we got is really acceptable. And still, we are working to improve our model to the next level.

In the future, we will try to incorporate this algorithm in a mobile application so that people can directly use it as much as possible. Also, it will make the whole process of predicting hand signs much easier. Technologies like OpenCV and Yolo3 will also be introduced. We want to make this whole process as simple as possible. We all have mobile phones with us and everyone uses and knows how to use various applications. Also in these recent years, the power of cloud computing has skyrocketed. We can do almost everything using the cloud from storing data sets, training and testing our model to using that model in our applications. Therefore, we will be making an application using Flutter framework and using cloud computing technology to train and deploy the model. Our application will send the image taken from the camera to the cloud and the cloud will return back the appropriate label. After this, we will also implement computer vision in the application itself.

REFERENCES

1. Ashish S. Nikam, and Aarti Ambekar. (2016). Sign language recognition using image based hand gesture recognition techniques, International Conference on Green Engineering and Technologies (IC-GET), pp. 1–5.
2. Virender Ranga, Nikita Yadav, and Pulkit Garg. (2018). American sign language fingerspelling using hybrid discrete wavelet transform-gabor filter and convolutional neural network, Journal of Engineering Science and Technology. 13(9):2655–2669.
3. Wenjin Tao, Ming Leu, and Zhaozheng Yin. (2018). American sign language alphabet recognition using convolutional neural networks with multiview augmentation and inference fusion. Engineering Applications of Artificial Intelligence. 76. 10.1016/j.engappai.2018.09.006.
4. Hyojoo Shin, Woo Kim, and Kyoung-ae Jang. (2019). Korean sign language recognition based on image and convolution neural network, ICIGP '19: Proceedings of the 2nd International Conference on Image and Graphics Processing, pp. 52–55. doi: 10.1145/3313950.3313967.

5. Zhi-jie Liang, Sheng-bin Liao, and Bing-zhang Hu. (2018). 3D convolutional neural networks for dynamic sign language recognition. Computer Journal. 61: 1725–1736. 10.1093/comjnl/bxy049.
6. Kian Lim, Alan Tan, Chin-Poo Lee, and Shing Tan. (2019). Isolated sign language recognition using convolutional neural network hand modelling and hand energy image. Multimedia Tools and Applications. 78. 10.1007/s11042-019-7263-7.
7. Sign Language MNIST Dataset Available in online: https://www.kaggle.com/datasets/datamunge/sign-language-mnist (Accessed on 10.10.2021).
8. Sign Language MNIST, Drop-In Replacement for MNIST for Hand Gesture Recognition Tasks, https://www.kaggle.com/datamunge/sign-language-mnist.
9. ASL Alphabet Image data set for alphabets in the American Sign Language, https://www.kaggle.com/grassknoted/asl-alphabet.
10. Hamid Reza Vaezi Joze and Oscar Koller (2018). MS-ASL: A Large-Scale Data Set and Benchmark for Understanding American Sign Language. arXiv 2018, arXiv:1812.01053.
11. Aditya Das, Shantanu Gawde, Khyati Suratwala and Dhananjay Kalbande. (2018). Sign language recognition using deep learning on custom processed static gesture images, 2018 International Conference on Smart City and Emerging Technology (ICSCET), pp. 1–6. doi: 10.1109/ICSCET.2018.8537248.
12. Andrew G. Howard, Menglong Zhu, Bo Chen, Dmitry Kalenichenko, Weijun Wang, Tobias Weyand, Marco Andreetto, Hartwig Adam. (2017). MobileNets: Efficient Convolutional Neural Networks for Mobile Vision Applications, https://arxiv.org/abs/1704.04861.
13. Christian Szegedy, Wei Liu, Yangqing Jia, Pierre Sermanet, Scott Reed, Dragomir Anguelov, Dumitru Erhan, Vincent Vanhoucke, Andrew Rabinovich. (2014). Going Deeper with Convolutions, https://arxiv.org/abs/1409.4842.
14. Becky Sue Parton. (2005). Sign language recognition and translation: A multidisciplined approach from the field of artificial intelligence. Journal of Deaf Studies and Deaf Education. 11(1):94–101.
15. Mukul Singh Kushwah, Manish Sharma, Kunal Jain, and Anish Chopra. (2017)."Sign language interpretation using pseudo glove". In Proceeding of International Conference on Intelligent Communication, Control and Devices, pages 9–18, Springer, 2017.
16. Runpeng Cui., Hu Liu, and Changshui Zhang. (2019). A deep neural framework for continuous sign language recognition by iterative training. IEEE Transactions on Multimedia. 21: 1880–1891.

9 Automated Kinship Recognition through Facial Feature Matching

Gunjan Chhabra
Department of Computer Science Engineering,
Graphic Era Hill University
Dehradun, Uttarakhand, India

Rashmi Sharma
Shree Vaishnav Vidyapeeth Vishwavidyalaya, Shri Vaishnav
Institute of Computer Application
Indore, Madhya Pradesh, India

CONTENTS

9.1 INTRODUCTION

Humans commonly identify and recognize each other by faces and facial features. In common saying that person X carries similar trait from his/her biological parents or from ancestors. Naturally, there is a similarity in the trait(s) among pair of family members like mother and son, known as a familial trait. In the field of computer vision, face recognition, age estimation, face emotion classification etc. archived huge achievements and many applications were built under this domain [1, 2]. On the other side, few attempts are made to develop automatic kinship verification systems based on human perception, due to lots of challenges and unavailability of public data. Kinship is defined as the relationship among family members who own biological and genetic relationships with each other. Naturally, humans can identify relationships even on unfamiliar faces and that perception is quite opposite from identity recognition. The psychological findings inspired many researchers to automate human perception of recognizing kinship from face similarity traits and develop applications. Thus, it generates a new classification problem to determine that whether a given pair of an image belongs to kin class to non-kin class.

DOI: 10.1201/9781003320340-9

The challenge under this umbrella is quite different from a typical face recognition system [3,4]. In face recognition, the objective is to match and recognize the features of the same person in an image gallery known as facial identity. Whereas in kinship verification, the objective is to extract similar features but from different individuals, i.e. two different people share some common traits. Hence, this problem should be observed in a different way to solve than a traditional facial recognition system. To understand this problem more accurately, it is required to understand the challenges behind the scene, which will act as a guide to develop an automated system. The related challenges are broadly divided into two categories: (1) Direct challenges, (2) Indirect challenges. The direct challenges include kinship-related challenges, i.e. traits are calculated among different age groups (father-son), among different sex (siblings) and even different in both (mother-son). There are some special cases, let us consider, parents have two daughters among which traits inherit from parents differently (one daughter has a similar trait, e.g. nose, to her father, whereas the other has a similarity with her mother). Hence, it proves that the kinship problem is stochastic. On the other hand, the indirect challenges include the challenges environmental factors, unavailability of a public database, ageing, resolution, makeup and so forth.

Kinship is related to the biological relationship among individuals or groups, i.e. between parents and children, siblings and others. In contrast to this, an adoptive child is excluded from this as it has no biological or genetic link with step-parents. Thus, under this problem, one can consider majorly two categories of relationship: (1) Relation based on blood or genetics overlapping, (2) Relation formed based on marriage. Another method of defining kinship is based on its degree i.e. how close a relationship is related to each other. Kinship has three classes: (1) Primary, which includes the direct relationship between individuals such as parents-children and between siblings, (2) Secondary, which refers to first-degree kinship includes brother's wife, father's brother, i.e. uncle, (3) Tertiary, which includes the wife of brother-in-law.

So far, kinship problem falls under the category of computer vision, therefore, automated kinship recognition is allowed to perform the dual-task; one for verification and the other for recognition. In terms of the verification process, the system can verify the blood relation between a given pair of images, whereas recognition process includes detection of the degree of that relationship. The computer vision domain works with various artificial intelligence (AI) techniques to give good results. It is widely used for various applications of robotics, biometric-based systems, human-computer interactions and many others. One of the commonly used computer vision applications is face recognition and is related to kinship recognition, where both require facial characteristics. However, the solution behind the scene is different in both. Face verification included 1:1 mapping, whereas face identification included 1:N mapping, thus both the techniques are uncorrelated. In contrast to this, in the case of kinship identification and verification, possess 1:N mapping and without verification, identification is not possible, thus both the processes are correlated means identification depends on verification. Hence, to solve this problem, this chapter includes a computational model to give enhanced results. In the coming section, the chapter includes a survey on previous work followed by proposed methodology with desired computation model. The chapter further includes the results section and ends with concluding remarks.

9.2   LITERATURE SURVEY

The main purpose of writing this chapter is to propose one more application of image processing with the help of computer vision. Computer vision, machine learning (ML), convolution neural network (CNN), AI [5–7] are few fields that attract researchers to develop something invincible. Here, the authors have used the existing algorithms of image processing along with computer vision and ML and intend to design one algorithm for extraction/matching [8] of features of biological parents with their kids. Computer vision and ML are two integral fields of image processing that work together for appropriate results.

Computer vision is a well-known field of computer science that uses for the processing and analysis of digital images with the help of some algorithms. These algorithms help machines to process an image at a pixel level and understand it. Image classification and identification are two main tasks that are taken care of while implementing computer vision algorithms [9]. Classification analyses the graphical contents and classifies the target image on a photo/video to the defined category. After classification, it identifies the image among the library of images. Pattern recognition [10] is the main concept based on mostly computer vision algorithms work. Machine trains on a huge amount of photographic data. Algorithms process images, identify the specific image on them and find the patterns in those objects [11,12]. For example, if we send a million images of people, the algorithm will analyse them, identify the features (specific pattern) of source person image that are similar to a specific group of people and, at the end, it will create a group of the same featured people. Additionally, ML algorithms use here for mining and matching purposes [13,14]. Fundamentals of image processing like object detection, noise removal are some integral methodologies of computer vision that are used here in this chapter. In [15] authors have explained the following working steps of computer vision:

1. **Image understanding:** Object detection, recognition and shape analysis.
2. **Image analysis:** Image segmentation, registration and matching.
3. **Image processing:** Image enhancement, noise removal, restoration, feature detection and compression.

Computer vision belongs to machine learning or is a subset of ML. In ML, some algorithms and statistical models are used to train the respective system and its working depends on patterns, not on explicit instructions. Therefore, it applies to computer vision, software engineering and pattern recognition. Pattern recognition and computer vision are the focus of this chapter where ML algorithms are used for analysis purposes. In [16] authors partitioned the complete working into two modules, i.e. computer vision and the designed architecture of both. Following,

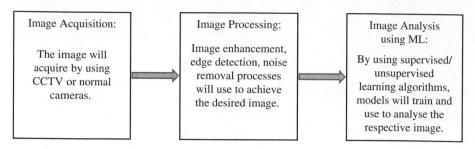

FIGURE 9.1 Role of machine learning in computer vision.

as shown in Figure 9.1, are the working of ML, image processing and computer vision together.

9.3 METHODOLOGY

This section elaborates proposed methodology to find a better solution for the state's challenges in the automated kinship recognition problem. As discussed earlier, kinship can be done by either or both ways, namely, **kinship authentication**, to verify the existence of a relationship, and **kinship identification**, to identify the degree of relationship. The procedure includes, input image (e.g. query image) and image (group or individual image) from the database, and follows the following steps:

1. Identify the features of query image and features of member(s) in the test image, if matched more than 70% then go to step 2 else stop.
2. Check the relationship between an input image and member(s) in the test image, if found then go to step 3 else stop.
3. Identify the type of relationship.

Although the present work does not focus on the specific degree of relationships such as grand-parent and grand-child, rather the task is to verify the kinship and identify the class of the relationship. The complete procedure of the method is shown in the flowchart as shown in Figure 9.2. The present work focuses on designing an automated system to verify and identify the kinship-based on genetics, i.e. parent-child. Further, the genetic relationship is represented as mother-son, father-son, mother-daughter and father-daughter pairing. In addition to these combinations, one can extend the process to sibling pairs, including three more relations as brother-brother, sister-sister and brother-sister.

Looking forward, after considering all the parameters and requirements, an automated kinship verification and identification system have been designed. This system includes different sub-modules that help in identifying the kinship. The stated problem is very complex and difficult; hence, to find a robust solution, the divide and conquer technique is followed, as shown in Figure 9.3. The whole system is divided into five major components, i.e. image or video preprocessing [17], extraction of features, feature selection [18] and similarity matching, classification, verification and recognition [19–22].

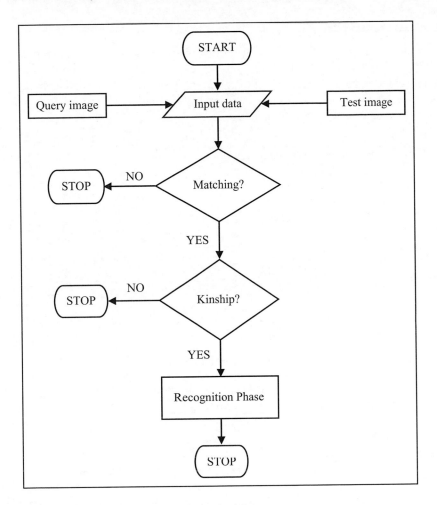

FIGURE 9.2   Flowchart to illustrate the methodology.

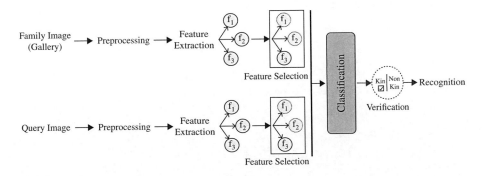

FIGURE 9.3   Kinship verification and recognition system.

9.4   ALGORITHM

As shown in Figure 9.3, the first phase of the working algorithm includes preprocessing of the input image. Preprocessing is a process to locate or detect and extract the facial region from an image. The face detection process includes some challenges like orientation, lighting and other environmental conditions. The following steps are used to detect the face(s) from an image:

1. $get\_face\_encodings(image\_path)$:
   $img = PIL.Image.open(image\_path)$
   $img = np.asarray(img, dtype = np.uint8)$
   $if \ len(img.shape) == 2$:
       $img = np.stack((img,)*3, axis = -1)$
   $face\_locations = face\_recognition.face\_locations(img, model = 'cnn')$
   $face\_encodings = face\_recognition.face\_encodings(img, face\_locations)$
   $if \ len(face\_encodings) > 0$:
       $return \ face\_encodings[0].astype(dtype = np.float32, copy = False)$
   $else$:
       $return \ np.zeros(shape = (128,)).astype(dtype = np.float32, copy = False)$

Preprocessing stage also includes the normalization process, which helps in extracting key points of the faces. The normalization process includes the conversion of a coloured image into a grayscale image to simplify the calculations. In addition to that normalization process also aimed to reduce the effect of other environmental effects like illumination, over brightness, image size and others. In the next stage, the process of feature extraction is performed to get the relevant and useful features. These features help the automated system to distinguish between the faces, hence, play an important role in the kinship verification system. The present work uses the ML method for feature extraction and feature selection to improve the accuracy of the results. The CNN technique is used to reduce redundancy and to discard non-relevant features and related errors. The deep learning techniques are capable of gathering relevant low-level and mid-level features. The deep learning method resolves the issues associated with traditional methods of feature extraction and enhanced the accuracy of computing for such complex tasks.

```
Calculate Euclidean distance (x1, x2)
Calculate Manhattan distance (x1, x2)
Find cosine similarity(x1, x2)
Find pearson correlation(x1, x2):
```
    $n = x1.shape[1]$
    $cov\_bias = np.mean(x1 * x2, axis = 1) - np.mean(x1, axis = 1)*$
      $np.mean(x2, axis = 1) \# cov\_bias = cov\_bias * n/(n-1)$
    $corr = cov\_bias/(np.std(x1, axis = 1) * np.std(x2, axis = 1))$
    $return \ corr$

After the process of feature extraction and feature selection, the algorithm is allowed to calculate the Euclidean and Manhattan distance for kin similarity measurement. Additionally, the cosine similarity index is calculated for the classification. For the classification model, K-means neural network (KNN) and support vector machine (SVM) are two algorithms that are commonly used by the researchers, here, in the present work; the accuracy of KNN-based classification shows better results. On the other hand, XGBoost is an open-source library for enhancing the performance of classification, which is used to make much better decisions and improvise accuracy.

```
get_score(img_path1, img_path2, model_path):
    im1 = get_face_encodings(img_path1).reshape((1, 128))
    im2 = get_face_encodings(img_path2).reshape((1, 128))
    data = pd.DataFrame(im1 - im2)
    data.columns = [str(x) for x in data.columns]
    data['euc'] = euclidean_distance(im1, im2)
    data['man'] = manhattan_distance(im1, im2)
    data['cos'] = cosine_similarity(im1, im2)
    data['cor'] = pearson_correlation(im1, im2)
    with open(model_path,'rb') as file:
        model = pickle.load(file)
    score = model.predict(xgboost.DMatrix(data),
            ntree_limit = model.best_ntree_limit,
            validate_features = True)
    return score
```

For the verification and recognition phase, the overall score is identified based on distance and similarity index. The observed score is then used to verify that whether the input image carries any kinship or not, i.e. person belongs to the same family or not. The verification phase is a one-to-one matching method. It also checks the similarity index between father-child and mother-child for the recognition purpose. The recognition phase is a one-to-many matching method; however, the degree of relationship is not covered in the present research work. The algorithm was tested in an uncontrolled environment. The participants include a different group of families and the training and test of the algorithm were performed by using the online available data sets.

9.5 RESULTS AND DISCUSSION

This subsection includes the discussion and evaluation of results obtained by the proposed method. The accuracy, precision and recall of the outcome are evaluated by the confusion matrix, shown in Table 9.1. The confusion matrix is used for classification problems in supervised learning for visualizing the performance of the algorithm.

TABLE 9.1
2 × 2 Confusion Matrix

True Positive	False Positive
Criteria: Noticeable Impact if accurately predicted	**Criteria:** Noticeable Impact if accurately predicted
False Negative	**True Negative**
Criteria: Un-Noticeable Impact if not accurately predicted	**Criteria:** Un-Noticeable Impact if not accurately predicted

$$Precision_{predict} = {True_{Positive}}\big/{True_{Positive} + False_{Positive}} \qquad (9.1)$$

$$Recall_{predict} = {True_{Positive}}\big/{True_{Positive} + False_{Negative}} \qquad (9.2)$$

$$Accuracy_{predict} = \frac{True_{Positive} + True_{Negative}}{True_{Positive} + False_{Positive} + True_{Negative} + False_{Negative}} \qquad (9.3)$$

$$F-Score_{predict} = 2.\frac{Precision.Recall}{Precision + Recall} \qquad (9.4)$$

The Equations 9.1, 9.2, 9.3 and 9.4 are used to evaluate precision, recall, accuracy and F-score. Precision signifies the accurate prediction of positive cases, whereas recall signifies the proportion of accurate prediction. The accuracy is to identify the accurate prediction of both positive and negative cases, whereas F-score identifies harmonic mean of model's precision and recall. To test the working of the proposed algorithm, a different group of participants were made and results are shared with them. On the other hand, participants were also allowed to verify and recognize the given set of facial images. The outcome of the proposed method was compared using various parameters along with some existing techniques.

The performance of the proposed method is evaluated based on accuracy, error, kappa, mean absolute error (MAE) and root mean square error (RMSE). Various existing techniques such as decision tree, SVM and histogram of oriented gradients were used to compare with the proposed method. Tables 9.2 and 9.3 showcase the results obtained of models using all features.

TABLE 9.2
Accuracy/Error/Kappa/MAE and RMSE of Models Using All the Features

Model	Accuracy (%)	Error Rate (%)	Kappa	MAE	RMSE
Proposed method	95.75	4.25	0.8461	0.2025	0.2651
Decision tree	83.30	16.69	0.6408	0.1915	0.4026
SVM	87.80	12.20	0.7129	0.1504	0.3235
HoG	85.40	14.59	0.7644	0.2277	0.3043

TABLE 9.3

TPR/FPR/Precision/Recall/F-Measure and ROC of Models Using All the Features

Model	Class	TPR	FPR	Precision	Recall	F-Measure
SVM	Yes	0.810	0.102	0.864	0.810	0.836
	No	0.898	0.190	0.856	0.898	0.876
Decision tree	Yes	0.788	0.149	0.808	0.788	0.798
	no	0.851	0.212	0.834	0.851	0.842
Proposed method	yes	0.894	0.052	0.933	0.894	0.913
	no	0.948	0.106	0.918	0.948	0.933
HoG	Yes	0.853	0.091	0.882	0.853	0.867
	no	0.909	0.147	0.886	0.909	0.897

Based on the calculations performed, Figure 9.4 shows the accuracy and error values. The graph shown below indicates that the accuracy is high for the prosed method, whereas the error rate is low. Hence one can use this algorithm for various applications to identify the kinship.

In Figure 9.5, MAE, RMSE and Kappa values have been visualized, and it clearly shows that the proposed method is performing better as compared to the other algorithms.

The performance of the proposed algorithm is measured based on various parameters. The comparison of the outcomes has been shown in Figure 9.6, indicating a good performance rate for the proposed algorithm.

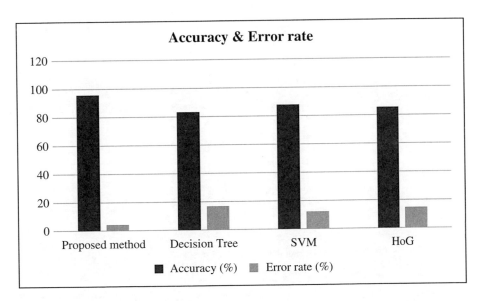

FIGURE 9.4   Comparison graph showing accuracy and error rate.

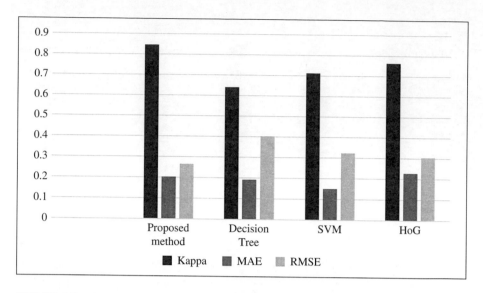

FIGURE 9.5   Comparison based on MAE, RMSE, Kappa value.

9.6   CONCLUSION AND FUTURE SCOPE

The objective of this research is to identify the kinship and can be applied to find the missing child, to stop child trafficking and other related crimes. The outcomes obtained from the experimentation show that proposed algorithm gives an accuracy of approximately 92% which is quite acceptable but one can enhance the accuracy by using more advanced AI-based techniques and by including more parameters for feature matching.

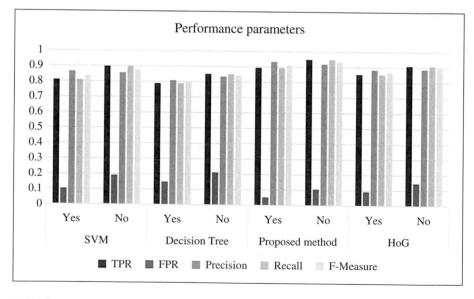

FIGURE 9.6   Performance measures based on various parameters.

Many other advancements in technology have opened up different methods to improve the results therefore computer vision domain has much more potential to overcome and solve the issues such as kidnapping, child labour, missing child identification and recognition and so on. The present work also highlights the challenges and overall difficulties in the practical implementation of the kinship-based model in terms of computer vision. Still, a lot of work has to be done to find the kinship in different levels of degree-of-relationship, and by other means of age, gender, illuminations, poses, etc. Due to the built-in complexity of this problem and wide real-world application, this area will draw amassed attention from a variety of fields that will be beyond computer vision, ML and their sub-domains.

REFERENCES

1. Algan, G., & Ulusoy, I. (2021). Image classification with deep learning in the presence of noisy labels: A survey. *Knowledge-Based Systems*, *215*, 106771.
2. Jähne, B., & Haussecker, H. (Eds.). (2000). Computer vision and applications: a guide for students and practitioners. Academic Press, Inc.
3. Mousavi, S., Charmi, M., & Hassanpoor, H. (2021). A distinctive landmark-based face recognition system for identical twins by extracting novel weighted features. *Computers & Electrical Engineering*, *94*, 107326.
4. Mathur, A. (2021). Face Recognition System.
5. Li, X., Lai, S., & Qian, X. (2021). DBCFace: Towards pure convolutional neural network face detection. *IEEE Transactions on Circuits and Systems for Video Technology*, *32*(4), 1792–1804.
6. Mehrabi, N., Morstatter, F., Saxena, N., Lerman, K., & Galstyan, A. (2021). A survey on bias and fairness in machine learning. *ACM Computing Surveys (CSUR)*, *54*(6), 1–35.
7. Manwar, R., Zafar, M., & Xu, Q. (2021). Signal and image processing in biomedical photoacoustic imaging: a review. *Optics*, *2*(1), 1–24.
8. Bonet-Solà, D., & Alsina-Pagès, R. M. (2021). A comparative survey of feature extraction and machine learning methods in diverse acoustic environments. *Sensors*, *21*(4), 1274.
9. Umbaugh, S. E. (2010). *Digital image processing and analysis: human and computer vision applications with CVIPtools*. CRC Press.
10. Saini, P., Kaur, J., & Lamba, S. (2021). A Review on Pattern Recognition Using Machine Learning. In *Advances in Mechanical Engineering* (pp. 619–627). Springer, Singapore.
11. Mohri, M., Rostamizadeh, A., & Talwalkar, A. (2018). *Foundations of machine learning*. MIT Press.
12. Sarker, I. H. (2021). Machine learning: Algorithms, real-world applications and research directions. *SN Computer Science*, *2*(3), 1–21.
13. Kumar, K. K., Kumar, M. D., Samsonu, C., & Krishna, K. V. (2021). Role of convolutional neural networks for any real time image classification, recognition and analysis. *Materials Today: Proceedings*.
14. Wang, P., Fan, E., & Wang, P. (2021). Comparative analysis of image classification algorithms based on traditional machine learning and deep learning. *Pattern Recognition Letters*, *141*, 61–67.
15. Awcock, G. J., & Thomas, R. (1995). Applied image processing (pp. 111–118). Basingstoke, UK: Macmillan.
16. Mahmoodpour, M., Lobov, A., Hayati, S., & Pastukhov, A. (2019). An Affordable Deep Learning Based Solution to Support Pick and Place Robotic Tasks. In *"Instrumentation Engineering, Electronics and Telecommunications-2019" Proceedings of the V International Forum* (Izhevsk, Russia, November 20–22). Kalashnikov Izhevsk State Technical University.

17. Bhosale, K. A., Kuk, S., & Park, S. H. (2021, August). Study on Deep CNN as Preprocessing for Video Compression. In *Applications of Digital Image Processing XLIV* (Vol. 11842, p. 118420V). International Society for Optics and Photonics.

18. Zhou, H., Zhang, J., Zhou, Y., Guo, X., & Ma, Y. (2021). A feature selection algorithm of decision tree based on feature weight. *Expert Systems with Applications, 164*, 113842.

19. Chen, L., Rottensteiner, F., & Heipke, C. (2021). Feature detection and description for image matching: from hand-crafted design to deep learning. *Geo-spatial Information Science, 24*(1), 58–74.

20. Cordonnier, J. B., Mahendran, A., Dosovitskiy, A., Weissenborn, D., Uszkoreit, J., & Unterthiner, T. (2021). Differentiable Patch Selection for Image Recognition. In *Proceedings of the IEEE/CVF Conference on Computer Vision and Pattern Recognition* (pp. 2351–2360).

21. Goyal, A., & Meenpal, T. (2021). Robust discriminative feature subspace analysis for kinship verification. *Information Sciences, 578*, 507–524.

22. Hassanin, M., Radwan, I., Khan, S., & Tahtali, M. (2021). Learning Discriminative Representations for Multi-Label Image Recognition. *arXiv preprint arXiv:2107.11159.*

10 Ensemble Convolutional Neural Network

A Bidimensional EMD Model for ECG Denoising

Parvathy Rema
and Manju Bhaskara Panicker Radha
Department of Mathematics, Amrita School of Arts and
Sciences, Amritapuri Campus
Vallikavu, India

CONTENTS

10.1 INTRODUCTION

Heart disorders are considered one of the leading causes of death in all populations worldwide. It is an alarming fact that at each minute, one person in the United States dies of heart diseases [1]. So, early detection and treatment for any heart-related irregularities is of uttermost importance. Electrocardiogram (ECG) is a diagnostic test that measures the heart's regular functioning. As our heart beats, it produces electrical signals which are acquired by the electrodes placed on one's body during the recording process. These electrodes could sense the small electrical changes happen during the heart muscle depolarization along with the repolarization during each heart beat [2, 3].

During the recording process, there are higher chances of accumulation of certain noises which hinders the accurate diagnosis process. There are mainly two types of noises that get added along with the original signal, which are high frequency

DOI: 10.1201/9781003320340-10

noises and low frequency noises [4]. High frequency noises include additive white Gaussian noise (AWGN) and powerline interference. AWGN is a white noise with normal distribution and average zero. It is considered to be a collection of noises that are present in our nature. Powerline interference lies under the frequency range of 50–60 Hz. It gets added through the electromagnetic interference from electro-magnetic induction of any nearby machines. These high frequency noises can in fact change the morphological structure of the original signal. Low frequency noises include baseline wander, which lies under the frequency of 1 Hz and get added by the breathing or body movements of the patient during the recording process [5].

There are various methods used for removing noises in ECG signals. A few of them include techniques called Empirical Mode Decomposition (EMD) [6], Non-Local Means (NLM) [7], Discrete Wavelet Transform (DWT) [8] and various filters [4, 9]. There are also techniques which are either a modified version of existing methods or a combination of two or more methods. Those include modified EMD (M-EMD) [10, 11], ensemble EMD (EEMD) [12] and Variational Mode Decomposition (VMD) [13].

EMD is a technique of decomposing a signal into certain functions of time, called intrinsic mode functions (IMFs) without leaving the time domain [6]. NLM is a denoising technique which works on the theory of self-similarity, by averaging the patches from different parts of the signal which have similar special structure [7]. M-EMD is a combination of both EMD and NLM, and EEMD and VMD are modi-fied versions of EMD technique where all of these are considered better methods of signal denoising [10, 12, 13].

Deep convolutional neural network is being used for medical image denoising recently. Convolutional denoising autoencoder is used in this domain which is a sta-tistical extension of regular autoencoders, where pure images are reconstructed from its noisy versions. The model randomly selects some of the parameters to be zero such that the denoising autoencoder predicts the missing values of the selected sub-sets of patterns. When compared to normal autoencoders, convolutional denoising autoencoder is found to be a better image preprocessing technique [14]. Generative adversarial network (GAN) is also found to be a better denoising technique [15].

For detection of ailments related to heart, ECG is utilized as a medical image modality and hence it is critical to find a denoising technique for two-dimensional ECG signal better performing than the aforementioned techniques with lesser latency in implementation. There exists a technique called bidimensional EMD (BEMD) which works for 2-D data or images where non stationary data is decomposed to zero mean image components or 2-D functions which are also named IMFs, like traditional EMD technique [16]. The number of IMFs iterated will depend on the data characteristics and may vary with images. The highest local spatial frequency components (mostly the noise) will be found in first few IMFs and denoising those IMFs will reduce the amount of noise of the entire image [17].

BEMD is seemed to underperform when a large amount of noise is present in the signal. It can be seen in the case of drifting noise which might be several times higher than the signal's magnitude. Denoising large image dataset in a short span of time is a difficult process [16]. To overcome this difficulty, a Convolutional Neural Network (CNN) model is used owing to its strong learning ability in combination with the BEMD approach, which identifies and removes noisy components from each IMF.

The CNN model stacks many convolution layers with pooling and batch normalization with respective activation functions which helps in blind denoising of images.

In the proposed work, BEMD is used to iterate out first few IMFs that are then fed to the CNN model, where each of the image IMFs is denoised and recombined back. The remaining of the paper is structured as follows: The proposed ECG denoising technique is presented in Section 10.2 Secin Section 10.3, the methodology of the proposed BEMD – CNN model is explained. Experimental evaluation is discussed in Section 10.4 which is followed by results and conclusion in Sections 10.5 and 10.6, respectively.

10.2 PROPOSED ENSEMBLE CNN-BEMD MODEL

The proposed model can be divided into two sections, the BEMD architecture and the denoising CNN model. EMD is considered one of the better denoising methods when compared to most of the existing techniques [10, 11], which was proposed by Huang et al. in 1998 [18]. It is the method of dissecting down a signal to functions called IMFs, without leaving the time domain. BEMD works in a similar way where an image is decomposed by an iterating process called sifting to image basis called 2-D IMFs and a residue. If an image is decomposed to a set of orthogonal basis of the original image (IMFs), then it is observed that the first few IMFs will have a higher frequency than the preceding ones. In addition, the high frequency IMFs will have the higher number of noisy features [17, 19]. The objective of the proposed model is to remove the high frequency noisy features from the first few IMFs.

After decomposing the image in to n number of IMFs, first few IMFs with maximum distortion are considered for denoising. For the training of the model, IMFs of pure ECG image along with their corresponding noisy IMFs are fed to the denoising CNN model. The proposed CNN model has an input layer followed by 19 successive convolution layers with pooling and batch normalization with rectified linear unit (ReLU) as the activation function. The model ends with a final regression layer and will output the mean squared error (MSE) values between the clean and noisy IMFs. The noisy features of each IMF are learned by the model in each layer and are removed from its respective IMF using Gradient Descent technique. The denoised IMFs are recombined together to retrieve the denoised ECG image.

10.3 METHODOLOGY

10.3.1 BIDIMENSIONAL EMPIRICAL MODE DECOMPOSITION (BEMD)

BEMD is a well-known and standard denoising technique for images, which disintegrates a given image to functions or basis called IMFs.

A function is called an IMF if it satisfies the following constraints:

a. The number of zero crossings and number of extremas of an IMF should be either same or differ at most by one.
b. The average value at any point of the lines defined by maximas and minimas should be zero [10].

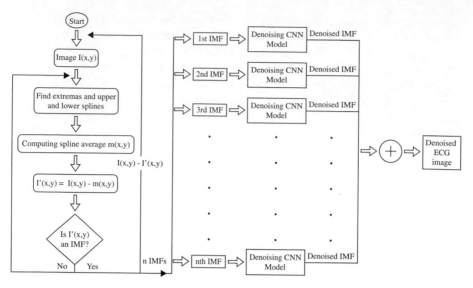

FIGURE 10.1 Flowchart of the CNN-BEMD technique.

Figure 10.1 shows the methodology flowchart of the proposed ECBEMD model. The first half of the figure represents the BEMD algorithm, while next half shows the working of the CNN model.

The methodology of the BEMD technique follows the preceding steps:

1. When an image $I(x,y)$ is considered, find all of its local extremas (minimas and maximas) and join them by cubic spline lines (I_{max} and I_{min}, respectively).
2. Calculate average of these spline lines at each point (I_{avg}), followed by finding the difference between the input signal and $m_1(x,y)$.

$$I(x,y) - m_1(x,y) = I^1(x,y) \qquad (10.1)$$

3. If $I^1(x,y)$ is an IMF, it undergoes a sifting process, where

$$I^{11}(x,y) = I(x,y) - I^1(x,y) \qquad (10.2)$$

4. The steps 1 and 2 are repeated for $I^{11}(x,y)$ and will find $I^{22}(x,y)$

$$I^2(x,y) = I^{11}(x,y) - m_2(x,y) \qquad (10.3)$$

$$I^{22}(x,y) = I^{11}(x,y) - I^2(x,y) \qquad (10.4)$$

The sifting process will continue until the conditions for a stoppage criterion is met, that is:

$$SD = \sum_{n=0}^{N} \frac{\left(I^{nn}(x,y) - I^{(n-1)(n-1)}(x,y) \right)^2}{\left(I^{(n-1)(n-1)}(x,y) \right)^2} \qquad (10.5)$$

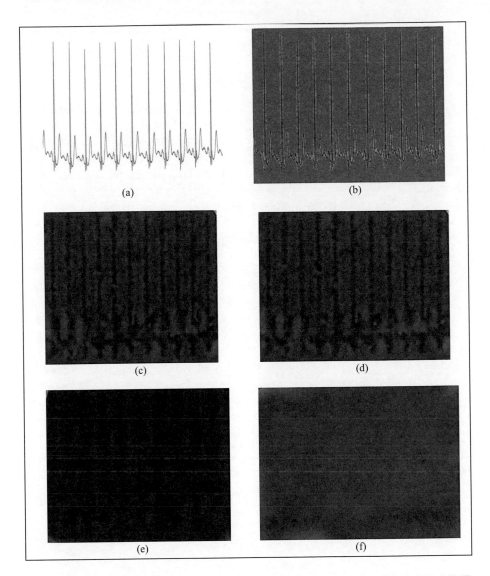

FIGURE 10.2   (a) The pure input image, (b) First IMF, (c) Second IMF, (d) Third IMF, (e) Fourth IMF and (f) Residue.

It should have value in between 0.2 and 0.3. The sifting process of the IMFs is continued until no more IMFs could be iterated out and the remaining signal is called residue [10]. All IMFs will have both high and low spatial frequency features, while the lower order IMFs (the first few IMFs) will have a greater number of higher frequency features than the remaining IMFs and residue.

Figure 10.2 shows the pure aka noiseless ECG image and its corresponding IMFs after treating it with BEMD algorithm. Here, Figure 10.2(a) shows the pure image, Figure 10.2(b) (the first IMF) shows edges and prominent features of the input image, while Figure 10.2(e) (fourth IMF) shows the shading and background of the input image. This is because the first IMF contains the high frequency features of the image while its preceding IMFs contain the lesser frequency features.

10.3.2 DENOISING CONVOLUTIONAL NEURAL NETWORK

In the proposed work, we consider a denoising CNN model for denoising each of the IMFs iterated out from the BEMD algorithm. For training the model, we constructed a 60 layer CNN architecture integrating convolution layers, ReLU which is the activation function and batch normalization (batch norm) in a repeating sequence ending with a fully connected layer and an output layer giving the MSE between the clean IMF and noisy IMF. There are 19 such convolution-batch norm-ReLU sequences in the model. Every layer, but the first convolution layer, is of the size 64x3x3x64 and the first convolution layer is of the size 64x3x3x1. ReLU is specifically used for avoiding vanishing and exploding gradient problem [20].

The ReLU function $f(x)$ is defined as:

$$f(x) = \max\{0, x\} \text{ where } x \in (-\text{infinity, infinity})   \quad (10.6)$$

In a CNN model, filters aka kernals slice or convolve through the images and learn their different features. In the proposed model, for the first convolutional layer, 64 such filters are used which are of the size 3 by 3 and depth 1 along with strides and layers of padding as 2 and 4, respectively. For the succeeding convolution layers, 64 filters with same size and depth of 64 are used with 2 strides and 4 layers of padding. From the first convolution layer, 640 parameters are being learned while from the second convolution layer, 36,928 parameters are being learned by the model.

Batch norm is introduced to standardize the input data each time it is fed to a new convolution layer to avoid the problem of internal covariate shift [21].

Batch norm transforms the data as:

$$\mu = \frac{1}{n}\sum x^i   \quad (10.7)$$

$$\sigma = \frac{1}{n}\sum x^i - \mu   \quad (10.8)$$

$$x_{norm} = \frac{x_i - \mu}{\sqrt{\sigma^2 - \varepsilon}}   \quad (10.9)$$

$$x^1 = \gamma * x_{norm} + \beta   \quad (10.10)$$

Here, x^i is the data, μ, σ, ε are the mean, standard deviation and a numerical constant used for stable calculation. α *and* β are two trainable parameters, where α adjusts the standard deviation and β adjusts the bias [20]. It normalizes the data using its mean and standard deviation (in eqn (10.7), (10.8) and (10.9)) and calculates the output by applying a linear transformation to it (in eqn (10.10)).

Figure 10.3 represents the proposed denoising CNN model. As shown in the figure, the IMFs iterated out using BEMD algorithm are fed to the convolution

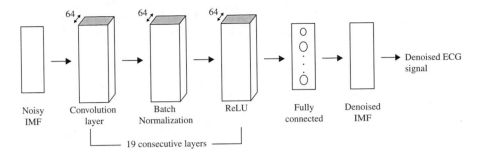

FIGURE 10.3   The denoising CNN model.

layer-batch norm-ReLU layers and then to a fully connected layer which maps the noisy components of the IMF and then minimizes it.

Here, for training the model, IMFs of clean aka noiseless ECG images are considered and fed into the CNN model along with the noisy IMFs. Throughout each convolution layers, the noisy features are learned and a noise mapping is done by the model.

Suppose we consider a clean ECG image $I(x,y)$ and the same image with the white Gaussian noise, $N(x,y)$.

$$N(x,y) = I(x,y) + noise \tag{10.11}$$

Let $I_1, I_2, \ldots, I_n$ are the IMFs from the clean image and $N, N_2, \ldots, N_n$ are the IMFs from the noisy image.

At each iteration, features of each IMFs are learned and the higher frequency components from the noisy IMFs (which will be the noisy features) are mapped as a separate function $W_n(x,y)$.

The aim of the proposed model is to minimize this function from the noisy IMFs with respect to its corresponding clean IMFs. Essentially this step will denoise the former.

MSE function is considered the cost function of the model to find the optimal parameters for the learning purpose. That is, if I_n is the clean IMF and N_n is its corresponding noisy IMF, the aim of the model is to find the mean of the square of the differences between features of the noisy IMF and the clean IMF, where the mean squared difference will be the noise function which is needed to be minimized.

The MSE function with two features x_1 *and* x_2 could be represented as:

$$MSE\ (cost\ function) = \frac{1}{m}\left(\sum_m I_i(x,y) - N_i(x,y)\right) \tag{10.12}$$

Since MSE function is a convex function [22], gradient descent technique could be used as the optimization technique to minimize the cost function.

Gradient descent is an optimization technique that tweaks the learning parameters in such a way that it minimizes the cost function. A convex function will have a unique minima point which will be its global minima and hence irrespective of the initialization, gradient descent algorithm could minimize the cost function [22, 23].

Gradient descent algorithm finds the slope of the cost function by finding its first derivative. If $\theta_1, \theta_2,...., \theta_k$ are the learning parameters used, then the cost function can be rewritten from eqn 10.12 as:

$$C\left(\theta_1, \theta_2,...., \theta_k\right) = \frac{1}{m}\sum_m\left(I_i\left(\theta_1, \theta_2,...., \theta_k\right) - N_i\left(\theta_1, \theta_2,...., \theta_k\right)\right) \quad (10.13)$$

Here, $C\left(\theta_1, \theta_2,...., \theta_k\right)$ is the cost function which then fed into gradient descent algorithm which is defined as:

Repeat until the convergence {

$$\theta_k := \theta_k - \alpha\frac{\partial}{\partial\theta_j}C\left(\theta_1, \theta_2,...., \theta_j\right), \text{ for } j = 1,2,...,k \quad (10.14)$$

}

Here, $\theta_1, \theta_2,...., \theta_k$ are the parameters to be learned and optimized for tuning the model and α is the learning rate used, where its value is assigned as 0.001 with 100 iterations.

This step is repeated for the entire training image dataset with n images, that is $\left(I_i\left(x,y\right), N_i\left(x,y\right)\right)$ for $i = 1,2,...,n$ where $I_i\left(x,y\right)$ is the clean ECG image and $N_i\left(x,y\right)$ is the noisy image. The optimum value of the parameters is learned and is used for denoising the test image dataset.

The denoised IMFs $D_i\left(x,y\right)$ and residue $r\left(x,y\right)$ are reconstructed to form the denoised image.

$$Output = \sum D_i\left(x,y\right) + r\left(x,y\right) \quad (10.15)$$

Where $\sum D_i\left(x,y\right)$ sums up the IMFs and $r\left(x,y\right)$ denotes the residue [10]. The process of denoising will not affect the morphology of the image and hence its spatial structure.

10.4   EXPERIMENTAL EVALUATION

In this session, the experimental setup and training of the proposed model are discussed and its performance evaluation is done.

10.4.1   EXPERIMENTAL SETUP AND TRAINING OF THE MODEL

For training the model, 1,000 noiseless ECG datasets are selected from MIT BIH Physionet Arrhythmia database which are simulated for 10 seconds. The one dimensional ECG datasets are then converted to their corresponding images using Matlab image processing toolkit. All the datasets are cropped to the size of 64 by 64 and are preprocessed to remove artifacts, if any. Three copies of each image dataset are made and a different level of noise is added separately for each sets.

Figure 10.4 shows a sample dataset used for training. Figure 10.4(a) represents the noise less ECG image while (b), (c) and (d) represents the same ECG image with 20%, 40% and 60% of noise in it. These three datasets with different noise levels are used for model training separately but together with its clean image.

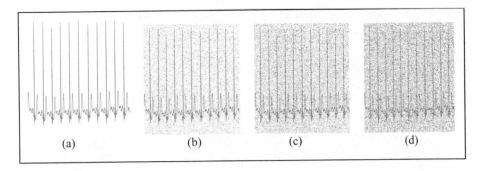

FIGURE 10.4 (a) Clean ECG image, (b) ECG image with 20% noise, (c) ECG image with 40% noise and (d) ECG image with 60% noise.

All the four sets of image datasets are fed to the BEMD algorithm and their IMFs are iterated out. Figure 10.2 represents the resulting IMFs of a pure ECG image.

Figure 10.5 shows the 1st IMFs of a sample image from the dataset with (a) no noise, (b) 20% noise, (c) 40% noise and (d) 60% noise each iterated out separately. From the figure, it is clear that the edges and other features of the ECG image are more prominently seen in the IMF of noiseless image. As the noise ratio increased,

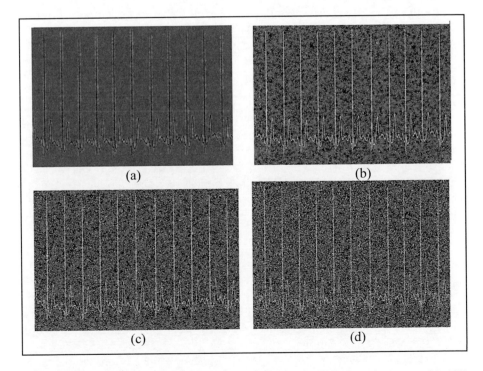

FIGURE 10.5 1st IMFs of (a) pure image, (b) image with 20% noise, (c) image with 40% noise and (d) image with 60% noise.

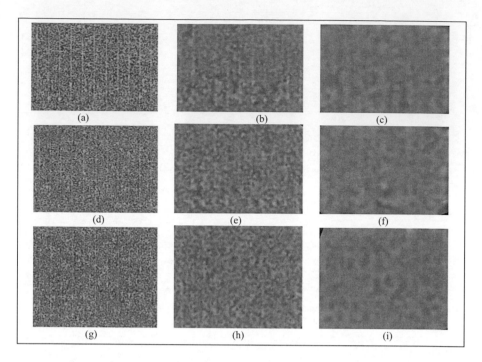

FIGURE 10.6   2nd IMF of (a) image with 20% noise, (b) 40% noise, (c) 60% noise, 3rd IMF of (d) image with 20% noise, (e) 40% noise, (f) 60% noise and 4th IMF of (g) image with 20% noise, (h) 40% noise and (i) 60% noise.

the image texture started to get distorted because the high frequency noise artifacts gained more importance.

Figure 10.6 shows the 2nd, 3rd and 4th IMFs of the same image sample used earlier. It can be noticed that as the order of IMFs iterated in each case increased, the distortion due to the noise in each of the IMFs decreased. The 2nd IMF in all the three cases look different and distorted when compared to the respective IMF of pure image, while 3rd and 4th IMFs look almost the same. The reason for the above is that as IMFs are iterated, the lower order IMF will have higher frequency components and hence will be noisy, whereas higher order IMFs will have relatively lesser noisy features.

Taking advantage of the above-mentioned characteristics of the IMFs, in the proposed work, only the first 3 IMFs are considered. The first three IMFs of each data are categorized into different sets where each set is a collection of noisy IMFs and their corresponding pure IMFs. IMFs with different noise levels are considered different sets. These sets are fed to the denoising CNN model and the remaining IMFs are kept aside. The learning rate of the gradient descent algorithm is kept as 0.001 with 100 epochs for the training.

Figure 10.7 represents the denoised IMFs of a sample image from the MIT-BIH dataset. The denoised IMFs do not show much morphological distortion when compared to its respective pure IMFs. The high frequency noisy components of the IMFs

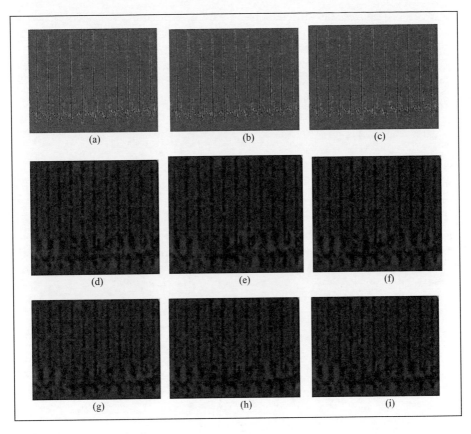

FIGURE 10.7 Denoised 1st IMF of (a) image with 20% noise, (b) 40% noise, (c) 60% noise, 2nd IMF of (d) image with 20% noise, (e) 40% noise, (f) 60% noise and 3rd IMF of (g) image with 20% noise, (h) 40% noise and (i) 60% noise.

are removed. The high frequency image features regain its importance; hence the lines and edges are clearly visible. These denoised IMFs along with the rest of the IMFs are recombined to form the denoised image.

10.4.2 Testing the Model and Performance Evaluation

In order to evaluate the performance of the proposed model, three best denoising techniques are considered which include NLM, DWT [24] and Wiener filter [25].

NLM filter works by weighting how the noisy pixels vary with respect to the desired pixels.

$$D(m) = \frac{1}{S_m} \int N(m) f(m,n) \, dm \qquad (10.16)$$

Where, $D(m)$ is the denoised value of the image at m, $N(m)$ is the noisy value at m, $f(m, n)$ is the weighting function and S_m is the normalizing factor [7].

DWT decomposes into different basis where each basis represents different space – frequency components. To suppress noises, thresholding and scaling is performed, which makes DWT an image denoising technique [24, 26].

Wiener filter uses the spectral property of the image and noise for denoising the image with the assumption that both have linear properties. The following equation is used for finding the denoised image:

$$D(x,y) = \sum_{i=0}^{M-1}\sum_{J=0}^{N-1} W_{ij}I(x-i,y-j)*n(x-i,y-j) \qquad (10.17)$$

Here, W_{ij} is the optimal weight, $I(x,y)$ is the input image, $n(x,y)$ is the noise and $D(x,y)$ is the denoised image [25].

Figure 10.8 shows the noisy ECG images along with its corresponding denoised images where each of the noisy images has different noise quantity. It is clear from the figure that even though the image (e) has more noise in it than the image (a), both of their denoised images look similar. This is true when comparing (a) and (b) and

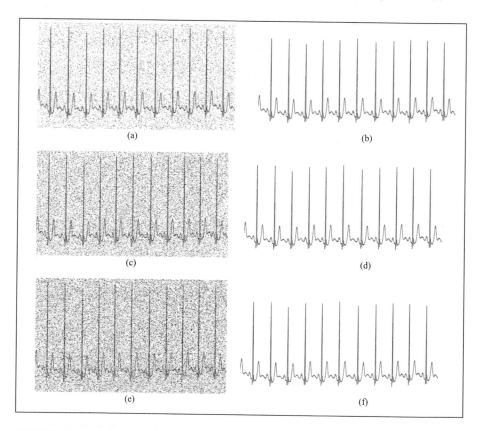

FIGURE 10.8 ECG noisy image with (a) 20% noise, (c) 40% noise and (e) 60% noise and denoised ECG images using proposed ECBEMD technique which had (b) 20% noise, (d) 40% noise and (f) 60% noise.

between (b) and (c). It is also noticeable that the morphological structure of the image is preserved in all the three cases.

In order to assess the efficiency of the proposed method, techniques like root MSE (RMSE) and peak signal-to-noise ratio (PSNR) are implemented.

PSNR is defined as:

$$PSNR = 10\log\left(\frac{Max\_I^2}{MSE}\right) \tag{10.18}$$

$$MSE = \frac{1}{N}\sum_m I_i(x,y) - N_i(x,y) \tag{10.19}$$

Here, Max_I is the maximum intensity vale of the input image $I_i(x,y)$, $N_i(x,y)$ represents the noisy image and MSE represents the MSE between the input image and the noisy image.

RMSE is defined as:

$$RMSE = \sqrt{\frac{1}{N}\sum_m I_i(x,y) - N_i(x,y)} = \sqrt{MSE} \tag{10.20}$$

Here, $I_i(x,y)$, $N_i(x,y)$ represents the clean and noisy image, respectively.

It is well known that if the technique has higher PSNR value and Lower MSE value, then it is considered to be a better technique in denoising [10].

After the model is trained, another datasets with 120 ECG images are acquired from MIT BIH Physionet Arrhythmia image database. All the images are of same size and dimension. Random amount of noise is added to the test dataset to check the denoising power of the proposed model with different noise level.

The test dataset is fed to the algorithms of the proposed model, NLM, DWT and Wiener filter. The respective resultant denoised images are then used separately to find the PSNR and MSE values between them and their noise-free images.

10.5   RESULTS

This section discusses the inference from the performance evaluation of the proposed method when compared with three of the powerful image denoising techniques.

Table 10.1 depicts the PSNR values between pure ECG images and its corresponding denoised images where all the three sets of images with different noise levels are considered. In the table, values of 10 randomly selected samples among the total 120 samples are given. Table 10.2 depicts the average PSNR values between the ECG images and its corresponding denoised images where all 120 samples are considered and their average PSNR value is found. Table 10.3 represents the RMSE values of the same samples used for Table 10.1 for the three different noise levels. Table 10.4 represents the average of the RMSE value of all the samples in the test set.

Figure 10.9 shows the noisy images with 205, 40% and 60% noise levels and their respective denoised images which are treated by Ensemble Convolutional Neural Network Bidimensional Empirical Mode Decomposition (ENBEMD), NLM, DWT and Wiener filter in their respective orders. The denoised images visually do not

TABLE 10.1

PSNR Values between the Pure ECG Images and Their Respective Denoised Images of 10 Samples of the Test Set

Samples	Image with 20% Noise				Image with 40% Noise				Image with 60% Noise			
	ECBEMD	NLM	DWT	WF	ECBEMD	NLM	DWT	WF	ECBEMD	NLM	DWT	WF
S1	8.546	4.287	4.785	6.574	8.334	4.052	4.551	6.41	8.147	3.984	4.231	6.25
S2	8.641	4.274	4.762	6.492	8.564	4.012	4.347	6.347	8.412	3.945	4.25	6.189
S3	8.246	4.241	4.727	6.442	8.201	4.045	4.345	6.348	8.195	3.97	4.28	6.148
S4	8.745	4.176	4.674	6.396	8.702	4.015	4.248	6.248	8.698	3.826	4.187	5.984
S5	8.647	4.295	4.802	6.653	8.541	4.152	4.520	6.547	8.502	4.086	4.487	6.421
S6	8.349	4.321	4.832	6.745	8.245	4.247	4.641	6.547	8.145	4.012	4.348	6.402
S7	8.45	4.226	4.569	6.334	8.425	4.145	4.324	6.214	8.341	3.943	4.247	6.024
S8	8.347	4.139	4.331	6.263	8.245	3.842	4.397	6.148	8.145	3.547	4.287	5.978
S9	8.524	4.269	4.74	6.539	8.347	3.921	4.854	6.475	8.245	3.645	4.578	6.270
S10	8.601	4.307	4.806	6.703	8.46	4.104	4.742	6.697	8.345	4.015	4.621	6.726

TABLE 10.2

Average PSNR Values between the Pure ECG Images and Their Respective Denoised Images of All Samples of the Test Set

Image with 20% Noise				Image with 40% Noise				Image with 60% Noise			
ECBEMD	NLM	DWT	WF	ECBEMD	NLM	DWT	WF	ECBEMD	NLM	DWT	WF
8.543	4.248	4.726	6.348	8.472	4.157	4.674	6.247	8.347	3.985	4.347	6.147

TABLE 10.3

RMSE Values between the Pure ECG Images and Their Respective Denoised Images of 10 Samples of the Test Set

Samples	Image with 20% Noise				Image with 40% Noise				Image with 60% Noise			
	ECBEMD	NLM	DWT	WF	ECBEMD	NLM	DWT	WF	ECBEMD	NLM	DWT	WF
S1	0.124	0.425	0.341	0.245	0.135	0.456	0.375	0.257	0.147	0.479	0.385	0.275
S2	0.145	0.457	0.347	0.275	0.157	0.467	0.351	0.284	0.168	0.478	0.367	0.297
S3	0.153	0.479	0.368	0.235	0.165	0.481	0.371	0.247	0.176	0.497	0.381	0.257
S4	0.134	0.467	0.387	0.278	0.148	0.472	0.397	0.287	0.167	0.498	4.002	0.297
S5	0.142	0.427	0.314	0.214	0.157	0.438	0.327	0.234	0.171	0.449	0.345	0.248
S6	0.137	0.428	0.357	0.219	0.148	0.446	0.367	0.227	0.167	0.479	0.376	0.243
S7	0.167	0.473	0.367	0.278	0.175	0.481	0.375	0.297	0.184	0.493	0.384	0.304
S8	0.176	0.476	0.357	0.237	0.185	0.482	0.367	0.247	0.192	0.491	0.378	0.267
S9	0.148	0.428	0.368	0.249	0.157	0.438	0.375	0.257	0.172	0.464	0.384	0.268
S10	0.113	0.437	0.327	0.276	0.134	0.447	0.347	0.284	0.142	0.458	0.3578	0.297

TABLE 10.4

Average RMSE Values between the Pure ECG Images and Their Respective Denoised Images of All Samples of the Test Set

Image with 20% Noise				Image with 40% Noise				Image with 60% Noise			
ECBEMD	NLM	DWT	WF	ECBEMD	NLM	DWT	WF	ECBEMD	NLM	DWT	WF
0.157	0.468	0.369	0.279	0.161	0.475	0.375	0.281	0.175	0.492	0.382	0.295

differ much from each other and all of them could be categorized as good denoised images irrespective of the algorithm used.

Even though the denoised images treated with the above-mentioned four denoising techniques visually look similar, when considering the PSNR and RMSE value, it is found that the proposed method, ECBEMD has the highest PSNR value, followed by Wiener filter, DWT and NLM (from Tables 10.1 and 10.2). Also it is found that ECEBMD has lesser RMSE values than the rest of the techniques (from Tables 10.3 and 10.4).

Higher PSNR implies that there are lesser noise components in the denoised image, while lesser RMSE value depicts that the error between the pure image and denoised image is less. Both these results imply that the proposed model, Ensemble CNN-BEMD is a better denoising technique when compared to the most used techniques like NLM, DWT and Wiener filter.

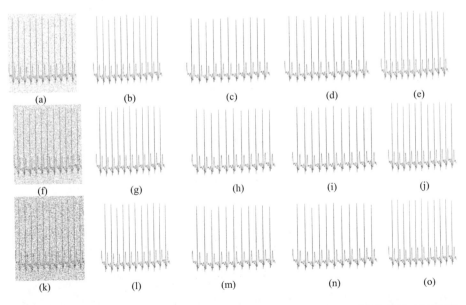

FIGURE 10.9 (a) Image with 20% noise level that is treated with (b) ECBEMD, (c) NLM, (d) DWT, (e) WF, (f) Image with 40% noise level that is treated with (g) ECBEMD, (h) NLM, (i) DWT, (j) WF and (k) Image with 60% noise level that is treated with (l) ECBEMD, (m) NLM, (n) DWT and (o) WF.

From Tables 10.1, 10.2, 10.3 and 10.4, it can be seen that the PSNR values decrease and the RMSE values increase by a small amount as the noise levels of the noisy input image increases for all the techniques. This guides us to the conclusion that even after training with different noisy images, the model along with the other models slightly fails to denoise images with higher degree of noise. This problem can be considered for a future work.

10.6 CONCLUSION

The accumulation of noise in the ECG images during its recording process can hinder the proper diagnosis of heart's functioning. It is important to develop an ECG denoising technique that can denoise huge ECG datasets while maintaining their morphological structure. The study proposes that the ECBEMD model, which combines deep learning with BEMD, is considered an effective denoising technique for ECG images. The working efficiency of the proposed model is evaluated with three other prominent and powerful denoising techniques, namely NLM, DWT and Wiener filter. The experimental evaluation conducted between the proposed model and the above-mentioned approaches indicates that the datasets treated with ECBEMD had a greater signal to noise ratio and lesser MSE values. This has been achieved without any distortions in the image morphology and with comparatively lesser computational latency. As a result, the suggested ECBEMD model can be deemed an effective denoising approach for ECG images.

REFERENCES

1. Sidney, Stephen, et al. "Heterogeneity in national US mortality trends within heart disease subgroups, 2000–2015." *BMC Cardiovascular Disorders* 17.1 (2017): 1–10.
2. Blackburn, Henry, et al. "The electrocardiogram in population studies: a classification system." *Circulation* 21.6 (1960): 1160–1175.
3. Syama, S., et al. "Classification of ECG signal using machine learning techniques." *2019 2nd International Conference on Power and Embedded Drive Control (ICPEDC).* IEEE, 2019.
4. Prakash, M. Bhanu, et al. "Noise reduction of ECG using Chebyshev filter and classification using machine learning algorithms." *2021 International Conference on Computing, Communication, and Intelligent Systems (ICCCIS).* IEEE, 2021.
5. Khaing, Aung Soe, and Zaw Min Naing. "Quantitative investigation of digital filters in electrocardiogram with simulated noises." *International Journal of Information and Electronics Engineering* 1.3 (2011): 210–216.
6. Rilling, Gabriel, Patrick Flandrin, and Paulo Goncalves. "On empirical mode decomposition and its algorithms." *IEEE-EURASIP Workshop on Nonlinear Signal and Image Processing.* Vol. 3. No. 3. NSIP-03, Grado (I), 2003.
7. Manjón, José V., et al. "MRI denoising using non-local means." *Medical Image Analysis* 12.4 (2008): 514–523.
8. Lang, Markus, et al. "Noise reduction using an undecimated discrete wavelet transform." *IEEE Signal Processing Letters* 3.1 (1996): 10–12.
9. AlMahamdy, Mohammed, and H. Bryan Riley. "Performance study of different denoising methods for ECG signals." *Procedia Computer Science* 37 (2014): 325–332.

10. Manju, Bhaskara Panicker Radha, and Parvathy Rema. "A Performance based comparative study on the Modified version of Empirical Mode Decomposition with traditional Empirical Mode Decomposition." *Procedia Computer Science* 171 (2020): 2469–2475.

11. Singh, Pratik, Syed Shahnawazuddin, and Gayadhar Pradhan. "An efficient ECG denoising technique based on non-local means estimation and modified empirical mode decomposition." *Circuits, Systems, and Signal Processing* 37.10 (2018): 4527–4547.

12. Wu, Zhaohua, and Norden E. Huang. "Ensemble empirical mode decomposition: a noise-assisted data analysis method." *Advances in Adaptive Data Analysis* 1.01 (2009): 1–41.

13. Dragomiretskiy, Konstantin, and Dominique Zosso. "Variational mode decomposition." *IEEE Transactions on Signal Processing* 62.3 (2013): 531–544.

14. Gondara, Lovedeep. "Medical image denoising using convolutional denoising autoencoders." *2016 IEEE 16th International Conference on Data Mining Workshops (ICDMW)*. IEEE, 2016.

15. Chen, Jingwen, et al. "Image blind denoising with generative adversarial network based noise modeling." *Proceedings of the IEEE Conference on Computer Vision and Pattern Recognition*. IEEE Xplore, 2018.

16. Nunes, Jean Claude, et al. "Image analysis by bidimensional empirical mode decomposition." *Image and Vision Computing* 21.12 (2003): 1019–1026.

17. Bhuiyan, Sharif M. A., Reza R. Adhami, and Jesmin F. Khan. "A novel approach of fast and adaptive bidimensional empirical mode decomposition." *2008 IEEE International Conference on Acoustics, Speech and Signal Processing*. IEEE, 2008.

18. Huang, Norden E., et al. "The empirical mode decomposition and the Hilbert spectrum for nonlinear and non-stationary time series analysis." *Proceedings of the Royal Society of London. Series A: Mathematical, Physical and Engineering Sciences* 454.1971 (1998): 903–995.

19. Haritha, C., M. Ganesan, and E. P. Sumesh. "A survey on modern trends in ECG noise removal techniques." *2016 International Conference on Circuit, Power and Computing Technologies (ICCPCT)*. IEEE, 2016.

20. Hanin, Boris. "Which neural net architectures give rise to exploding and vanishing gradients?." *arXiv preprint arXiv:1801.03744* (2018).

21. Santurkar, Shibani, et al. "How does batch normalization help optimization?." *Proceedings of the 32nd International Conference on Neural Information Processing Systems*. Advances in neural information processing systems, 2018.

22. Cai, T. Tony, and Mark G. Low. "A framework for estimation of convex functions." *Statistica Sinica* (2015): 25: 423–456.

23. Ruder, Sebastian. "An overview of gradient descent optimization algorithms." *arXiv preprint arXiv:1609.04747* (2016).

24. Shensa, Mark J. "The discrete wavelet transform: wedding the a trous and Mallat algorithms." *IEEE Transactions on signal processing* 40.10 (1992): 2464–2482.

25. Shamsollahi, Mohammad Bagher. "ECG denoising and compression using a modified extended Kalman filter structure." *IEEE Transactions on Biomedical Engineering* 55.9 (2008): 2240–2248.

26. Bnou, K., S. Raghay, and A. Hakim, A wavelet denoising approach based on unsupervised learning model. *EURASIP J. Adv. Signal Process*. 2020, 36 (2020). https://doi.org/10.1186/s13634-020-00693-4.

11 Wrapper-Based Feature Selection for Big Data Using a Multi-Core Environment

Subhash Kamble
and Arunalatha Jakkanahally Siddegowda
Department of Computer Science and Engineering,
University Visvesvaraya College of Engineering
Bengaluru, India

Venugopal Kuppanna Rajuk
Bangalore University
Bengaluru, India

CONTENTS

DOI: 10.1201/9781003320340-11

143

11.1   INTRODUCTION

Big data is a term used to describe large amounts of data that are too vast and complex to be contained in traditional databases. In addition, it refers to any data that exceeds a device's processing power. Many disciplines now have to deal with huge databases that contain a broad range of features. Feature selection strategies tend to reduce the number of noisy, redundant, or irrelevant characteristics that can degrade the classification accuracy. Traditional methods, on the other hand, lack the scalability needed to handle datasets with millions of instances and deliver results in a timely manner. Furthermore, for large datasets like big data, traditional methods for selecting features, such as the wrapper approach, are just as expensive as computerized. When constructing a predictive model, selection of feature ensures that the number of input variables is minimized. The selection of features for the models has an important area of data mining research, with a subset of unique features being selected for the models. Reducing the number of input variables would be an advantageous for both reducing the computational cost of modeling and increasing the model performance in terms of classification accuracy [1, 2]. The purpose of data extraction is to obtain and use information, the dimensions of which are defined by handling large quantities of data. It is difficult to deal with datasets that include high time for building the models, redundant data, and noisy data. The use of features is a key stage in preprocessing a subset of the larger dataset, as well as classification accuracy. The features are selected based on the results of a search and a subsets success evaluation. This work has been tested on six datasets, the obtained result indicates better accuracy as compared to existing technique.

11.1.1   MOTIVATION

The main shortcomings of high-dimensional datasets take more time for creation of the model with redundant information, and it degrades the quality of the model that makes data analysis task difficult [3, 4]. To overcome this problem, for any high-dimensional datasets, the feature selection plays very important role since it removes any type of irrelevant or duplicate features from the dataset, which increases the classification accuracy and reduces the computation time.

11.1.2   CONTRIBUTIONS

The main contribution of the proposed work includes:

1. The wrapper-based feature selection is proposed to select the best features of the data.
2. The proposed work has been implemented on multi-core environment.
3. The performance of the proposed work has been analyzed by considering six various datasets as described in the following sections.

11.1.3   ORGANIZATION

The chapter has been organized as follows, Section 11.2 provides related works, Section 11.3 describes the proposed system, and the result has been explained in Section 11.4 with analysis of efficiency and effectiveness of the proposed methodology.

11.2 RELATED WORKS

In the contemporary big data feature selection research domain, there have been many attempts to achieve better accuracy while selecting the features. Therefore, this section provides insights on various related works.

Hasnony et al. [4] suggested a novel approach for establishing and minimizing the feature selection barriers by employing the combination of particle swarm optimization (PSO) and grey wolf optimization (GWO). For determining the optimal results method considered the k-nearest neighbor (KNN) classifier along with Euclidean partition matrices. The K-fold cross-validation is used in resolving the overfitting issue. The proposed model used 20 datasets for the experiments and statistical analysis to achieve the efficiency and persuasiveness of the work. The average accuracy obtains 90% as compared to 81.6% and 86.8% of other methods. It takes more time for the computation. In future, model can be used on various datasets along with combinations of other functionalities. Also, to improve the efficiency, model can be built by combining the modern metaheuristics algorithms such as whale swarm and salp optimization algorithm [5].

Kong et al. [6] introduced a novel feature selection using distributed fuzzy rough set (DFRS), which splits and assigns the jobs to multiple nodes for parallel computation. The main key challenge is to keep the global data on each assigned node without conserving the whole fuzzy relation matrix. Using multiple real datasets, extensive experiments are conducted and demonstrated that DFRS significantly improves the execution time and its feature selection accuracy is nearly the same as the traditional approach. It performs well on single class datasets but fails to handle multi-class datasets.

Sun et al. [7] have addressed single label issues by presenting a hybrid filter-wrapper multi-label feature selection approach with the Lebesgue measure for multi-label neighborhood decision systems. Moreover, the proposed algorithm using Novel Correlation-Based Feature Selection (NCFS)-Binary Particle Swarm Optimization (BPSO) prevents redundant features from decreasing complexity and improves efficiency. Further, this work can be extended to achieve better multi-label classification performance using semi-supervised algorithms [8].

Wang et al. [9] proposed automated search-based breadth and attention mechanisms to expedite wrapper feature selection. They simulated actual datasets using various machine learning bases and observed that their strategies produce a more important feature set with improved efficiency.

Elhariri et al. [10] used a hybrid Filter-Wrapper, which is trained and tested through the use of crack photos and UCI databases. The proposed solution outperforms other methods with traditional methodologies for the collection of features in terms of reduced rates and computational time. Ghosh et al. [11] introduced a framework that incorporates various techniques for obtaining effective prediction result with the usage of Relief, and Least Absolute Shrinkage and Selection Operator (LASSO) method. The proposed model is not suitable when the missing data is more.

Tu et al. [12] initially presented an improved hierarchy strengthened GWO (HSGWO) algorithm, dominant, and omega wolves. Secondly, the updated best learning plan for dominant wolves is being introduced to escape misdirection and increase group performance by low ranking wolves. The result obtained shows improved accuracy and convergence of other algorithms for the solution in most experiments. In future, this can be applied to various methods that handle various constraints for the real-world problems.

Haz *et al.* [13] introduced a modern simplified two-dimensional method for the collection of characteristics depending on the particle swarm. The central principle of the solution proposed is the cardinality subset and is incorporated into the learning system by expanding the speed dimension. The findings of the comparative study with genetic algorithm (GA), Ant Colony Optimization (ACO), and five other PSO variants show that the suggested 2D learning method provides a functional subset with comparatively smaller cardinal characteristics and higher success in classification with shorter running times.

11.3 PROPOSED SYSTEM

The proposed system is a parallelized exhaustive feature selection (PEFS) technique, which is a wrapper method of feature selection, and it is parallelized in a multi-core CPU environment for minimizing execution time and computing power. The proposed work analyzes the feature importance of each of dataset. The KNN algorithm is used classify the obtained feature subsets. Throughout the model training, 10-fold cross-validation used to escape from the overfitting problem. The architecture of proposed model is shown in the Figure 11.1.

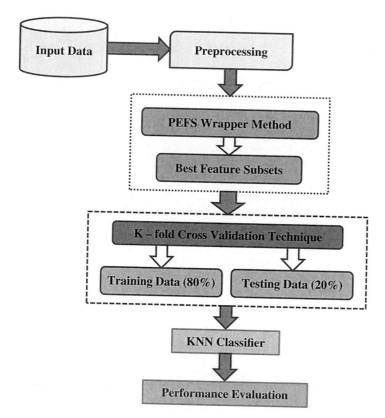

FIGURE 11.1   Architecture of proposed model.

11.3.1 PROBLEM STATEMENT

The problem considered in the proposed work is to develop an optimized feature selection mechanism for big data which is computationally less expensive and to achieve better efficiency.

11.3.2 OBJECTIVES

1. Minimize the number of features,
2. Maximize the output accuracy, and
3. Reduce the computational time.

11.3.3 PREPROCESSING

In this step missing values, redundant and noisy data will be cleaned using integer scaling normalization technique.

$$X = \frac{|A| - (10^{n-1}) * |B|}{10^{n-1}} \tag{11.1}$$

where X = scale one value between 0 and 1, A = data element, N = number of digits in element A and, B = first digit of the data in element A.

11.3.4 WRAPPER METHOD

In this step, the best feature of the given dataset will be selected. In the proposed Wrapper-based PEFS framework, the datasets are independently provided as input data by bifurcating the number of features present in the respective datasets in the form of batches. Each batch will be parallelizing the CPU of the system for the computation of the best possible subsets by checking all the possible combinations of feature sets and then all the batches will return the best identified feature subsets. Finally, the best identified feature subsets are again inputted to EFS in a sequential manner and it gives the best feature subset of the given input dataset. The algorithm steps are given below.

**ALGORITHM 1   WRAPPER-BASED PARALLELIZED
EXHAUSTIVE FEATURE SELECTION**

Input: Dataset DS with n Features
Output: Best Features Subset
1: Bifurcate the n Features in the form of *batches*
2: $b \leftarrow batches$
3: Best_Features [] = $EFS()$
4: **while** $b \leftarrow batches$ **do**
5: Best_Features [] $\leftarrow Parallelize(EFS(), CV)$
6: $Seq(EFS(), CV)$
7: **end**
8: **return** Selected Best Feature Subset

11.3.5 K-FOLD CROSS-VALIDATION TECHNIQUE

The proposed work uses KNN Algorithm with K = 5 and the K-fold cross-validation approach with exhaustive feature selection to get better results. The dataset specifies the value of K in K-fold cross-validation. The K-fold method produces a less biased model than other methods. As any observation from the original dataset has a chance of turning up in the training and test sets.

After K-fold cross-validation, the proposed work divides the data into K folds at random. At higher values of K, the model is less biased. Whereas, the lower the value of K, the more similar the model is to the train-test split method. Later by using the K-1 fold, fit and validate the model. Then, the list of the scores and mistakes will be created. Repeat procedure until every K-fold is used as a test set. Then take the average of all the ratings. This gives the performance metric of the model.

11.3.6 KNN CLASSIFIER

KNN uses a Euclidean distance for finding distance equation to evaluate the K-nearest neighbors for the given datasets.

$$E_k(x,y) = b \pm \sqrt{\sum_{i=1}^{k}(y_i - x_i)^2}$$ (11.2)

where y_i and x_i are particular feature selected from the input data, and i is a variable from 1 to k, and k is the complete number of features used.

11.4 EXPERIMENTAL RESULTS AND DISCUSSION

The algorithm is implemented using python library and Ray framework is used for distributing the task among different cores of the CPU.

11.4.1 DATASETS

The datasets in this work were considered from the machine learning library [14]. For the proposed work, the selected six datasets are depicted in Table 11.1, in which

TABLE 11.1

Dataset Description

Datasets	Instances	Features	Classes
KC1	2110	21	2
Ionosphere	0351	34	2
Sonar	0208	60	2
WDBC	0561	30	2
Breast cancer	0699	09	2
Page blocks	5473	10	2

among the six datasets, the sonar dataset is considered a big dataset [4]. In order to test the model individually, the training and testing samples for every datasets are separated, and it is employed according to the proposed work.

11.4.2 Performance Evaluation

The proposed model performance with respect to the classification accuracy can be calculated using Equation (11.3)

$$Accuracy = \frac{TP + TN}{TP + TN + FP + FN} \quad (11.3)$$

11.4.3 Performance Analysis

The performance of the implemented model related to the accuracy, execution time, and features selected is compared to the existing methods [4, 5, 8].

11.4.3.1 Accuracy

Table 11.2 shows the classification accuracy using KNN classifier for six datasets that are used during the conduction of the experiments. The proposed model provides better in accuracy for most of the datasets. However, the impact of the accuracy is more on ionosphere dataset as compared to other datasets. The result in Table 11.2 is graphically depicted in Figure 11.2.

11.4.3.2 Execution Time

Table 11.3 shows the execution time using KNN classifier for six datasets that are used during the conduction of the experiments. The proposed model minimizes the execution time as compared to the traditional approach as proposed model is parallelized on multi-core environment. The result in Table 11.3 is graphically represented in Figure 11.3.

11.4.3.3 Feature Selection

Table 11.4 shows the selection of feature using PEFS for six datasets that are used during the conduction of the experiments. The proposed model provides more impact

TABLE 11.2

Comparison of Accuracy

Datasets	PSO [4]	GWO [4]	bGWO2 [5]	BPSO [8]	PSO+GWO [4]	Proposed Method
KC1	80.85	80.45	79.00	79.05	82.10	83.40
Ionosphere	86.55	85.40	83.00	84.00	90.10	94.40
Sonar	79.00	78.00	72.00	74.00	85.5.0	85.70
WDBC	92.25	95.05	83.00	84.00	92.00	94.70
Breast cancer	95.68	95.38	97.00	95.00	96.70	97.90
Page blocks	94.60	94.15	93.60	94.00	96.00	96.80

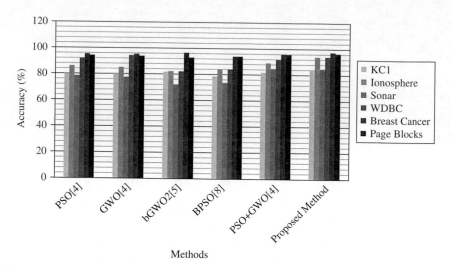

FIGURE 11.2   Comparison of accuracy on various datasets.

TABLE 11.3
Comparison of Execution Time

Datasets	PSO [4]	GWO [4]	bGWO2 [5]	BPSO [8]	PSO+GWO [4]	Proposed Method
KC1	11.75	12.85	14.06	13.50	09.40	04.65
Ionosphere	09.05	08.35	10.50	09.54	06.10	03.32
Sonar	08.83	07.98	09.65	09.80	06.30	04.35
WDBC	08.70	08.60	10.90	10.40	06.75	04.60
Breast cancer	08.80	08.48	10.69	12.30	07.00	02.58
Page blocks	15.50	16.40	18.70	15.50	13.75	11.93

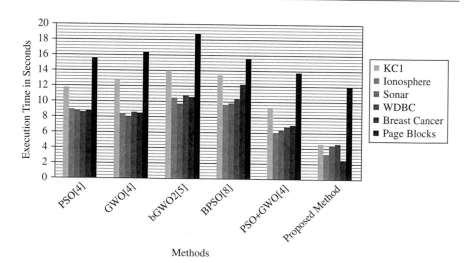

FIGURE 11.3   Comparison of execution time on various datasets.

TABLE 11.4

Comparison of Selected Features

Datasets	PSO [4]	GWO [4]	bGWO2 [5]	BPSO [8]	PSO+GWO [4]	Proposed Method
KC1	02.35	03.60	16.10	20.40	04.65	3
Ionosphere	10.45	15.25	15.20	19.20	03.90	2
Sonar	26.20	30.05	32.00	31.00	14.65	3
WDBC	13.15	14.00	32.00	31.20	03.80	3
Breast cancer	02.35	03.60	05.20	05.70	02.25	3
Page blocks	07.50	09.80	07.90	08.40	02.30	3

on selecting feature subsets of the datasets. The result in Table 11.4 is graphically represented in Figure 11.4.

11.5 CONCLUSIONS

This work introduces a new paradigm based on KNN and wrapper-based approaches with Euclidean separation matrices. The proposed model employs a KNN classifier with an integrated exhaustive feature selection, which is a wrapper method of feature selection that is parallelized in a multi-core CPU environment which solves the feature selection problem. The feasibility and consistency of experiment and predictive analysis of six datasets were carried out. The proposed technique resulted in a substantial reduction in feature size, and extremely effective in terms of accuracy and processing time. The secured accuracy measured up to 83.4%, 94.4%, 85.7%, 94.7%, 97.9%, and 96.7% for the Software Defect Prediction Dataset (KC1), ionosphere, sonar, Wisconsin Diagnostic Breast Cancer (WDBC), breast cancer, and page blocks of datasets.

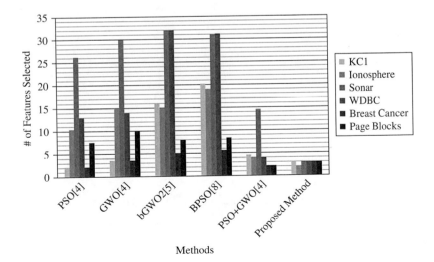

FIGURE 11.4 Comparison of selected features on various datasets.

REFERENCES

[1] Rong, M., Gong, D., Gao, X.: Feature Selection and Its use in Big Data: Challenges, Methods, and Trends. IEEE Access, **7**, pp. 19709–19725 (2019).

[2] Tang, R., Zhang, X.: CART Decision Tree Combined with Boruta Feature Selection for Medical Data Classification. In: 5th International Proceedings on Big Data Analytics, pp. 80–84. IEEE, (2020).

[3] Chen, K., Zhou, F. Y., Yuan, X. F.: Hybrid Particle Swarm Optimization with Spiral Shaped Mechanism for Feature Selection. IEEE Transactions on Expert System Applications, **128**, pp. 140–156 (2019).

[4] El-Hasnony, I. M., Barakat, S. I., Elhoseny, M., Mostafa, R. R.: Improved Feature Selection Model for Big Data Analytics. IEEE Transactions on Knowledge and Data Engineering, **8**, pp. 66989–67004 (2020).

[5] Emary, E., Zawbaa, H. M., Hassanien, A. E.: Binary Grey Wolf Optimization Approaches for Feature Selection. Journal of Neurocomputing, **172**, pp. 371–381 (2016).

[6] Kong, L., Qu, W., Yu, J., Zuo, H., Chen, G., Xiong, F., Pan, S., Lin, S., Qiu, M.: Distributed Feature Selection for Big Data using Fuzzy Rough Sets. IEEE Transactions on Fuzzy Systems, **28**(5), pp. 846–857 (2019).

[7] Sun, L., Yin, T., Ding, W., Xu, J.: Hybrid Multilabel Feature Selection using BPSO and Neighborhood Rough Sets for Multilabel Neighborhood Decision Systems. IEEE Access, **4**(7), pp. 175793–175815 (2019).

[8] Mafarja M. M., Mirjalili, S.: Hybrid Whale Optimization Algorithm with Simulated Annealing for Feature Selection. Journal of Neurocomputing, **260**, pp. 302–312, (2017).

[9] Wang, Z., Xiao, X., Rajasekaran, S.: Novel and Efficient Randomized Algorithms for Feature Selection. Journal of Big Data Mining and Analytics, **3**(3), pp. 208–224, (2020).

[10] Elhariri, E., El-Bendary, N., Taie, S. A.: Using Hybrid Filter-Wrapper Feature Selection with Multi Objective Improved Salp Optimization for Crack Severity Recognition. IEEE Access, **1**(8), pp. 84290–84315, (2020).

[11] Ghosh, P., Azam, S., Jonkman, M., Karim, A., Shamrat, F. J., Ignatious, E., Shultana, S., Beera-volu, A. R., De Boer, F.: Efficient Prediction of Cardiovascular Disease Using Machine Learning Algorithms with Relief and LASSO Feature Selection Techniques. IEEE Access, **22**(9), pp. 19304–19326, (2021).

[12] Tu, Q., Chen, X., Liu, X.: Hierarchy Strengthened Grey Wolf Optimizer for Numerical Optimization and Feature Selection. IEEE Access, **7**, pp. 78012–78028, (2019).

[13] Haz, F., Swain, A., Patel, N., Naik, C.: A Two Dimensional (2D) Learning Framework for Particle Swarm based Feature Selection. Pattern Recognition, **76**, pp. 416–433, (2018).

[14] Dheeru, D.: Karra taniskidou e, UCI Machine Learning Repository (2017).

12 MDAKB
A Metadata-Driven Approach for Multilingual Knowledge Base Generation for Agricultural Domains in the Indian Context

Arulmozhi Varman Murugesan
Department of Electronics and Electrical Engineering,
SASTRA Deemed University
Thanjavur, Tamil Nadu, India

Gerard Deepak
Department of Computer Science and Engineering,
National Institute of Technology
Tiruchirappalli, Tamil Nadu, India

CONTENTS

12.1   INTRODUCTION

India is a multilingual country; it is well known for its diverse cultures and traditions. The country's chief occupation is agriculture, and India's official languages are 22 in number, and unofficially the numbers of languages are unknown to the world. Agriculture is known as the backbone of the Indian economy, more than 50% of India's working populations are farmers, and agriculture shares 17–18% of the country's gross domestic product (GDP). In this chapter, we propose a method to predict the crop according to the time of the year, type of the soil and suggest the type of fertilizer and chemical to utilize and the time to harvest using grey wolf

DOI: 10.1201/9781003320340-12

optimization algorithm [1] by computing the semantic similarity of entropy, Morita's overlap index and normalized point wise mutual induction and presenting user the biological names of the ideal crop to cultivate in Kannada knowledge base, Tamil knowledge base, and Hindi knowledge base with the help of IndoWordNet [2].

Motivation: When users search from ontologies regarding crop farming, the specific terms are extracted from the searches. Metadata is generated using OpenCalais, PyRdfa, GRDDL, Resource Description Framework (RDF) Distiller in three ways; by Level of Detail (LOD) clouds, Wiki data/DBpedia/Google Graph application programming interface (API), or matching them in specialized crop ontology portals. The metadata is evaluated for relevancy with term frequency-inverse document frequency (TF-IDF) that gets its reference from data crawled through the World Wide Web into a Web Document Corpus. The evaluated data is now sent into a recursive neural network to retrieve terms from the top 20% of the classified documents. The semantic similarity of the retrieved terms is computed. This computed semantic similarity is used to link all the ontological terms hierarchically. From a list containing the biological names of all crops, the final crop names are extracted. The crop names are provided to the user through IndoWordNet in the Kannada knowledge base, Tamil knowledge base, and Hindi knowledge base.

Contribution: A novel framework to recommend knowledge base crop prediction is proposed in this work. The proposed model's accuracy and efficiency are better than the base model as the biological taxonomy of crops is being encompassed to improve the recommendation. Crop ontology portals are incorporated with seed ontology and are classified using recurrent neural networks (RNNs). The results are optimized using the grey wolf algorithm, and the most relevant crops are recommended to the user.

Organization: The chapter put out is structured in the following way. Related works are in Section 12.2, and Section 12.3 encircles the proposed framework. Section 12.4 contains implementation and performance evaluation, while Section 12.5 carries the results. Conclusively, the chapter is terminated in Section 12.6.

12.2   RELATED WORK

Bhattacharyya et al. [2] proposed wordnet for Indian languages, namely Marathi, Sanskrit, Bodo, and Telugu. The rules to develop wordnet are described in this chapter, and the primary methodology to construct wordnet is explained to the lexicographers in a detailed manner. Also, the benefits of IndoWordNet are compared with the EuroWordNet. Mirjalili et al. [1] proposed the grey wolf algorithm that is inspired from the grey wolves by their leadership and hunting methods. The outcome obtained by the algorithm is validated through a comparative study with many optimization techniques and algorithms and provides a contentious result. It also gave solutions to three design problems of many real applications in the field of optical engineering. Burrows et al. [3] examined the use of RNNs in such applications. Their work demonstrates the feedback connections' contribution as a smoothing process, which is accomplished by shifting the class boundary of an analogous feed forward system classifier. Almiani et al. [4] introduced an ostensibly fully automated detection mechanism for Fog protection to combat cyberattacks. Their approach employs multi-layered RNNs that are intended to be used for Fog computing protection that is similar to Internet of Things (IoT) applications. The primary objective of this research by Tikhamarine et al. [5] is to propose an effective hybrid system that incorporates the optimization algorithm of grey wolves with several models of artificial intelligence (AI). Xingjun et al. [6] proposed a model that employs the grey wolf optimization algorithm to design a novel fuzzy-based approach for data congestion control in the cloud-based IoT technology. Ndikumana et al. [7] developed a framework to use deep learning techniques to gain a deeper understanding of the attributes of Sentinel-1 radar data for farmland cover mapping. Amin et al. [8] introduced a hybrid framework for detecting Dengue fever focused primarily on social media messages. Based on tweets, the system derives the involvement of patients diagnosed with Dengue infection and determines if that is a general conversation about the infection without anyone infected or afflicted with the infection. Zhang et al. [9] presented a minimally supervised system for categorizing text with metadata based on a generative process to describe the interactions among terms, records, marks, and metadata. Franz et al. [10] present the complexity and deficiencies in designing a biological taxonomy that can be incorporated into an ontological reasoning system. Sinha et al. [11] proposed a practical method for the construction of Marathi WordNet using Hindi WordNet by synset identity.

12.3 PROPOSED WORK

The input is collected as seed ontology. The relevant terms are extracted from the input. Metadata is generated using OpenCalais, PyRdfa, GRDDL, RDF Distiller by Linked Open Data Cloud, Google graph API/Wiki data/DBpedia, or coordinating the extracted terms with specialized ontology portals such as the Agroportal. Linked Open Data Cloud is a data set that consists of 1255 data sets along with 16174 links. This quantitative data of Linked Open Data Cloud is as of May 2020. Agroportal is an online repository for ontologies as of several domains related to agriculture. Agroportal contains almost 64 ontologies related to agriculture. Google knowledge graph API provides information and data that are more relevant to the user search and Wikidata is a multilingual knowledge graph which is a source of open data for the projects such as Wikipedia. DBpedia keeps the structured contents from numerous Wikimedia projects.

The metadata is evaluated for relevancy with TF-IDF that gets its reference from data crawled through the World Wide Web into a Web Document Corpus. The evaluated data is classified with RNN and the top 20% terms are retrieved from the classified documents. The grey wolf algorithm is applied to compute semantic similarity of the retrieved terms. Entropy, Morisita's overlap index, and normalized point wise mutual induction are calculated, respectively. A statistic evaluation metric measures the dispersion of the data set to correlate and determine the samples overlapping. Point wise mutual information is a tool employed in information theory to estimate association. Normalized point wise mutual induction can be obtained when point wise mutual induction carry a limit of [−1]. The mean uncertainty in the potential outcomes of the parameters is used to estimate the entropy of a random variable. A neural network in which the input for the node in the current layer is obtained from the previous hidden layer is known as RNN (see Figures 12.1, 12.2, and 12.3).

By linking all the terms hierarchically, which is classified based on the semantic similarity computed by the grey wolf optimization algorithm. The crop's final names are extracted, and the entire crop's name is being changed to their biological nomenclature in taxonomy. All the biological terms are converted into Kannada, Tamil, and Hindi knowledge base with the help of IndoWordNet. IndoWordNet is a

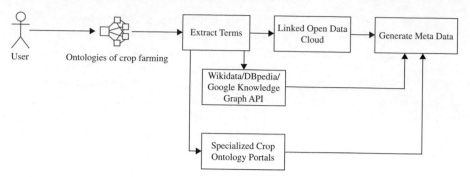

FIGURE 12.1 Phase one of proposed MDAKB architecture.

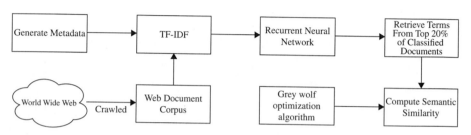

FIGURE 12.2 Phase two of proposed MDAKB architecture.

combined knowledge base of 18 scheduled languages of India. The crops' names are then sent to the user in their respective Kannada, Tamil, and Hindi knowledge base.

12.4   IMPLEMENTATION AND PERFORMANCE EVALUATION

12.4.1   DATA SET PREPARATION

Terms were collected from the datasheets of "Agriculture crops production in India," ontology is formed dynamically using Onto Collab. Terms from the Independent Communications Authority of South Africa (ICASA) data dictionary were crawled, and ontology was modelled. Many documents from agriculture and horticultural books were taken, and terms were collected. The terms from all these documents

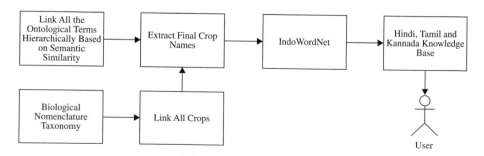

FIGURE 12.3 Phase three of proposed MDAKB architecture.

were combined to make the proposed Metadata-Driven Approach for Multilingual Knowledge Base (MDAKB) ontology (see Algorithm 1).

ALGORITHM 1   PROPOSED ALGORITHM
OF THE MDAKB FRAMEWORK

Input: Seed ontology
Output: Crops those are most suitable to the need of the user.

Start
Step 1: The input seed ontologies are formalized to obtain enriched seed terms.
Step 2: Generate metadata terms using OpenCalais, PyRdfa, GRDDL, RDF Distiller
Step 3: Classification using RNN on the webservice data set and enriched queries.

           Initialize the algorithm for classification
           RNN is operated for updating weights
           Error percentage is calculated
           Causing some disturbance to the weights
           RNN is used again to update weights
           Error percentage is calculated after the disturbance caused
           Final weights is updated

Step 4: Calculation of semantic similarity using grey wolf optimization measure
Step 5: Employ grey wolf optimization on the classified documents.

           Randomly launch the population of the grey wolves
           Set c, C, and A
           Estimate the fitness for each agent
           Y_α = Entropy, T1
           Y_β = Morisita's overlap index, T2
           Y_δ = Normalized Point Wise Mutual Information, T3
             While (x < Maximum number of iterations)
             For each search agent
               Modify the location for T
             end for;
             Modify c, C, and A
             Evaluate the fitness of all T
             Modify Y_α, Y_β, and Y_δ
             x = x + 1
           end while;
        return Y_α;

Step 6: Biological nomenclature in taxonomy are obtained from the final terms.
Step 7: Biological terms are translated into Kannada, Tamil, and Hindi information bases.
End

The grey wolf optimization algorithm is inspired from the hunting mechanism and the leadership hierarchy of the grey wolves. There are four divisions of grey wolves, namely P, Q, R, and S that are engaged in the leadership hierarchy. The hunting mechanism of grey wolf consists of three main steps through which optimization is implemented. The three steps are searching for prey, encircling prey, and attacking prey. The first optimal solution is taken as P. The second optimal solution is taken as Q and a third solution is taken as R, respectively. The S wolves go behind these three wolves. Here, t specifies the current iteration. The prey's location vector is denoted by $\vec{G_q}, \vec{G}$. In Equations (12.3) and (12.4), r1 and r2 are vectors of random value from [0, 1].

$$\vec{Y} = \left| \vec{A} \cdot \vec{G_q} - \vec{G}(t) \right| \tag{12.1}$$

$$\vec{F}(t+1) = \vec{G_q} - \vec{C} \cdot \vec{Y} \tag{12.2}$$

$$\vec{C} = 2\vec{c} \cdot \vec{r1} - \vec{c} \tag{12.3}$$

$$\vec{A} = 2 \cdot \vec{r2} \tag{12.4}$$

$$\vec{Y_\alpha} = \left| \vec{A_1} \cdot \vec{G_\alpha} - \vec{G} \right| \tag{12.5}$$

$$\vec{Y_\beta} = \left| \vec{A_2} \cdot \vec{G_\beta} - \vec{G} \right| \tag{12.6}$$

$$\vec{Y_\delta} = \left| \vec{A_3} \cdot \vec{G_\delta} - \vec{G} \right| \tag{12.7}$$

$$\vec{G_1} = \vec{G_\alpha} - \vec{C_1} \cdot \left(\vec{Y_\alpha} \right) \tag{12.8}$$

$$\vec{G_2} = \vec{G_\beta} - \vec{C_2} \cdot \left(\vec{Y_\beta} \right) \tag{12.9}$$

$$\vec{G_3} = \vec{G_\delta} - \vec{C_3} \cdot \left(\vec{Y_\delta} \right) \tag{12.10}$$

$$\vec{G}(t+1) = \frac{\vec{G_1} + \vec{G_2} + \vec{G_3}}{3} \tag{12.11}$$

The search agent updates the location of P, Q, and R with the help of the Equations (12.8), (12.9), and (12.10). Only P, Q, and R modify its location of the prey. Other wolves randomly modify their location in the region of the prey. The first three best search agent's solutions have been saved and other search agents will update their location with respect to the best search agent's location.

12.5   RESULTS AND PERFORMANCE EVALUATION

The seed ontology is collected from the user, and metadata terms are extracted using OpenCalais, PyRdfa, GRDDL, and RDF Distiller with linked data cloud and specialized crop ontology portals. The RNN classifies the Web Document Corpus, and top 20% is retrieved, and semantic similarity is computed using the grey wolf optimization algorithm. The computed semantic similarity terms are linked hierarchically, and biological taxonomy is applied to all the terms, and the terms are translated to Kannada knowledge base, Tamil knowledge base, and Hindi knowledge base using IndoWordNet.

$$F - measure = \frac{2 * Precision * Recall}{Precision + Recall} \qquad (12.12)$$

$$Precision \% = \frac{True\ Number\ of\ positive}{True\ Number\ of\ positives + False\ Number\ Of\ Positives} \qquad (12.13)$$

$$Recall \% = \frac{True\ Number\ of\ positive}{True\ Number\ of\ positives + False\ Number\ Of\ Negatives} \qquad (12.14)$$

$$Accuracy \% = \frac{(Precision + Recall)}{2} \qquad (12.15)$$

From Figure 12.4, the proposed model performs superior to DOIAE [11]. The proposed model has a better value for precision, F-measure, and accuracy. The precision value proposed is better than DOIAE by 8.07%. The F-measure of the proposed

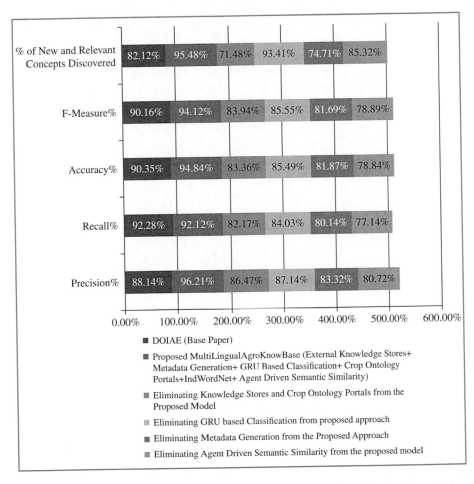

FIGURE 12.4 Observation of the proposed approach with the baseline model and other alternatives.

model has a better score of 3.96% than DOIAE. The accuracy of the proposed model is better than DOIAE by 4.49%. The percentage of new and relevant concepts discovered is better in the proposed model than DOIAE by 13.36%. The proposed model has been very effective with the combined functions of knowledge-based and crop ontology portals, metadata generation, RNN-based classification, and grey wolf algorithm-driven semantic similarity. By eliminating the knowledge-based and crop ontology portal from the proposed model, the accuracy, precision, recall, F-measure, and per cent of new and relevant concept discovered are reduced by 11.48%, 9.74%, 9.95%, 10.18%, and 24%, respectively. By removing RNN-based classification from the proposed model, the accuracy, precision, recall, F-measure, and per cent of new and relevant concept discovered are declined by 9.35%, 9.07%, 8.09%, 8.62%, and 2.07%, respectively. By eliminating the metadata generation from the proposed model, the accuracy, precision, recall, F-measure, and per cent of new and relevant concept discovered are reduced by 12.67%, 12.89%, 11.98%, 12.43%, and 20.77%, respectively. By removing grey wolf optimization, algorithm-driven semantic similarity from the proposed model, the accuracy, precision, recall, F-measure, and per cent of new and relevant concept discovered are declined by 16%, 15.49%, 14.98%, 15.23%, and 10.16%, respectively.

The graphical representation of the base paper values and other alternatives are depicted in Figure 12.5. The F-measure is enumerated as portrayed in Equation (12.12). The precision and recall values are calculated using the Equations (12.13) and (12.14). The accuracy percentage is calculated through the Equation (12.15) (see Table 12.1).

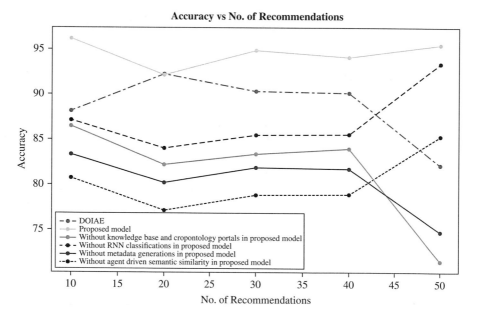

FIGURE 12.5   Graphical representation of the proposed work and other baseline models.

TABLE 12.1

Number of Concepts in the Seed Domain and the Proposed
MultiLingualAgroKnowBase for a Single Language

Specialized Domain	Seed Ontology	Proposed MultiLingualAgroKnowBase
Crop ontology	471	12458
Climate ontology	125	7822
Soil ontology	854	11486
Fertilizer ontology	1024	17586
Taxonomy of biological terms	2122	24695
Horticultural ontology	1154	9653
Geological ontology	1254	15684

12.6 CONCLUSION

The outcomes obtained prove the adequacy of the proposed knowledge base for intended purposes. It achieves an average accuracy of 94.84% with a percentage of new and relevant concept discovered being more than DOIAE by 13.36%, implying that it is by far the most effective solution. The high accuracy accomplished is due to the incorporation of crop ontology portals, grey wolf optimization algorithm, and Agro knowledge base and the optimization of classified data. As the future scope of the work, further hybridization of meta-heuristic algorithms would be explored in future to enhance the model's efficacy.

REFERENCES

1. Mirjalili S, Mirjalili SM, Lewis A. Grey wolf optimizer. Advances in Engineering Software. 2014 Mar 1;69:46–61.
2. Bhattacharyya P. IndoWordNet. In Proceedings of the Seventh International Conference on Language Resources and Evaluation (LREC-10) 2010.
3. Burrows TL, Niranjan M. The use of recurrent neural networks for classification. In Proceedings of IEEE Workshop on Neural Networks for Signal Processing 1994 Sep 6 (pp. 117–125). IEEE.
4. Almiani M, AbuGhazleh A, Al-Rahayfeh A, Atiewi S, Razaque A. Deep recurrent neural network for IoT intrusion detection system. Simulation Modelling Practice and Theory. 2020 May 1;101:102031.
5. Tikhamarine Y, Souag-Gamane D, Ahmed AN, Kisi O, El-Shafie A. Improving artificial intelligence models accuracy for monthly streamflow forecasting using grey wolf optimization (GWO) algorithm. Journal of Hydrology. 2020 Mar 1;582:124435.
6. Xingjun L, Zhiwei S, Hongping C, Mohammed BO. A new fuzzy-based method for load balancing in the cloud-based Internet of things using a grey wolf optimization algorithm. International Journal of Communication Systems. 2020 May 25;33(8):e4370.
7. Ndikumana E, Ho Tong Minh D, Baghdadi N, Courault D, Hossard L. Deep recurrent neural network for agricultural classification using multitemporal SAR Sentinel-1 for Camargue, France. Remote Sensing. 2018 Aug;10(8):1217.

8. Amin S, Uddin MI, Hassan S, Khan A, Nasser N, Alharbi A, Alyami H. Recurrent neural networks with TF-IDF embedding technique for detection and classification in tweets of dengue disease. IEEE Access. 2020 Jul 13;8:131522–131533.

9. Zhang Y, Meng Y, Huang J, Xu FF, Wang X, Han J. Minimally supervised categorization of text with metadata. In Proceedings of the 43rd International ACM SIGIR Conference on Research and Development in Information Retrieval 2020 Jul 25 (pp. 1231–1240).

10. Franz NM. Biological taxonomy and ontology development: scope and limitations. Biodiversity Informatics. 2010;7(1).

11. Sinha M, Reddy M, Bhattacharyya P. An approach towards construction and application of multilingual indo-wordnet. In 3rd Global Wordnet Conference (GWC 06). Jeju Island, Korea 2006 Jan.

13 Melanoma Prediction from Skin Lesions Using Convolutional Neural Network against the Support Vector Machine Learning Algorithm to Achieve Maximum Accuracy and Minimum Loss

Saravanan Madderi Sivalingam
Department of Artificial Intelligence, Saveetha
School of Engineering, Saveetha Institute
of Medical and Technical Sciences
Chennai, India

Pradnya Patil
K. J. Somaiya Institute of Engineering
and Information Technology
Mumbai, India

Sivakumar Ramachandran
Department of Electronics and Communication
Engineering, College of Engineering
Trivandrum, India

CONTENTS

DOI: 10.1201/9781003320340-13

13.1   INTRODUCTION

Skin lesions are abnormal conditions of the skin [1]. The skin lesion has different types of dermatoscopic and related types of classified diseases. Skincare is the thing that needs more care when considering temperature and climate change in the recent past decade [1]. Some unknown skin lesions are still not classified under any type; this is under research [2]. The melanoma skin lesions are classified into 24 groups with benign and malignant tumors [3]. The importance of skin lesion predictions is using it to find the exact treatment by classifying the bacterial infection and related issues [1]. The skin lesion is used to predict automatic segmentation and also find the reason for the color change with various temperature changes [4].

Healthcare is the hot trending research area for the next decade and also needs a lot of research focus; this skin lesion classification prediction is also one among these. The melanoma from skin lesion classification uses machine learning algorithms and an evaluation process using skin images [5]. The logistic regression machine learning algorithm predicted clinical information modules with the skin lesion of dermoscopy information with melanoma classification using a fusion technique and predicted accuracy of 77% [5]. The ResNet-50 deep learning algorithm-based classifier predicted 87% with accuracy [6]. The conventional image processing method classified the area under the ROC curve (AUC) with 79% of accuracy [7]. The basal cell carcinoma (BCC) lesion images classified using 35 images achieved 80.2% accuracy using neural network-based machine learning algorithms [8].

The existing research study predicted the classified melanoma type of skin cancer from the skin lesion dataset with maximum accuracy of 81% using the support vector machine (SVM) machine learning algorithm. Therefore, the research gap will be identified to improve the accuracy of prediction. Hence, we propose to introduce a convolutional neural network (CNN) machine learning algorithm on the skin lesion dataset to achieve better accuracy and reduce the loss. The aim is to predict the correctly classified melanoma with the skin lesion datasets from the CNN machine learning algorithm against the SVM machine learning algorithm for better accuracy and worse loss.

13.2   MATERIALS AND METHODS

This research study was carried out in the Artificial Intelligence Laboratory at the Department of Computer Science and Engineering, Saveetha School of Engineering, Chennai. This research study uses two groups: the SVM algorithm and the CNN algorithm. Each group sample size was predicted using the g-power tool with version 3.1.10, resulting in 104 samples with an 80% of g-power value, and the threshold value is set to 0.05 and the confidence interval as 95% [8]. Each group has 104 samples. If we apply the algorithms with 104 samples, it cannot give different results. Therefore, we are restricting machine and deep learning algorithms by changing the data size to 10 samples instead of 102 samples.

```
candidateSV = { closest pair from opposite classes}
while there are violating points do
        Find a violator
        candidateSV = U candidate SVS violator
        if any ap < 0 due to addition of c to S then
                candidateSV = candidateSVP
                repeat till all such points are pruned
        end if
end while
```

FIGURE 13.1   Pseudocode of support vector machine algorithm.

The dermatoscopic innovative image capture dataset was downloaded from the Kaggle website. The downloaded dataset was used for the implementation of two groups of algorithms to identify the better accuracy for melanoma disease. The name of the dataset is HAM10000_metadata-new [9]. That dataset has a list of columns such as "lesion_id" is a row identification of the dataset, "image_id" is to represent the lesion number, "dx" is to represent the lesion such as "melanoma vascular" or basal cell carcinoma (bcc) or melanocytic nevi (nv), benign keratosis (bkl) or actinic keratoses called solar keratoses) and intraepithelial carcinoma called Bowen's disease) (akiec), "dx_type" is representing histopathological lesion (histo), consensus is a typical benign case of lesion [10], confocal is a type of facial bkl, follow-up is to represent nevi monitored by digital dermoscopy did not show any changes during three follow-up visits or 1.5 years we accepted this as evidence of biologic benignity, "age", "sex", and "localization" is to represent the location of a lesion such as scalp, ear, face, back, trunk, chest, neck, and genital, these columns are used in this experimental setup. The total number of rows in this dataset is 10016. The last update of this dataset was in November 2020.

The pseudocode used for the support vector machine algorithm to apply to the skin lesion dataset is shown in Figure 13.1. The pseudocode works with multiple neurons, and with randomizing property, it will repeat the iterations n times with the distance vector. The final outcome of the pseudocode will be sent through the parameters x and c.

The following pseudocode explains about convolutional neural network algorithms as shown in Figure 13.2, all the input values are taken from the for loop statements, and output is taken from the activation_function(sum), which is given below.

The minimum requirements of hardware are Intel Core 3 processor, 50-gigabyte hard disk capacity, and 4-gigabyte random access memory sufficient to implement this experimental setup. Also, the software required to run the algorithms is any of the operating systems with Python application or Anaconda with spyder version 4.1.5.

First, we need to apply the first group of algorithms called SVM on the dataset to predict melanoma with better accuracy. For this, the training dataset took about 70% of the data on the overall dataset and the testing with 30% of data on the overall dataset. This will be repeated ten times by varying the data size, varying the number of rows count, and recording the respective results.

```
for (1=0;1<L;1++){
    for (m=0;m<M;m++){
        for (n=0;n<N;n++){
            sum=bias[1];
            for (k=0;k<K;k++){
                for (s1=0;s1<S1;s1++){
                    for (s2=0;s2<S2;s2++){
                        sum+=weight[k] [1] [s1] [s2] × input[k] [m+s1] [n+s2];
}}}
    output [1] [m] [n] = activation_func (sum);
}}}
```

FIGURE 13.2   Pseudocode of convolutional neural network algorithm.

Second, we are applying the second group of algorithms called CNN on the data-set to predict the accuracy of melanoma skin disease with 70% of training data and 30% of testing data on the overall dataset. This will be tested for ten samples and will be recording the respective results. The independent variables "lesion_id", "image_id", "dx_type", "age", "sex", and "localization" and the dependent variable "dx" of the melanoma dataset are used for experimentation. Finally, the results collected from the group one and group two algorithms will be applied on the Statistical Package for Social Sciences (SPSS) tool for the result analysis.

13.3   RESULTS

Before applying the prediction of the accuracy rate on the skin lesion dataset, first, we need to preprocess the data before dividing it for training and testing dataset to apply the machine learning algorithms on it and shown in Figure 13.3 and it has the melanoma skin lesion extracted from the dataset of 10016 records.

The SVM machine learning algorithm and CNN machine learning algorithm are compared with ten samples by applying various 70% of training and 30% of testing datasets by varying the number of records of the dataset, and the outcomes are depicted in Table 13.1. Overall, 70% of training data and 30% of testing data are taken into consideration to get optimal accuracy, and if the data are less or higher than 70% of training data, it will yield bad prediction of accuracy vice versa testing data.

	lesion_id	image_id	dx	dx_type	age	sex	localization
0	HAM_0000118	ISIC_0027419	bkl	histo	80	male	scalp
1	HAM_0000118	ISIC_0025030	bkl	histo	80	male	scalp
2	HAM_0002730	ISIC_0026769	bkl	histo	80	male	scalp
3	HAM_0002730	ISIC_0025661	bkl	histo	80	male	scalp
4	HAM_0001466	ISIC_0031633	bkl	histo	75	male	ear

FIGURE 13.3   First 5 records of melanoma skin lesion dataset out of 10016 and having the features as columns of lesion_id, image_id, dx, dx_type, age, sex, and localization.

TABLE 13.1

Comparison between SVM and CNN Algorithm with N = 10 Samples of the Dataset with the Highest Accuracy of, Respectively, 81% and 92% in the Sample (When N = 1) Using the Dataset Size = 10016 and the 70% of Training and 30% of Testing Data

Sample (N)	Dataset Size	SVM Accuracy in %	CNN Accuracy in %
1	10016	81.0	92.0
2	9016	73.4	88.0
3	7016	70.2	84.0
4	6616	65.4	82.0
5	5416	60.4	80.2
6	4916	58.4	78.8
7	4716	56.2	76.2
8	4616	54.8	75.3
9	4416	53.5	73.1
10	4016	50.5	70.0

The skin lesion of melanoma shown in Figure 13.4 has a variety of skin images and has severe and less infected samples. Figure 13.5 shows the various types of skin lesions infected on the patient such as bkl, nv, df, mel, vasc, bcc, and akiec.

Figure 13.6 has the results predicted after the classification of skin lesions of melanoma using various sizes of datasets and epochs with CNN machine learning algorithm, and the predicted accuracy is shown in y-axis for each sample. Figure 13.7 shows the loss of classification on melanoma skin lesions.

In Table 13.2, we observed after performing statistical analysis of ten samples that CNN obtained 6.779 standard deviations with 2.114 standard error, while the SVM algorithm obtained 9.853 standard deviations with 3.116 standard error. The

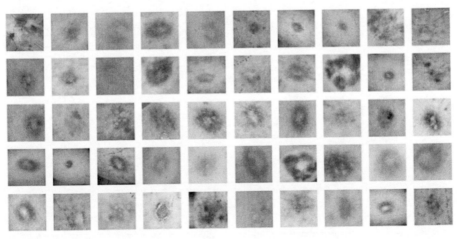

FIGURE 13.4 Dataset sample of skin images of a melanoma lesion.

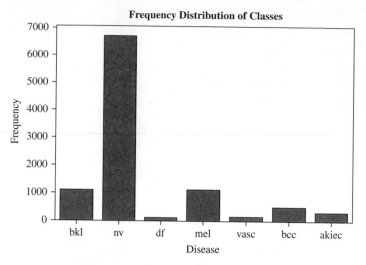

FIGURE 13.5 Representation of various types of a melanoma skin lesion with and respective frequency of occurrences.

significance value 0.000 is smaller than 0.05 and showed that our hypothesis holds good. For changes in the input values (independent variables), the corresponding output values (dependent variables) also change, and it is depicted in Table 13.3.

An independent t-test was used to compare the accuracy of two algorithms and a statistically significant difference was noticed $p < 0.000$. The CNN model obtained 92% accuracy and the SVM algorithm obtained 81% of accuracy; it is shown in Figure 13.8. Finally, we compared the mean accuracy of CNN and SVM algorithms (Figure 13.9) and it shows that the CNN is significantly better than the SVM algorithm.

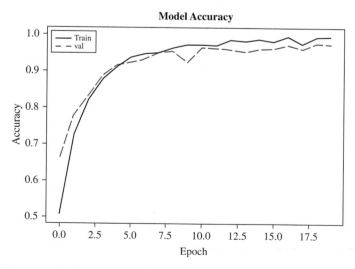

FIGURE 13.6 Result of melanoma skin lesion classification shown in x-axis: epochs and y-axis: accuracy.

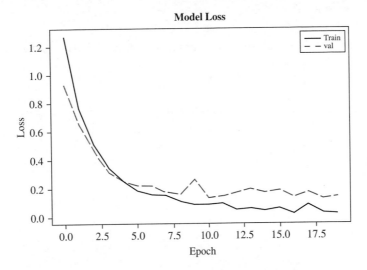

FIGURE 13.7 Result of melanoma skin lesion classification shown in x-axis: epochs and y-axis: loss.

13.4 DISCUSSION

This research study found 92% of accuracy for melanoma skin lesion detection using the CNN algorithm against the 81% of accuracy by the SVM algorithm and it is shown in Figure 13.6 and also we observed that the CNN algorithm is significantly better than the SVM algorithm with ($p < 0.000$). In Table 13.3, the calculated value of "p" is greater than the value of alpha; the results corresponding to equal variances assumed are considered for analysis. The negative value of "t" implies that the mean of CNN is statistically greater than the mean of SVM. Hence, this research study found that the CNN algorithm is significantly better than the SVM algorithm with ($p < 0.000$) using an independent t-test.

To support this research study, logistic regression for machine learning uses tree analysis using the CART algorithm to classify the skin lesion information to reduce the risk of infection at 78% of prediction [9]. Most of the studies were changing

TABLE 13.2
Statistical Results of CNN and SVM Algorithms

Algorithms	Sample (N)	Mean	Std Deviation	Std Error Mean
Accuracy				
SVM	10	62.38	9.853	3.116
CNN	10	79.96	6.779	2.144

Note: Mean accuracy value, standard deviation and standard error mean for CNN and SVM algorithms are obtained for ten iterations. It is observed that the CNN algorithm performed better than the SVM algorithm.

TABLE 13.3

Independent Sample Test for Significance and Standard Error Determination

	Levene's Test for Equality of Variances		T-test of Equality of Means					95% of the Confidence Interval of the Difference	
	F	Sig.	T	df	Sig (2-tailed)	Mean Difference	Std Error Difference	Lower	Upper
Accuracy									
Equal variance assumed	2.021	0.172	−4.648	18	0.000	−17.580	3.7821	−25.526	−9.634
Equal variance not assumed			−4.648	15.961	0.000	−17.580	3.7821	−25.599	−9.561

Note: P value is less than 0.05 which is considered to be statistically significant, and 95% confidence intervals were calculated.

the percentage size of learning and testing data. But this research study is taken by changing the size of the records for each sample. The classification of malignant melanoma and benign skin lesions using backpropagation neural networks proposed the earlier prediction of classification using health informatics discussed in this research study with an accuracy of 80% [11]. The stochastic gradient estimation algorithm was used for melanoma skin lesion classification using dual-rate stochastic systems and predicted results with only 69% of accuracy [12]. Therefore by comparing the other algorithms' performance of the proposed CNN machine learning algorithm

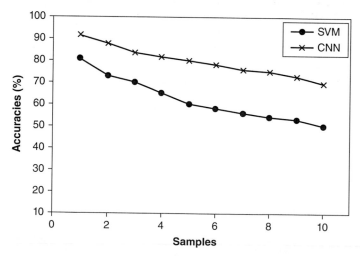

FIGURE 13.8 Comparison of accuracies of CNN algorithm (orange in color with 92%) and SVM (blue in color with 81%) across the samples.

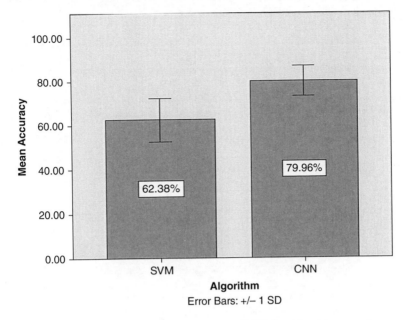

FIGURE 13.9   Comparison of SVM algorithm and CNN algorithm in terms of mean accuracy. The mean accuracy of CNN is better than the SVM algorithm and the standard deviation of CNN is slightly better than the SVM algorithm. x-axis: CNN vs SVM algorithm y-axis: mean accuracy detection.

to achieve better performance than other algorithms, this research study compared only the SVM algorithm.

To oppose this study, some other findings treat the skin lesion classification using manual labeling on melanoma data and involve the prediction process, but this study used a machine, learning-based classification model [13]. The preprocessed melanoma data used in this study and feature extraction of melanoma skin lesions classified the data using research study; therefore, we achieved significant improvement in the accuracy.

This research study is limited to the CNN algorithm applied on 10016 cases of melanoma skin lesion as input. But if you use more case studies, there may be a chance of more accuracy than this research finding. This research study is only applicable to the age group from 5 to 50. In the future, other range of age groups of skin lesions will be taken and can compare the performances for better results.

13.5   CONCLUSION

The research study found 92% of the accuracy of classification of melanoma from skin lesions using an innovative dermatoscopic image capture dataset against the SVM algorithm prediction about 81% of accuracy; therefore, this research study says the CNN algorithms significantly work better than the SVM algorithms and they will help the healthcare practitioners to take good decision-making for further treatment.

REFERENCES

[1] Ayan, Enes, and Halil Murat Unver. 2018. "Data Augmentation Importance for Classification of Skin Lesions via Deep Learning." *2018 Electric Electronics, Computer Science, Biomedical Engineerings' Meeting (EBBT)*. https://doi.org/10.1109/ebbt.2018.8391469.

[2] Park, Gunhyuk, Byeong Cheol Moon, Seung Mok Ryu, Wook Jin Kim, and Hye-Sun Lim. 2021. "Cicadidae Periostracum Attenuates Atopic Dermatitis Symptoms and Pathology via the Regulation of NLRP3 Inflammasome Activation." *Oxidative Medicine and Cellular Longevity* 2021 (January): 8878153.

[3] Martin-Gorgojo, A., M. Á. Descalzo-Gallego, S. Arias-Santiago, A. Molina-Leyva, Y. Gilaberte, P. Fernández-Crehuet, H. Husein-ElAhmed, et al. 2021. "What Proportion of the Caseload at Dermatology Outpatient Clinics in Spain Do Skin Tumors Account for? Results from the DIADERM National Random Sampling Project." *Actas Dermo-Sifiliográficas*, February. https://doi.org/10.1016/j.ad.2021.02.004.

[4] Ramella, Giuliana. 2020. "Automatic Skin Lesion Segmentation Based on Saliency and Color." *Proceedings of the 15th International Joint Conference on Computer Vision, Imaging and Computer Graphics Theory and Applications*. https://doi.org/10.5220/0009144904520459.

[5] Kaur, Navdeep, and Priya Kapoor. 2017. "Study of Techniques Used For Segmentation and Classification of Skin Lesion." *International Journal of Scientific Research and Management*. https://doi.org/10.18535/ijsrm/v5i6.41.

[6] Hagerty, Jason R., R. Joe Stanley, Haidar A. Almubarak, Norsang Lama, Reda Kasmi, Peng Guo, Rhett J. Drugge, Harold S. Rabinovitz, Margaret Oliviero, and William V. Stoecker. 2019. "Deep Learning and Handcrafted Method Fusion: Higher Diagnostic Accuracy for Melanoma Dermoscopy Images." *IEEE Journal of Biomedical and Health Informatics* 23 (4): 1385–91.

[7] Emre Celebi, M., Teresa Mendonca, and Jorge S. Marques. 2015. *Dermoscopy Image Analysis*. CRC Press.

[8] Feng, Xu, Austin J. Moy, Hieu T. M. Nguyen, Yao Zhang, Jason Zhang, Matthew C. Fox, Katherine R. Sebastian, Jason S. Reichenberg, Mia K. Markey, and James W. Tunnell. 2018. "Raman Biophysical Markers in Skin Cancer Diagnosis." *Journal of Biomedical Optics* 23 (5): 1–10.

[9] Mancini, Silvia, Emanuele Crocetti, Lauro Bucchi, Nicola Pimpinelli, Rosa Vattiato, Orietta Giuliani, Alessandra Ravaioli, et al. 2019. "Melanoma Survival with Classification and Regression Trees Analysis: A Complement for the Communication of Prognosis to Patients." *Giornale Italiano Di Dermatologia E Venereologia: Organo Ufficiale, Societa Italiana Di Dermatologia E Sifilografia*, June. https://doi.org/10.23736/S0392-0488.19.06402-2.

[10] Pereira, Pedro, Luis Tavora, Rui Fonseca-Pinto, Rui Paiva, Pedro Assuncao, and Sergio M. de Faria. 2019. "Image Segmentation Using Gradient-Based Histogram Thresholding for Skin Lesion Delineation." *Proceedings of the 12th International Joint Conference on Biomedical Engineering Systems and Technologies*. https://doi.org/10.5220/0007354100840091.

[11] Rosendahl, Cliff, and Aksana Marozava. 2019. *Dermatoscopy and Skin Cancer: A Handbook for Hunters of Skin Cancer and Melanoma*. Scion Publishing.

[12] Sharma, Varun. 2020. "Classification of Malignant Melanoma and Benign Skin Lesion with the Aid of Using Back Propagation Neural Network and ABCD Rule." *International Journal of Psychosocial Rehabilitation*. https://doi.org/10.37200/ijpr/v24i5/pr201802.

[13] Tschandl, Philipp, Cliff Rosendahl, and Harald Kittler. 2018. "The HAM10000 Dataset, a Large Collection of Multi-source Dermatoscopic Images of Common Pigmented Skin Lesions." *Scientific Data* 5: 180161. doi: 10.1038/sdata.2018.161.

14 Fusion-Based Morphological Watershed Segmentation Algorithm for Medical Images

Kavitha Kattigehalli Jayanna
GM Institute of Technology
Davangere, India

Priestly B. Shan
Chandigarh University
Ajitgarh, Punjab, India

CONTENTS

14.1 INTRODUCTION

Medical image watermarking (MIW) plays an important role in healthcare systems to ensure authenticity, integrity, confidentiality and security to electronic health record (EHR) which embodies the medical images (MIs) and related patient information details. The medical information is very crucial, and any changes in such information are not acceptable in medical systems. A slight modification of information may harm the patient's health, and to avoid such cases, most of the researchers perform embedding process in region of non-interest (RONI) part of MI while preserving and securing region of interest (ROI) in many ways. So, it becomes necessary to separate ROI and RONI parts in MIs, which in turn is a very challenging task for most of the medical image researchers. Even though most of the implemented MIW techniques adopted a segmentation procedure, more than 90% of the authors have not specified which segmentation algorithm is used in the work, and as the features of MIs are very much different from natural images, extra care must be taken to ensure that there is no loss of critical information. Medical image segmentation (MIS) is a process of segmenting objects of interesting region to make per-pixel predictions in MIs [1] and this process should be stopped once the ROI objects are isolated and these segmentation techniques can be classified as follows:

- Manual
- Semi-manual and
- Fully automatic segmentation techniques [2, 3]

Manual segmentation is a tidy and time-consuming process and more over segmentation results are entirely based on the skill of person who is involved in it; although fully automatic segmentation does not require human interaction, it may not be suitable for MIs as the generalization of these techniques is not a good idea. Semi-manual segmentation is more suitable in case of MIs, so that the results will be under the control of user and also able to maintain trade-off between précised results. Although there is no exact method available for segmentation classification, based on the properties of intensity values such as discontinuity and similarity, they can be categorized as threshold, edge and region-based segmentation techniques [4], and in this chapter, MIs are subjected to fusion-based watershed segmentation algorithm based on morphological processing and their efficiencies are evaluated using certain quality metrics. In the following section, a brief discussion about morphological MIS is provided.

14.2   MORPHOLOGICAL-BASED MEDICAL IMAGE SEGMENTATION

In healthcare systems, analysis of MIs plays an important role as it helps to identify abnormalities and segmentations based on threshold or edge detection doesn't yield a good-quality image which is not desirable for inspection of objects under suspect. One of the effective segmentation methods is watershed morphological method, which partitions grey image based on its topographic surface and helps in extracting useful image components required for its representation and description.

The presented segmentation process is based on texture and modulated intensity gradient and it uses a simple Sobel kernel to detect edges as well as their orientation and achieves good smoothness by giving more importance to the centre pixel and its sensitivity based on its threshold and dual-tree complex wavelet transform (DTCWT); watershed algorithm and the methodology used are shown in Figure 14.1.

Initially, the MIs are read from the database and subjected to pre-processing stage. In this stage, if the image is red-green-blue (RGB), it is converted to grey and 64-bit double precision data type and resized to 512×512. This process involves

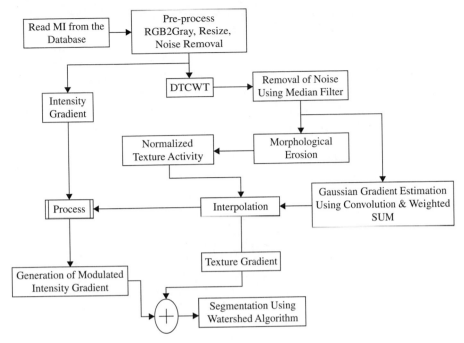

FIGURE 14.1   Segmentation methodology based on watershed algorithm and DTCWT.

boundary detection and is done with modulated intensity and texture gradient (TeG) components (MIG & TeG). The MIG involves the following steps:

- The Sobel kernel is generated as defined by the following Equations (14.1) and (14.2):

$$\nabla x = \frac{\partial I}{\partial m} = (p7 + 2p8 + p9) - (p1 + 2p2 + p3) \tag{14.1}$$

$$\nabla y = \frac{\partial I}{\partial n} = (p3 + 2p6 + p9) - (p1 + 2p4 + p7) \tag{14.2}$$

- As the derivatives are involved, these are linear operations and the kernel is generated by Equation (14.3):

$$M(x, y) = \sqrt{(\nabla x)^2 + (\nabla y)^2} \tag{14.3}$$

- This kernel is used for generating horizontal and vertical intensity gradients for input MI as indicated by Equation (14.4):

$$grad(I) = \sqrt{(Ix)^2 + (Iy)^2} \tag{14.4}$$

where Ix and Iy are filtered MIs computed by considering the nearest array border value.

In the next step, the procedure for generation of TeG of image is explained: Here the MI is subjected to DTCWT as it gives improved results than discrete wavelet transforms (DWT). Although DWT is a very effective tool in many image processing applications, it suffers from various limitations such as fractional loss, very sensitive to shifting of input which results in large variations in the filter coefficients and poor directivity, i.e. this wavelet is unable to distinguish in the phase angles. These drawbacks are overcome with DTCWT which will generate image with separate row and column filters comprising real and imaginary frequency components [5]. Because of such attractive features, complex wavelets are more suitable for texture analysis rather than any other filters and detailed coefficients of this wavelet orientation, and complex magnitude is used for the MIG analysis [6].

14.2.1 MODULATED INTENSITY GRADIENT (MIG) ANALYSIS

Basically, MIG is used to obtain description about sharpness of an image and act as high pass filter. Earlier, Gabor filter was the default choice for analysing the texture or intensity details of an image as it helps in analysing specific frequency component of image in precise directions in a restricted region around the point or region of analysis. But as this method results in undesired ridges and valleys which make the system less effective in removing noise, although high value of standard deviation makes the system stable and robust, it also smoothens the system such that it vanishes the information of the presence of ridges and valleys in it, whereas the lower value of standard deviation results in non-operativeness and inefficiency to remove noise and more over this filter is computationally burden.

The limitations of Gabor filter are overcome with the use of DTCWT, as it is very sensitive to the direction in 2-D, shift invariance, good reconstruction capability of images and computational efficient. These features lead to the use of DTCWT in this work instead of Gabor filter.

The DTCWT applied to MI results in total of six pass-bands and complex magnitude is computed for these bands and is defined by Equation (14.5):

$$\left|D_{i,\theta}\left(m,n\right)\right| = \sqrt{\left(w_{real}\right)^2 + \left(w_{img}\right)^2} \tag{14.5}$$

Separable median filter (SMF), a special class of median filter, i.e. which is implemented as a product of two more simple median filters, is used to remove noise by operating simultaneously over row and column vector components of $\left|D_{i,\theta}\right|$, while preserving edges and thereby avoids the generation of false region around the boundary during watershed algorithm run and its implementation is given by Equation (14.6):

$$SF_{i,\theta}\left(m,n\right) = SMF\left(\left|D_{i,\theta}\left(m,n\right)\right|\right) \tag{14.6}$$

The smoothed MI's texture features obtained from the above step respond to a larger area than required and are hence subjected to a morphological erosion process using a square structural element of dimension $n \times n$, where a shrunken image is thus formed by removing irrelevant pixel details and leads to the thinning of image and thereby this process is treated as a morphological filter and is implemented using Equation (14.7):

$$I_{erod} = [i \ominus se](m,n) = \min_{(s,t)\in se}\{I(m+s,n+t)\} \tag{14.7}$$

And, variation in wavelet filter is controlled during erosion by dividing complex magnitudes by a factor 2^i and is followed by separable interpolation operation to achieve up-sampling and is done using Equation (14.8):

$$I_{tex\_energy} = \sum_{i,\theta} sep_{interpol}\left(I_{erod}\right)/2^i \tag{14.8}$$

To avoid negative exponent value, i.e. to remove systematic distortions in an image, the texture energy is subjected to half-wave rectification process with rectification factors ε and ω with and MIG is computed as given by Equation (14.9):

$$MIG = \left|\frac{grad(I)}{e^{\left(\frac{I_{texenergy}}{\varepsilon}-\omega\right)\geq 0}}\right| /Max(grad(I)) \tag{14.9}$$

14.2.2 Texture Gradient (TeG) Analysis

The texture of an image gives spatial information regarding the framing of image intensities over a certain region of it, which can be obtained naturally by capturing it or created artificially using some techniques and this method is very useful in image segmentation as it can be used to analyse the description of a region.

To get TeG, horizontal and vertical Gaussian gradients are used to reduce noise and blur edges, using which weighted average is computed in both directions and is defined by Equations (14.10)–(14.12):

$$[dx \ dy] = grad(gaussian(I)) \tag{14.10}$$

$$Ix = convolution(wx, dx)$$

$$Iy = convolution(wy, dy)$$

$$M_\theta = \sqrt{(I_x)^2 + (I_y)^2} \tag{14.11}$$

$$TEG = \sum sep_{interpol}\left|\frac{size(M_\theta)}{sum\left(\frac{M_\theta}{max(M_\theta)}\right)^2}\right| * w_i \tag{14.12}$$

Now, the overall result of morphological method is the weighted sum of MIG and TeG and is defined by Equation (14.13) and this net result is applied with the watershed algorithm explained in the next section:

$$grad_{sum} = \sum (MIG + TEG)$$ (14.13)

14.3　WATERSHED SEGMENTATION ALGORITHM

In this work, an optimal spanning forest topological-region-based watershed algorithm has been used to segment MIs. The basic idea behind this algorithm is a water drop falling on a topographical surface following a sliding path and ultimately reaching the minimum and the watershed acts as a ridge to separate catchment basins [7, 8], as shown in Figure 14.2.

The algorithm used in this work is explained below: In this algorithm, the region boundary lines in terms of watershed lines are identified by marking the pels which are having a maximum magnitude of gradient intensity values, whereas the water positioned on pels enclosed by watershed lines tends to flow downwards to a common local intensity minimum (LIM), and those pels which are exhausting to a common minimum forms catch basin representing a segment in an image. The detailed steps which are used in the algorithm are given below:

- Read the image obtained in the previous stage $grad_{sum}$ and original image.
- Erode $grad_{sum}$ image using disk shaped structuring element which typically performs the function of eroding the white pels of forefront boundary regions and thereby shrunken its pels size and enlarging holes within its area.

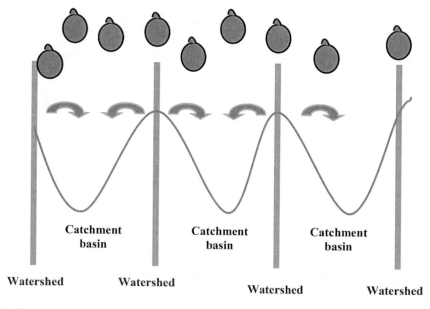

FIGURE 14.2　An optimal spanning forest topological-region-based watershed algorithm.

- As an effect of this process results in an image marked with places at which intensity rapidly changes without affecting the regions with uniform intensity.
- The above step is followed by the reconstruction of an image with dilation process using the same structuring element which helps in bridging gap/ repairs in an image.
- Compute regional maxima from the resulting figure, which is used for superimposing on the original image.
- Compute threshold from the above step, using which watershed ridge lines are constructed.
- Now, superimpose the regional maxima superimposed on original image with the ridge lines, and watershed regions are identified.

14.4   RESULTS

In the proposed work, nearly 1000 magnetic resonance imaging (MRI) images were used for segmentation purpose. The results of watershed segmentation technique employed in the presented chapter are depicted in Figure 14.3 and the corresponding histogram of modulated intensity gradient, TeG, their sum and segmented images is as shown below in Figure 14.4. In the segmentation process carried out in the present work, it involves the use of modulated intensity gradient to detect abrupt changes in intensities between two regions and in fact high-intensity valued pixels act as edge pels to form closed boundaries as shown in the first column of Figure 14.3, whereas TeG provides spatial distribution of grey levels in neighbourhood pels and thereby helps in determining shape and properties by extracting certain features from respective regions as shown in second column of Figure 14.3; and thereby combining these two results provides segmented images as shown in third and fourth columns of Figure 14.3.

In the work presented, the segmentation technique algorithm uses the various desirable quality metric measures based on human perception such as contrast, correlation, energy, homogeneity, standard deviation, mean, root mean square (RMS) value, entropy, variance, smoothness, kurtosis, skewness and also peak signal-to-noise ratio (PSNR), mean square error (MSE), normalised correlation coefficient (NCC) and normalized absolute error (NAE) [9, 10].

As it is known that most of the quality watershed segmentation technique is based on image contrast, which in turn may be degraded during image capturing. The watershed segmentation on such poor contrasted images results in over or under segmentation results which is not desirable in medical image analysis. In the proposed work, to avoid the effect of poor contrast, images are enhanced with morphological operators in square shape and thereby segmentation is evaluated in terms of contrast ratio (CR). In practical, many factors connive for increase in black luminance and thereby result in decreased contrast and quality of the images and CR may be termed the ratio between the measures of peak luminance reference of white to the black reference [11, 12] as defined by Equation (14.14).

$$CR = \frac{lum\_white_{ref}}{lum\_black_{ref}} = \frac{\cup w}{\cap b} \qquad (14.14)$$

MODULATED INTENSITY GRADIENT	TEXTURE GRADIENT	TOTAL GRADIENT	SEGMENTED IMAGE

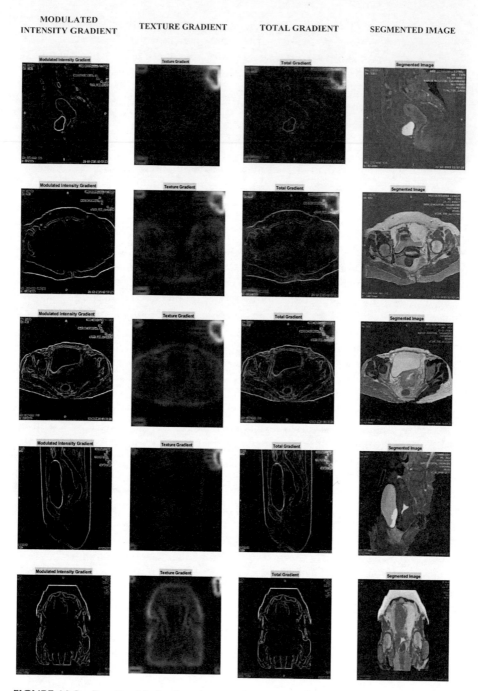

FIGURE 14.3   Results of fusion-based morphological watershed segmentation.   *(Continued)*

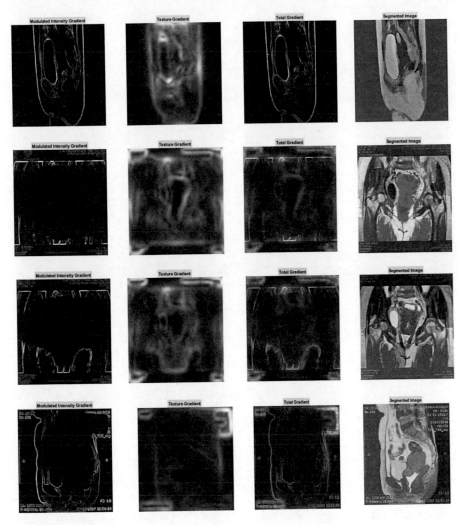

FIGURE 14.3   *(Continued)*

Basically, correlation concept is used to measure shifts or variations in data sets, and in case of segmentation, correlation factor (CF), and in case of morphological watershed segmentation used in the work, it is measured as the ratio of data shift in segmented image ζ_{seg} to the data shift in original image ζ_{org} as defined by Equation (14.15).

$$CF = \frac{\zeta_{seg}}{\zeta_{org}} \tag{14.15}$$

Energy of a segmented image is the measure of localized changes in the pels of an image or it is also expressed as the rate of change in pels parameters such as

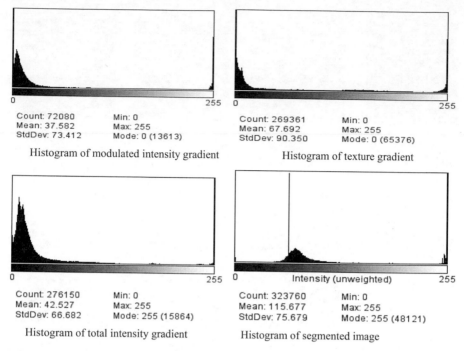

Count: 72080   Min: 0
Mean: 37.582   Max: 255
StdDev: 73.412   Mode: 0 (13613)

Histogram of modulated intensity gradient

Count: 269361   Min: 0
Mean: 67.692   Max: 255
StdDev: 90.350   Mode: 0 (65376)

Histogram of texture gradient

Count: 276150   Min: 0
Mean: 42.527   Max: 255
StdDev: 66.682   Mode: 255 (15864)

Histogram of total intensity gradient

Count: 323760   Min: 0
Mean: 115.677   Max: 255
StdDev: 75.679   Mode: 255 (48121)

Histogram of segmented image

FIGURE 14.4   Histogram of segmentation results.

luminance/brightness of local pels with respect to initial pel values as defined by Equation (14.16).

$$E = \frac{\upsilon_{lum\_local_{pel}}}{\mathsf{v}_{initial_{pel}}} \qquad (14.16)$$

Other useful metrics in the analysis of image segmentation are skewness and kurtosis; skewness measures symmetry or lack of symmetry and the distribution of dataset is symmetric if it resembles the same on left and right at the centre point of image, whereas kurtosis is an actual statistical measure of skewness for defining heavy or light tails to indicate excess or lack of outliers. So, we may define kurtosis as the pictorial representation of frequency distribution about its mean rather than with respect to its normal distribution.

The results of morphological watershed segmentation are shown in Table 14.1 and are measures using various quality metrics which are evaluated using modulated intensity gradient and TeG-based analysis for the proposed system.

14.5   CONCLUSION

In the implemented work, auto-segmentation is done using modulated gradient and texture-based fusion techniques based on DTCWT and watershed segmentation algorithm at reduced execution time. Although this technique provides good perceptive images, it requires good fusion segmentation map techniques, and thereby it might

TABLE 14.1
Evaluation of Implemented Segmentation Technique

Images	Image1	Image2	Image3	Image4	Image5	Image6	Image7	Image8	Image9
Contrast	0.2569	0.4116	0.4753	0.5070	0.5679	0.7133	0.5222	0.2915	0.4017
Correlation	0.8952	0.9231	0.8975	0.9101	0.9163	0.9544	0.9485	0.8994	0.9448
Energy	0.5045	0.4115	0.4290	0.4891	0.2000	0.4598	0.1313	0.3379	0.4230
Homogeneity	0.9828	0.9773	0.9769	0.9765	0.9687	0.9737	0.9777	0.9817	0.9768
Mean	182.96	162.130	133.61	182.891	165.224	82.5241	117.892	185.568	148.612
SD	33.740	51.2829	47.780	54.9262	60.1303	80.1109	70.1994	41.9679	57.3249
Entropy	1.9389	3.1033	2.0215	1.9887	3.3273	1.8759	3.7588	2.4452	2.3661
RMS	15.968	15.9687	15.9687	15.9687	15.9687	15.9687	15.9687	15.9687	15.968
Variance	1.0844	2.4023	2.1255	2.2168	3.3097	3.5333	4.4625	1.6659	1.3897
Smoothness	1.0000	1.0000	1.0000	1.0000	1.0000	1.0000	1.0000	1.0000	1.0000
Kurtosis	9.3285	3.6287	4.18C2	3.8572	2.7818	2.0934	1.6977	5.0616	3.3260
Skewness	-1.6182	-0.9377	-0.1227	-1.4807	-0.9520	0.9477	0.1383	-1.5821	-1.1383
PSNR	7.4245	10.8202	13.367	6.9599	9.6209	20.7892	13.2265	8.2066	13.598
MSE	2.7660	1.8710	1.3955	2.9180	2.1480	5.9378	1.4183	2.5278	1.3588
NCC	2.5137	1.1956	1.0961	1.0385	1.2413	1.1408	0.9471	1.1771	1.1726
NAE	6.5665	2.0535	2.6554	3.2527	2.2806	1.3891	2.5786	2.4593	1.5219

not be suitable for MIs as we may observe from the quality metrics values obtained in Table 14.1. And also we can observe that the proposed algorithm provides good results for images with fewer edges and at the same time it is shift invariant and does not consider directional edge information. The metric standard deviation acts as a salient feature for the best segmentation. So, it is necessary to come up with a new segmentation algorithm with salient features of neural networks which may be well suitable for MIs for more precise analysis.

REFERENCES

1. R. El Jurdia, C. Petitjeana, P. Honeinea, V. Cheplyginab, and F. Abdallahc, "High-Level Prior-Based Loss Functions for Medical Image Segmentation: A Survey", Computer Vision and Image Understanding (CVIU2020), pp. 1–24, Vol. 210, September 2021, 103248, ISSN 1077–3142, https://doi.org/10.1016/j.cviu.2021.103248.
2. T. Sakinis, F. Milletari, H. Roth, P. Korfiatis, P. M. Kostandy, K. Philbrick, Z. Akkus, Z. Xu, D. Xu, and B. Erickson, Interactive Segmentation of Medical Images through Fully Convolutional Neural Networks. Computer Vision and Pattern Recognition, pp. 1–10, Vol. 1903, March, 2019, *ArXiv, abs/1903.08205.*
3. P. V. Supe, K. S. Bhagat, and J. P. Chaudhari, "Image Segmentation and Classification for Medical Image Processing", International Journal on Future Revolution in Computer Science & Communication Engineering, pp. 45–52, Vol. 5, Issue 1, January 2019.
4. J. Gopinath and R. Krishnan, "A Survey on Different Types of Segmentation Techniques", International Journal of Modern Trends in Engineering and Research, pp. 420–425, Vol. 2, Issue 10, October 2015, ISSN: 2349–9745.
5. H. Paulose and H. Singh, "Finger Knuckle Analysis: Gabor vs DTCWT", IOSR Journal of Engineering (IOSRJEN), pp. 1–9, Vol. 5, Issue 6, June 2015, ISSN (e): 2250–3021.
6. S. Chourasia and A. V. Bhalla, "MRI Medical Image Enhancement using Modulated Intensity Gradient and Texture Gradient Based Segmentation", International Journals of Advanced Research in Computer Science and Software Engineering, pp. 26–32, Vol. 9, Issue 5, May 2019, ISSN: 2277–128X.
7. J. K. Chaithanya, and T. Ramashri, "Image Segmentation of Multi-focused Images using Watershed Algorithm", International Journal of Current Engineering and Technology, pp. 344–350, Vol. 2, Special Issue–2, February 2014, ISSN: 2277–4106.
8. S. Derivaux, G. Forestier, C. Wemmert, and S. Lefèvre, "Supervised Image Segmentation Using Watershed Transform, Fuzzy Classification and Evolutionary Computation", Pattern Recognition Letters, pp. 2364–2374, Vol. 31, Issue 15, 2010, ISSN 0167–8655.
9. F. Meyer and P. Maragos, "Multiscale Morphological Segmentations Based on Watershed, Flooding, and Eikonal PDE", Conference: Scale-Space Theories in Computer Vision, Second International Conference, Scale-Space, Corfu, Greece, pp. 351–362, September 26–27, 1999.
10. C. C. Benson, V. L Lajish, and Rajamani Kumar, "Brain Tumor Extraction from MRI Brain Images Using Marker Based Watershed Algorithm", 3189 78-1-4799-8792- 4/15/ $31.00 c 2015 IEEE.
11. P. Thakur, K. Pahwa, and R. Gupta, "Brain Tumor Detection, Segmentation Using Watershed Segmentation And Morphological Operation" International Journal of Computer Applications (0975–8887), Vol. 58, Issue 16, November 2012.
12. Z. Akkus, J. Sedlar, L. Coufalova, P. Korfiatis, T. L. Kline, J. D. Warner, J. Agrawal, and B. J. Erickson, "Semi-automated Segmentation of Preoperative Low Grade Gliomas in Magnetic Resonance Imaging," Cancer Imaging, pp. 1–12, Vol. 15, Issue 1, 2015.

15 Music Recommendation System to Address the Problem of Long Tail Using Multi-Stage Graph

Mallannagari Sunitha, Thondepu Adilakshmi, and Yashfeen Zehra
Vasavi College of Engineering
Hyderabad, India

CONTENTS

15.1 INTRODUCTION

Because of expanded prevalence of music streaming services such as Spotify, Apple Music, Pandora, Last.fm and so forth, music listeners now have access to millions of digital tracks. This growth led to information overloading [1] and the listeners often find it difficult to choose a right song. Music recommendation systems (MRSs) help users to deal with the huge search space. Lately, research in MRSs have gained popularity both in industry and academia [2].

Recommendation systems research approaches are divided into collaborative filtering, content-based filtering and hybrid approach [3]. The core concept in collaborative filtering [4] is the interaction between user and item, whereas content-based filtering is dependent on the features of the item. Hybrid approach combines collaborative and content-based methods.

DOI: 10.1201/9781003320340-15

185

MRS learns from the user's listening history and recommends songs which they are most likely to listen in future. It constantly mines the user behaviour to better understand their preferences and make reasonable recommendations. But the listening habits of the users can be complicated and can vary depending upon several factors. A user may favour diverse sorts of music in the part of the day and distinctive sorts in the evening. So, it is quite difficult to produce satisfactory results always.

Recommendation system tends to be biased towards mainstream artists, ignoring the less popular items that might be intriguing to the users. This ignorance gives rise to the long tail problem of recommendation systems. Long tail in MRSs refers to the tracks that are rare and have few or no recommendations. The tail data requires special dealing, and some of the methods for handling this issue are described in [5].

This chapter addresses the problem of long tail by considering a multi-stage graph. The rest of the chapter is coordinated as follows. Related work is described in Section 15.2. Proposed algorithm and methodology is explained in Section 15.3. Section 15.4 describes conclusion and future scope.

15.2   RELATED WORK

Music utilization is biased towards a couple of popular artists. For instance [6], in 2007, only 1% of digital tracks addressed 80% of the relative multitude of sales. Moreover, 1000 albums represented half portion of all album deals, and 80% of all albums sold were bought under hundred times.

As per Chris Anderson [7, 8], the item distribution is isolated into two distinct sections namely the head and the tail as shown in Figure 15.1. The definition emphasizes on the existence of two sectors: the well-known one (the head) and the since a long time ago disregarded and now developing (the long tail). His goal was to make everything accessible to the users and help the users find all the items available. Today, everything is accessible due to the presence of online services, but the latter must be satisfied by the recommender systems that exploit the songs from the long tail items.

Recommendation systems follow popular items and suggest only the best selling items to all the users. But they often leave out novel or less popular items that the users might like. And this constitutes the problem of long tail. The long tail of item

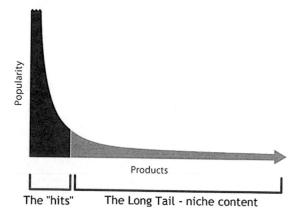

FIGURE 15.1   The long tail.

distribution consists of the items that are novel and less popular. It consists of items that have very few ratings. There is a need to assist the music listeners to find and recommend music items from the colossal proportion of music content available along the long tail.

This chapter proposes a novel method to recommend the items from the long tail of the distribution.

15.3 METHODOLOGY

The long tail comprises small number of well-known items (hits) and of unpopular and novel items which form the tail. The item could be a book, film, piece of music or whatever else. This project addresses the issue of long tail by using the multi-stage graph.

The user item matrix is generated after data preprocessing. The matrix consists of 200 users as rows and songs along with their playcounts as the columns. After obtaining the matrix, the next step is to fit the data present in the long tail of item distribution.

15.3.1 FITTING THE DATA OF LONG TAIL

To use the idea of long tail and make helpful and pragmatic examination of the phenomenon, long tail information is addressed by utilizing a numerical model proposed by Kilkki.

A large portion of the research work done in MRSs is dependent on popular items. Mainly the research approaches are classified into three namely collaborative filtering approach, context-based approach and hybrid approach.

The initial step is to resolve the issue of long tail is fitting a model to address data distribution. In this project, data is obtained from users' implicit feedback and represented by user-item rating matrix. After pre-processing the user logs from the Last. fm dataset, the number of items obtained are 14458. The items in MRS are modelled by using the formula given by Kilkki. Only a couple of items out of the 14458 items are extremely popular and will be recommended by collaborative filtering-based recommendation systems, rest of the items fall into the long tail. These items may not be mainstream/hit but they might be intriguing to the users. The long tail items should be isolated from the popular items. This is accomplished by modelling average item frequency data by using Equation (15.1) proposed by Kilkki [9]. The graph is plotted with respect to F and average frequency of items.

$$F(X) = \frac{\beta}{\left(\dfrac{N_{50}}{X}\right)^{\alpha} + 1} \tag{15.1}$$

where F(x) denotes portion of data under the frequency x, β is the total volume of data, α decides the shape of the long tail curve and $0 \le \alpha \le 1$, N_{50} represents 50th percentile or median of the data.

At the point when the items average frequency is shown using F(x), items are isolated into three areas head, mid and tail to exhibit three section of the curve. The head involves the most popular items, the mid and tail parts include items having relatively few assessments or novel items.

The definition for boundaries that isolate head, mid and tail parts are given by conditions (15.2) and (15.3), respectively.

$$\text{Boundary between}(\text{Head}->\text{Mid}) = Q_2{}^{2/3} \qquad (15.2)$$

$$\text{Boundary between}(\text{Mid}->\text{Tail}) = Q_2{}^{4/3} \qquad (15.3)$$

15.3.2 MULTI-STAGE GRAPH CONSTRUCTION

After modelling item average frequency data to fit long tail, given the limits characterized by Equations (15.2) and (15.3), items are divided into three sections head, mid and tail. A three-stage graph is constructed with items in the head as the first stage of the graph, items in the mid form the second stage of the graph and the items in the tail form the third stage of the graph. The graph construction is exhibited by considering the sample user-item matrix demonstrated in Table 15.1.

Consider the average frequencies of the sample items in the increasing order as 1, 1, 2, 3, 3, 4, 5, 6, 8 and median of this distribution is 3. $\alpha = 0.95$ and $\beta = 1$ are considered for the project. The average frequency vs percentage share of data is shown in Table 15.2.

The graph is plotted between the average frequencies and percentage of data till x. It is demonstrated below.

Based on the long tail data fitting in Figure 15.2, the items with the frequency rank 2 form the tail part of the curve, items with the frequency rank till 4 form the mid part of the curve and the items with frequency rank more than 4 form the head part of the curve.

Considering the sample user-item matrix, the head consists of three songs namely S3, S5, S7, the mid consists of the songs S4, S6 and S8 and the tail comprises the songs S1, S2 and S9. A multi-stage graph is constructed with items in the head part comprising the principle stage (first stage), items in the mid part establishing the subsequent second stage and items in the tail part establishing the third stage of the graph.

TABLE 15.1

Sample User-Item Matrix

Users/Songs	Song1	Song2	Song3	Song4	Song5	Song6	Song7	Song8	Song9
User1	1	0	0	3	6	4	0	4	0
User2	0	0	6	4	0	3	8	4	0
User3	1	1	0	3	6	0	0	0	3
User4	0	1	6	1	0	0	0	4	2
User5	2	1	0	0	6	3	8	0	1
User6	0	0	4	3	5	2	0	0	3
Average frequency (after rounding)	1	1	5	3	6	3	8	4	2

TABLE 15.2

Average Frequency vs Percentage Share of Data Till Rank x

Average Frequency(x)	% Share of Data Till x: F(x)
1	26.79
1	26.79
2	41.88
3	51.76
3	51.76
4	58.76
5	63.99
6	68.03
8	73.89

15.3.3 EDGE WEIGHTS CALCULATION

Weights of the edges interfacing the head, mid and tail sections are calculated depending upon four factors:

1. Number of users who have listened to the same items
2. Album of the items
3. Context of the items
4. Degree of similarity between the items

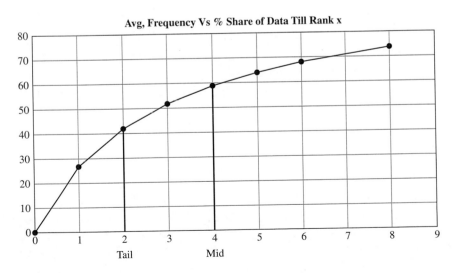

FIGURE 15.2   Long tail fitting data using F(x).

$$W_{ij} = \text{Weight}\left(\text{no of common users}\left(S_i, S_j\right)\right) + \text{Album}\left(S_i, S_j\right)$$
$$+ \text{Context}\left(S_i, S_j\right) + \text{Item\_Clusters}\left(S_i, S_j\right) \qquad (15.4)$$

where

$$\text{Weight}\left(\text{no of common users}\left(S_i, S_j\right)\right)$$
$$= \frac{\text{Number of users listened}\left(S_i, S_j\right)}{\text{No. of users listened}\left(S_i\right) + \text{No. of users listened}\left(S_j\right)}$$

$$\text{Album}\left(S_i, S_j\right) = 1 \text{ if } \text{Album}\left(S_i\right) = \text{Album}\left(S_j\right)$$
$$= 0 \text{ if } \text{Album}\left(S_i\right) \neq \text{Album}\left(S_j\right)$$

$$\text{Context}\left(S_i, S_j\right) = 1 \text{ if } \text{Context}\left(S_i\right) = \text{Context}\left(S_j\right)$$
$$= 0 \text{ if } \text{Context}\left(S_i\right) \neq \text{Context}\left(S_j\right)$$

Weights of common users: The weight of the common users is calculated by dividing the total number of users who have heard both the songs by the summation of the total number of users who have heard first song and the total number of users who have heard second song.

Album weight: Album similarity is also considered for calculating the weight of the edges. If both the songs are of the same, album weight one is assigned and if both the songs are not of the same album, then weight zero is assigned to the edge.

Context-based weight calculation: The context considered for the recommendation was the time of the day the song was listened to by the user. Three contexts were created namely morning, afternoon and evening. The time in the dataset is in 24-hour format.

Item cluster weight: Sklearn library has inbuilt K-means algorithm. The number of clusters taken into consideration is denoted by k and the value of k is taken 60 for this project. Then the item (song) clusters and user clusters are formed. K-means clustering was used to create the cluster of items for all the users using their listening history.

Sample multi-stage graph with weights determined by using Equation (15.4) appears in Figure 15.3.

15.3.4   GRAPH TRAVERSAL FOR RECOMMENDATION

As an initial move towards the proposal, the user-item rating matrix is developed from the listening history of 200 users. The matrix consists of 200 users and 14458 songs, it is of 14458 X 200 size. For each item, the average frequency is calculated. We consider the items in increasing order of their average frequency to demonstrate the data distribution of each and every item. Fit the item avg. frequency data by utilizing F(x) to feature long tail. In the light of the limits recognized from the data

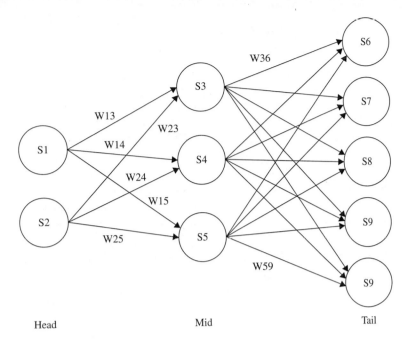

FIGURE 15.3   Weighted three stage graph.

distribution curve for some given α, β values, separate the items into three sections head, mid and tail.

A three-staged graph is built using these three sections. The first section (head) has fewer songs when compared to the second section (mid) and the second section (mid) has less number of songs than the third section (tail). In our project after division into three sections, we got 15 songs in head, 50 songs in the mid region and 14393 songs in the tail.

Music taste of a user differs dependent on the hour of a day. A user may favour diverse sorts of music in the first part of the day and distinctive sorts in the evening. To include these data for music suggestion, the context of song is characterized into morning, afternoon and night and is demonstrated in Table 15.3.

An example context information table for the user-item matrix is shown in Table 15.3.

TABLE 15.3
Items with Context Information

User/Item	Frequency (S1)	Context	....	S14458	Context
U1	12	Evening		6	Afternoon
U2	8	Morning		....	....
....					
U200				9	Evening

TABLE 15.4

Artist Information of Items

Item	Artist
SI	Pezet
S2	Garbage
....	....
S14458	Rantanplan

The dataset obtained from Last.fm consists of the features such as album name and timestamp along with userID, TrackID, TrackName. Album information table is constructed and is shown in Table 15.4 with item and artist as columns.

Context of the item is acquired depending on the timestamp. Timestamp demonstrates the time when a specific item has been listened. It is addressed by utilizing 24 hours of a day.

15.3.5 RECOMMENDATION ALGORITHM

Weights of the edges are calculated by using Equation (15.4) and these weights are utilized in traversing the three-stage graph during the recommendation phase as shown in Figure 15.3. For any test user, we start traversing the multi-stage graph from the head items preferred by a test user. Traversal is also starts at mid-level, if test user does not contain any item from the head list.

The algorithm used for traversing the graph and recommending song items is as follows:

Algorithm CF_LONGTAIL ()

Input: Three-stage graph, Artist table, Context table

Output: Recommendation Vectors for test users

Methodology

1. For each test_user belongs to $Ut=\{U_1, U_2,....U_{60}\}$
2. For each item of test user $I_k \in$ Head
3. Start from the item I_k in the first stage of the graph
4. Add an item I_{k+1} from mid to the recommendation vector if and only if Weight (I_k, I_{k+1}) is highest from all I_{k+1} possible
5. From I_{k+1} at second stage, add an item I_{k+2} from tail to the recommendation vector if and only if Weight (I_{k+1}, I_{k+2}) is highest from all I_{k+2} possible
6. Repeat steps 4 and 5 until the size of the recommendation vector exceeds a threshold N
7. End

The algorithm takes 60 test users. The graph traversal starts from the head region and moves to the mid item having the maximum weight. From the second stage, the traversal moves to the third stage, i.e. the tail part having the maximum weight. The songs are added to the recommendation vector. The graph is traversed until a threshold N is reached.

15.4 RESULTS

MRSs are the software algorithms that help users to find relevant music. The research work done in this project proposed and implemented novel approach for MRS. We have used three evaluation parameters obtained based on the confusion matrix shown in Table 15.5 for evaluation of our algorithm namely precision, accuracy and recall. These measures are obtained by using the confusion matrix.

True positives (TP) indicate that the songs which are recommended by the recommendation systems and are listened by the test user. True negatives (TN) indicate that the songs which are not recommended by the recommendation systems and are not listened by the test user. False positives (FP) indicate that the songs which are recommended by the recommendation systems and are not listened by the test user. False negatives (FN) indicate that the songs which are not recommended by the recommendation systems but are listened by the test user.

Precision: Precision is used to indicate how many songs that are recommended by the recommendation system are liked by the test user. It is given in Equation (15.5)

$$Precision(Ui) = \frac{Number\ of\ songs\ listened\ by\ the\ test\ user(TP)}{Total\ number\ of\ songs\ recommended(TP+FP)} \quad (15.5)$$

For every individual test user, precision is calculated utilizing the equation mentioned above. Average precision for all test users is calculated as given by Equation (15.6).

$$Average\ Precision(AP) = \sum_{i=1}^{m} \frac{Precision(U_i)}{m} \quad (15.6)$$

Accuracy: Accuracy is used to indicate how many songs that are recommended by the recommendation system have been listened by total number of songs present as shown in Equation (15.7).

TABLE 15.5
Confusion Matrix

Actual/Recommended	Recommended to Test User	Not Recommended to Test User
Listened by test user	True positive (TP)	False negative (FN)
Not listened by test user	False positive (FP)	True negative (TN)

$$\text{Accuracy}(\text{Ui}) = \frac{\text{Number of songs correctly predicted}(TP+TN)}{\text{Total Number of songs in the dataset}(TP+FN+FP+TN)} \quad (15.7)$$

Recall: Recall indicates fraction of songs recommended out of total songs listened by a test user. Recall is calculated by Equation (15.8).

$$\text{Recall}(\text{Ui}) = \frac{TP}{TP+FN} \quad (15.8)$$

Average recall for all test users is calculated by Equation (15.9).

$$\text{Average Recall}(\text{AR}) = \sum_{i=1}^{m} \frac{\text{Recall}(U_i)}{m} \quad (15.9)$$

After preprocessing the data logs from the Last.fm dataset, 200 users and 14458 songs were obtained. The songs were categorized into head, mid and tail regions using the mathematical formula proposed by Kilkki. A three-stage graph was constructed using the head, mid and tail regions as the three stages. Weights of the edges of the graph were calculated by taking common users, context, album and item similarity into consideration.

The graph was traversed and recommendations are made from mid and tail regions. The results are obtained by calculating the precision, accuracy, recall and average long tail precision as shown in Table 15.6.

The results obtained for the proposed method by using evaluation measures namely accuracy, precision, recall and average long tail precision are plotted for different values of N. N is the threshold for the number of recommended songs from mid and tail regions. Figure 15.4 shows the accuracy of the model for different N values. Model obtained highest accuracy at N = 3.

In Figure 15.5, recall values are showcased. Model has highest recall at N = 5. Recall increased as the number of neighbours increased.

Figure 15.6 showcases the precision obtained for the proposed multi-stage graph model. Precision of the model is high at N = 1. Precision decreased with N value increased.

Figure 15.7 shows average tail precision obtained by the proposed model. Multistage graph model is able to identify tail songs efficiently as the highest tail precision is 0.35.

15.5   CONCLUSION AND FUTURE SCOPE

Effective recommendation systems should promote novel and relevant items, primarily from the tail of the popularity distribution. We have used Kilkki model to describe the cumulative distribution of the curve. This method allows us to define song popularity. The popularity curve is divided to head, mid and tail regions and a multistage graph is constructed. Recommendations are made by traversing the graph from head

TABLE 15.6

Performance of Multi-Stage Graph Model

Alpha	Beta	Total Songs	No. of Head Songs	No of Mid Songs	No. of Tail Songs	Recommended Mid Song for Each Head Song	Recommended Tail Song for Each Mid Song	Average Precision	Average Accuracy	Average Recall	Average Long tail Precision
0.95	1	14458	15	50	14393	1	1	0.499855515	0.759105685	0.00149270	0.28333333
0.95	1	14458	15	50	14393	2	2	0398138528	0.708400194	0.001BS919	032500000
0.95	1	14458	15	50	14393	3	3	0.449823279	0.768662102	0.00254069	0.36111111
0.95	1	14458	15	50	14393	4	4	0375719073	0.739833771	0.00336496	0.33333333
095	1	14458	15	50	14393	5	5	0363511707	0.734217504	0.00356261	0.30000000

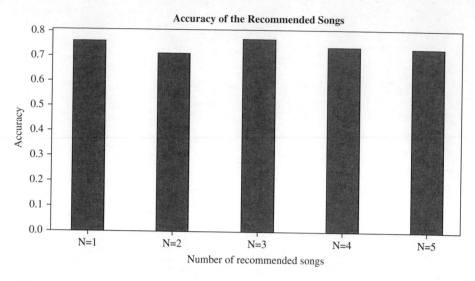

FIGURE 15.4   Accuracy of the proposed multi-stage graph method.

to mid and mid to tail parts. Proposed method is evaluated on the benchmark dataset obtained from Last.fm and results obtained prove the ability of proposed system in identifying tail songs. The accuracy, precision and recall and average long tail precision of the recommendations are measured.

As music taste of a user depends on multiple parameters, the proposed recommendation approach can be improved by considering other parameters of users and songs to identify the long tail songs more efficiently.

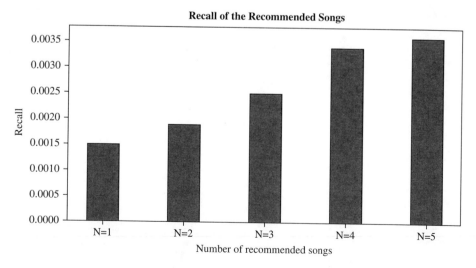

FIGURE 15.5   Recall of the proposed multi-stage graph model.

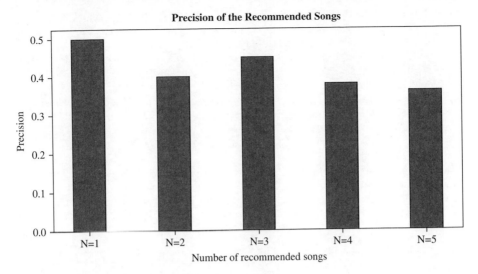

FIGURE 15.6   Precision of the proposed multi-stage graph.

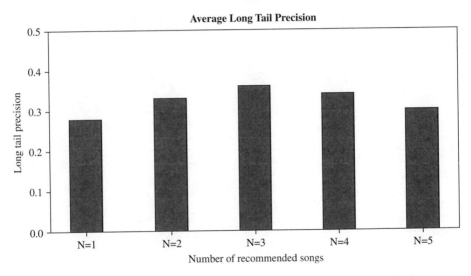

FIGURE 15.7   Average long tail precision the proposed multi-stage graph method.

REFERENCES

[1] B. Sarwar, G. Karypis, J. Konstan, J. Riedl, Item-Based Collaborative Filtering Recommendation Algorithms, Hong Kong: ACM, May 1–5, 2001 1-58113-348-0/01/000

[2] M. Schedl, P. Knees, B. McFee, D. Bogdanov, M. Kaminskas, "Music Recommender Systems", In: Ricci F, Rokach L, Shapira B, Kantor PB (eds) Recommender Systems Handbook, chap. 13, 2nd edn. Berlin: Springer, 2015, pp 453–492

[3] P. Nagarnaik, A. Thomas, "Survey on Recommendation System Methods", International Conference on Electronics and Communication System (ICECS), 2015 IEEE International, 26–27 Feb. 2015

[4] M. Nilashi, M. Salahshour, O. Ibrahim, A. Mardani, M. Dalvi Esfahani, N. Zakuan, A New Method for Collaborative Filtering Recommender Systems: The Case of Yahoo! Movies and TripAdvisor Datasets, 2013

[5] A. Schein, A. Popescul, L. Ungar, D. Pennock, "Methods and Metrics for Cold-Start Recommendations," Proceedings of the 25th Annual International ACM SIGIR Conference on Research and Development in Information Retrieval, 2002

[6] Celma, Ò. (2010). The Long Tail in Recommender Systems. In: Music Recommendation and Discovery. Springer, Berlin, Heidelberg. https://doi.org/10.1007/978-3-642-13287-2_4.

[7] Chris Anderson, "The Long Tail: Why the Future of Business is Selling Less or More", Hyperion, New York (2006), $24.95, ISBN: 1-4013-0237-8, VL - 43, DO - 10.1016/j.ipm.2006.10.002

[8] N. Sundaresan, "Recommender Systems at the Long Tail", Fifth ACM Conference on Recommender Systems, pp 1–5, 2011

[9] K. Kilkki, A practical model for analyzing long tails. First Monday, 12(5), 2007

16 Speech-Based Access of Agricultural Commodity Prices and Weather Information in the Kannada Language and Its Dialects

Thimmaraja Yadava Gopalappa
Nitte Meenakshi Institute of Technology
Bengaluru, Karnataka, India

Nagaraja Benageri Gnaneshwara
Vidyavardhaka College of Engineering
Mysuru, Karnataka, India

Haradagere Siddaramaiah Jayanna
Siddaganga Institute of Technology
Tumkur, Karnataka, India

CONTENTS

16.1 INTRODUCTION

One of the most desired means of communication among people is speech. It includes multiple steps, beginning with the coding of thought or information in the talker's brain and ending with the effective decoding of that thought or information

DOI: 10.1201/9781003320340-16

by the listener's brain. It has a wide range of applications, such as automatic speech recognition (ASR), speaker recognition, speech encoding and spoken inquiry systems. Upgrading a spoken inquiry system using a telephone web-based ASR framework offers a better solution to the many issues in [1]. The ASR systems developed in the early 1950s were sufficiently proficient to recognize only vowels and consonants. Their potentialities later progressed for phonemes including irregular phrases. Today's ASR systems are able to interpret constant random speech independently of speakers. However, there is still a good amount of feasibility for the end user to boost their precision, pace, reproducibility, terminology and functionality. Work throughout the ASR region has generally concentrated on different accents, such as English, French, Spanish, Chinese and Japanese, whereas most other dialects, mainly African, South Asian and Eastern European, have gained the least consideration [2]. Study operations lately containing conjugative Slavic languages, such as Czech, Polish, Serbo-Croatian, Russian and Ukrainian under resourced European languages have been steadily increasing. An automatic phonetic transcription based on guidelines is typically used to build a large vocabulary of identification. For the Russian language transformation, guidelines regarding orthographic to phonemic content depiction are not so difficult. The biggest challenge is, determining the place of tension within dictionary shapes. Here are no specific guidelines to identify the tension places and composite words that have multiple stressed vowels too.

The International Phonetic Alphabet (IPA) is commonly included as a standardized descriptive phoneme list for different cultures. This consists of 55 phonemes for the Russian, 17 vowels and 38 consonants. Meanwhile, the American English IPA package includes 49 phonemes, 24 consonants and 25 diphthongs and vowels. In Russian, the predominant palatalization activates a significant volume of consonants. Some attempts are made to develop an ASR program with a broad vocabulary for the Russian language [3, 4]. Russian is perhaps a virtual language with multiple roots albeit affixes. When modeling the acoustic, lexical and language models, the authors have paid greater emphasis to the particulars for the Russian dialect in their work. A specialized software framework was created for the development of pronunciation lexicons. In the acoustic model, the authors have tested a mixture of information-based and mathematical approaches, generating many dissimilar phoneme ranges. The choice of these was calculated experimentally. They have implemented a latest approach to develop better n-gram models, which integrates syntactic and regression interpretation for the language model and instruction script. Two independent Russian speech repositories gathered and internally were used to conduct assessment tests. Scientific studies were performed with 204000 ASR words to contrast typical n-gram language models, and hence, the language models were generated leveraging a syntactic-statistical method. Test findings showed that the proposed vernacular simulation technique has become very effective in curbing machine translation errors.

When researchers deal with the key machine translation lookup problem, they were very often faced with the issue of the required development of a whole system from scratch, even if they only want to investigate one aspect of the field. Open-source machine translation tools, including hidden Markov model toolkit (HTK) [5], audiovisual continuous speech recognition (AVCSR) [6] and earlier Sphinx [7] systems versions, are available. These systems are mostly advanced to build speech systems for a one-time operation. As a consequence, these structures are ultimately creating barriers to potential research works that differ from the true purpose of the program. Furthermore, some of these systems are restricted by licensing contracts that make it hard for non-academic instituting to join the research arena. The authors distributed a cross-disciplinary team to create Sphinx-4 to encourage new advances in the science of speech recognition [7]. It needs one open-source network that meets the need for evolving research fields and integrates state-of-the-art methodologies. Due to the researchers' diversity and their technical aspirations, they published Sphinx-4 in JAVA™ programming language, providing access to that of a wide range of devices. Firstly, Sphinx-4 has become a flexible and plug-in architecture, which assimilates current device model trends with enough flexibility to serve evolving fields of study in science. Since it includes distinguishable elements assigned for different functions. The architecture is flexible because it is composable since the elements may be quickly changed throughout initialization. Sphinx-4 even provides a range of tools incorporating state-of-the-art machine translation strategies for application experiments and providing researchers with a working program.

Kaldi is a well-known machine translation toolbox for building language and acoustic models [8]. Kaldi is a machine translation toolkit that is directly accessible and designed for computer language C++. The Kaldi software contains C++ executables, as well as multiple shell commands. The keys shown here are versatile and innovative but cannot be easily comprehensible. Kaldi's key purpose of extracting features is to establish regular mel-frequency cepstral coefficients (MFCC). It backups traditional modeling techniques, including Gaussian mixture model (GMM), subspace Gaussian mixture model (SGMM), and extends to other techniques, such as SGMM and deep neural networks (DNN). Therefore, the Kaldi toolkit is being used by many researchers all over the world to develop robust ASR systems for various types of applications. A spoken inquiry system was created to obtain commodity prices particulars in the Assamese language [9]. The implemented system authorizes the speaker/farmers/user to reach the current service price by using a landline/mobile phone to dial the device. The spoken inquiry framework consists of integrated voice response (IVR) and ASR models that are generated using the Kaldi open-source toolkit. The voice information was gathered from various Assam Vernacular sectors for ASR models production. Problems of test information adaptation are illustrated, and a restricted data-unseen speaker adaptation technique is applied on baseline results, which has provided a relative improvement in word error rate (WER) of 8%. Conventional approaches such as maximum likelihood linear regression (MLLR) [10] have struggled to allow for improved results, because they need a necessary volume of records for adaptation. The literature defined that the strategies for Eigen voice and cluster adaptive training [11] are better adapted when the data for adaptation is smaller. Thus, the authors used Eigen voice and cluster adaptive training strategies because of its adjustment knowledge for constructing an Assamese language query system [9].

In [12], an Arabic speech recognition system has been introduced, which has a very wide vocabulary and message slenderness. Traditional forms like GMM and SGMM have been used for the design of a system for the detection of Arabic voice. The authors handed down 36 phonemes as well as 200 hours of voice content. Its accomplished WER seems to be 15.81% for broadcast reports to the relative source results. Analysis of voice translation technologies with a limited volume of voice data transmitted in Arabic dialects was examined in [13]. Its 50 hours of translated voice information was drawn via the Al-Jazeera news channel. Experimental WERs obtained were 29.85% for radio interactions, 17.86% for television broadcast reproductions and 25.60% for total voice using i-vector-deployed speaker adaptation. Alexey *et al.* established a method for the recognition of Russian voice via a big speech corpus using syntactic statistical vocabulary [4]. The sampling frequency of 16 kHz and cumulative speaking data of 26 hours were used for Kaldi preparation. The WER obtained was 26.90%. An end-to-end, uninterrupted machine translation network focused on recurrent neural networks (RNN) was proposed in [14]. The authors used the Texas instruments/Massachusetts institute of technology (TIMIT) dataset to direct the simulations. Kaldi and voice detection algorithms were used for software planning as well as development.

An end-to-end voice identification system had been acquired using RNN [15,16]. The authors in [16] suggested a process for designing a framework that becomes a hybrid with deep bidirectional long short-term memory (LSTM) RNN architecture with its analytical feature of connectionist temporal classification (CTC). Synthesis of the character level was achieved using RNN. Through contrasting the current model with a reference for speaker-independent identification on both the Wall Street Journal corpus, the authors achieved state-of-the-art precision. The enhancements in the Assamese spoken inquiry system were described in [17] to access the prices of agricultural resources. A spoken question framework comprises an IVR request flow, ASR templates as well as a server with the agricultural marketing network (AGMARKNET) information database. Various forms of noises corrupted the speech data that had an impact on the identification levels of the base version of the spoken question method. The writers presented one methodology dealing with zero frequency filtering to eliminate the background distortions, to overcome this barrier as well as to achieve high precision.

In [18], the authors presented a strong accent, microphone-independent, simultaneous speech recognition framework focusing on phonetic transcription. The Viterbi beam scan decoding was used, and the segmental approximation of k-means was substantiated as a guideline for the calculation of the clustered frame process. The TIMIT database was chosen for the analytical reason, with a vocabulary scale of 855 words. For the words of 25, 105 and 855, the translating term accuracy was 91%, 87.0% and 63%, respectively. The writers in [19] investigated a fusion of complementary origins of perceptual action with large-vocabulary continuous speech recognition (LVCSR). The attributes obtained when paired with the duration of the vocal tract using the pitch synchronous measurements were especially captivating. The obtained WER is significantly better compared to the WER of conventional modeling techniques.

The research work reported in this work exploits two factors (issues in speech enhancement and performance of ASR models) at the acoustic signal level for developing speech enhancement methods and robust ASR systems. The suggested approaches were used to analyze deteriorated speech data using spectral and statistical methods, as well as to create robust ASR models for noisy and enhanced speech data. Spectral processing involves the estimation and elimination of corrupted components in the degraded speech data. Developing a robust end-to-end ASR system involves the following:

- Collection of speech data under corrupted conditions.
- Transcription and validation of collected speech data.
- Eliminating the corrupted components in the degraded speech data by proposed speech enhancement technique [20].
- Speech feature extraction using MFCC.
- Creating lexicon and phoneme set for Kannada dialects.
- Creating robust ASR models at various phoneme levels for corrupted and enhanced speech data.
- Collection of information of agricultural commodity prices and weather forecasting from AGMARKNET and IMD websites using web crawler.
- Development of end-to-end spoken inquiry system using interactive voice response system (IVRS) call flow.

16.2 BASIC STRUCTURE OF AUTOMATIC SPEECH RECOGNITION SYSTEM

Implementation of a robust ASR system comprises different phases. They are as follows:

- Speech data as input.
- Features extraction of speech corpus.
- Preparation of lexicon and phoneme set for a particular language.
- Creating acoustic models for the extracted features.
- Training acoustic models to obtaining language models.
- Decoding the trained models.

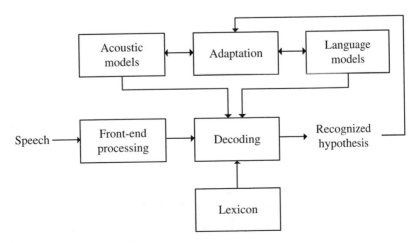

FIGURE 16.1 Basic structure of ASR system.

The block-wise representation of the fundamental ASR system is shown in Figure 16.1. To obtain better accuracy of speech recognition, a large amount of data needs to be given as input for the extraction of speech features. The speech features extraction part can also be called front-end processing. Using extracted features, one can develop acoustic models using different modeling techniques. The lexicon/dictionary plays an important role while training and decoding the system. The lexicon comprises both phoneme level and word level transcriptions of speech data. With the help of lexicon and language models, the decoding process could be done. On the basis of the recognized hypothesis, one can estimate the accuracy of speech recognition.

16.3 DEVELOPMENT OF END-TO-END KANNADA SPOKEN INQUIRY SYSTEM

Speech data was collected from 2500 speakers/farmers across Karnataka under degraded conditions in order to construct strong ASR models [21]. Totally, 430 speech words have been used for the collection of speech corpus, which includes 30 districts names, 250 mandi names and 150 commodity names. The speaker-independent ASR models were created by Kaldi for degraded speech data. Using Kaldi and Kannada language/dialects dictionary resources, the obtained WERs were 9.95%, 11.84% and 18.40% for district names, names of mandis and names of commodities, respectively. The spoken inquiry system was developed by taking the least WER ASR models of degraded speech data. The online and offline speech recognition accuracies were compared and given an inference that speech recognition accuracy could be further improved by eliminating various types of degradations/noises in the corrupted speech data. The proposed algorithm has given better improvement in terms of speech, audibility, quality and intelligibility. The degraded speech data was enhanced by proposed noise elimination technique and developed ASR models for enhanced speech data using Kaldi. The achieved WER was 9.60% for mixed enhanced speech data. By taking these least WER ASR models, we have developed a spoken inquiry system to get the real-time weather information and prices of agricultural commodities in Kannada dialects. For completeness of the proposed work, we have reproduced some of the experimental results from [20]. The speech files utilized for training and testing are shown in Table 16.1.

The robust ASR models for Kannada language were obtained at following phoneme levels (modeling techniques):

- MFCC technique was used for speech feature extraction.
- Training and decoding at single phone level.
- Triphone 1: Delta + Delta-Delta training and decoding.

TABLE 16.1
The Speech Files Utilized for Training and Testing

Speech Database	Train Files	Test Files
Noisy speech	68523	2180
Enhanced speech	67234	2180

- Triphone 2: linear discriminant analysis (LDA) + maximum likelihood linear transform (MLLT) training and testing.
- Triphone 3: LDA + MLLT + speaker adaptation training (SAT) and testing.
- SGMM training and testing.
- Hybrid training and testing using DNN (DNN + hidden Markov model (HMM)).

Using the various modeling techniques, Kannada dialect resources and Kaldi features, the achieved WERs for noisy and enhanced Kannada speech data are shown in Tables 16.2 and 16.3, respectively.

16.3.1 SPOKEN INQUIRY SYSTEM CALL FLOW STRUCTURE

The spoken inquiry interface was added to the AGMARKNET to give more value. The website stated in the Karnataka section provides the medium, maximum and minimum prices of 250 different commodities disseminated over several mandis in various Karnataka districts. The Asterisk server was installed to connect the telephone/mobile calls to a server. It consists of an IVRS flow structure and a computer mobile/telephone interface card (CTIC). The fundamental block diagram of the spoken inquiry system is depicted in Figure 16.2. The implemented system gives the privilege to the speaker/user to give a query/question about the information of commodity prices and weather forecasting. It receives the input data from speaker/farmer, records, processes and distributes the current price of asked commodity and weather information through pre-recorded voice messages. The proposed noise elimination algorithm is introduced at each step where the user is prompted to utter district name, mandi name and commodity name. Therefore, the speech data given by the user is subjected to enhancement before the feature extraction part.

TABLE 16.2
The WERs for Noisy Speech Data

Phoneme Level	WER
Mono	31.61
tri1_2000_8000	16.15
tri1_2000_16000	14.95
tri1_2000_32000	14.63
tri2_2000_8000	15.14
tri2_2000_16000	13.85
tri2_2000_32000	13.12
tri3_2000_8000	14.91
tri3_2000_16000	13.78
tri3_2000_32000	13.17
SGMM	12.78
tri4_nnet_t2a (DNN)	**10.80**

Note: Bold value indicates the best result.

TABLE 16.3

The WERs for Enhanced Speech Data

Phoneme Level	WER 1
Mono	30.55
tri1_2000_8000	15.52
tri1_2000_16000	13.90
tri1_2000_32000	13.48
tri2_2000_8000	14.79
tri2_2000_16000	12.91
tri2_2000_32000	12.29
tri3_2000_8000	13.97
tri3_2000_16000	12.60
tri3_2000_32000	12.01
SGMM & 11.78	11.797
tri4_nnet_t2a (DNN)	**9.60**

Note: Bold value indicates the best result.

The spoken inquiry system consists of two major parts. One for information of commodity prices and the other for information of weather forecasting. Firstly, the farmer/speaker needs to call the server to get a connection with it. Once the call is connected to the server, it will play out the welcome prompt that "Welcome to agricultural commodity prices and weather information center, please tell the name of commodity (dhavasadhaanya) or weather (havamaana) to know the information of commodity price or weather information". If the farmer/speaker says commodity, then it will go to the first branch, or else, it will go to the second branch.

In the first section, the user/farmer is instructed to speak the name of the district in which he wanted to know the information of commodity price. If the district name is successfully identified, the server will tell the user to say the mandi's name. If the name of the mandi is correctly identified, the user will be instructed to pronounce the name of the commodity. If the commodity's name is also recognized, the server will look up the name in the commodity pricing information table. If the information of commodity price is available in the table, then the server will play out the price information through pre-recorded voice messages. If the user's inputs, such as

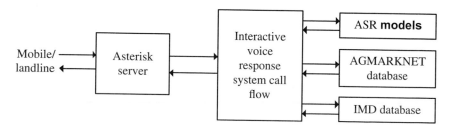

FIGURE 16.2   Block diagram of spoken inquiry system.

district names, mandi names and commodity names, are not recognized correctly, the user may be prompted to speak two more times. Even if it is not correctly recognized, the system/server expresses regret! After a while, try it! In the second part, the user/farmer is advised to say just the name of the district for which weather forecasting information is required. If the district name is successfully identified, the server will search the weather information database for the recognized district name. If it exists, the server will retrieve the most recent weather-predicting data from the database. The schematic representation of the spoken inquiry call flow structure for getting commodity price information and weather information is shown in Figure 16.3.

16.3.2   COMMODITY PRICES AND WEATHER INFORMATION DATABASES

The information of various commodity prices is available at www.agamrknet.gov.in website for various states of India. The information of commodity prices is represented in English for all the states. This could be the major problem for the farmers of India as most of them are illiterate and not having awareness about the computer, internet and website information. In order to provide the information of commodity prices to farmers from the website, a complete ASR system is developed. The text-based information of commodity prices was crawled from the mentioned website using a web crawler and stored it in the postgreSQL database. The database is updated for every 24 hours using a web crawler. The Indian Meteorological Department (IMD: www.imd.gov.in) disseminates weather forecasting information for all Indian districts. The weather information is also available in English on this page. The same web crawler and postgreSQL databases are used to crawl and store the weather information. The information of commodity price and weather forecasting are read out through pre-recorded voice messages.

16.3.3   TESTING OF IMPLEMENTED SPOKEN INQUIRY SYSTEM BY SPEAKERS/FARMERS IN THE FIELD

To compare the online and offline accuracy rates of speech recognition, 300 farmers tested the designed end-to-end spoken inquiry system in corrupted situations. Table 16.4 shows the online speech recognition accuracies under uncontrolled environment. From the table, it can be observed that the online and offline speech recognition accuracies are almost matched with each other.

16.4   CONCLUSIONS

This work describes some approaches to speech recognition under degraded conditions. These approaches are used to enhance the degraded speech data and to improve the performance of the ASR system. Firstly, the 2500 farmers' Kannada speech data was collected under degraded conditions throughout the various dialect areas/regions of Karnataka to gather all pronunciations for each speech sentence. The names of districts, mandi and commodities are used as words for the speech corpus collection. We have studied, implemented and analyzed the impact of spectral subtraction with voice activity detection (SS-VAD) and magnitude-squared

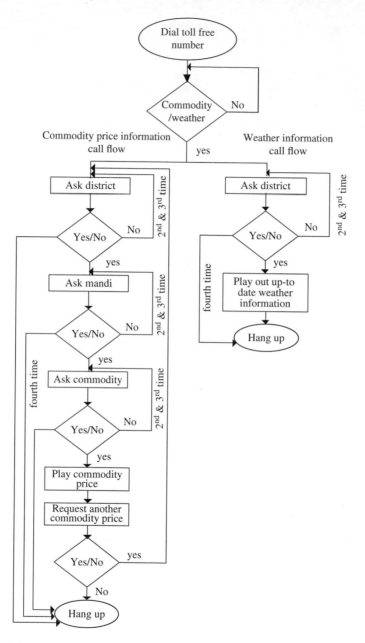

FIGURE 16.3 Call flow structure of spoken inquiry system.

spectrum estimators (MSSE) for speech enhancement. Three types of MSSE meth-ods (MMSE-SP, minimum mean square error spectrum power estimator based on zero crossing [MMSE-SPZC] and maximum a posteriori (MAP)) are tested with TIMIT and Kannada speech corpus databases. Among three MSSE techniques, the MMSE-SPZC gives better speech quality and intelligibility for the speech data

TABLE 16.4

Online Speech Recognition Accuracies Obtained after System Testing by Users/Farmers

Language: Kannada	Total No. of Farmers	Attempts			Total No. of Recognitions	Recognition in %
		1	2	3		
District names	300	242	16	13	271	90.20
Mandi names	300	240	23	12	271	90.20
Commodity names	300	240	21	09	268	89.26

degraded by musical and other types of noises. Therefore, we proposed a technique by amalgamating an SS-VAD with MMSE-SPZC to suppress the musical, babble and other types of noises. The experimental results revealed that the proposed algorithm has given much improvement in speech quality and intelligibility compared to existing techniques. The proposed technique was applied on a large noisy Kannada speech database, and it was enhanced. A toolkit called Kaldi was used for creating ASR models for degraded and enhanced speech data. Using least WER ASR models, a spoken inquiry system was developed for accessing the information of commodity prices and weather forecasting. The implemented system was tested on 300 farmers, and the accuracies of online and offline speech recognitions were also presented in this chapter. The future scope of this work is to improve the accuracy of speech recognition by enhancing the degraded Kannada speech data using DNN-based speech enhancement techniques and recent acoustic modeling techniques using Kaldi.

REFERENCES

[1] L. R. Rabiner, "Applications of speech recognition in the area of telecommunications," in IEEE Workshop on Automatic Speech Recognition and Understanding Proceedings, pp. 501–510, 1997.

[2] P. Kotkar, W. Thies, and S. Amarasinghe, "An audio wiki for publishing user-generated content in the developing world," in HCI for Community and International Development, Florence, Italy, April 2008.

[3] A. Karpov, I. Kipyatkova, and A. Ronzhin, "Speech recognition for east Slavic languages: The case of Russian," in Proc. 3rd International Workshop on Spoken Languages Technologies for Under-resourced Languages SLTU, Cape Town, RSA, pp. 84–89, 2012.

[4] A. Karpov, "Large vocabulary Russian speech recognition using syntacticostatistical language modeling," Speech Communication, vol. 56, no. 3, pp. 213–228, 2014.

[5] S. Young, "The HTK hidden Markov model toolkit: Design and philosophy," Cambridge University Engineering Department, UK, Tech. Rep. CUED/FINFENG/TR152, 1994.

[6] X. Liu, Y. Zhao, X. Pi, X. Liang, and A. V. Nefian, "Audio-visual continuous speech recognition using a coupled hidden Markov model," in Proceedings of the 7th International Conference on Spoken Language Processing, Denver, pp. 213–216, 2002.

[7] W. Walker and P. Lamere, "Sphinx-4: A flexible open source framework for speech recognition," Sun Microsystems, Inc., 2004.

[8] D. Povey, A. Ghoshal, G. Boulianne, L. Burget, O. Glembek, N. Goel, M. Hannemann, P. Motlicek, Y. Qian, P. Schwarz, J. Silovsky, G. Stemmer, and K. Vesely, "The Kaldi speech recognition toolkit," in IEEE 2011 Workshop on Automatic Speech Recognition and Understanding, IEEE Signal Processing Society, 2011.

[9] S. Shahnawazuddin, D. Thotappa, B. D. Sarma, A. Deka, S. R. M. Prasanna, and R. Sinha, "Assamese spoken query system to access the price of agricultural commodities," in 2013 National Conference on Communications (NCC), India, pp. 1–5, 2013.

[10] C. J. Leggetter and P. C. Woodland, "Maximum likelihood linear regression for speaker adaptation of continuous density hidden Markov models," Computer, Speech and Language, vol. 9, no. 2, pp. 171–185, 1995.

[11] R. Kuhn, J.-C. Junqua, P. Nguyen, and N. Niedzielski, "Rapid speaker adaptation in eigenvoice space," IEEE Trans. on Speech and Audio Processing, vol. 8, no. 6, pp. 695–707, 2000.

[12] A. Ali, Y. Zhang, P. Cardinal, N. Dahak, S. Vogel, and J. Glass, "A complete KALDI recipe for building Arabic speech recognition systems," in 2014 IEEE Spoken Language Technology Workshop (SLT), South Lake Tahoe, pp. 525–529, 2014.

[13] P. Cardinal, "Recent advances in ASR applied to an Arabic transcription system for Al-Jazeera," pp. 2088–2092, 2014.

[14] K. C. Jan Chorowski, Dzmitry Bahdanau and Y. Bengio, "End-to-end continuous speech recognition using attention-based recurrent NN: First results," arXiv preprint arXiv:1412.1602, 2014.

[15] A. Hannun, et al., "Deep speech: Scaling up end-to-end speech recognition," arXiv preprint arXiv:1412.5567, 2014.

[16] M. G. Yajie Miao and F. Metze, "End-to-end speech recognition using deep (RNN) models and WFST-based decoding," pp. 167–174, 2015.

[17] S. Shahnawazuddin, et al. "Improvements in IITG Assamese spoken query system: Background noise suppression and alternate acoustic modeling," Journal of Signal Processing Systems, vol. 88, no. 1, pp. 91–102, 2017.

[18] Y. Zhao, "A speaker-independent continuous speech recognition system using continuous mixture Gaussian density HMM of phoneme-sized units," IEEE Transactions on Speech and Audio Processing, vol. 1, no. 3, pp. 345–361, 1993.

[19] G. Garau and S. Renals, "Template-based continuous speech recognition," IEEE Transactions on Audio, Speech, and Language Processing., vol. 16, no. 3, pp. 508–518, 2008.

[20] T. Yadava Gopalappa and H. S. Jayanna, "Enhancements in automatic Kannada speech recognition system by background noise elimination and alternate acoustic modelling," International Journal of Speech Technology, vol. 23, no. 1, pp. 149–167, 2020.

[21] T. Yadava Gopalappa and H. S. Jayanna, "A spoken query system for the agricultural commodity prices and weather information access in Kannada language", International Journal of Speech Technology (IJST), vol. 20, no. 3, pp. 1–10, 2017.

17 Weather Classification
Image Embedding Using Convolutional Autoencoder and Predictive Analysis Based on Stacked Generalization

Anish Sudhir Ghiya, Vaibhav Vijay,
Aditi Ranganath, Prateek Chaturvedi,
and Sharmila Banu Kather
School of Computer Science and Engineering, VIT
Vellore, Tamil Nadu, India

Balakrushna Tripathy
School of Information Technology and Engineering, VIT
Vellore, Tamil Nadu, India

CONTENTS

17.1 INTRODUCTION

Weather is an important component in day-to-day activities. This is also an important aspect of planning future actions. Understanding the weather is an essential component of computer vision tasks. The use of a digital camera for surveillance transmitting to the computers helps to keep check of the environment to carry out the task of weather classification to produce intelligent computer vision systems [1, 2]. Feature extraction techniques are essential to predict weather, and autoencoders (AE) are normally used for this purpose. In recent days, due to the advent of deep neural network (DNN) methods, one of its variants the convolutional neural networks (CNN) is hybridized with AE to carry out the feature extraction process [3–5]. Sometimes stacked generalisation, which is an ensemble algorithm, is used to have better results based upon two or more models [6].

Limited vision because of the bad weather might cause problems in self-driving car applications and other computer vision tasks. To enhance machine view in these drastic weather situations, a reliable detection system is especially important to set as a baseline. Vision assistance systems are designed in such a way so as to perform decently well under good weather conditions. Unfortunately, limited visibility occurs more regularly on a daily basis and needs to be handled (e.g., heavy rain or cloudy weather). As these heavily affect the overall accuracy or even the general functioning of the vision system designed, the information from the weather condition is important information for these systems [7].

Most current applications are based on the assumption of clear weather, whereas this might not always be the case. Hence, to ensure better versions of these applications where they can be deployed in the real world, weather conditions must be taken into consideration as the first step towards development.

The works that have classified weather focus on a supervised approach to classification based on a pixel-wise feature extraction [2, 7]. In order to deal with classification-based applications, DNNs have been found to be the most suitable techniques [8–10]. DNNs have been applied to audio signal classification [11], text-based image retrieval [12], in healthcare [13], brain MRI segmentation techniques [14], gene characteristic and their applications [15] and computational biology [16]. Convolutional neural networks (CNNs) are neural networks where the convolutional operator is used instead of matrix multiplication [17]. Hence, we propose a semi-supervised method for abstract feature extraction using CNN-based AE.

17.2   RELATED WORK

The previous work in this field has mostly taken a pixel-level feature extraction method to get to the classifiers [2, 7]. However, in this chapter, we focused on more abstract image-level feature vector representation using transfer learning (Figure 17.1) pertained models (VGG16, ResNet50, etc.) to extract features (Figure 17.2). Furthermore, an unsupervised CNN-based AE model is also analysed to measure the difference in the vector encodings of the images. Ensemble-based learning is applied in order to

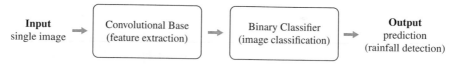

FIGURE 17.1   Transfer learning pipeline.

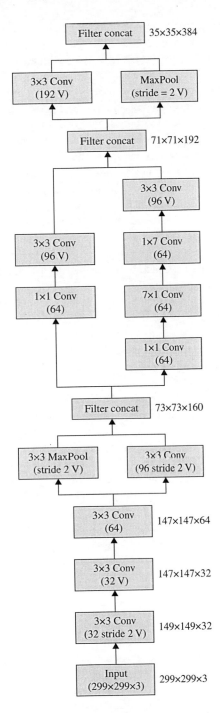

FIGURE 17.2   Inception-ResNet-V2 architecture.

boost the machine learning models that are used for classification using stacking generalization. In order to analyse the output from the AE correlation, analysis is done.

AEs are a form of representation learning which leverages neural networks for compressed knowledge embedding using unsupervised techniques. AEs are an important part of the neural network toolset where efficient encodings are learnt from unlabelled data. They are a set of neural networks that consist of two parts, an encoder and a decoder. These (AE) are trained by reconstructing data images after encoding them into a latent space representation. Nevertheless, AEs have enabled major applications in real world along with the advancement in the field of research [4]. CNNs have led to significant improvement in performance on a spread of image recognition tasks [18–20] and hence we have used a convolution-based architecture for our AE architecture.

The non-trivial nature of the task at hand and therefore the small size of the available image data set meant that one among the foremost effective strategies was the transfer learning [21, 22] approach. The major advantage of re-utilizing a neural network architecture which was previously trained on a large-scale image classification task using benchmark data sets such as ImageNet [20] is the transferability of the abstract features learnt during training.

StackNet is a computational, scalable and analytical framework implemented in the programming language Java with an architecture that resembles a feedforward neural network and uses [6] stacked generalization in a number of levels to enhance accuracy within machine learning tasks. With respect to feedforward neural networks, instead of being trained through backpropagation, the network architecture is made iteratively one layer at a time (using stacked generalization), each of which uses the penultimate target as its target. Given some input data set files, a neural network usually applies a perceptron along with any activation function like ReLU, SeLU, ELU, sigmoid among others. StackNet assumes that this activation function can take the shape of a supervised machine learning algorithm. Weighted inputs are provided to every neuron a bit like any neural network where the weights are trained to reduce the value of the loss; weighted outputs of every neuron can be fed onto the subsequent layers.

Global average pooling (GAP) is employed to get one feature map for every category present in the data set of the classification task from the last convolutional layer. Rather than adding fully connected (FC) layers over the feature maps, we take average of every feature map, and resulting vector is directly fed into the final softmax layer. One advantage of GAP over the FC layers is that it is a lot more native when compared to the convolution structure which by putting correspondences between the feature maps and output labels. Thus, the feature maps can be easily interpreted as label confidence maps, which can be used to visualize the activations based in the target. Overfitting is avoided because there are no trainable variables. Furthermore, GAP retains the spatial information; thus, it is more competent at spatial translations of the input variables to be mapped to the target [23].

Transfer learning is an essential technique wherein a model that was prepared to classify on one task is repurposed for another downstream task. From the novel architectures presented in [24–26], very deep convolutional networks are central to the most important advances in image recognition tasks in recent years. One example is that the inception architecture has been shown to realize excellent performance at

TABLE 17.1

Data Set Distribution between Classes

Sunrise	Cloudy	Shine	Rain
356	300	252	212

a relatively low computational cost [25]. Dense Convolutional Network (DenseNet) is a neural network that connects every layer to each other layer in a feedforward manner while training and evaluation [26].

17.3 METHODOLOGY

17.3.1 DATA SET

The data set originally contains 1120 images belonging to the four categories (distribution as in Table 17.1, samples in Figure 17.3). Each image in the data set contained different dimensions, and to uniformize the whole data set, we converted them to 256×256 dimensions RGB images. The distribution of the images between the classes is imbalanced which can be handled by the ensemble method proposed based on multiple models to increase the accuracy.

17.3.2 IMAGE EMBEDDINGS

For this chapter, we have used a deep convolutional reconstruction AE (Figure 17.4) for generating the vector embeddings of latent space representation of the images which represent the feature mappings. Our model consists of four strided convolution layers (each convolution layer contains a convolutional layer and a max pooling

FIGURE 17.3 Data set sample from each class.

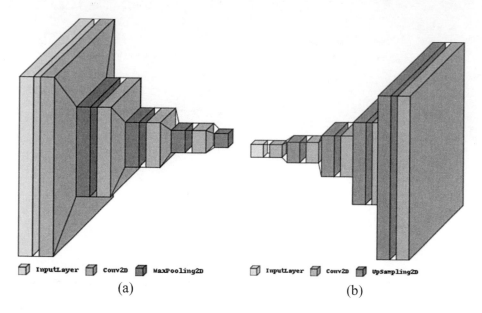

(a)   (b)

FIGURE 17.4   (a) Encoder and (b) decoder parts of the autoencoder.

layer) in an encoder (Figure 17.4 (a)) and four up-sampling convolution layers, each of which contains bilinear up-sampling layer followed by padded convolutional layer as part of the decoder (Figure 17.4 (b)). The latent space representation from the encoder is of size 16 × 16 × 4 or 1024 dimensions. The reconstruction of the images (Figure 17.5) from the embedding is generated from the encoder using the decoder. The reconstructed images had some blur associated with it. The reconstruction loss while training was 0.53. The AE was trained for 30 epochs with a reconstruction loss of 0.5931 and an accuracy of 0.7236.

$$Loss\ function = -\frac{1}{N}\sum_{i=1}^{N} y_i \log\big(p(y_i)\big)+\big(1-y\big)\log\big(1-p(y_i)\big) \qquad (17.1)$$

There were a few correlations present in the 1024-dimensional output from the AE. There was a slight case of entanglement in the representation Figure 17.6 (a), and in order to reduce this, principal component analysis (PCA) (Figure 17.6 (b)) was

FIGURE 17.5   Reconstruction of image (row 1) from embeddings generated from autoencoder (row 2).

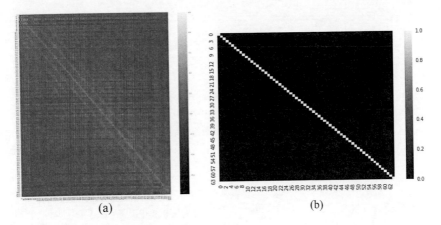

FIGURE 17.6   (a) Entanglement analysis using correlations of latent space representation of images from autoencoder and (b) correlation after applying PCA.

applied in order to reduce the correlation and intern producing a more disentangled representation of the embeddings.

17.3.3 TRANSFER LEARNING

For the chapter, we have taken base architectures and used it for the downstream task of weather classification. The classification layer from the proposed architecture in the papers is scraped and replaced by GAP in order to maintain the spatial information inferred from the model architecture followed by a classification layer.

17.3.4 MODELLING

The model parameters were chosen based on hyperparameter tuning with the help of grid search. Each model was trained on a stratified tenfold cross-validated data set and the results are based on the stratified test set which was held out before training.

To evaluate the predictions from the models with respect to one another, we used Cohen's kappa coefficient.

$$K = \frac{P_0 - P_e}{1 - P_e} \tag{17.2}$$

$$P_0 = \frac{Number\ in\ agreement}{Total\ number}, \quad P_e = P_{correct} + P_{incorrect} \tag{17.3}$$

Cohen's kappa score depicts how the models have similarity in their predictions. XGB and LGBM have very similar (Table 17.2). Support vector classifiers are the most different from the rest of the model. Logistic regression which was used as the baseline also has very little similarity with any other models, especially to depict the difference between logistic regression and SVC has the lowest kappa score.

TABLE 17.2

Cohen's Kappa Score between Models

Kappa Score	Model 1	Model 2
0.8318	Logistic Regression	XGB
0.844	Logistic Regression	LGBM
0.7837	Logistic Regression	SVC
0.9519	XGB	LGBM
0.8374	XGB	SVC
0.8497	LGBM	SVC

For the StackNet architecture (Figure 17.7) for this chapter, we have used a baseline model in terms of logistic regression and multiple boosting models like Extreme Gradient Boosting and Light Gradient Boosting. Bagging models like random forest are also used. Support vector machines are also used to classify the projection into a higher dimensional space using radial basis function kernels. And for the meta model, we have used a basic logistic regression model.

17.3.5 EVALUATION METRICS

Accuracy was used as a basic measure of performance evaluation of models. It describes the ratio between the correctly predicted observations and total observations.

$$Accuracy = \frac{TP + TN}{TP + FP + FN + TN} \tag{17.4}$$

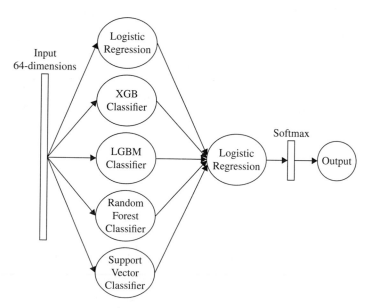

FIGURE 17.7 StackNet schematic diagram.

TABLE 17.3

Comparison with SAID Method Proposed in [2]

| Class | Accuracy | |
	SAID II	IESG
Cloudy	81.5	86.04
Rainy	95.2	95.77
Sunshine	88.4	94.00
Sunrise	81.7	88.33

F1 score is weighted average of precision and recall. Since we have an uneven class distribution, F1 score is another metric used.

$$F1\ Score = 2.\frac{Precision + Recall}{Precision * Recall} \tag{17.5}$$

The area under curve (AUC) is a measure of the ability of a classifier to distinguish between classes and uses the summary of the receiver operator characteristic (ROC).

Confusion metrics are also used to analyse the output from the models for each class and hence understanding the accuracies from each class per model.

17.4 EXPERIMENTAL RESULTS AND DISCUSSION

The Image Embedding-based Stacked Generalization (IESG) method gains advantageous inputs in terms of outputs from each of contributing models. This makes the proposed system gain higher accuracy. For each class present in the data set, the proposed method performs superior to the existing method tabulated in Table 17.3.

Logistic regression is taken as the baseline model for the work in this chapter (Table 17.4, Figure 17.8). Key point to note is that the random forest depicts lower accuracy when compared to logistic regression. The support vector classifier performed the best of all classifiers. While performing the grid search, the RBF kernel proved to be the best option for the SVM classifier.

TABLE 17.4

Scoring of Machine Learning Models

Model Name	Train Accuracy	Test Accuracy	F1 Score	ROC-AUC Score
Logistic regression	0.821523	0.830357	0.830595	0.969846
XGB	0.844894	0.857143	0.857231	0.997407
LGBM	0.847104	0.883929	0.883964	0.998591
Random forest	0.756729	0.803571	0.802188	0.990327
SVC	0.864007	0.888393	0.889324	0.997789
StackNet	0.998884	0.919643	0.9201	0.978447

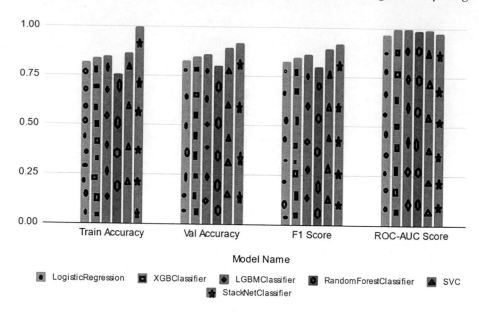

FIGURE 17.8   Comparison of ML models.

The confusion matrix in Figure 17.9 shows the classification of each model of each class. Most models perform well on the class rain. Cloudy and sunrise are mostly misclassified during predictions.

Table 17.5 depicts a comparative analysis between the SAID method as published in [2] and IESG method that we have proposed in this chapter. There is a 5% increase in the accuracy with respect to the SAID method.

Each model architecture has been taken wherein the FC layers are replaced by a GAP in order to retain the spatial information of the convolutional output. From Table 17.6, it is clearly visible that the proposed architecture performs better than some transfer learning models.

17.5   CONCLUSION

We proposed in our work a novel approach to feature extraction using AEs for weather classification. We first adapted the idea of convolutional AE to apply an architecture to generate image embeddings into a 1024 latent space representation. The embeddings generated from the encoder have slight entanglement in the representation and hence PCA is used in order to disentangle the representation. This is then passed onto machine learning models wherein bagging and boosting models are used to classify these disentangled embeddings. We conducted experiments with different combinations of models and evaluated the difference in outputs generated using the Cohen's Kappa coefficient. The models are then used to generate an ensemble using the StackNet architecture. This brought an increase in the model's accuracy by 3% when compared to the best model SVC and the whole approach gained an accuracy of 5% when compared to the existing

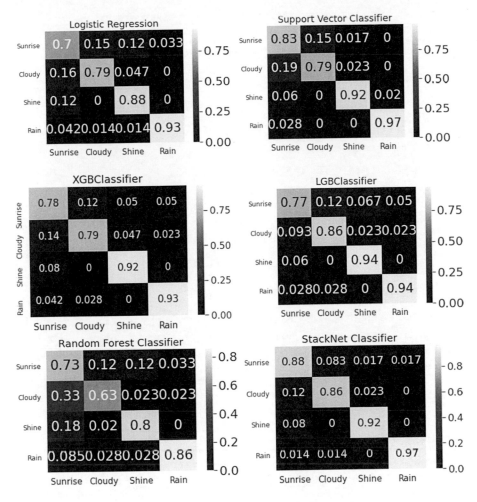

FIGURE 17.9   Comparison of ML models based on confusion matrix.

TABLE 17.5

Comparison with Previous Work

Method	Accuracy
Random forest	80
SAID Method I	85
SAID Method II	86
IESG	91

TABLE 17.6

Transfer Learning Models Classification Scores

Model Name	Accuracy
MobileNetV2	84.38
Densenet201	87.05
VGG16	89.73
ResNet152V2	95.00
Inceptionresnetv2	95.09

research on this data set. Furthermore, to compare the architecture proposed in the chapter, pre-trained model architectures are used for comparison, wherein the proposed architectures perform better than a few but are inferior when compared to others.

17.6 LIMITATIONS AND FUTURE WORK

The data set is small and so classification scores are lower than human levels. In order to increase the accuracy, a greater number of images are required. For this, beta-variational AEs (β-VAE) can be used in order to generate synthetic samples from the probability distribution function generated from the VAE. Also, to analyse the effective areas during encoding using AEs, the visualization technique of GRAD-LAM [27] can be used.

REFERENCES

1. Ajayi, G.: Multi-class weather dataset for image classification. Mendeley Data version 1 (2018). https://doi.org/10.17632/4drtyfjtfy.1
2. Oluwafemi, A. G., Zenghui, W.: Multi-class weather classification from still image using said ensemble method. Southern African universities power engineering conference/robotics and mechatronics/pattern recognition association of South Africa (SAUPEC/RobMech/PRASA), pp. 135–140 (2019). https://doi.org/10.1109/RoboMech.2019.8704783.
3. Zhang, Y.: A better autoencoder for image: convolutional autoencoder. In: ICONIP17-DCEC (2018). URL: http://users.cecs.anu.edu.au/Tom.Gede-on/conf/ABCs2018/paper/ABCs2018_paper_58.pdf (accessed on 23 March 2017).
4. Manakov, I., Rohm, M, Tresp, V.: Walking the tightrope: an investigation of the convolutional autoencoder bottleneck (2019). arXiv preprint arXiv:1911.07460.
5. Baldi, P.: Autoencoders, unsupervised learning, and deep architectures. Proceedings of ICML workshop on unsupervised and transfer learning (pp. 37–49). JMLR Workshop and Conference, Bellevue, WA, United States (2012).
6. Wolpert, D.H.: Stacked generalization. Neural Networks 5(2), 241–259 (1992). https://doi.org/10.1016/S0893-6080(05)80023-1
7. Roser, M., Moosmann, F.: Classification of weather situations on single color images. 2008 IEEE intelligent vehicles symposium, pp. 798–803 (2008). https://doi.org/10.1109/IVS.2008.4621205.

8. Bhattacharyya, S., Snasel, V., Hassanian, A. E., Saha, S., Tripathy, B. K.: Deep Learning Research with Engineering Applications, De Gruyter Publications, Berlin, Germany, 2020.

9. Adate, A., Tripathy, B. K.: A Survey on deep learning methodologies of recent applications, in: Acharjya D.P., Mitra A., Zaman N. (eds.) Deep Learning in Data Analytics: Recent Techniques, Practices and Applications, Springer Publications, Cham, Switzerland, 2021, pp. 145–170.

10. Adate, A., Tripathy, B. K.: Deep learning techniques for image processing, in: Bhattacharyya S., Bhaumik H., Mukherjee A., De S. (eds.), Machine Learning for Big Data Analysis, Berlin, Boston: De Gruyter, 2018, pp. 69–90.

11. Bose, A., Tripathy, B. K.: Deep learning for audio signal classification, in: Bhattacharyya S., Hassanian A.E., Saha S., Tripathy B.K. (eds.), Deep Learning Research and Applications, De Gruyter Publications, Berlin, Germany, 2020, pp. 105–136.

12. Singhania, U., Tripathy, B. K.: Text-based image retrieval using deep learning, in: Encyclopedia of Information Science and Technology, Fifth Edition, IGI Global, 2021, p. 11, DOI: 10.4018/978-1-7998-3479-3.ch007

13. Kaul, D., Raju, H. Tripathy, B. K.: Deep learning in healthcare, in: Acharjya D.P., Mitra A., Zaman N. (eds.), Deep Learning in Data Analytics: Recent Techniques, Practices and Applications, Springer Publications, Cham, Switzerland, 2021, pp. 97–115.

14. Tripathy, B. K., Parikh, S., Ajay, P., Magapu, C.: Brain MRI segmentation techniques based on CNN and its variants, in: Chaki J. (ed.), Brain Tumor MRI Image Segmentation using Deep Learning Techniques, pp. 161–182, Elsevier Publications, London, UK, 2021.

15. Gupta, P., Bhachawat, S., Dhyani, K., Tripathy, B. K.: A study of gene characteristics and their applications using deep learning, in: Handbook of Machine Learning Applications for Genomics, to be published by Springer Nature, Berlin, Germany, 2021.

16. Bhardwaj, P., Guhan, T., Tripathy, B. K.: Computational Biology in the lens of CNN, in: Roy S.S., et al. (Eds.), Handbook of Machine Learning Applications for Genomics, to be published by Springer Nature, Berlin, Germany, 2021.

17. Maheswari, K., Shaha, A., Arya, D., Tripathy, B. K., Rajkumar, R.: Convolutional neural networks: a bottom-up approach, in: Bhattacharyya S., Hassanian A. E., Saha S., Tripathy B.K. (eds.), Deep Learning Research with Engineering Applications, De Gruyter Publications, Berlin, Germany, 2020, pp. 21–50.

18. Deng, J., Dong, W., Socher, R., Li, L.J., Li, K., Fei, L.: ImageNet: A large-scale hierarchical image database. Proceedings of the 2009 IEEE conference on computer vision and pattern recognition, Miami, FL, United States, pp. 248–255 (2009).

19. Krizhevsky, A., Sutskever, I., Hinton, G.E.: ImageNet classification with deep convolutional neural networks. Advances in Neural Information Processing Systems 25(1), 1097–1105 (2012).

20. Zhou, B., Lapedriza, A., Xiao, J., Torralba, A., Oliva, A.: Learning deep features for scene recognition using places database. Advances in Neural Information Processing Systems 27(1), 487–495 (2014).

21. Pan, S.J., Yang, Q.: A survey on transfer learning. IEEE Transactions on Knowledge and Data Engineering 22(10), 1345–1359 (2010). https://doi.org/10.1109/TKDE.2009.191.

22. Yosinski, J., Clune, J., Bengio, Y., Lipson, H.: How transferable are features in deep neural networks? 27th international conference on neural information processing systems, Lake Tahoe, NV, United States, 2 (ICIP), pp. 3320–3328 (2015).

23. Girshick, R., Donahue, J., Darrell, T., Malik, J.: Rich feature hierarchies for accurate object detection and semantic segmentation. Proceedings of the IEEE conference on computer vision and pattern recognition, Columbus, OH, United States, pp. 580–587 (2014).

24. Lin, M., Chen, Q., Yan, S.: Network in network, arXiv preprint arXiv: 1312.4400 (2013).

25. Simonyan, K., Zisserman, A.: Very deep convolutional networks for large-scale image recognition, arXiv preprint arXiv: 1409.1556 (2014).
26. Szegedy, C., Ioffe, S., Vanhoucke, V.: Inception-v4, inception-ResNet and the impact of residual connections on learning. Thirty-first AAAI conference on artificial intelligence, San Francisco, CA, United States, pp. 4278–4284 (2017).
27. Huang, G., Liu, Z., Van Der Maaten, L., Weinberger, K.Q.: Densely connected convolutional networks. Proceedings of the IEEE conference on computer vision and pattern recognition, Honolulu, HI, United States, pp. 4700–4708 (2017).

18 COVID-19 Confirmed Case Prediction after Vaccination Using Deep Learning Models

Nigam Patel
Department of Information Technology,
Government Engineering College
Gandhinagar, Gujarat, India

*Sahil Kumar Narola, Shubham Chaudhari,
and Vishwa Dave*
Department of Electronics and Communication,
Lalbhai Dalpatbhai College of Engineering
Ahmedabad, Gujarat, India

CONTENTS

DOI: 10.1201/9781003320340-18

18.1 INTRODUCTION

Severe acute respiratory syndrome coronavirus 2 (SARS-CoV-2) and novel coronavirus, also known as COVID-19, has infected 151661490 people and claimed 3193123 lives as of 30 April 2021 [1, 2]. The disease was first diagnosed in December 2019 in Wuhan, China, and the name "COVID-19" was given by the World Health Organization (WHO) afterward. Current research suggests that the virus spreads mainly between people who have been in close contact. The severity of this disease can range from mild or no symptoms to shortness of breath, pneumonia, or permanent damage to the lungs, heart, and other organs [3]. Shereen et al. investigated the origins of COVID-19 and findings on the comparative study of coronavirus emergence and dissemination, primary reservoirs and hosts of coronaviruses, characteristics and entrance mechanisms of human coronaviruses, genomic variants in SARS-CoV-2, as well as the critical barriers to research advancement, prospective COVID-19 therapy options, and vaccines [4]. COVID-19 has affected not only the mental and physical health of humans but the economy, culture, politics, and education have also been affected drastically. As of now, solutions to this pandemic are precautionary measures taken by every individual, government restrictions, social distancing, and sanitization. Due to the lack of an absolute cure for the disease, basic treatment, hospitalization, ventilation, and various therapies are currently being used. In late 2020, some vaccines that have been approved by the WHO started being used for vaccination. The UK and the USA started vaccination on 8th and 15th December, respectively, and the effect of the same is noticeable in the curve of the confirmed cases which started to decline.

Researchers from different fields are trying to contribute as much as they can in this complex and hazardous situation. Many studies have been conducted with various methods and models, such as Susceptible-Exposed-Infectious and Recovered (SEIR)-based models [5–7], statistical models [8–13], and deep learning models [13–19], to investigate the trend of COVID-19 cases.

COVID-19 confirmed cases are analyzed using long short-term memory (LSTM) and gated recurrent units (GRU) deep learning models to forecast the time-series data. The dataset used in this study contains data from six countries, including daily new confirmed cases, the total confirmed cases, daily new vaccinations, and total vaccinations. The data includes 242 samples from 1 September 2020 to 30 April 2021. Since January 2021, most countries have started vaccination, which helps in getting a clear trend after vaccination and with the time-series analysis of vaccination effects. To determine the performance of these models, metrics such as mean absolute error (MAE) and root mean squared error (RMSE) are used.

Pandemics are generally exponential in nature, and the prediction of the same has always been a challenge for researchers [20]. Our research is also being conducted with the motive of finding out clear estimates about COVID-19 cases after the vaccination and which deep neural network (DNN)-based model performs better with time-series data for training and predictions.

18.2 LITERATURE REVIEW

We will look at the available literature on pandemic prediction using various approaches in this section. Many research initiatives have been undertaken in recent times to estimate the COVID-19 cases. Some researchers worked on the

SEIR model [5–7]. He et al. [5] studied the SEIR model based on the data from Hubei province. The particle swarm optimization algorithm was used to estimate the model parameters for the SEIR model to fit the real solution. The authors looked into the dynamics of SEIR and discovered that it varies upon selected parameters. Mwalili et al. [6] modified the SEIR model using the Runge-Kutta technique, integrating environmental and social distancing elements. The reproduction number was derived using a generation matrix methodology. The authors investigated how quarantining contacts and isolating patients might help prevent the spread of COVID-19. Yang et al. [7] examined the population migration data from China after 23 January 2020 to create an epidemic graph using the SEIR model and then utilized an LSTM-based model to forecast fresh infection peaks.

Roimi et al. [8] provided a study on determining predicted cases of COVID-19 and hospital utilization based on individual characteristics. The model forecasts the patient's illness trajectory into critical, severe, or moderate clinical states. It was observed that their model accurately predicts cases of total and critical care measured by MAE. The data used for this research was provided by the Israeli ministry of health on hospitalized patients from 1 March 2020 to 2 May 2020 was used in this study.

Time-series forecasting using various statistical and deep learning models has been used in many studies. Khan et al. [9] worked on ARIMA and NAR-based models for time-series forecasting of COVID-19 cases in India. The models were trained on a dataset of two months and validated on a dataset of ten days. The ARIMA model (1,1,0) on Bayesian information criteria and the NAR model consisting of ten neurons with Levenberg-Marquardt optimization were also studied. Kim [10] studied two statistical models, ARIMA and GARCH, and a deep learning model, LSTM DNN. The author found that LSTM DNN outperforms statistical models in terms of MAE and RMSE; a dataset of 420 days was used, provided by WHO. Singh et al. [11] worked on a hybrid methodology, including ARIMA and discrete wavelet decomposition. They observed the hybrid model performed well rather than the simple ARIMA, and the authors used a dataset of 82 days. Singh et al. [12] and other researchers focused on COVID-19 case prediction using ARIMA and least square SVM; here, data of five countries, including Italy, Spain, France, UK, and USA were collected from 21 January 2020 to 9 May 2020 and predicted cases for one month period. Kirbaş et al. [13] used ARIMA, NARNN, and LSTM models, with six performance metrics like MSE, PSNR, RMSE, NRMSE, MAPE, and SMAPE. The authors found that LSTM performed best in terms of accuracy. The dataset of European countries was used to predict for 14 days and found that cases were declining.

Shahid et al. [14] worked on the prediction of cases based on models like Bi-LSTM, GRU, SVR, and ARIMA. The authors measured performance by the RMSE, MAE, and R2 score indices, which indicated that Bi-LSTM outperformed. The dataset used in this study was from 22 to 27 January 2020 and contained 158 samples. For forecasting, Zeroul et al. [15] used GRU, LSTM, Bi-LSTM, RNN, and VAE. The dataset covers six countries, Italy, Spain, France, China, the USA, and Australia, and spans a period of 148 days, ending on 17 June 2020. The researchers said VAE outperformed other deep learning approaches. Rasjid et al. [16] did forecasting on the dataset of Indonesia provided by Humanitarian Data Exchange (HDX) for 147 days with models like Savitzky-Golay smoothing and LSTM neural network. The authors found that LSTM-NN performed better by plotting inclination with the curve. Chimmula et al. [17] investigated LSTM to forecast cases. The data used for this research was till 31 March 2020 in Canada. The model predicted 2-, 4-, 6-, 8-, 10-, 12-, and 14-day predictions for two successive days. Pal et al. [18] did the country-wise risk prediction with shallow LSTM based on NN with Bayesian optimization and designed a country-specific network. They proposed a shallow LSTM model with few layers, search space definition, network search, and fuzzy rule-based risk categorization. They used the dataset of the number of recovered cases and number of deaths later combined with weather data. Arora et al. [19] worked on the case study of Indian states for predicting COVID-19 confirmed cases with deep LSTM, convolution LSTM, and bi-directional LSTM. MAPE was used as a performance indicator. In their work, the error rate of 3% on daily and 8% on weekly cases was observed. Dataset used in this chapter was stochastic in nature and duration from 14 March to 8 May 2020 with testing data from 9 May to 14 May 2020. Vadyala et al. [21] developed a K-means-LSTM-based model to forecast the confirmed cases. The authors used data from Louisiana, USA, and found good accuracy in the K-means-LSTM-based model compared to SEIR, but their model can predict very short-term trends only. Dealing with the data, which is large and contains many records, is challenging.

18.3 PROPOSED APPROACH

Our approach is divided into four parts. The first part is the data availability and preprocessing. The second part is about methods that have been applied for prediction. The third part consists of error-evaluating methods to validate the performance measure of the models. The last part shows the results of the experiment.

18.3.1 DATA AVAILABILITY AND PREPROCESSING

The data of per day new cases and total cases is required for forecasting the confirmed cases of COVID-19. The dataset of the same was gathered from the ourworldindata. com website [2]. This includes daily new confirmed cases, total confirmed cases, daily new vaccination and total vaccination, and many more features. It contains the data of 242 days from 1 September 2020 to 30 April 2021. Data from 15 January 2021 to 30 April 2021, a total of 105 days is used for testing purposes.

For data preprocessing, we used feature scaling. It is generally implemented on the independent feature (i.e., total_cases and new_cases) of our dataset. It normalizes the data within a particular range (e.g., In this case (0, 1)). The main advantage of feature scaling is to increase the calculation speed of the network while training.

$$X_{\text{normalised}} = \frac{(X_i - X_{min})}{(X_{max} - X_{min})} \tag{18.1}$$

18.3.2 METHODOLOGY

Deep learning is a subset of artificial intelligence. In deep learning, recurrent neural network (RNN) is widely used for time-series prediction. To begin with, both

LSTM [22] and GRU are RNNs [23]. The main benefit of utilizing these RNN architectures is that they can deliver high-accuracy predicted results with sequential data that simple neural networks and other machine learning algorithms cannot. Another aspect to consider is that these two methods were created to address the classic RNN's fundamental problem of vanishing and exploding gradients [24], where problems regarding the weights of neurons occur. The cell state or memory cell is the central concept in both GRUs and LSTMs. It enables both networks to keep any information without suffering significant loss. Gates are also included in the networks, which help to control the flow of data to the cell state. These gates can determine which data in a series is significant and which is not. Due to these properties, we have developed both LSTM- and GRU-based models to predict the confirmed cases of COVID-19.

18.3.2.1 LSTM Neural Network

A RNN with an LSTM cell is a special category of DNN. It works well for a variety of issues, including time-series prediction, speech recognition, handwriting recognition, and others. The LSTM network is made up of some layers which contain LSTM cells. The forget gate, input gate, and output gate are the three gates of the basic LSTM cell. Each cell has a memory state C_t and a hidden state h_t. Figure 18.1 illustrates the architecture of the LSTM cell.

Forget gate. This gate determines which information should be discarded from the memory of our cell. It is composed of the current input step X_t as well as the previously hidden state h_{t-1}.

Input gate. This gate determines what information should be added to our memory. It is also composed of the previously hidden state h_{t-1} and current input step X_t.

Output gate. It determines what should be the output of the current step.

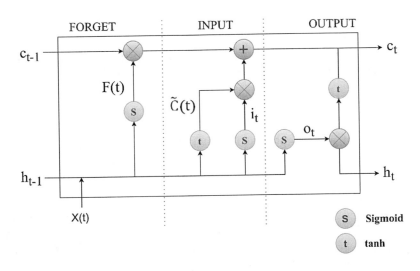

FIGURE 18.1   LSTM cell architecture.

Equations that implement these gates are given below:

$$F_t = \sigma\left(W_{xf} \cdot X_t + W_{hf} \cdot h_{t-1} + b_f\right) \qquad (18.2)$$

$$i_t = \sigma\left(W_{xi} \cdot X_t + W_{hi} \cdot h_{t-1} + b_i\right) \qquad (18.3)$$

$$O_t = \sigma\left(W_{xo} \cdot X_t + W_{ho} \cdot h_{t-1} + b_o\right) \qquad (18.4)$$

$$\tilde{C}_t = tanh\left(W_{xc} \cdot X_t + W_{hc} \cdot h_{t-1} + b_c\right) \qquad (18.5)$$

$$C_t = F_t \otimes C_{t-1} + i_t \otimes C_t \qquad (18.6)$$

$$h_t = O_t \otimes tanh(C_t) \qquad (18.7)$$

S = sigmoid

$$\sigma(x) = \frac{1}{1+e^{-x}} \qquad (18.8)$$

t = hyperbolic tangent

$$tanh(x) = \frac{e^x - e^{-x}}{e^x + e^{-x}} \qquad (18.9)$$

C_t is known as a cell state. It is a memory of LSTM. It contains all the information which was learned and also contains unnecessary information which is not useful for the current time step output. It is updated by the forget gate and the input gate. h_t is the hidden state or output of the current cell. The variable W_{xf}, W_{xo}, W_{xi}, W_{xc} are the weight metrics of the current input, and W_{hf}, W_{ho}, W_{hi}, W_{hc} are the weight metrics of previous hidden states, and b_f, b_i, b_o, b_c are the biased terms.

18.3.2.2 Stacked LSTM

Multiple layers of LSTM cells form stacked LSTM. The key benefit of stacking the LSTM layers is that sometimes it improves the model's performance. This method is also utilized in this chapter. The architecture of stacked LSTM is shown in Figure 18.2.

18.3.2.3 GRU Neural Network

The GRU is an LSTM variation. GRU is similar to LSTM except that it has only two gates, a reset gate and an update gate, whereas LSTM has three gates. It does not have a distinct cell state C_t like LSTM. It just has a single hidden state h_t. Although GRU is not as complicated as LSTM, it is quicker than LSTM in model training. GRU is also suitable for small datasets rather than LSTM. Figure 18.3 illustrates the architecture of the GRU cell.

Reset gate. This gate is utilized by the model to determine how much information from the past should be forgotten. A fresh vector will be passed into the update gate.

Update gate. The update gate aids the model in determining how much previous data (from previous time steps) needs to be passed on to the next time step. It changes the value for the new state of h_{t-1} to h_t.

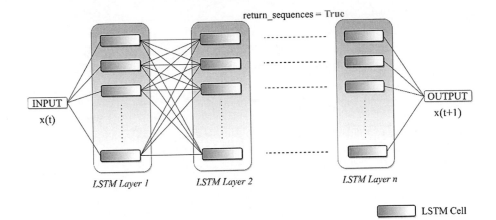

FIGURE 18.2   Stacked LSTM architecture.

The equations of these gates are given below:

$$Z_t = \sigma\left(W_{xz} \cdot X_t + W_{hz} \cdot h_{t-1} + b_z\right) \tag{18.10}$$

$$r_t = \sigma\left(W_{xr} \cdot X_t + W_{hr} \cdot h_{t-1} + b_r\right) \tag{18.11}$$

$$\tilde{h}_t = \tanh\left(W_{xh} \cdot X_t + W_{hh} \cdot h_{t-1} + b_h\right) \tag{18.12}$$

$$h_t = \left(1 - Z_t\right) \otimes h_{t-1} + Z_t \otimes \tilde{h}_t \tag{18.13}$$

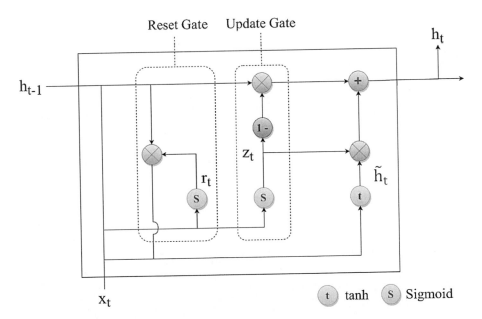

FIGURE 18.3   GRU cell architecture.

18.3.2.4   Stacked GRU Neural Network

The stacked GRU network can be used to improve the performance of our model like the stacked LSTM. In addition, the design of stacked GRU is similar to that of stacked LSTM, with the exception that GRU cells are used instead of LSTM cells.

18.3.3   PERFORMANCE MEASURES

There are several methods for evaluating the deep learning model's performance [25]. As we get the optimum results for the model, RMSE and MAE methods are used to validate our models. Both MAE and RMSE are used to calculate the average prediction error of a mode; we have used both in our circumstances. These two metrics provide average predictions error for total confirmed cases and new confirmed cases. It has the same units as the dependent variable, allowing us to quickly analyze our model in comparison to MSE and other statistical methods (kappa, etc.) of performance measures. RMSE is referred to as the L2 norm and MAE is referred to as the L1 norm. Both are effective methods for evaluating the model's performance. In the situation of extremely high precision, where the high error is considerable, RMSE is preferable to MAE for evaluating performance. We may observe from the RMSE equation that the large errors are given more weight compared to small errors. Another key point is that RMSE is a differential function that makes it easy to perform mathematical calculations. Particularly, the RMSE is used to calculate the difference between the actual value and the value predicted by the model. It calculates the root of the average squared difference between the predicted and actual cases. MAE is also used to evaluate the performance of regression models. It calculates the absolute value of the difference between actual and predicted cases each day.

Equations of RMSE and MAE are given below:

$$\sqrt{\sum_{i=1}^{n} \frac{\left(y_{actual} - y_{predicted}\right)^2}{n}} \tag{18.14}$$

$$\text{MAE} = \sum_{i=1}^{n} \frac{\left|y_{actual} - y_{predicted}\right|}{n} \tag{18.15}$$

where y_{actual} is the number of actual cases per day, $y_{predicted}$ is the number of predicted cases per day, and n is the number of days. Figure 18.4 demonstrates the basic approach from training to testing our model for both LSTM and GRU.

18.3.4   RESULTS

The results of our research experiment are mentioned in this section.

18.3.4.1   Device and Platform Availability

All of the training is carried out on an Intel Core i5 8th Gen computer with 8GB of RAM. Python 3.7.6 was used to train the models. The required Python Libraries, as

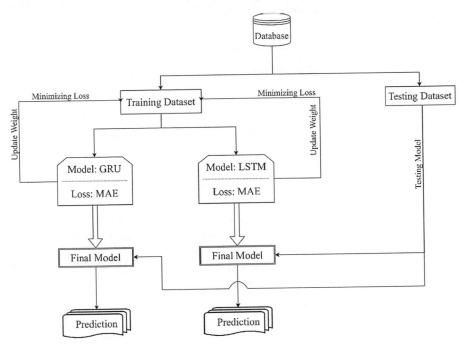

FIGURE 18.4 Flowchart of the proposed approach.

well as the version we utilized in our training, are TensorFlow – 1.14.0, Sklearn – 0.22.1, Keras – 2.3.1, Matplotlib – 3.1.3, Pandas – 1.0.1, and NumPy – 1.18.1.

18.3.4.2 Target Countries

These models forecast total cases and new cases per day in six countries (i.e., Brazil, Canada, India, Israel, the UK, and the USA). The dataset we used for training the model is of 242 days starting from 1 September 2020 to 30 April 2021. The date from this period is taken into consideration because it includes the most recent vaccination data. The goal of this prediction is to see how the overall number of daily cases in the above-mentioned countries changes after the vaccination starts.

18.3.4.3 Training and Testing

These models forecast total cases as well as daily new cases for various countries (see Section 18.3.4.2). As mentioned in Section 18.3.2, LSTM and GRU are implemented to train the models. If the performance of the model with single-layer LSTM/ GRU is not much adequate, stacked LSTM/stacked GRU (e.g., the UK, Israel) can be used. The models' parameters are also fine-tuned to get the best performance out of it. Tables 18.1 and 18.2 list several significant parameters and their values for total confirmed cases. The initialization of the connection weights is a significant stage in the training of any neural network. Weight initialization is essential for avoiding vanishing and exploding gradient problems. Consequently, it can affect the performance of the models; hence, the weights must be initialized. In our models, we have utilized glorot_uniform weight initializer. Another key component of any neural

TABLE 18.1

Parameter Configuration of LSTM Models

	Brazil	Canada	Israel	India	UK	USA
Time step	25	5	5	5	25	5
LSTM layer	1	1	2	1	2	1
LSTM units per layer	150	100	100	100	200	150
Epoch	30	30	30	30	30	30
Batch size	35	35	35	35	35	35
Learning rate	0.001	0.001	0.001	0.001	0.001	0.001

network's training is the optimizer. The job of an optimizer is to update weights, which reduces the loss function. The Adam optimizer suited the best in this model out of all other optimizers.

18.3.4.4 Models' Performance

In this section, we have mentioned the experimental output results of the models. LSTM and GRU models are used for prediction, while RMSE and MAE are used to evaluate the performance of this model. These models are tested on data from 15 January to 30 April 2021 (105 days). Most countries had begun the vaccination during this period. Figure 18.5 shows the graph of actual new cases vs predicted new cases by LSTM and GRU for Brazil, Canada, India, Israel, the UK, and the USA. It is visible that new cases are increasing in most countries, except in Israel, the UK, and the USA; this might be due to early vaccination. In Table 18.3, a comparison of LSTM and GRU is demonstrated in terms of RMSE and MAE measures for countries Brazil, Canada, India, Israel, the UK, and the USA on testing data. It can be observed that they produce significantly lower errors for most of the cases, and GRU is slightly more efficient.

In Figure 18.6, total cases of COVID-19 predicted by LSTM and GRU vs actual total cases are plotted for considered six countries on testing data.

In Table 18.4, a comparison of the models concerning RMSE and MAE on total confirmed cases for considered six countries is given. For total confirmed cases, GRU outperforms LSTM and produces lower errors for most of the countries.

TABLE 18.2

Parameter Configuration of GRU Models

	Brazil	Canada	Israel	India	UK	USA
Time step	25	5	5	5	25	5
GRU layer	1	1	1	1	2	1
GRU units per layer	100	60	60	100	150	100
Epoch	30	30	30	30	30	30
Batch size	35	35	35	35	35	35
Learning rate	0.001	0.001	0.001	0.001	0.001	0.001

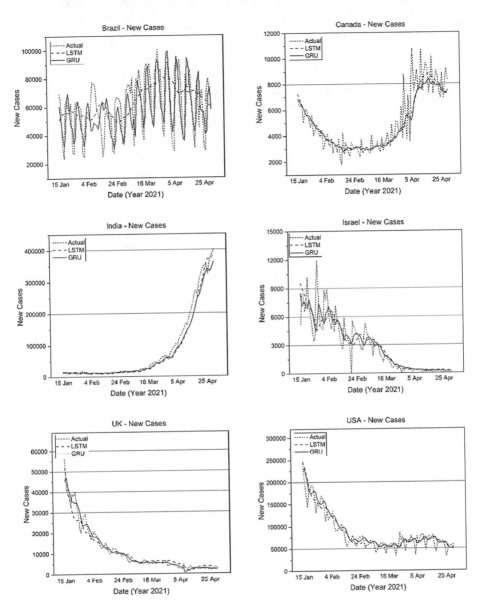

FIGURE 18.5 Predicted new daily confirmed cases with actual new cases in six considered countries for both LSTM and GRU.

18.4 RESULTS ANALYSIS AND DISCUSSION

We have investigated the deep learning models to see if they can predict confirmed cases of COVID-19 with a data-driven approach. It demonstrates that both models can adapt to this nonlinear, time-series data for the countries under consideration. In the case of Israel, the experiment shows that the GRU model outperforms the LSTM

TABLE 18.3

RMSE and MAE according to the Models for New Cases in Six Countries

Country	Model	RMSE	MAE
Brazil	LSTM	19799	16062
	GRU	16167	13164
Canada	LSTM	1045	727
	GRU	1119	752
India	LSTM	16503	10586
	GRU	17984	10914
Israel	LSTM	1380	833
	GRU	1264	770
UK	LSTM	2989	1899
	GRU	2392	1477
USA	LSTM	16477	11840
	GRU	16362	11884

model in terms of performance measures such as RMSE and MAE (1264, 770) for daily new cases (Table 18.3). On the other hand, in the case of Canada, LSTM performs better than GRU with the same performance measures (1045, 727) for daily new cases (Table 18.3). GRU has also been found to be better at adapting to daily case trends over LSTM. One more fact, there are fluctuations in predictions due to factors like a sudden change in confirmed COVID-19 cases, different population densities, and the different numbers of cases across the countries. For instance, due to lower confirmed total cases, models of Canada (5691, 5107) (Table 18.4) and Israel (9602, 7227) (Table 18.4) have the lowest amount of errors in terms of numbers about the prediction of new cases for RMSE and MAE, respectively, whereas in countries like India (347734, 193523) (Table 18.3) and Brazil (107216, 62443) (Table 18.3), due to higher confirmed total cases and exponential rise in cases, the numbers in error seem to be a bit larger on the scale of the prediction, but still it is inclined with the curve. Furthermore, by making small changes in the training process of these models, we can forecast confirmed COVID-19 cases for desired time intervals and hence determine the future trajectory.

Some research has been done to predict the confirmed cases of COVID-19 using deep learning models [13–19]. Direct comparison with these studies seems challenging due to the datasets used which contain different parameters, times, sizes, and countries. These models were used to forecast cases before the vaccination started. It is noticeable that the results of our models compared to Zeroual et al. [15] are much better in terms of MAE and RMSE, as mentioned in Table 18.5. Because their models were only tested for 17 days and countries were not common, we only compared the USA's data. It's worth noting that even with big testing data our models are pretty accurate, and this is almost comparable with most of the existing studies. In such a massive outbreak, higher accuracy in predictions is desirable because the number

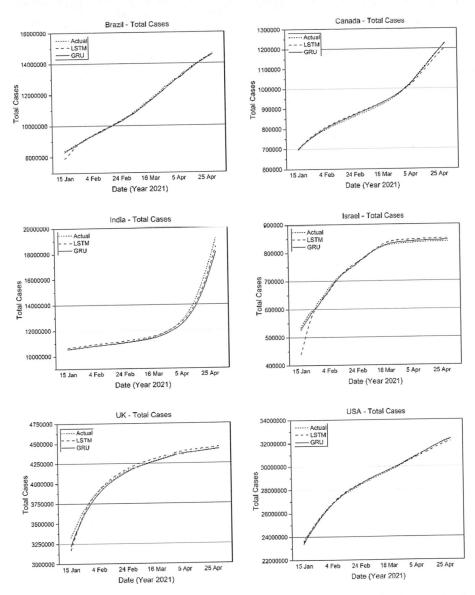

FIGURE 18.6 Predicted total confirmed cases with actual new cases in six considered countries for both LSTM and GRU.

of people getting infected is large. With low errors, predictions can be more beneficial. Most of the recent studies mentioned in the literature survey show theoretical approaches and a very high number of errors in predictions. Some of the causes could be data utilized before vaccination, different models that may or may not be efficient in time-series analysis, and different orders and parameters.

According to the data we have gathered [2], the daily confirmed cases of COVID-19 tend to decrease significantly when the vaccination rate reaches around 20% in

TABLE 18.4

RMSE and MAE according to the Model for Total Cases in Six Countries

Country	Model	RMSE	MAE
Brazil	LSTM	107216	62443
	GRU	70792	62863
Canada	LSTM	11603	10189
	GRU	5691	5107
India	LSTM	236445	167059
	GRU	347734	193523
Israel	LSTM	7687	6577
	GRU	9602	7227
UK	LSTM	38226	29047
	GRU	31475	19673
USA	LSTM	103870	91126
	GRU	79978	62783

countries like Israel, the UK, and the USA. We can expect from this observation that COVID-19 cases will decline as more people get vaccinated. Due to the low errors and accurate predictability of these models, it would be helpful for the people in authority in the decision-making of future events. Also, other researchers and science enthusiasts can take it as a reference and can gain some insights into using different deep learning algorithms and what are the benefits of using these particular techniques or how our chapter is more reliable in accuracy aspects as we have studied and analyzed many research papers for thorough guidance.

18.5 CONCLUSIONS AND FUTURE WORK

In this study, we have proposed LSTM- and GRU-based deep learning models with optimal parameters to predict the confirmed cases of COVID-19. Our models show promising results. We used the latest dataset, including the countries that started vaccination early. As a pandemic is exponential in nature, a sudden rise in cases is

TABLE 18.5

Comparison with Existing Studies

Comparison	Data	Model	USA RMSE	USA MAE
Our models	1 January–30 April 2021 (4 months)	LSTM	103870	91126
		GRU	79977	62783
Existing models [15]	1–17 June 2020 (17 days)	LSTM	1129183	1123909
		GRU	4369108	4240145

a bit of a challenge to predict in some countries because multiple factors affect the spread of disease, like social distancing, masking, sanitization, government restrictions, immunity of an individual, and, much more still, the performance of our models is impressive. The data used for testing was from the period when vaccination started. We observed that GRU performs better than LSTM-based RNN in most cases, but both the models are pretty accurate in error measures such as MAE and RMSE. These models are adaptive in nature; the dynamic incorporation of data is the main feature compared to total cases, and they produce low errors. Hence, they can learn on their own given the continuous time-series data provided; this eliminates the need to retrain the models for new data. Government agencies can use these models to forecast the upcoming confirmed cases of COVID-19, which will help them take precautionary measures, and medical facilities can be available at the time. Furthermore, in the future, God forbid, if such kinds of casualties occur, researchers and scientists of that time can refer to COVID-19-related articles that can help them to analyze the situation then.

As a part of future work, we plan to expand this study with more elements like hospitalization period, required medical care, forecasting the daily number of deaths, lung damage recovery with other meta-learning methods, generative adversarial networks, and other methods for time-series analysis.

REFERENCES

1. Coronavirus Update (Live): 151,661,490 Cases and 3,193,123 Deaths from COVID-19 Virus Pandemic – Worldometer (2021). Available: https://www.worldometers.info/coronavirus/ [Accessed 1-May-2021].
2. Covid.ourworldindata.org (2021). [Online]. Available: https://covid.ourworldindata.org/data/owid-covid-data.csv. [Accessed: 1-May-2021].
3. "Getting your workplace ready for COVID-19: How COVID-19 spreads", Who.int (2021). [Online]. Available: https://www.who.int/publications-detail-redirect/getting-your-workplace-ready-for-covid-19-how-covid-19-spreads. [Accessed: 1-May-2021].
4. M. Shereen, S. Khan, A. Kazmi, N. Bashir and R. Siddique: COVID-19 infection: Emergence, transmission, and characteristics of human coronaviruses, Journal of Advanced Research, vol. 24, pp. 91–98, Available: 10.1016/j.jare.2020.03.005 (2020).
5. S. He, Y. Peng and K. Sun: SEIR modeling of the COVID-19 and its dynamics, Nonlinear Dynamics, vol. 101, no. 3, pp. 1667–1680, Available: 10.1007/s11071-020-05743-y (2020).
6. S. Mwalili, M. Kimathi, V. Ojiambo, D. Gathungu and R. Mbogo: SEIR model for COVID-19 dynamics incorporating the environment and social distancing, BMC Research Notes, vol. 13, no. 1, Available: 10.1186/s13104-020-05192-1 (2020).
7. Z. Yang et al: Modified SEIR and AI prediction of the epidemics trend of COVID-19 in China under public health interventions, Journal of Thoracic Disease, vol. 12, no. 3, pp. 165–174, Available: 10.21037/jtd.2020.02.64 (2020).
8. M. Roimi et al.: Development and validation of a machine learning model predicting illness trajectory and hospital utilization of COVID-19 patients: A nationwide study, Journal of the American Medical Informatics Association, Available: 10.1093/jamia/ocab005 (2021).
9. F. Khan and R. Gupta: ARIMA and NAR based prediction model for time series analysis of COVID-19 cases in India, Journal of Safety Science and Resilience, vol. 1, no. 1, pp. 12–18, Available: 10.1016/j.jnlssr.2020.06.007 (2020).

10. M. Kim: Prediction of COVID-19 confirmed cases after vaccination: Based on statistical and deep learning models, SciMedicine Journal, vol. 3, no. 2, pp. 153–165, Available: 10.28991/scimedj-2021-0302-7 (2021).

11. S. Singh, K. Parmar, J. Kumar and S. Makkhan: Development of new hybrid model of discrete wavelet decomposition and autoregressive integrated moving average (ARIMA) models in application to one month forecast the casualties cases of COVID-19, Chaos, Solitons & Fractals, vol. 135, p. 109866, Available: 10.1016/j.chaos.2020.109866 (2020).

12. S. Singh, K. Parmar, S. Makkhan, J. Kaur, S. Peshoria and J. Kumar: Study of ARIMA and least square support vector machine (LS-SVM) models for the prediction of SARS-CoV-2 confirmed cases in the most affected countries, Chaos, Solitons & Fractals, vol. 139, p. 110086, Available: 10.1016/j.chaos.2020.110086 (2020).

13. İ. Kırbaş, A. Sözen, A. Tuncer and F. Kazancıoğlu: Comparative analysis and forecasting of COVID-19 cases in various European countries with ARIMA, NARNN and LSTM approaches Chaos, Solitons & Fractals, vol. 138, p. 110015, Available: 10.1016/j.chaos.2020.110015 (2020).

14. F. Shahid, A. Zameer and M. Muneeb: Predictions for COVID-19 with deep learning models of LSTM, GRU and Bi-LSTM, Chaos, Solitons & Fractals, vol. 140, p. 110212, Available: 10.1016/j.chaos.2020.110212 (2020).

15. A. Zeroual, F. Harrou, A. Dairi and Y. Sun: Deep learning methods for forecasting COVID-19 time-Series data: A comparative study, Chaos, Solitons & Fractals, vol. 140, p. 110121, Available: 10.1016/j.chaos.2020.110121 (2020).

16. Z. Rasjid, R. Setiawan and A. Effendi: A Comparison: Prediction of death and infected COVID-19 cases in Indonesia using time series smoothing and LSTM neural network, Procedia Computer Science, vol. 179, pp. 982–988, Available: 10.1016/j.procs.2021.01.102 (2021).

17. V. Chimmula and L. Zhang: Time series forecasting of COVID-19 transmission in Canada using LSTM networks, Chaos, Solitons & Fractals, vol. 135, p. 109864, Available: 10.1016/j.chaos.2020.109864 (2020).

18. R. Pal, A. Sekh, S. Kar and D. Prasad: Neural network based country wise risk prediction of COVID-19, Applied Sciences, vol. 10, no. 18, p. 6448, Available: 10.3390/app10186448 (2020).

19. P. Arora, H. Kumar and B. Panigrahi: Prediction and analysis of COVID-19 positive cases using deep learning models: A descriptive case study of India, Chaos, Solitons & Fractals, vol. 139, p. 110017, Available: 10.1016/j.chaos.2020.110017 (2020).

20. Y. Hu, J. Jacob, G. Parker, D. Hawkes, J. Hurst and D. Stoyanov: The challenges of deploying artificial intelligence models in a rapidly evolving pandemic. Nature Machine Intelligence, vol. 2, pp. 298–300. Available: 10.1038/s42256-020-0185-2 (2020).

21. S. Vadyala, S. Betgeri, E. Sherer, and A. Amritphale: Prediction of the number of COVID-19 confirmed cases based on K-means-LSTM. Array, vol. 11, p. 100085, Available: 10.1016/j.array.2021.100085 (2021).

22. F. A. Gers, J. Schmidhuber, and F. Cummins,: Learning to forget: Continual prediction with LSTM. Neural computation, vol. 12, no. 10, pp. 2451–2471 (2000).

23. J. Chung, et al.: Empirical evaluation of gated recurrent neural networks on sequence modeling., arXiv preprint, arXiv:1412.3555 (2014).

24. R. Pascanu, T. Mikolov, & Y. Bengio,: On the difficulty of training recurrent neural networks. In International conference on machine learning, pp. 1310–1318, PMLR (2013).

25. A. Botchkarev: Performance metrics (error measures) in machine learning regression, forecasting and prognostics: Properties and typology, arXiv preprint, arXiv:1809.03006. (2018).

19 Recognition Model for Facial Expression Using Machine Learning

Shanmuganathan Chandrasekaran
and Menaka Suman
SRM Institute of Science and Technology
Ramapuram, Chennai, India

N. V. S. K. Vijayalakshmi Kathari
Annamalai University
Chidambaram, India

CONTENTS

19.1 INTRODUCTION

19.1.1 IMAGE PROCESSING

There has been a great deal of progress in face detection and recognition in the last few years, but many problems remain unsolved. Research on face detection must deal with many challenging problems, especially when dealing with outdoor

DOI: 10.1201/9781003320340-19

illumination, pose variation with large rotation angles, low image quality, low resolution, occlusion, and background changes in complex real-life scenes.

Image of pre-processing is a common name for operations with images at the lowest level of abstraction. Its input and output are intensity images. The aim of pre-processing is an improvement of the image data that suppresses unwanted distortions or enhances some image features important for further processing. When an image is corrupted/noisy, it is restored to its original state. Errors include motion blur and camera focusing issues as well as noise in the audio and video streams. It differs from image enhancement in that the latter is meant to accentuate elements of the image that make it more attractive to the spectator, but not necessary to provide realistic data from a scientific point of view. For example, "Imaging packages" do not employ a priori models of the process that generated the image. By surrendering some resolution, noise may be successfully eliminated from images via image enhancement, but this is not an option in many situations. In a fluorescence microscope, the z-direction resolution is already poor. Recovering the item requires the use of more complex image processing algorithms. For example, the de-convolution method is a method for picture restoration: increasing resolution, especially in the direction of travel; removing noise; and improving contrast. This would be followed by (low-level) feature extraction in order to find lines, regions, and potentially places with particular textures. For example, automobiles on a road, items on a conveyor belt, or malignant cells under the microscope may all be seen as groupings of these forms. Because an item might seem quite different when seen from multiple angles or under varied illumination, this is an issue with artificial intelligence [1]. Identifying which characteristics belong to which item and which are backdrop or shadows, etc., is another challenge to overcome. When it comes to the human visual system, these activities are carried out mainly subconsciously, but to achieve human-like performance, computers require expert programming and a lot of processing power. A variety of approaches may be used to manipulate data into a picture. One of the most common ways that images are portrayed is through photographic prints, slides, television screens, and movie screens. In a computer, you may process a picture in two ways: visually or digitally.

An image must be reduced to a sequence of numbers before it can be processed digitally. A picture element, or pixel, is an integer that represents the brightness value of an image at a certain point. Even while considerably bigger pictures are becoming more popular, the usual digital image may only contain 250,000 pixels (512×512). Once the image has been digitized, the computer may execute three basic operations on it. Because of this, the output image's pixels are determined by only one input image's pixels. The value of a pixel in the output picture depends on the value of many surrounding pixels in the input image. In a global operation, all of the input picture pixels contribute to a pixel value for the output image based on the global operation.

19.2   RELATED WORKS

19.2.1   IMAGE FEATURE EXTRACTION

By converting the image into the normal coordinate system instead of the global coordinate system, parameter estimation is done based on a current average of shape.

After that, the retrieved features are used to lead to a fall and recalculate the shape parameter vectors until convergence is reached [2]. To find key face regions in images, this technique employs cascaded regression trees. To discriminate among distinct areas of the face, 68 feature points are determined using segmentation results [3, 4].

Figure 19.1a shows the point with different features, and Figure 19.1b shows the face landmark detection using 68 different locations. After the features are in place, the dislocation proportions of these 19 feature locations are calculated using pixel measurements. When it comes to displacement ratios, it's the variation in given pixels in between starting and finishing expressions. Table 19.1 [3] shows the distances that may be determined for each of the 12 categories of distances. Instead of directly using these distances, displacement ratios are utilized since pixel distances change based on the distance between the camera and the human. As illustrated in Figure 19.1a, the author [3] uses just 19 of the 68 recovered features, focusing solely on the eyes, mouth, and brows. After under 3 milliseconds, the regression tree ensemble yielded 68 characteristics. Some algorithm parameters have worked really well.

19.2.2   RATIO OF THE DISPLACEMENT

Once the features are in place, the displaced proportions among these 19 feature locations are calculated with pixel values. Displacement ratios are defined as the difference in pixel location between the first and last expressions in a picture. Table 19.1 [3] illustrates the distances that may be calculated for each of the 12 distance categories. Because pixel distances change based on the distance between the camera and the human, displacement ratios are used instead of using these values directly.

The iBug-300W data set, which contains approximately 7,000 pictures, and the CK+ data set, which contains 593 facial expression sequences from 123 different people, were used in this work [5].

19.2.3   MACHINE LEARNING ALGORITHM

Now that the data set contains the essential properties, it is time to employ a good classification technique. This is the most crucial stage in data analysis. When it comes to human expression classification, the use of support vector machines (SVMs) is almost solely restricted to multi-class categorization [6–8]. Some of them are used in combination with other approaches for extracting features [7].

19.2.4   SUPPORT VECTOR MACHINE

Most powerful classification methods are based on SVMs. Ideally, a hyperplane that separates the two classes properly will be found. Margin refers to how much space should be left between two classes in order to avoid any overlap [2]. A greater dimension is used to map data that cannot be separated linearly. In the case of non-linear data, kernel functions such as radial basis function (RBF) and polynomial are utilized [8].

Loconsole et al. [7] used principal component analysis (PCA) to reduce the number of attributes before they were input into SVM. By using an Eigen matrix [9], the

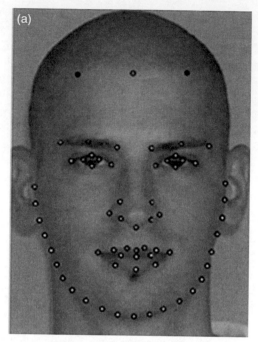

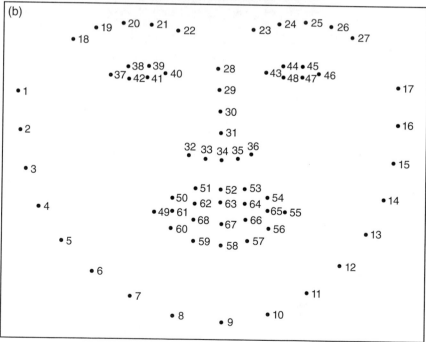

FIGURE 19.1   (a) Feature points of the image. (b) Face landmark detection template.

TABLE 19.1

Distances Computed for Displacement Ratios

Range	Description
R1–R2	Between the upper and lower eyelids of the right and left eye
R3	Left and right eyebrows are separated by a little distance
R4–R5	A distance between the nose tip and the inner tips of the brows on the left and right
R6–R8	A distance between the nose tip and the corners of the lips on the right and left
R7–R9	Measurement of distance between the tip of the middle of the upper and lower lips, and also the nose
R10	The distance between the mouth corners on the right and left
R11	The distance between the midpoints of the upper and lower lips
R12	Circumference of the mouth
R13	Distance between eyes
R14–R15	Distance between eyes and nose

picture feature space is converted to Eigenspace [10]. In addition to kernel design, SVM provides strategies for modifying parameters such as C and y [6]. In this example, C represents a result of misclassification, whereas gamma assists in decision boundary optimization [11]. Both of these parameters have an influence on classifier performance and may be tweaked to achieve the best results in both binary and multi-class classification.

19.3 PROPOSED METHOD

The proposed system stages are explained in the flowchart in Figure 19.2. The first level is the facial identification of an instructor from lecture recordings. Unnecessary frames are removed, keeping only the mid-frames of each emotion [12]. These key frames must be further processed in order to extract deep characteristics from different levels of a region of interest (ROI).

To extract features, the new face ROI is performed. The output of the face detection or facial expression recognition (FER) processes will be the same as the input if there is no classified region. Images of angry, joyful, and neutral individuals make up each person's data collection. The steps are described in the following subsection.

19.3.1 FACE DETECTION

Because it differs from normal FER algorithms, recognizing an instructor's facial expressions is difficult. Face invisibility (for example, when the teacher is writing on the board), occlusion (for example, when the instructor is reading a slide from a laptop and part of his or her face is covered behind the screen), and variable lighting conditions are all problems that must be overcome.

The suggested method is constructed in such a way as to address these issues. Faces of teachers are recognized in a picture using the Viola–Jones face detection

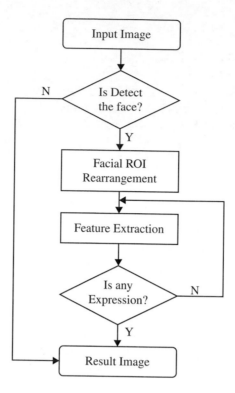

FIGURE 19.2   Flow diagram of proposed systems.

technique [13], which seeks complete upright frontal faces while reducing nonra-
cial emotion frames [14]. Each expression's initial and end frames are generally
neutral, while the middle frame captures the emotion of the image well [15]. As
illustrated in Figure 19.3, the center frames for each expression label are chosen.
The excessive frames are reduced to only a few frames that exhibit the peak expression using this key frame selection method. Only the frames that best characterize
the mood are chosen for expressive portrayal. Many levels of expressiveness may
be found in frames.

19.3.2 EXTRACTION OF CHARACTERISTICS

Because it differs from normal FER algorithms, recognizing an instructor's facial
expressions is difficult. Face invisibility (for example, when the teacher is writing
on the board), occlusion (for example, when the instructor is reading a slide from a
laptop and part of his or her face is covered behind the screen), and variable lighting
conditions are all problems that must be overcome.
    The suggested method is constructed in such a way as to address these issues.
Faces of teachers are recognized in a picture using the Viola–Jones face detection
technique [13], which seeks complete upright frontal faces while reducing non-racial
emotion frames [16]. Each expression's initial and end frames are generally neutral,

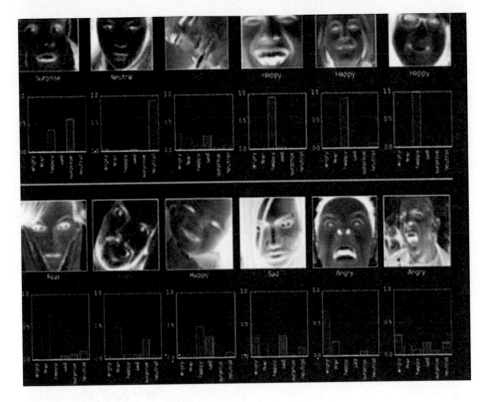

FIGURE 19.3   Facial feature extraction.

while the middle frame captures the emotion of the image well. As illustrated in Figure 19.3, the center frames for each expression label are chosen. The excessive frames are reduced to only a few frames that exhibit the peak expression using this key frame selection method. Only the frames that best characterize the mood are chosen for expressive portrayal. Many levels of expressiveness may be found in frames.

19.3.3   Face Expression

Once recognized, the ROI and important facial features are extracted from the face. There are several features that may be used to identify emotions [17, 18]. This work focuses on facial features, such as the eyes, lips, and brows. We are working with a multi-class classification problem as opposed to a multi-label classification challenge. There is a distinction since a collection of characteristics might belong to many labels but only one distinct class. SVM is used to integrate the collected facial features in order to find multi-class expressions. To compare the outcomes of different techniques, we used machine learning algorithms such as random forest and logistic regression to analyze the output. It is possible to visualize the processing pipeline. Furthermore, not all pictures evoke emotion; just 327 image networks graphic files induce emotion [19]. Despite having the same name, the emotion labels are stored in a separate place than the image files. Creating the database, The CK+ database

FIGURE 19.4   Different emotions of images data set from FER2013.

picture files are organized into separate folders and subdirectories, each of which correlates to one of the seven emotions. According to the individual and session number, all of the files were portable. The distance formula can be used to compute the distance between any two locations on the face using formulae (19.1) and (19.2):

$$\sqrt{(x2-x1)^2+(y2-y1)^2} \tag{19.1}$$

$$\left|\left((x1y2-y1x2)+(x2y3-y2x3)+\cdots(xny1-ynx1)\right)/2\right| \tag{19.2}$$

As a result, when we run the file through our system, we'll obtain the emotion label for it. We utilized Dlib's 68 landmark facial feature predictors to extract face features. The facial expression detection method takes a window containing the x, y, width, and height of the recognized face as x, y, width, and height. The features prediction technique is used to analyze the detected face. Figure 19.1a depicts the 68 markers discovered for a specific face. The 68 points on the left and right eyes, mouth, brows (both left and right), nose, and jaw are returned by the predictor function. The 68 points were transformed into an array of 68 x and y coordinates showing their position using the NumPy array. These are the features of the face that we are looking for. As seen in Figure 19.4, the FER2013 data sets include seven emotions that have been used to predict emotion. The many classes include anger, disgust, fear, joy, sadness, surprise, and neutral. Figure 19.5 displays the happy image sequences, whereas Figure 19.6 depicts the angry image sequences.

19.4   RESULTS AND DISCUSSIONS

19.4.1   EXPERIMENTAL SETUP

For the simulation, MATLAB version 8.5 was used for the experiments on an Intel Core (TM) i3-4005U CPU@1.70 GHz 1700 MHz, 2 Core(s) computer with 8 GB DDR4 RAM and a graphics card. Figure 19.7 shows the screenshot of our execution process. The suggested architecture was evaluated using four common metrics: precision, recall, F1 score, and accuracy. SVM using a linear kernel outperformed the other

FIGURE 19.5   Happy sequence of images expression data set from FER2013.

FIGURE 19.6   Angry sequence of images expression data set from FER2013.

FIGURE 19.7   Screenshot of process execution.

kernels in our testing. RBF performed the poorest, whereas poly performed as well as a linear kernel. We aimed to keep the same test set percent that both divided and cross-validated data to create consistency in results. The overall cross-validation value was nearly comparable toward the accuracy score of the split.

Table 19.2 displays the experimental outcomes here CN stands for conventional system and PRO stands for proposed system. A test set was used to calculate the F1 score [8]. The person classifier and the facial expression classifier were merged

TABLE 19.2

Facial Recognition Score for Proposed System w.r.t. Conventional System

System	Precision		Recall		F1 Score	
	CN	PRO	CN	PRO	CN	PRO
Angry	0.81	0.83	0.92	0.94	0.81	0.85
Happy	0.77	0.80	0.91	0.95	0.82	0.84
Neutral	0.76	0.80	0.84	0.86	0.85	0.87
Total	0.76	0.82	0.88	0.93	0.83	0.86

TABLE 19.3

Face Expression with Number of Samples

Face Expression	Total Images Depicting
Anger	51
Disgust	60
Sadness	27
Contempt	20
Happy	71
Fear	28
Surprise	80

in the traditional system. As a result, each person's expression was labeled in a single layer. Table 19.3 shows that the traditional system had a total F1 score of 0.81. Even though the facial expression classifier was just for one person, at the traditional system's classifier, facial expression information from both the subject and others impacted FER and the comparison results are shown in Figure 19.8.

Table 19.3 lists the number of samples in each class. Figure 19.9 clearly shows that the number of classes differs. As a result, certain classes may be falsely labeled. For example, fear has a small total amount of samples (16), making it challenging to identify the class fear in the testing data set if none of the examples are present in training. Furthermore, because there are fewer training samples, the class might be considered an anomaly. The algorithm may grow biased toward the emotion of surprise and label the majority of photos as such. There was no bias favoring any one class in the RaFD database. In several situations, the disgust and sadness samples were misidentified as anger. This might be because of the fact that both emotions have comparable facial characteristics.

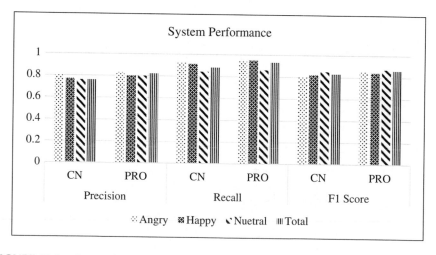

FIGURE 19.8   Comparison of proposed system performance with conventional.

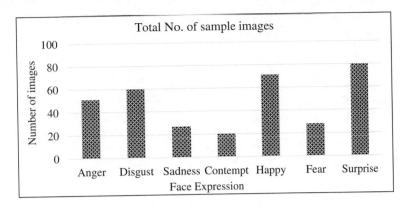

FIGURE 19.9   Number of samples in each category of images.

The rate of detection of sadness was the same as in the previous trial. A logical assumption is that the individuals' sadness feels similar to those of anger. We fine-tuned the results to improve them. We adjusted the data split to 70:30 and increased the number of cross-validation folds to five. For the split, we utilize stratified sampling. We also retrieved additional features from the 68 face point landmarks that were accessible.

19.5   CONCLUSION AND FUTURE WORK

The system mainly deals with several sorts of emotions with picture clarity or black-and-white photos taken from various sources in this article, and it recognizes the image configuration. It exclusively takes photos of the frontal face. The system employs an adaptive method, and cascade helps in the quicker identification of recorded pictures. It also enhances the face recognition system in low-light and non-frontal views, as well as the recognition speed. It primarily detects faces in a variety of environments using various detection methods. The system correctly recognized a person's facial expression in the simulation, and the suggested approach earned an F1 score of 0.83. Finally, machine learning techniques as well as extraction of features techniques are examined, and the system assists us in recognizing human emotions with greater accuracy.

To enhance the results in the future, a more robust face identification algorithm with some excellent characteristics might be investigated. It just looked at a few distances and regions, but there are likely to be many more relevant characteristics on the face that may be statistically computed and utilized to train the algorithm.

REFERENCES

1. D. C. B. Silva, P. P. Cruz, A. M. Gutiérrez and L. A. S. Avendaño, *Applications of Human-Computer Interaction and Robotics Based on Artificial Intelligence*, Editorial Digital del Tecnológico de Monterrey, Monterrey, México, 2020.
2. X. Jiang, "A facial expression recognition model based on HMM," Proceedings of 2011 International Conference on Electronic & Mechanical Engineering and Information Technology, Harbin, Heilongjiang, China, 2011.

3. V. Kazemi and J. Sullivan, "One millisecond face alignment with an ensemble of regression trees," 2014 IEEE Conference on Computer Vision and Pattern Recognition, Columbus, OH, 2014.

4. S. Park, S. W. Lee, and M. Whang, "The analysis of emotion authenticity based on facial micromovements", Sensors-MDPI, vol. 21, no. 13, 4616, 2021 Jul.

5. K. Wang, X. Peng, J. Yang, S. Lu and Y. Qiao, "Suppressing uncertainties for large-scale facial expression recognition," Proceedings of the IEEE/CVF Conference on Computer Vision and Pattern Recognition, Seattle, WA, USA. 14–19 June 2020.

6. K. M. Rajesh and M. Naveenkumar, "A robust method for face recognition and face emotion detection system using support vector machines," 2016 International Conference on Electrical, Electronics, Communication, Computer and Optimization Techniques (ICEECCOT), Mysuru, 2016.

7. C. Loconsole, C. R. Miranda, G. Augusto, Λ. Frisoli and V. Orvalho, "Real-time emotion recognition novel method for geometrical facial features extraction," 2014 International Conference on Computer Vision Theory and Applications (VISAPP), Lisbon, Portugal, 2014.

8. W. Swinkels, L. Claesen, F. Xiao and H. Shen, "SVM point-based real-time emotion detection," 2017 IEEE Conference on Dependable and Secure Computing, Taipei, 2017.

9. Neerja and E. Walia, "Face recognition using improved fast PCA algorithm," 2008 Congress on Image and Signal Processing, Sanya, Hainan, 2008.

10. C. Shanmuganathan and P. Raviraj, "Performance analysis of secure group key mechanism in mobile ad hoc networks," International Journal of Engineering and Technology(UAE), 7, no. 4.10 Special Issue 10, pp. 344–348, 2018.

11. C. Shanmuganathan and P. Raviraj, "A comparative analysis of demand assignment multiple access protocols for wireless ATM networks," Communications in Computer and Information Science, 204 CCIS, pp. 523–533, 2011.

12. M. E. Ayaadi, F. Karraeand and M. S. Kamal, "Survey on emotion recognitions: Features, classification scheme, and database," Pattern Recognition, vol. 44, no. 3, pp. 572–587, 2011.

13. P. Viola and M. J. Jones, "Robust real-time face detection," International Journal of Computer Vision, vol. 57, no. 2, pp. 137–154, 2004.

14. F. Noruzi, G. Anbarjafaari and N. Akraami, "Expression-based emotion recognition and next reaction prediction," 2017 25th Signal Processing Communications Applications Conference (SIU), no. 1, 2017

15. S. Hickson, N. Dufour, A. Sud, V. Kwatra and I. A. Essa, Eyemotion: Classifying facial expressions in VR using eye-tracking cameras. arXiv 2017, arxiv:1707.07204

16. K. Weint and C.-W. Huaang, Characterizing types of convolution in deep convolutional recurrent neural networks for robust speech emotion recognition, pp. 1–19, 2017.

17. K. Li, Y. Jin, M. W. Akram, R. Han and J. Chen, "Facial expression recognition with convolutional neural networks via a new face cropping and rotation strategy," De Visual Computer, vol. 36, no. 2, pp. 391–404, 2020.

18. M. Yu, H. Zheng, Z. Peng, J. Dong and H. Du, "Facial expression recognition based on a multi-task global-local network," Pattern Recognition Letters, vol. 131, pp. 166–171, 2020.

19. E. Jensen, M. Dale, P. J. Donnelly et al., "Toward automated feedback on teacher discourse to enhance teacher learning," Proceedings of the 2020 CHI Conference on Human Factors in Computing Systems, pp. 1–13, Florence, Italy, April 2020.

20 Sentiment Analysis and Sarcasm Detection in Indian General Election Tweets

Arpit Khare, Amisha Gangwar,
Sudhakar Singh, and Shiv Prakash
Department of Electronics and Communication,
University of Allahabad
Prayagraj, India

CONTENTS

20.1 INTRODUCTION

In the digital era of modern times, everything is shifting towards online mode, and in the pandemic time of COVID-19, this shift towards online mode has increased drastically. Let it be studies, work, doctors' practice, banking, shopping, fitness, surveys, etc., everything has started working online. In today's world, to share our opinion with other people, we use online social networking platforms like Twitter, Facebook, YouTube, etc. Very often, people use these platforms to share their experiences about some incidents or issues they are facing. The usage of these platforms allows the user to increase the range of audience to which they can share their thoughts, as compared to the offline method for opinion sharing. The analysis of the opinion of the common public is very important for a wide range of organizations; let it be a political party, businessmen, investors, or working professionals, everyone tries to understand the opinion and trends getting followed by the public.

DOI: 10.1201/9781003320340-20

When it comes to politics and elections, many parties try to recognize the trend of opinions getting followed among the citizens. Even news channels and different media houses perform various kinds of opinion polls and survey polls to understand the opinions and sentiments of the common person. But, in the pandemic time of COVID-19, reaching out to someone physically is not possible sometimes [1]. Because elections are a periodic activity that will occur regularly, even during the pandemic time, so to reduce the risk of the field workers of the polling agency for performing survey polls, sentiment analysis of political tweets is very significant. In this chapter, we have used the political tweets of the Lok Sabha elections 2019 for getting the political sentiments of the people by performing the sentiment analysis techniques along with handling the sarcastic tweets which is not yet considered in the state-of-the-art works in this domain. Training and testing are done on election 2019 data where tweets are taken from the data science platform "Kaggle" [2]. The chapter presents the analysis of the tweets of the major political parties participating in the elections. It applied the transfer learning approach for handling the unsupervised nature of the problem. The main contributions of this chapter are as follows:

- Developing a robust sentiment analysis model for election data.
- Making the model capable enough to handle the sarcastic tweets.
- Implementing the transfer learning approach for handling the unsupervised nature of the problem.
- Analysing the results of the model with respect to the actual election results.

The chapter is structured section-wise as follows: Section 20.1 introduces the chapter; Section 20.2 presents the literature review, in which the related works in the domain of sentiment analysis and election results predictions are reviewed; Section 20.3 contains materials and methods including the approaches proposed for handling the sentiment analysis and sarcasm detection of textual data; Section 20.4 is the experimental evaluation of the sentiment analysis and sarcasm detection model; finally, Section 20.5 concludes the chapter with the scope of future work.

20.2   RELATED WORKS

Various researchers have been doing sentiment analysis of Twitter data in various application fields from past times, which is not limited to only political tweets. Pang and Lee [3] in 2008 developed an algorithm to mine the opinions of different people and analyse types of words. Jhanwar and Das [4] proposed a technique for studying the sentiments of the people of India by analysing the texts written in mixed languages of Hindi-English. Go et al. [5] tried to train a sentiment analysis algorithm to detect whether a tweet is a positive tweet about any specific subject by using emoticons. In the same domain, Pak and Paroubek [6] tried to expand the functionality by means of subjectively and objectively of different words which can create classifiers. These classifiers can be used to collect data to regulate a tweet's sentiment. In [7], an open-source application called Valence Aware Dictionary for sEntiment Reasoning (VADER) [7] was introduced. This is a rule-based application for finding the sentiment scores for textual data. Zhang et al. [8] examined the COVID-19 tweets in four cities in Canada and four cities in the USA. Sentiment intensity scores are examined through VADER [7] and National Research Council Canada (NRC) [9] methods and visualized the data during the pandemic. Das and Bandyopadhyay [10] tried many approaches for concluding the sentiments behind various tweets. They used the approaches of interactive game, bilingual dictionary, and WordNet library. In the literature [11] and [12], the authors have used a dictionary-based approach in which they created a small set of opinion words and then searched in a large collection of texts for growing the dictionary, in the same way as is done in WordNet [13]. Taboada et al. [14] also introduced a sentiment analysis method using the lexicon-based approach. The authors used a dictionary of positive or negative visualized words to analyse the tweets. Bhadane et al. [15] reviewed various methods used to perform analysis on some natural language textual data, as per the sentiments expressed in that data, i.e. whether the text is of positive emotion or negative emotion.

Political tweets have been a centre of attraction for many stakeholders. A number of authors have contributed towards sentiment analysis on election and political tweets. Hamling and Agrawal [16] analysed the 2016 US election–related tweets. These tweets were used to find a correlation between the tweet sentiments and the election results. They used the SentiWordNet library [17] for finding out the sentiment scores. Values for positive words ranged from +0.0625 to +1.0 and −0.0625 to −1.0 for negative values. For instance, positive keyword like "helpful" would receive a value of +0.125 from the sentiment algorithm, or a strongly negative word like "unhappy" would receive a value of −0.25. In their algorithm, they were not able to handle the sarcastic tweets done by some of the users, since sarcasm is also a general form of expression of opinion, so the importance of sarcasm detection can't be overlooked in this domain. In [18], the authors tried to extract the positive and negative sentiments and emotions of the people for the common political parties by computing a distance measure. It denotes the closeness of various tweets. More closely the tweets are for different political parties, it indicates the chances of a tough and close fight among the different parties.

What people think is directly related to what they post over social media; many investigations have proved to predict election results by performing sentiment analysis of Twitter data, such as using the lexicon method for the Swedish elections [19]. Jose and Chooralil [20] implemented a new method by using Twitter's streaming application programming interface (API) for the data collection process. They tried to extract the sentiments and information from the tweets by using lexical tools like WordNet [13] and SentiWordNet [10]. Also, to increase their efficiency, they used a method for handling negation in the data pre-processing stage.

The usage of Twitter by politicians and their political campaigns has been a subject of interest for researchers. In the 2008 USA elections, the campaign routines of Barack Obama have increased the interest in the role of Twitter in political battles [21, 22]. In [23] and [24], it is reported that many US Congress members in their Twitter venture posted their opinions about political issues on Twitter and the issues related to their election area.

Sharmistha Chatterjee in her post on HackerNoon [25] used crawling twitter data through API for performing the sentiment analysis of the two major parties Bharatiya Janata Party (BJP) and Indian National Congress (INC). She used standard machine learning and deep learning algorithms for mood classification of the two major parties. She crawled and merged the tweets every week for some months. The word clouds and n-gram model [26] was used for sentiment representation. She also added an additional location mapping feature for the tweets and used the retweet frequency distribution. Sharma and Moh [27] attempted to predict Indian election results using sentiment analysis on Hindi Twitter data. They fetched a total of 42345 tweets in Hindi language. Then they performed data cleaning to remove irrelevant tweets and left with a total of 36465 tweets and, after that, labelled the data manually on these 36465 tweets, making the unsupervised problem a supervised one. Then they used Naïve Bayes, a support vector machine (SVM) on the Twitter data.

Gaikar and Sapare [28] also predicted the results of general elections 2019 in India using the long short-term memory (LSTM) neural network approach. They used over 1500 labelled tweets, which were labelled with labels like positive, negative, and neutral for the training of their model. In real time, they used the Twitter API to extract a total of 40000 tweets from Jan 2019 to Mar 2019 related to elections to test their model. They also visualized their results using word clouds and compared them with ABP-C and India Today survey results for the elections. Ansari et al. [29] also performed a classification of the tweets related to the general elections 2019 in India; they employed the LSTM model to perform the classification process of the Twitter text. They used the classification model to predict the inclination of tweets to infer the results of elections. With respect to the Indian election, Sharma and Ghose [30] performed text mining using the named entity recognition to filter out the unrelated tweets. For performing sentiment analysis on the related tweets, they used the model RapidMiner AYLIEN [31]. Naiknaware and Kawathekarm [32] used the sentiment analysis score method of R programming language to execute the sentiment analysis on the election related tweets for general election 2019 of India. Bose et al. [33], in the context of political tweets, used the NRC emotion lexicon approach for finding the overall tone of the event. Then they used the deep learning tool ParallelDots that can categorize the tweets into positive, negative, and neutral categories. A strategy known as adaptive neuro-fuzzy inference system (ANFIS) is proposed by Katta and Hegde [34]. The fuzzy-based ontology is made by implementing non-linear SVM classifier analysis to improve the fuzzy principles. They concluded that an ANFIS non-linear SVM-based model for sentiment analysis of social media text is less complex and provides high accuracy. In [35], Bansal and Srivastava used a lexicon-based approach for Twitter sentiment analysis for the vote share prediction using the emojis and n-gram features. Hitesh et al. [36] performed real-time sentiment analysis of the 2019 general elections in India using Word2vec and random forest models. Joseph [37] used the decision tree classifier approach for predicting the outcomes for Indian general elections 2019. He considered the tweets of the English language. His approach was to perform the mood mapping of people over a timely basis during different phases of elections. Prediction of Indonesia's election results was performed by Kristiyanti et al. [38] using the SVM with selection features of particle swarm optimization (PSO) and genetic algorithm (GA). They tried to perform predictions for the post of President and Vice president of Indonesia. Hidayatullah et al. [39] also performed the prediction of Indonesia's election results using the deep learning approach using various algorithms like convolutional neural network (CNN), LSTM, CNN-LSTM, gated recurrent unit (GRU)-LSTM, and bidirectional LSTM. They compared the results with various traditional machine learning algorithms and concluded that the bidirectional LSTM achieved the best accuracy.

Various methodologies have been introduced for opinion and sentiment mining, but all these are broadly classified into two major groups. One is a machine learning approach and the second one is a lexicon-based method, a linguistically inclined method [40]. In this chapter, we have used the machine learning approach for opinion mining. There are two significant types of machine learning algorithms, supervised learning and unsupervised learning. The supervised learning approach requires labelled data for the particular domain targeted to build a machine learning model. In contrast, the unsupervised approach is used when there is no labelled data for training the model. Sentiment analysis of tweets lies in the category of unsupervised learning since we do not have any assigned labels to the 2019 Loksabha election–related tweets dataset. To solve this lack of having the desired labelled dataset, we have used the transfer learning approach. Transfer learning is a type of approach for solving unsupervised problems. In this approach, the model is trained using some other problems' dataset (labelled dataset), and then the trained model is used for predictions on some new dataset which is not having any class labels attached to it. Although several works have been done on sarcasm detection [41], none of them have been performed in the domain of political tweets, so this chapter contributes in that direction. It applies sarcasm detection in the domain of election-related tweets.

20.3 MATERIALS AND METHODS

20.3.1 DATASET

The testing of our trained model is done using the India Lok Sabha elections 2019 tweets. During elections, people used to express their views, opinions, and experiences related to major political parties of that time, i.e. BJP and INC. The complete dataset of the election-related tweets is available on the data science platform Kaggle [2]. The dataset consists of the following fields:

Last_updated: This column contains the information about the time stamp at which the particular tweet was last updated.

Tweet_id: The unique id which is assigned to every tweet.

Created_at: This column contains the timestamp at which the tweet was created.

Full_text: The column contains the complete tweet text on which we will perform the text analysis.

Quote_count: This column contains the frequency of the current tweet that was retweeted with a comment.

Reply_count: This column contains the frequency of the current tweet that was replied to or commented on by any user.

Retweet_count: This column contains the frequency the current tweet was retweeted.

Favorite_count: This column contains the frequency of likes the current tweet is having.

In this chapter, we have considered only the column with textual data for the sentiment analysis process, i.e. "full_text" column.

20.3.2 Machine Learning Algorithms

Term frequency-inverse document frequency (TF-IDF). TF-IDF [42] is a matrix that provides the word frequency table in a document/sentence. Term frequency $(TF(t,d))$ is the measure for the word occurring in a document (d), whereas document frequency $(DF(t))$ is counter for the number of documents the word is occurring. Inverse document frequency $(IDF(t))$ gives the relative weight for a word. If the word is occurring often, its $IDF(t)$ measure will be low, whereas the $IDF(t)$ will be high for less occurring words. Hence, it can be mathematically defined as Equation (20.1) [43, 44].

$$IDF(t) = \frac{N}{DF(t)} \tag{20.1}$$

where N is number of documents, $DF(t)$ is document frequency, and $IDF(t)$ is inverse document frequency.

In Equation (20.1), N can be a large value hence it will explode the value of $IDF(t)$ or $DF(t)$ can possibly be 0 during query time. Hence, the log function is taken to control the former once, and the latter one is resolved by adding 1. Then the new equation for $IDF(t)$ will be as Equation (20.2) [43, 44].

$$IDF(t) = \log \frac{N}{DF(t)+1} \tag{20.2}$$

Finally, from Equation (20.2), *TF-IDF* can be mathematically expressed as Equation (20.3) [43, 44].

$$TF-IDF(t,d) = TF(t,d) * \log \frac{N}{DF(t)+1} \tag{20.3}$$

Linear support vector classifier (SVC). SVM is a machine learning algorithm that can perform classification, regression, and outliers identification. Linear SVC is a classifying algorithm that gives out the best fitting line or hyperplane depending upon the dimensions of the problem. Dimension refers to the number of features. SVC is chosen because it ignores all the outliners and only chooses the best hyperplane to distinguish between the classes. Figure 20.1 shows a Linear SVC example in two-dimensional space [45].

Proposed model. In this chapter, we have tried to tackle the unsupervised nature of analysing sentiments of elections 2019 tweets by using transfer learning. We have used the standard Twitter review dataset available on Kaggle [2] for training our model using the Linear SVC and then performed the sentiment analysis on the actual data. Since the data was of textual format, we have used the TF-IDF method for creating the TF-IDF matrix to deal with the textual data. This work improves over the study conducted on the US Presidential elections in which Sarcasm was not handled [16]. Figures 20.2 and 20.3 illustrate the workflow of training of sentiment analysis and sarcasm detection model, and testing of the trained models on the election's dataset, respectively.

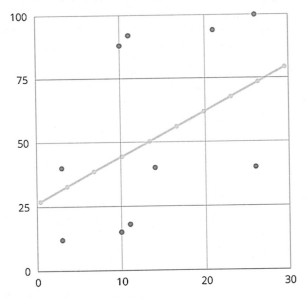

FIGURE 20.1   Linear SVC example in 2-D space.

Algorithms for training the sentiment analysis model, training of the sarcasm detection model, and transfer learning approach for sentiment analysis and sarcasm detection of the election's dataset are presented in Algorithms 1, 2, and 3, respectively.

We have introduced an extra feature of sarcasm detection to the existing methodologies for performing sentiment analysis of political tweets. Since the nature of the incoming data makes the problem an unsupervised problem, i.e. it is not known beforehand which tweet is sarcastic and which one is not, we applied the transfer learning approach to resolve this problem. For the training of the sarcasm detection model, a standard sarcasm detection dataset available on Kaggle is used, and then the trained model can be used to predict results on the actual tweets.

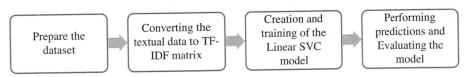

FIGURE 20.2   The flow of work for the training of sentiment analysis and sarcasm detection model.

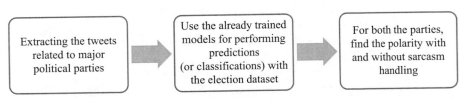

FIGURE 20.3   The flow of work for the testing of the trained models on the election's dataset.

ALGORITHM 1   PROCEDURE FOR THE TRAINING OF THE SENTIMENT ANALYSIS MODEL

1. Split the dataset into training and the testing data by the ratio of 70:30, setting the random state to be 42.
2. Use the TFIDFVectorizer of the sklearn library, transforming the textual data into the TFIDF matrix.
3. Create a pipeline passing the two phases for it as TFIDF and the LinearSVC model.
4. Fit the newly created pipeline with the training dataset along with the labels.
5. Perform the predictions using the testing data.
6. Compare the predicted results with the actual results by using the confusion_matrix and the classification_report which provides the accuracy score for the model.

ALGORITHM 2   PROCEDURE FOR THE TRAINING OF THE SARCASM DETECTION MODEL

1. Use the TFIDFVectorizer of the sklearn library, transforming the textual data into the TFIDF matrix.
2. Create a pipeline passing the two phases for it as TFIDF and the LinearSVC model.
3. Fit the newly created pipeline with the training dataset along with the labels.
4. Perform the predictions using the testing data.
5. Compare the predicted results with the actual results using the confusion_matrix and the classification_report provides the accuracy score for the model.

ALGORITHM 3   PROCEDURE FOR USING TRANSFER LEARNING APPROACH FOR SENTIMENT ANALYSIS AND SARCASM DETECTION

1. Use the already created sentiment analysis and sarcasm detection models for performing predictions (or classifications) with the election dataset.
2. Add two new columns with the prediction results for both the models, i.e. one column having the sentiment result, whether positive or negative, while the second column holds the result for whether the tweet is sarcastic or not.
3. For both the parties, find the positive and negative popularity with and without sarcasm detection and display the results of both.
4. Plot the results for both the parties as bar graphs and pie charts.

20.4 EXPERIMENTAL EVALUATION

20.4.1 SYSTEM CONFIGURATION AND PROGRAMMING ENVIRONMENT

The experimentation is carried out on the Windows 10 operating system installed on a machine having an Intel Core i5 processor, 8 GB RAM, and a 2 TB hard disk drive. The implementation was done using the programming environment of Python 3.7 along with the Jupyter Notebook 6.4.3. The other adopted tools/libraries are as follows:

Sklearn (Version 0.22): Scikit-learn is a free software machine learning library in Python which provides various machine learning algorithms for regressions, classifications, and clustering.

Matplotlib (Version 3.4.3): MatplotLib is a plotting library in Python which provides the API for plotting embedded plots for the data passed to it.

pandas (Version 1.3.2): pandas is a data table handling library in Python which provides the methods to perform all the operations on the data tables conveniently.

Pipelines (Version 1.0): Pipelines in python provide a sequence of transformation and prediction on the data as per the machine learning models passed to it.

JSON library: The JSON library can parse JSON from strings or files. The library parses JSON Python dictionary or list. It can also convert Python dictionaries or lists into JSON strings.

20.4.2 RESULTS AND DISCUSSIONS

After the successful training of the model, to check the accuracy and classification quality of the model, we have used the confusion_matrix and classification_report methods available in the Python library sklearn. A confusion matrix is the tabular representation of the number of correct and incorrect classifications performed by the algorithms, whereas a classification report is a table that is used to find out the quality of the classifications performed by the classification algorithms. The results for the sentiment analysis model are as follows in Tables 20.1 and 20.2.

Table 20.1 shows that our sentiment analysis model gets an accuracy of 80%, which is good to be used for transfer learning. Table 20.2 indicates that the sarcasm

TABLE 20.1
Classification Report of Sentiment Analysis Model

Type	Precision	Recall	F1-Score	Support
Negative	0.80	0.79	0.79	239819
Positive	0.79	0.80	0.80	240181
Accuracy			0.80	480000
Macro accuracy	0.80	0.80	0.80	480000
Weighted average	0.80	0.80	0.80	480000

TABLE 20.2

Classification Report of Sarcasm Detection Model

Type	Precision	Recall	F1-Score	Support
0	0.85	086	0.86	4498
1	0.82	0.81	0.82	3515
Accuracy			0.80	8013
Macro accuracy	0.80	0.80	0.80	8013
Weighted average	0.80	0.80	0.80	8013

detection model achieves an accuracy of 84%, which makes it suitable for transfer learning.

We have used the above trained models for performing election tweets analysis for both without sarcasm handling and with sarcasm handling. The results for both the major parties BJP and INC for both the cases, i.e. without and with sarcasm are shown in Figures 20.4–20.6 and 20.7–20.9, respectively.

The terms like positive tweets or positive polarity tweets indicate that the tweets are conveying some positive emotions about the particular political party. Similarly, on the other hand, terms like negative tweets or negative polarity tweets indicate that the tweets have some negative emotions/sentiments about the political party.

Figure 20.4 shows that 25.58% of the total tweets analysed without the sarcasm detection model were of positive polarity for the BJP. In the same manner, 13.16% of the total tweets were of negative polarity for the BJP, whereas Figure 20.7 shows the results after handling sarcasm, i.e. 23.76% of the total tweets were actually of positive polarity for BJP, and 20.01% of the total tweets were of negative polarity for BJP.

Similarly, for the second major party, Indian National Congress, in Figure 20.4, we can see that when we analysed the tweets without handling sarcasm, we got 6.50% of the total tweets to be of positive polarity, while 4.88% of the total tweets were of negative polarity. But when we handled the sarcasm using the transfer learning technique, 6.34% of the total tweets were of positive polarity, while 6.64% of the tweets were of negative polarity for INC as shown in Figure 20.7. The above observations are represented in Table 20.3.

To better understand the results, we plotted the bar graph for the positive to negative tweets for both political parties. Both the graphs for the cases without sarcasm

Popularity Spread without Sarcasm Handling

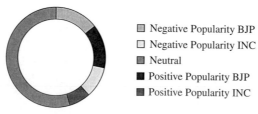

☐ Negative Popularity BJP
☐ Negative Popularity INC
■ Neutral
■ Positive Popularity BJP
■ Positive Popularity INC

FIGURE 20.4   Popularity spread of tweets without sarcasm handling.

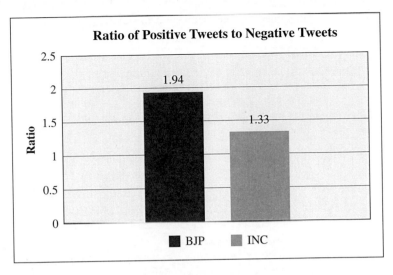

FIGURE 20.5   Ratio of positive to negative tweets without sarcasm handling.

handling and with sarcasm handling are shown in Figures 20.5 and 20.8, respectively. The ratio of positive-to-negative tweets for the BJP party is 1.94, while that of INC is 1.33 without sarcasm handling, but when we handled the sarcasm using our trained model, the results changed for both cases. It became 1.19 for the BJP party, while for the INC party also dropped to 0.96. All the result values for the ratios can be represented using Table 20.4.

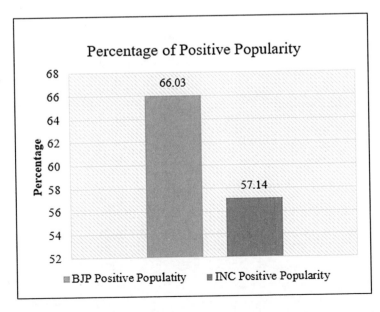

FIGURE 20.6   Percentage of positive tweets among total tweets without sarcasm handling.

Popularity Spread with Sarcasm Handling

☐ Negative Popularity BJP
☐ Negative Popularity INC
■ Neutral
■ Positive Popularity BJP
■ Positive Popularity INC

FIGURE 20.7   Popularity spread of tweets with sarcasm handling.

Then, we generated another bar graph for the percentage of positive tweets for a political party, with respect to the total tweets about that particular political party. The graphs for this value are represented in Figure 20.6 (without sarcasm handling) and Figure 20.9 (with sarcasm handling). We found in our prediction that 66.03% of the total tweets about the BJP party and its leaders were positive polarity, and 57.14% of the total tweets about the INC party were positive polarity when sarcasm handling is not considered. But when we tried to handle the sarcasm, we got the results that 54.28% of the total tweets about the BJP party were of positive polarity, while 48.87% of the total tweets about the INC party were of negative polarity. The above results are summarized in Table 20.5.

20.5   CONCLUSION AND FUTURE WORKS

This chapter proposed an idea of transfer learning for handling sarcastic tweets and analysing the tweets for positive and negative polarities. It is observed that our trained models are working very well. When we compared our model's results

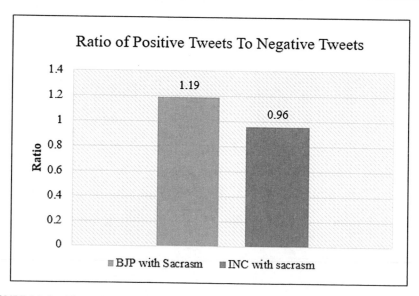

FIGURE 20.8   The ratio of positive to negative tweets with sarcasm handling.

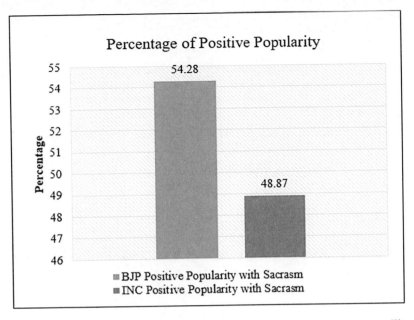

FIGURE 20.9   Percentage of positive tweets among total tweets with sarcasm handling.

with the actual election results, about 37.4% of the votes of the whole country were in the favour of the BJP party, while around 19.5% of the total votes were in favour of the INC party. Our model also predicted that the BJP party wins the election with a vote share difference of around 19% which is approximately similar to elections-2019 results.

The vote percentage difference in our model's results and the then election results are almost the same. Although the actual vote percentage for any party is having a difference with our model's predictions, the reasons behind this difference may be the following points, which need to be considered for a diversified country like India. There is a digital divide problem, which means that not an entire population has access to the Internet. Even among the people having access to the Internet, not everyone uses Twitter. Also, it could be the case that there could be some discrepancies while collecting the dataset. Further, in a society, many people avoid sharing negative emotions on public platforms due to many political and personal reasons.

TABLE 20.3
Polarity Percentage of Tweets with Respect to Total Tweets

Party	Positive Polarity of Tweets (without Sarcasm Handling)	Positive Polarity of Tweets (with Sarcasm Handling)	Negative Polarity of Tweets (without Sarcasm Handling)	Negative Polarity of Tweets (with Sarcasm Handling)
BJP (%)	25.58	23.76	13.16	20.01
INC (%)	6.50	6.34	4.88	6.64

TABLE 20.4

Positive: Negative Polarity Ratio of Tweets

Party	Positive: Negative (without Sarcasm Handling)	Positive: Negative (with Sarcasm Handling)
BJP	1.94	1.19
INC	1.33	0.96

TABLE 20.5

Percentage of Positive Tweets for a Political Party

Party	Percentage (without Sarcasm Handling)	Percentage (with Sarcasm Handling)
BJP (%)	66.03	54.28
INC (%)	57.14	48.87

In the future, the work can be extended to include the following. It can identify the concerned category for any negative tweets, like Agriculture, Education, Infrastructure, Price hike, which will be useful for the country's development. It can filter out the hate speech and abusive content-related tweets, such that only constructive criticism related tweets will be considered. Further, to improve the model, instead of the transfer learning approach, some other more efficient unsupervised learning algorithm can be applied for upgrading the model.

REFERENCES

1. Mohamed Ridhwan, K., Hargreaves, C.A.: Leveraging Twitter Data to Understand Public Sentiment for the COVID-19 Outbreak in Singapore. Int. J. Inf. Manag. Data Insights. 1, 100021 (2021). https://doi.org/10.1016/J.JJIMEI.2021.100021.
2. Indian Political Tweets 2019 (Feb to May) | Kaggle. (2019) https://www.kaggle.com/datasets/codesagar/indian-political-tweets-2019-feb-to-may-sample.
3. Pang, B., Lee, L.: Opinion Mining and Sentiment Analysis. Found. Trends® Inf. Retr. 2, 1–135 (2008). https://doi.org/10.1561/1500000011.
4. Jhanwar, M.G., Das, A.: An Ensemble Model for Sentiment Analysis of Hindi-English Code-Mixed Data. arXiv preprint arXiv:1806.04450. (2018 Jun 12).
5. Go, A., Bhayani, R., Huang, L.: Twitter Sentiment Classification Using Distant Supervision. CS224N project report, Stanford, 1(12), 2009 (2009). https://www-cs-faculty.stanford.edu/people/alecmgo/papers/TwitterDistantSupervision09.pdf
6. Pak, A., Paroubek, P.: Twitter as a Corpus for Sentiment Analysis and Opinion Mining. undefined. In Proceedings of the Seventh International Conference on Language Resources and Evaluation (LREC'10) (2010 May).
7. Hutto, C., Gilbert, E.: VADER: A Parsimonious Rule-Based Model for Sentiment Analysis of Social Media Text. Proc. Int. AAAI Conf. Web Soc. Media. 8, 216–225 (2014).
8. Zhang, Q., Yi, G.Y., Chen, L.-P., He, W.: Text Mining and Sentiment Analysis of COVID-19 Tweets. arXiv preprint arXiv:2106.15354. (2021 Jun 26).

9. Mohammad, S.M., Kiritchenko, S., Zhu, X.: NRC-Canada: Building the State-of-the-Art in Sentiment Analysis of Tweets. *SEM 2013 – 2nd Jt. Conf. Lex. Comput. Semant. 2, 321–327 (2013).

10. Das, A., Bandyopadhyay, S.: SentiWordNet for Indian Languages. 21–22 (2010).

11. Kim, S.-M., Hovy, E.: Determining the Sentiment of Opinions. 1367-es (2004). https://doi.org/10.3115/1220355.1220555.

12. Parrott, W. G. (Ed.). *Emotions in Social Psychology: Essential readings. – PsycNET.* Psychology Press. (2001). https://psycnet.apa.org/record/2000-12576-000.

13. George A. Miller. WordNet I A Lexical Database for English. Commun. ACM 38(11), 39–41 (1995 Nov). https://doi.org/10.1145/219717.219748.

14. Taboada, M., Brooke, J., Tofiloski, M., Voll, K., Stede, M.: Lexicon-Based Methods for Sentiment Analysis. Comput. Linguist. 37, 267–307 (2011). https://doi.org/10.1162/COLI_A_00049.

15. Bhadane, C., Dalal, H., Doshi, H.: Sentiment Analysis: Measuring Opinions. Procedia Comput. Sci. 45, 808–814 (2015). https://doi.org/10.1016/J.PROCS.2015.03.159.

16. Agrawal, A., Hamling, T.: Sentiment Analysis of Tweets to Gain Insights into the 2016 US Election. (2021). https://doi.org/10.52214/cusj.v11i.6359.

17. Baccianella, S., Esuli, A., Sebastiani, F.: SentiWordNet 3.0: An Enhanced Lexical Resource for Sentiment Analysis and Opinion Mining. In Proceedings of the Seventh International Conference on Language Resources and Evaluation (LREC'10) (2010 May).

18. Tumasjan, A., Sprenger, T., Sandner, P., Welpe, I.: Predicting Elections with Twitter: What 140 Characters Reveal about Political Sentiment. In Proceedings of the International AAAI Conference on Web and Social Media, 4(1), 178–185 (2010 May 16).

19. Liu, B.: Sentiment Analysis and Opinion Mining. In Synthesis Lectures on Human Language Technologies 5, 1–184 (2012). https://doi.org/10.2200/S00416ED1V01Y201204HLT016.

20. Jose, R., Chooralil, V.S.: Prediction of Election Result by Enhanced Sentiment Analysis on Twitter Data Using Word Sense Disambiguation. 2015 Int. Conf. Control. Commun. Comput. India, ICCC 2015. 638–641 (2016). https://doi.org/10.1109/ICCC.2015.7432974.

21. Abroms, L.C., Lefebvre, R.C.: Obama's Wired Campaign: Lessons for Public Health Communication. J Health Commun. 14, 415–423 (2009). https://doi.org/10.1080/10810730903033000.

22. Jarvis, S.E.: Communicator-in-Chief: How Barack Obama Used New Media Technology to Win the White House – Edited by John Allen Hendricks and Robert Denton, Jr. Pres. Stud. Q. 40, 800–802 (2010). https://doi.org/10.1111/J.1741-5705.2010.03815.X.

23. Glassman, M.E.: Social Networking and Constituent Communication: Member Use of Twitter during a Two-Week Period in the 111th Congress. Congressional Research Service, Library of Congress (2009). https://www.everycrsreport.com/files/20090921_R40823_bcce5c35c467082e181d6557c4d0d3e1ebbfdfe9.pdf.

24. Golbeck, J., Grimes, J.M., Rogers, A.: Twitter Use by the U.S. Congress. J. Am. Soc. Inf. Sci. Technol. 61, 1612–1621 (2010). https://doi.org/10.1002/ASI.21344.

25. Twitter Sentiment Analysis for the 2019 Lok Sabha Elections I HackerNoon. (2020). https://hackernoon.com/twitter-sentiment-analysis-for-the-2019-lok-sabha-elections-b43o320e.

26. Cavnar, W.B., Trenkle, J.M.: N-Gram-Based Text Categorization. In Proceedings of SDAIR-94, 3rd Annual Symposium on Document Analysis and Information Retrieval, 161175 (1994 Apr 11). https://www.let.rug.nl/vannoord/TextCat/textcat.pdf.

27. Sharma, P., Moh, T.S.: Prediction of Indian Election Using Sentiment Analysis on Hindi Twitter. Proc. – 2016 IEEE Int. Conf. Big Data, Big Data 2016. 1966–1971 (2016). https://doi.org/10.1109/BIGDATA.2016.7840818.

28. Gaikar, D., Sapare, G., Vishwakarma, A., Parkar, A., Professor, A.: Twitter Sentimental Analysis for Predicting Election Result Using LSTM Neural Network. Int. Res. J. Eng. Technol. 6(4), 3665–3670 (2019).

29. Ansari, M.Z., Aziz, M.B., Siddiqui, M.O., Mehra, H., Singh, K.P.: Analysis of Political Sentiment Orientations on Twitter. Procedia Comput. Sci. 167, 1821–1828 (2020). https://doi.org/10.1016/J.PROCS.2020.03.201.

30. Sharma, A., Ghose, U.: Sentimental Analysis of Twitter Data with Respect to General Elections in India. Procedia Comput. Sci. 173, 325–334 (2020). https://doi.org/10.1016/J.PROCS.2020.06.038.

31. Das, S., Kolya, A.K.: Sense GST: Text Mining & Sentiment Analysis of GST Tweets by Naive Bayes Algorithm. Proc. – 2017 3rd IEEE Int. Conf. Res. Comput. Intell. Commun. Networks, ICRCICN 2017. 2017-Decem. 239–244 (2017). https://doi.org/10.1109/ICRCICN.2017.8234513.

32. Naiknaware, B.R., Kawathekar, S.S.: Prediction of 2019 Indian Election Using Sentiment Analysis. Proc. Int. Conf. I-SMAC (IoT Soc. Mobile, Anal. Cloud), I-SMAC 2018. 660–665 (2019). https://doi.org/10.1109/I-SMAC.2018.8653602.

33. Bose, R., Dey, R.K., Roy, S., Sarddar, D.: Analyzing Political Sentiment Using Twitter Data. Smart Innov. Syst. Technol. 107, 427–436 (2019). https://doi.org/10.1007/978-981-13-1747-7_41.

34. Katta, P., Hegde, N.P.: A Hybrid Adaptive Neuro-Fuzzy Interface and Support Vector Machine Based Sentiment Analysis on Political Twitter Data. Int. J. Intell. Eng. Syst. 12(1), 165–173 (2019). https://doi.org/10.22266/ijies2019.0228.17.

35. Bansal, B., Srivastava, S.: Lexicon-Based Twitter Sentiment Analysis for Vote Share Prediction Using Emoji and N-Gram Features. Int. J. Web Based Communities. 15, 85–99 (2019). https://doi.org/10.1504/IJWBC.2019.098693.

36. Hitesh, M.S.R., Vaibhav, V., Kalki, Y.J.A., Kamtam, S.H., Kumari, S.: Real-Time Sentiment Analysis of 2019 Election Tweets Using Word2vec and Random Forest Model. 2019 2nd Int. Conf. Intell. Commun. Comput. Tech. ICCT 2019. 146–151 (2019). https://doi.org/10.1109/ICCT46177.2019.8969049.

37. Joseph, F.J.J.: Twitter Based Outcome Predictions of 2019 Indian General Elections Using Decision Tree. Proc – 2019 4th Int. Conf. Inf. Technol. Encompassing Intell. Technol. Innov. Towar. New Era Hum. Life, InCIT 2019. 50–53 (2019). https://doi.org/10.1109/INCIT.2019.8911975.

38. Kristiyanti, D.A., Normah, Umam, A.H.: Prediction of Indonesia Presidential Election Results for the 2019-2024 Period Using Twitter Sentiment Analysis. Proc. 2019 5th Int. Conf. New Media Stud. CONMEDIA 2019. 36–42 (2019). https://doi.org/10.1109/CONMEDIA46929.2019.8981823.

39. Hidayatullah, A.F., Cahyaningtyas, S., Hakim, A.M.: Sentiment Analysis on Twitter Using Neural Network: Indonesian Presidential Election 2019 Dataset. IOP Conf. Ser. Mater. Sci. Eng. 1077, 012001 (2021). https://doi.org/10.1088/1757-899X/1077/1/012001.

40. Mehta, P., Pandya, S.: A Review on Sentiment Analysis Methodologies, Practices and Applications. Int. J. Sci. Technol. Res. 9, 2 (2020).

41. Joshi, A., Bhattacharyya, P., Carman, J.: Automatic Sarcasm Detection. ACM Comput. Surv. 50 (2017). https://doi.org/10.1145/3124420.

42. Das, B., Chakraborty, S.: An Improved Text Sentiment Classification Model Using TF-IDF and Next Word Negation. arXiv preprint arXiv:1806.06407. (2018 Jun 17). https://doi.org/10.48550/arXiv.1806.06407.

43. TF-IDF: A Single-Page Tutorial - Information Retrieval and Text Mining. http://www.tfidf.com/.

44. Salton, G., Buckley, C.: Term-Weighting Approaches in Automatic Text Retrieval. Inf. Process. Manag. 24, 513–523 (1988). https://doi.org/10.1016/0306-4573(88)90021-0.

45. sklearn.svm.LinearSVC—scikit-learn 0.24.2 documentation. https://scikit-learn.org/stable/modules/generated/sklearn.svm.LinearSVC.html.

21 Image Generation Using Deep Convolutional Generative Adversarial Networks

Abhishek Aryan, Vignesh Kashyap, and Anurag Goel
Delhi Technological University
New Delhi, India

CONTENTS

21.1 INTRODUCTION

Data is being the most crucial resource of 21st century. If we could replicate similar data to generate synthetic data, it would be the ideal solution for the extensive amount of data required to improve and further provide new features with the same. With the emerging applications of machine learning in various fields, the need for data is increasing, which emerges the requirement of generative adversarial networks (GANs) [1], which is a very attractive method to achieve synthetic data generation.

GANs have proved to be quite efficient in generating data that mimic the data in the training set. The training of GANs is complex since two different networks must be trained against each other. As per our knowledge, the research work towards understanding the GANs and visualizing the intermediate representations of multi-layer GANs is limited. Hence, in this chapter, we intend to explore and describe the process of GANs with respect to image generation.

Convolutional networks are ideal in identifying spatial correlation within the image. Although GANs architecture can be used for any type of data but since we

DOI: 10.1201/9781003320340-21

are primarily focusing on image generation, we are using deep convolutional GAN (DCGAN) instead of GANs.

The rest of the chapter is structured as follows – Section 21.2 details the related work, while Section 21.3 describes our methodology, including the dataset, GANs architecture and the evaluation metrics used. The experiments and results are explained in Section 21.4, while Section 21.5 concludes the chapter.

21.2 RELATED WORK

Unsupervised representation learning is a widely studied subject in computer vision research in general, as well as in the domain of images. Hierarchical clustering of picture patches can be used to learn powerful image representations in the context of images [2]. Another common way is to train auto-encoders that use a convolutional stack to encode a picture [3], dividing what and where code components [4] and ladder structures [5].

We intend to use deep convolution GANs, an area where the research has not been as extensive. Image generative models can be classified into two: parametric and non-parametric.

Painting [6] and texture synthesis [7] have been achieved using non-parametric models, wherein they patch different images from the training set.

The usage of parametric models to generate images is well explored [8]. After that, the research into the generation of natural images came into the picture recently. Another approach for the same was with the usage of variational sampler [9], but the images obtained were quite blurred. Images generated from GANs were quite disturbed and noisy to understand clearly [1]. The iterative forward diffusion process is another method to generate images that was discussed in [10]. Due to the chaining of multiple models in the Laplacian pyramid extension [11] approach to GAN, the generated images looked unclear even though the resolution of images improved significantly.

DCGAN has been implemented in [12] to generate the images of chairs, tables and cars and in [13] to generate the faces and implemented on CIFAR 10 dataset.

In this research, we have utilized differentiable augmentation for data-efficient GAN training [14].

21.3 METHODOLOGY

21.3.1 DATASET

We have used the Fruits 360 dataset, which contains 131 distinct classes of fruits and vegetables. Each fruit image in this dataset is of size 100*100. This dataset was developed by recording short videos (of around 20 seconds duration) of various fruits which were placed on a slow motor shaft. There are 90,483 images consisting of 67,692 images in the training set, while 22,688 images are in the test set. The different variations of fruit were placed in different classes. They also employed the use of a novel algorithm that extracts the food from the background as the variations in lighting conditions produced unsatisfactory results. A few sample images from the dataset are shown in Figures 21.1–21.4.

FIGURE 21.1   Apple (6,405 images).

21.3.2   Architecture of the GAN

The GAN architecture proposed in [1] consists of two networks, namely the generator network and the discriminator network, which are trained simultaneously. After training, the discriminator network is eliminated, while only the generator network is saved in the model. Due to this nature, GANs have been largely unstable to train and often result in outputs that are random. Hence, we chose to use DCGAN [13] over GAN for our work. The architecture of the Generator and Discriminator network is shown in Figures 21.5 and 21.6, respectively.

DCGAN was developed by Radford et al. in [13], which made the modern convolutional GANs more stable by using some topological architectural restrictions.

FIGURE 21.2   Grape (3,419 images).

FIGURE 21.3   Banana (1,430 images).

FIGURE 21.4   Tomato (5,103 images).

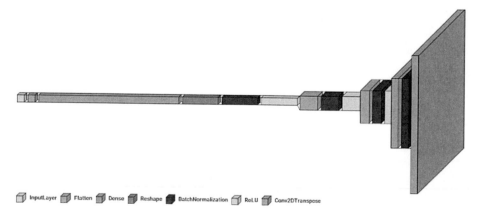

InputLayer   Flatten   Dense   Reshape   BatchNormalization   ReLU   Conv2DTranspose

FIGURE 21.5   Architecture of the generator network.

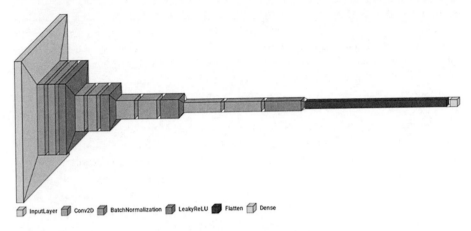

InputLayer   Conv2D   BatchNormalization   LeakyReLU   Flatten   Dense

FIGURE 21.6   Architecture of the discriminator network.

The first is the convolutional net [12], which learns by using strided convolutions rather than deterministic spatial pooling functions like max-pooling to facilitate network learning of spatial down-sampling on its own.

In addition to convolutional features, we have tried to remove all connected layers, like the latest image classification in [15]. The first layer of the GAN is fed an input of uniform noise distribution Z, which can be considered fully completely connected as it is simply matrix multiplication. Convolutional stack, in the beginning, utilizes the input matrix, which has been reshaped into a four-dimensional tensor. Output for the discriminator is received through a sigmoidal output, which has been fed the flattened final convolutional layer.

We were then able to stabilize the learning by using batch normalization [16], which facilitated the input normalization resulting in a zero mean and unit variance. The gradient in the model had a slow flow because of the utilization of the above technique [13] and also combated the issues that had arisen as a result of imperfect initialization. We had not applied batch normalization to input layer of discriminator as well as output layer of generator, as it seemed to cause oscillation of the sample and rendered the model unstable.

As discussed in their paper, the usage of ReLU activation [17] is used for all except the output layer that used Tanh instead. Bounded activations allow the model to learn more quickly and expand to the whole domain's colour space. For discriminator training, leaky ReLU performed better instead of the maxout activation discussed by [1].

A major part of the architecture was as per the DCGAN guidelines provided by [13], with some extra layers of convolutions added and the input and output layers tweaked according to the dataset we had in use. We also tried to reduce the operational memory and expedite the process. During the model architecture process, we were able to remove ~3 convolutions without much harm to the generator, but as it was just generated over ~50 epochs, we are quite uncertain about its long-term effects.

To augment the training data in an effective manner, we used ideas proposed by [14] to produce the significant diversity of data required by the GANs. This was especially useful in the context of some fruits like bananas which had only 1,430 images available for training. Many large-scale and successful models require a huge amount of training data to train. To name a few, the FFGQ dataset used by StyleGAN contains 70,000 selective high-resolution images of human faces. The collection of training data of this scale requires months or even years of considerable human efforts to be able to be procured. In various cases, it might not even be possible to have that number of samples, like in the case of a landmark, a rare species or a localized object. Reducing the amount of available data causes the quality of the generator to decrease drastically. A study done by [14] showed that using a small subset of the CIFAR dataset (around 20%) caused the training accuracy of the discriminator to quickly saturate to nearly 100%, but the validation accuracy then kept decreasing. This leads us to believe that in small datasets, the discriminator simply memorizes all the images in the data. This overfitting adversely affects the training of the generator and causes the generator to only learn a few images due to the positive feedback loop.

21.3.3 EVALUATION METRICS

Since the convergence of GAN training is very unpredictable, using a measurable metric like maximum likelihood error (MLE) may not be a good idea. We use the metrics inception score [18] and Fréchet inception distance (FID) [19] to evaluate the performance of the generator model. The first metric uses the Kullback-Leibler (KL) divergence to combine two criteria, the marginal and the conditional probability of the images from the generated set, which reflects the diversity and the quality of the images, respectively. A higher value is preferred as it represents a high KL divergence between the two compared distributions.

$$\text{IS(G)} = \exp\left(E_{x \sim p_g} D_{KL}\left(p\left(y \mid x\right) \| p\left(y\right)\right)\right) \tag{21.1}$$

$$p\left(y \mid x\right) \tag{21.2}$$

$$p\left(y\right) = \int_x p\left(y \mid x\right) p_g\left(x\right) \tag{21.3}$$

where y is the label for a given sample image x, and IS(G) gives the inception score of a generator.

FID uses an inception network as well but extracts the features from an intermedia layer instead. Lower FID is better.

$$\text{FID} = \|\mu_{real} - \mu_{gen}\|^2 + \text{Tr}\left(\Sigma_{real} + \Sigma_{gen} - 2\left(\Sigma_{real}\Sigma_{gen}\right)^{1/2}\right) \tag{21.4}$$

where $X_{real} \sim \mathcal{N}\left(\mu_{real}, \Sigma_{real}\right)$ are the 2,048-dimensional activations of InceptionV3's pool3 layers for real samples and $X_{gen} \sim \mathcal{N}\left(\mu_{gen}, \Sigma_{gen}\right)$ consist of the same but for generated samples instead.

The combination of these metrics gives us a good peek into the real-world performance of our GAN.

TABLE 21.1

Fréchet Inception Distance and Inception Score of the Four Fruit GANs

Fruit	Inception Score	Fréchet Inception Distance
Apple	(2.475, 0.112)	129
Banana	(2.556, 0.291)	270
Grape	(3.001, 0.078)	250
Tomato	(1.382, 0.036)	236

21.4 EXPERIMENTAL RESULTS

We trained the model on four different fruit image distributions. We tried to capture some different scales and shapes by picking these examples.

The embedded GIFs show the training progress of the generator model and are made by reusing the same seed to generate an image after every training epoch. The images are not temporally stable over the duration of the full training cycle, and we can see some significant changes that are only present in that epoch. Due to the low number of epochs, we also see some significant background noise and a noise texture overlay as well.

Table 21.1 shows the inception score and FID for all the four fruits, namely apple, banana, grape and tomato. The results obtained are very peculiar indeed. In human trials, the bananas were expressed to be the most realistic looking and diverse, while the results obtained are showing the reverse of it, i.e., the FID score obtained for the bananas is highest, while for the apples, the FID score obtained is the lowest. This also correlates with the findings in [20]. Figures 21.7–21.10 show the performance of GAN on fruit apple, grape, banana and tomato, respectively.

21.5 CONCLUSION

In this work, we have used the DiffAugment approach to generate the fruit images. We have used the Fruits 360 dataset for training the DCGAN model. We have trained our model on four different fruit images distributions. From the results, we can interpret that the generator has achieved a good inception score.

FIGURE 21.7   Performance of apple GAN over the training cycle.

FIGURE 21.8   Performance of grape GAN over the training cycle.

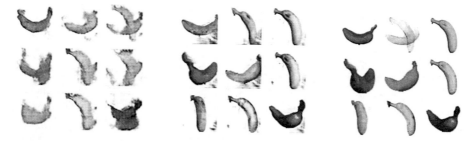

FIGURE 21.9   Performance of banana GAN over the training cycle.

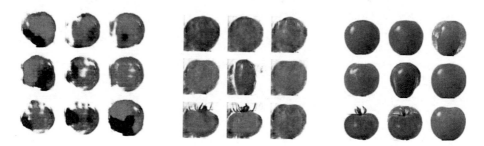

FIGURE 21.10   Performance of tomato GAN over the training cycle.

REFERENCES

1. Goodfellow, Ian, Jean Pouget-Abadie, Mehdi Mirza, Bing Xu, David Warde-Farley, Sherjil Ozair, Aaron Courville, and Yoshua Bengio. "Generative adversarial networks." Communications of the ACM 63, no. 11 (2020): 139–144.
2. Coates, Adam, and Andrew Y. Ng., "Learning feature representations with k-means", In Neural networks: Tricks of the trade, pp. 561–580. Springer, Berlin, Heidelberg, 2012.
3. Vincent, Pascal, Hugo Larochelle, Isabelle Lajoie, Yoshua Bengio, and Pierre-Antoine Manzagol. "Stacked denoising autoencoders: learning useful representations in a deep network with a local denoising criterion." Journal of Machine Learning Research 11 (2010): 3371–3408.
4. Zhao, Junbo, Michael Mathieu, Ross Goroshin, and Yann Lecun. "Stacked what-where auto-encoders." arXiv preprint arXiv:1506.02351 (2015).

5. Rasmus, Antti, Harri Valpola, Mikko Honkala, Mathias Berglund, and Tapani Raiko. "Semi-supervised learning with ladder networks." arXiv preprint arXiv:1507.02672 (2015).

6. Hays, James, and Alexei A. Efros. "Scene completion using millions of photographs." Communications of the ACM 51, no. 10 (2008): 87–94.

7. Efros, Alexei A., and Thomas K. Leung. "Texture synthesis by non-parametric sampling." In Proceedings of the Seventh IEEE International Conference on Computer Vision, vol. 2, pp. 1033–1038. IEEE, 1999.

8. Portilla, Javier, and Eero P. Simoncelli. "A parametric texture model based on joint statistics of complex wavelet coefficients." International Journal of Computer Vision 40, no. 1 (2000): 49–70.

9. Kingma, Diederik P., and Max Welling. "Auto-encoding variational Bayes." arXiv preprint arXiv:1312.6114 (2013).

10. Sohl-Dickstein, Jascha, Eric Weiss, Niru Maheswaranathan, and Surya Ganguli. "Deep unsupervised learning using nonequilibrium thermodynamics." In International Conference on Machine Learning, pp. 2256–2265. PMLR, 2015.

11. Denton, Emily, Soumith Chintala, Arthur Szlam, and Rob Fergus. "Deep generative image models using a Laplacian pyramid of adversarial networks." arXiv preprint arXiv:1506.05751 (2015).

12. Dosovitskiy, Alexey, Jost Tobias Springenberg, Maxim Tatarchenko, and Thomas Brox. "Learning to generate chairs, tables and cars with convolutional networks." IEEE Transactions on Pattern Analysis and Machine Intelligence 39, no. 4 (2016): 692–705.

13. Radford, Alec, Luke Metz, and Soumith Chintala. "Unsupervised representation learning with deep convolutional generative adversarial networks." arXiv preprint arXiv:1511.06434 (2015).

14. Zhao Shengyu, Zhijian Liu, Ji Lin, Jun-Yan Zhu, and Song Han. "Differentiable augmentation for data-efficient GAN training." Advances in Neural Information Processing Systems 33 (2020): 7559–7570.

15. Mordvintsev, Alexander, Christopher Olah, and Mike Tyka. "Inceptionism: Going deeper into neural networks." http://googleresearch.blogspot.com/2015/06/ inceptionism-going-deeper-into-neural.html (2015).

16. Ioffe, Sergey, and Christian Szegedy. "Batch normalization: Accelerating deep network training by reducing internal covariate shift." In International Conference on Machine Learning, pp. 448–456, PMLR (2015).

17. Nair, Vinod, and Geoffrey E. Hinton. "Rectified linear units improve restricted Boltzmann machines." In ICML'10: Proceedings of the 27th International Conference on International Conference on Machine Learning, pp. 807–814 (June 2010).

18. Salimans, Tim, Ian Goodfellow, Wojciech Zaremba, Vicki Cheung, Alec Radford, and Xi Chen. "Improved techniques for training GANs." Advances in Neural Information Processing Systems 29 (2016): 2234–2242.

19. Heusel, Martin, Hubert Ramsauer, Thomas Unterthiner, Bernhard Nessler, and Sepp Hochreiter. "GANs trained by a two time-scale update rule converge to a local Nash equilibrium." Advances in Neural Information Processing Systems 30 (2017): 6629–6640.

20. Barratt, Shane, and Rishi Sharma. "A note on the inception score." In arXiv preprint arXiv:1801.01973 (2018).

22 Human Activity Identification Using Artificial Intelligence

Srikanth Bethu, Machikuri Santoshi Kumari,
Chintha Sravani,
and Srinivasulu Gari Bhargavi Latha
Department of Computer Science and Engineering, GRIET
Hyderabad, India

Suresh Mamidisetti
Department of Computer Science Engineering,
Government Polytechnic
Hyderabad, India

Anurag University
Hyderabad, India

CONTENTS

DOI: 10.1201/9781003320340-22

22.1   INTRODUCTION

Person and activity identification is one of the important areas of computer vision research and applications. Activity identification plays a major role in video as well as image understanding. So, in recent years, it has been one of the active research areas. Basically, it deals with the recognition of the activity that is being performed by a person in an image. Actions are divided into two categories. The first one is atomic actions and the other is non-atomic actions. A group of atomic actions leads to non-atomic actions. Walking, sitting, standing, waving etc. are some examples of atomic actions.

Machine learning (ML) [1] term is given by Arthur Samuel, a computer scientist, in 1959, who stated that "it gives computers the ability to learn without being explicitly programmed." ML is one of the most interesting subfields of computer science. ML is a scientific study of algorithms and statistical methods that make a computer system order to perform a specific task efficiently without using any explicit instructions, relying on inference and patterns instead. Depending on the nature of learning, ML implementations are classified into three categories.

22.1.1   SUPERVISED LEARNING [1]

In this supervised learning, the machine is trained using a labeled training data, and it predicts the output based on that data. The input data which is already tagged with the output is called labeled data, and this data acts as a supervisor for the machine, which teaches how to predict the output. The main goal of this supervised learning is to map the input variable (X) to an output variable (Y). Some applications of supervised learning are risk assessment, image classification, fraud detection, etc.

22.1.2   UNSUPERVISED LEARNING [2]

In this unsupervised learning, the machine is not supervised with the training data. Instead, the machine itself must find all the hidden patterns from the dataset. The main goal of this learning is to find the structure of the dataset underlying and group the data according to their similarities and then represent that dataset in the required format. Regression and classification problems cannot be solved by using this algorithm.

22.1.3   SEMI-SUPERVISED LEARNING [2]

The combination of unsupervised and supervised learning is known as semi-supervised learning. In this type of learning, both unlabeled and labeled data are used for training the model. In a typical situation, the algorithm would use a large amount of unlabeled data with a small amount of labeled data.

22.1.4 REINFORCEMENT LEARNING [2]

Reinforcement learning is a feedback-based ML technique, in which the machine learns automatically from the feedbacks without using any labeled data. It is used for the problems where decision-making is sequential, and the goal is long-term. For example, game-playing and robotics. Based on the output of a system, there is another type of classification of ML tasks.

22.1.5 CLASSIFICATION [2]

By using this classification technique, the entire dataset can be divided into classes based on some criteria, and this division is done by finding a function. So, a classification algorithm is used to find a function that maps an input (X) to a desired output (Y). Some of the algorithms are support vector machines (SVM), k-nearest neighbors, decision tree classification and kernel SVM.

22.1.6 REGRESSION [2]

It is the process of obtaining the correlation between the independent and the dependent variables. The continuous variables can be predicted with the help of regression. Some of the algorithms are simple linear regression, multiple linear regression, support vector regression and decision tree regression.

22.1.7 CLUSTERING [2]

With the help of clustering, all the similar data points can be grouped together to form different clusters. The objects with the similarities remain in a group that has no similarities or less similarities with other groups. Some clustering methods in ML are partitioning clustering, density-based clustering, hierarchical clustering and fuzzy clustering.

Real-time advertisements on mobiles and web pages, web search results, network intrusion detection, email span filtering, image and pattern recognition are some of the examples of ML applications. To analyze the huge volumes of data, ML is applied, and all the above applications are by-products of ML. Data analysis was being characterized by trial and error. This approach becomes impossible when datasets are heterogenous and large. ML acts as a solution to all these by introducing clever approaches to analyze those huge volumes of data. ML can produce accurate results and analysis by developing data-driven models for real-time processing of the data and developing efficient and fast algorithms.

The goal of person and activity identification is to identify the person and examine the atomic activity of a person from the still images. The objectives of our work are identifying the presence of a person in the image, plotting the key points in the image, joining those key points to form a skeleton and identifying the action of person using the skeleton.

22.2 LITERATURE SURVEY

Human action identification is one of the most important and trending research in computer vision. There is a lot of research going on in this field from the past two decades. There are many papers being published every year on this area. The following are a few of them.

Human action recognition using multilevel depth motion maps (DMM): In this chapter, they presented a novel framework for person activity identification. This model is trained on depth images. The main two problems that are faced during action recognition are old motion history is covering the new motion, and DMM ignore static information, which is useful for motion recognition, while extracting motion information from depth sequence. From the input depth images, three levels of temporal samples are captured by making use of multilevel frame select sampling (MFSS). Then, each depth image is projected onto three perpendicular Cartesian planes. Then to identify the static posture and motion posture, the static history image and the motion history image are retrieved by using the motion and static maps (MSM). After that, the texture information is extracted by using the block-based Local Binary Patterns (LBP) feature extraction. In this process, all the key parameters involved are analyzed. The datasets used for this are the Skeleton-Based Action Recognition (MSR Action3D) dataset, the MSR Gesture3D dataset and the UTD Multimodal Human Action Dataset (UTD-MHAD).

Challenges observed: This approach works fine if the action to be recognized is from a depth image. But nowadays, most of the images are RGB images, and this will not work for those images. Also, this approach makes use of classical feature extraction methods. But neural networks show better results than these classical methods.

Action recognition using attention-joints graph convolutional neural networks: In this chapter, an innovative idea of activity identification through graph convolutional neural network (CNN) and skeleton images using attention-joints is presented. First, from the graph nodes, the spatial features are devised as Euclidian distances, and then, from the video sequence, the temporal features are introduced as attention-joints flow features. For activity recognition, these attention-joints, which are equipped with temporal and spatial features, are excited to graph neural network. Because of the consideration of the graph nodes and edges, spurious details are incurred. All these details and the noise can be reduced by this approach. The attention-joints represent only those joints that contribute to the required set of actions. The node features of the graph are the one that corresponds to only these attention-joints. These features include joints flow features, the distances between the neighboring attention-joints and the distance of attention-joints from the center of gravity of human body. The datasets used for this model evaluation are single-image Standford-40 Actions dataset, PKU-MDD dataset and NTU-RGBD dataset.

Challenges: This approach makes use of temporal signatures of video sequences, i.e., it works good for video-based action recognition. It cannot be implemented for images. The joints that are responsible for that action are only considered for feature extraction. This might not recognize all the activities that can be performed by a person.

Spatial temporal graph convolutional networks for skeleton-based action recognition: In this chapter, they presented a new model for skeleton-based activity identification and the spatial temporal graph convolutional network (ST-GCN). Based on the skeleton sequences, a spatial temporal graph convolution set is developed by the model. The complementary to RGB modality is dynamic skeleton sentences. This information related to the motion is captured by the ST-GCN. The datasets used in this model are Kinetics and NTU-RGBD. While implementing ST-GCN, the adjacent matrix and an identity matrix are used to represent the intra-body joint connections in a single frame. While performing actions, joints move in group, and one joint can appear in many body parts. For this, a mask, which is learnable, is added on each layer of spatial temporal graph convolution. This mask will reduce the contributions of node features to the adjacent nodes. The neighbor set is divided into three subsets: (1) the centrifugal group, (2) the centripetal group and (3) the root node.

Challenges: The one and only challenge with this approach was it can be used only for video-based action recognition. It is not suitable for activity recognition in images.

Human action recognition using support vector machine and 3D convolutional neural network: In this study, they proposed a support vector machine approach for human activity identification. They used a 3D CNN model to extract the features like temporal and spatial from the adjacent video frames. For training the model, they used the KTH dataset. A 3D CNN is used for feature extraction from the stacked video frames. These extracted features are used by SVM to classify the action. The overfitting problem was reduced by using a dropout technique where the output of each hidden neuron is set to zero with a probability of 0.5.

Challenges: Weight optimization is not possible with this approach. This can be achieved by integrating SVM with logistic regression. Another one is, it is not suitable for images.

22.3 METHODOLOGY

22.3.1 HUMAN ACTIVITY RECOGNITION APPROACHES

Human activity recognition is the problem of predicting what a person is doing. To predict the activity, there are mainly two approaches: wearable-based approach and vision-based approach.

Wearable-based approach: Wearable-based approach is based on some wearable electronic gadgets like smartphones, smartwatches and fitness bands. To recognize the activity, sensor data will be collected from the accelerometer and gyroscope sensors of these gadgets. This approach makes use of several techniques like support vector machine (SVM) and feature selection algorithms like sequential floating forward search.

SVM: SVM [3] is used for classification and regression problems. It is a supervised learning algorithm and a very popular algorithm, mainly used for classification problems in ML. For example, SVM is used for face detection, image classification problems, etc. The aim of the SVM algorithm is to develop the best line that divides the n-dimensional space into classes so that any new data points can be classified to its best in the future. There are two types of SVM's:

> **Linear SVM:** It is used for the data that can be classified linearly, i.e., the data that can be divided into two classes by a single straight line. The classifier used will be termed Liner SVM classifier.
>
> **Non-linear SVM:** It is used for the data that cannot be classified linearly, i.e., the data that cannot be divided by a single straight line. The classifier used will be termed non-linear SVM classifier.

SVM algorithm has two main components. They are hyperplanes and support vectors. There can be more than one line or decision boundary that can classify the data points.

But out of these lines, we must identify the best boundary that classifies the datapoint. This best boundary is called SVM hyperplane. The datapoints that are nearer to the hyperplane and affects the hyperplane position are called support vectors.

The dimensions of the hyperplane are dependent on the number of features of the dataset. If there are two features, then hyperplane is a straight line. If there are three features, then hyperplane is a 2D plane.

A straight line, which is a hyperplane, can separate the two-dimensional linearly separable data. The equation of this line be y = ax + b, which is same as ax − y + b = 0. This can be rewritten as w · x + b = 0, where x = (x, y) and w = (a, −1), and w · x means dot product. Hence, the equation of hyperplane is w · x + b = 0. This works for any number of dimensions. By using this hyperplane, we can make the predictions. The hypothesis function can be defined as

$$h(x) = +1 \ if \ w \cdot x + b \geq 0$$

i.e., the point above or on the hyperplane is given as class +1.

$$h(x) = -1 \ if \ w \cdot x + b \leq 0$$

i.e., the point below the hyperplane is given as class −1. The steps to implement the SVM are data pre-processing, fitting the SVM classifier to training step, predicting the test set result, creating the confusion matrix, visualizing the training set result and visualizing the test set result.

Sequential floating forward search: The sequential floating search algorithm [3] is the most effective feature selection algorithm. There are two types of this. One of them is Sequential Floating Forward Search. The algorithm starts with an empty feature set, and for each step, the best feature that satisfies some criteria is added to the current feature set, i.e., first, the best single feature is selected from the set of all features and added to the empty set. Then by using this best feature and remaining features, all the possible pairs are formed. From these pairs, the best feature pair is selected. Then, triplets are also formed in the same way, and the best one is selected. This process is continued until a predefined number of features are selected. Improvement possibility in the case if some features is removed is also verified by this algorithm. In this wearable-based approach, the entire dataset is divided into two parts, feature analysis dataset and train and validation dataset.

After dividing the dataset, the first step is to extract the heterogeneous features, i.e., feature selection from the feature analysis dataset using the sequential floating forward search, which results in an optimal feature vector. By using this vector, the optimal features from the train and validation dataset are extracted, which are used to train the SVM. By training the SVM, we can classify or recognize the activity.

22.3.2 VISION-BASED APPROACH

Vision-based approach [3] is based on images and videos. Human activity can be recognized by making use of images and videos. Image-based action recognition is a comparatively less studied area than video-based recognition. Generally, video is a group of frames that are displayed one after the other while playing a video. In video-based, the video is divided into frames, and each frame is analyzed separately. Then by comparing results of each frame, the activity is recognized. Most of the video-based approaches make use of CNN for each frame.

Convolutional neural networks: CNN [3] is one of the mostly used technique for image classification, object detections etc. CNN has many layers like convolution, pooling and fully connected layers (FCLs). Each image will pass through all these layers, and for the classification of the object, a Soft-max function is applied at the end. The input for each layer is an array of numbers, and output of each layer is also an array of numbers. The array is a multi-dimensional array, and the output of a layer will act as an input for other layers.

Convolution layer: Convolution layer is the main building block of the CNN, and the major computational work is done in this layer. The input for this layer is an image, and from this image, all the required features are extracted through this layer. To preserve the relationship between the pixels, this layer is meant to learn the features of the image. This learning happens by making use of the small squares of the image, which is given as input.

A CNN can have more than one convolutional layer. A set of learnable neurons are used in these layers to convolute the input image. This convolution will result in a feature map, and these are given as an input to the other convolutional layer. All the neurons are connected to the regions of the input image and a dot product between the weights and the regions of the input image is calculated in the convolutional layer.

Pooling layer: The convolutional layer produces a feature map. The dimensions of this feature map can be reduced by making use of these pooling layers. Though the dimensions of the activation map are reduced, the required information retains with the activation map. The non-linear operations like average and maximum are applied on the input images. To apply these operations, the input image must be splinted into small rectangles, and these rectangles should be non-overlapping. This pooling layer is generally placed between convolutional layers, and this layer will produce the best results and gives robustness for translation and distortion.

FCL: FCL helps to connect the filters of adjacent layers. The convolutional and pooling layers produce the combinations of features of the input image. These features are given as input to the FCL, and this layer will convert these inputs into a vector. The main goal to employ this layer is to classify the input image into classes of the network. The FCL is considered the final pooling layer, and the sum of the output probabilities from this layer is 1.

Some of the video-based approaches and their issues are listed below.

ConvNet architecture search for spatiotemporal feature learning: In this, a 3D convolutional network is used for the feature extraction from the video frames. They trained the network using the Sports 1M dataset and then used this model to extract features from the other datasets. The focus of this network is on the spatial appearance of the first frames, and in the next frames, it tracks the motion, i.e., the activity. The classifier they developed was a simple linear classifier like SVM. Challenges: The long-range temporal modeling is a problem. Another problem is to train that much big networks is a complex task.

3D CNNs for human action recognition: In this, a 3D convolution is used to extract the spatial and temporal features from the video. These convolutions are used by the CNN model that generates multiple channels of information from adjacent video frames and convolution and subsampling of each channel is performed separately.

Challenges: It makes use of supervised learning. So, the labeling of data is complex. This can be avoided by making use of unsupervised learning algorithm.

Action recognition by dense trajectories: In this, dense sampling and feature tracking are combined to analyze the videos. While capturing the video, there will be the camera motion. The computation of motion boundaries descriptors along the dense trajectories is performed to remove the camera motion. To decrease the content regarding to the motion, descriptors within a space-time volume are computed.

Challenges: There might be chance for trajectory drifting, from starting position, during tracking.

Large-scale video classification with CNN: CNN models require a fusion of time information. In this, they introduced late, slow and early fusion connectivity. They gave a conclusion that among these three fusions, slow fusion works better. To reduce the computation cost, they used a multi-resolution architecture of CNN, which will affect the performance. Two streams of processing over two spatial resolutions are used. Challenges: High cost. Performance improvement is very low.

So, action recognition from videos can be done by examining each frame separately. But that is not possible with images. So, action recognition from images is a bit difficult compared to videos. But we can implement action recognition from still images using ML techniques like pose estimation, skeleton-based action recognition and MLP classifier. This approach will produce more accurate results than the methods discussed above.

22.4   IMPLEMENTATION

Person and activity detection [4] deals with the recognition of activity of a person from images. The constraints for this system are that the input image should have either a single person or no person, and also, the person in the image should appear completely. The actions that are recognized in this person and activity identification [5] are wave, stand, squat, punch and kick.

To detect the activity, first we must check for the presence of a person in the image. Person presence can be decided from the face detection. So, for face detection, the Haar-Cascade algorithm [6] is used. Confirmation of the person in the image makes sure that there is some activity to be recognized from that image. After that, we can recognize the activity.

Generally, by seeing images of a person, we can recognize the activity based on his/her pose in the image [7]. Similarly, we can develop a system that can recognize the activity [8] based on the pose of that person. So, person and activity identification can be divided into three parts, human detection, pose estimation [9] and activity identification.

22.4.1 HUMAN DETECTION

Immediately after providing the image as input, first the system will check for the presence of a person in the image. If a person is present, then we will proceed to detect the activity. Otherwise, the respective message indicating the absence of person in the image is displayed, and the process terminates. In this chapter, CUHK01 (http://www.ee.cuhk.edu.hk/~xgwang/CUHK_identification.html) and INRIA Person (https://paperswithcode.com/dataset/inria-person) datasets are used to generate the results. Experiments conducted on both public datasets and customized datasets shown in the Results section.

Person presence can be confirmed by face detection. To identify the face, we have used the Haar-Cascade algorithm, which is developed by using python and OpenCV. The two modules required for this implementation are cv2 and sys. sys imports some common python methods like argparse, which is used to take input from command prompt, and cv2 imports OpenCV library. To identify faces in the image, first the image is converted into grayscale using the cvtColor() method of cv2. Then the Haar-Cascade algorithm can be implemented by loading that file into memory. To load the file, the cascadeClassifier() method of cv2 is used, which will detect the faces in the image. To convert an image from one color space to another, the cv2.cvtColor() method is used.

22.4.2 ALGORITHM

Step 1: import all the necessary packages.

Step 2: Read input i.e., image from command line.

Step 3: Load the Cascade Classifier XML file.

Step 4: Convert the image into gray scale.

Step 5: Apply the Haar-Cascade algorithm on the gray scale image.

Step 6: If face is detected go to step-6. Otherwise, print no face message and terminate.

Step 7: Draw a rectangle around the detected face and display the image.

Step 8: For pose estimation, load the prototxt and Caffe model files into the memory.

Step 9: Convert the OpenCV image into the blob format and send it as input to Caffe model.

Step 10: For every key point, compare the threshold value to the confidence map value. If threshold value is less than the confidence value, plot the key point and store the coordinates of that key point as a tuple in the points list. Otherwise, store null for that key point.

Step 12: Display the image with key points plotted on it.

Step 13: Draw the skeleton based on the pose pairs and key points detected.

Step 14: Display the skeleton image.

Step 15: Convert the key points list into a numpy array and form skeleton data from it.

Step 16: Extract the features head reference, pose2angles, normalization from numpy array.

Step 17: Load the action classifier model into the memory and input features to the model.

Step 18: Predict the action based on the features.

Step 19: If predicted action is in the list, display the image along with the predicted action on the image. Otherwise, display unauthorized action on the image.

22.4.3 POSE ESTIMATION

Pose estimation means detecting the key points location that describes an object. Here, the object is human. To estimate the pose of a person, it is mandatory to identify and localize the major joints/parts (like shoulders, knees, wrists etc.) of the body. To estimate the pose of a person, we can make use of the deep-learning-based Caffe model and OpenCV techniques.

22.4.4 PRE-PROCESSING

For pose estimation of a person, joints are considered key points and bones as connecting lines. The system will first detect the key points and then all these key points are joined to form a skeleton. This completes the pose estimation.

The Caffe model that is trained on COCO dataset is used to estimate the pose. This model will produce 18 key points. The 18 key points are as follows:

Nose – 0, Neck – 1, Right shoulder – 2, Right elbow – 3, Right wrist – 4, Left shoulder – 5, Left elbow – 6, Left wrist – 7, Right hip – 8, Right knee – 9, Right ankle – 10, Left hip – 11, Left knee – 12, Left ankle – 13, Right eye – 14, Left eye – 15, Right ear – 16, Left ear – 17.

After the confirmation of a person in the image, we load the Caffe model into the memory. Input for this network should be in the Caffe blob format. So, convert the input image, which is in OpenCV format, into that format using the blobFromImage() method of cv2 and pass the image to network.

22.4.5 KEY POINT DETECTION AND DRAWING THE SKELETON

After the image is passed to the model, key points have to be identified. This is achieved by calling the forward () method of the network. This method returns a 4D matrix as output. The four dimensions of this matrix are image ID, index of key points, height and width of image. The 4D matrix is the confidence map of all key points, and global maxima of every Key point are obtained, which gives the information about key point presence. Then we will check whether each key point is present or not, and all the detected key points are marked on the image along with their index values. The image after key points pointing will be like Nose, 1 – Neck, 2 – RShoulder, 3 – RElbow, 4 – RWrist, 5 – LShoulder, 6 – LElbow, 7 – LWrist, 8 – RHip, 9 – RKnee, 10 – RAnkle, 11 – LHip, 12 – LKnee, 13 – LAnkle, 14 – REye, 15 – LEye, 16 – REar and 17 – LEar.

Ather the identification of the key points, as we already know the indices and positions of key points, all the possible pairs for that image are joined to form a skeleton. The possible pairs for the 18 key points are as follows:

[Nose, Neck], [Neck, Right Shoulder], [Right Shoulder, Right Elbow], [Right Elbow, Right Wrist], [Neck, Left Shoulder], [Left Shoulder, Left Elbow], [Left Elbow, Left Wrist], [Neck, Right Hip], [Right Hip, Right Knee], [Right Knee, Right Ankle], [Neck, Left Hip], [Left Hip, Left Knee], [Left Knee, Left Ankle], [Right Ear, Right Eye], [Right Eye, Nose], [Left Ear, Left Eye] and [Left Eye, Nose].

To identify the activity, we have to collect data from the skeleton. The data is nothing but the position of each key point, i.e., x and y coordinates of each key point and score of each key point. By using this data, required features are extracted and then the classification of activity is done. In order to train our model to classify the activity, we have to form the dataset using this data. This dataset in csv format is given as input to train the model. The dataset, which is used to train the model for action classification, is downloaded from GitHub. To train the model, 3916 training images are collected. Each image has a single person performing any of the five activities. Among 3916 images, 711 are squat, 907 are stand, 583 are punch, 784 are kick and 931 are wave images. For all these images, skeletons are drawn, and the required data is extracted. This dataset has two types of data, Skeleton_filtered data and skeleton_raw data. Raw data contains of original data, and filtered data contains data without the data of the skeletons whose pose is incomplete, and these skeleton data is eliminated. Size of raw data is 2.44 MB, and filtered data is 2.05 MB. The below gives the sample of dataset used to train the model.

By using the data obtained from the skeleton, three features are extracted to classify the activity, and the data is given as the input to the neural network. The three features are as follows:

Head reference: All joint positions are converted to the x-y coordinates relative to the head joint. This feature represents the relative position of other key points to the head key points.

Pose to angle: The 18 joint positions are converted to 8 joint angles. They are left knee, right knee, lefts shoulder, right shoulder, left elbow, right elbow, left hip and right hip. This feature represents the angle between joints, which helps a lot to classify the activity. During this feature extraction, joint angles for elbow, hip, knee and shoulder are calculated.

Normalization: All joint positions are converted to x-y coordinates relative to the skeleton bounding box. This feature is used for best result and robustness. During this feature extraction, original data is separated into x and y lists. Then unwanted data (undetected data) is removed from the lists. Then the remaining data is normalized according to the bounding box of skeleton.

22.5   RESULTS AND DISCUSSION

In this case, the input image is given on the right side of the above image. As the image does not have any person in it, no face is identified, and hence, there is no activity being performed in that image. As there is no face identified in the image, the system had not proceeded to pose estimation. Figures 22.1, 22.2 and 22.3 are customized datasets created and taken using camera. Figures 22.4 and 22.5 are taken from INRIA Person dataset and CUHK01 (CUHK Person Re-Identification). Both are public datasets.

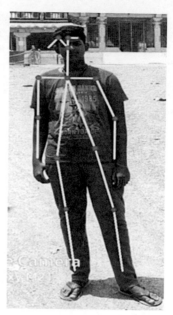

FIGURE 22.1   Illustration of key points and skeleton of a person.

FIGURE 22.2   Stand action. Face, key points detection, skeleton and standing activity detection.

FIGURE 22.3   Punch action. Face, key points, skeleton and punch activity detection.

FIGURE 22.4   Squat action. Face, key points, skeleton and squat activity detection.

FIGURE 22.5   Wave action. Face, key points, skeleton and wave activity detection.

22.6   CONCLUSION

In this chapter, a system is developed, which accepts the image as input. First, the system identifies the presence of a person in the image by face detection using the Haar-Cascade algorithm. If the presence is confirmed, then it will detect all the key points, i.e., body joints of that person and plots them on the image. These key points are joined as per the pairs, which results in the skeleton. This completes the pose estimation. From this skeleton, all the required details like x-y coordinates of the key points and their scores are extracted. By using this data, all the required features are extracted, which are passed to the activity classification model. This model will predict the activity of that person. Thus, activity recognition is done. This system can be used for smart homes, health-care monitoring, sports, security and surveillance, human-computer interaction, virtual reality, robotics, annotating images, searching an image database, searching images based on action queries, frame tagging etc.

REFERENCES

1. Abhay Gupta, Kshama Gupta, Kuldeep Gupta, Kapil Gupta, "Human Activity Recognition Using Pose Estimation and Machine Learning Algorithm," ISIC'21: International Semantic Intelligence Conference, February 25–27, 2021, New Delhi, India.
2. Deeptha Girish, Vineeta Singh, Anca Ralescu, "Understanding action recognition in still images," IEEE Explorer, DOI: 10.1109/CVPRW50498.2020.00193, July 28, 2020.
3. Girija Shankar Behera, "Face Detection with Haar Cascade," towardsdatascience.com, 2018.

4. Vikas Gupta," Deep Learning based Human Pose Estimation using OpenCV," learnopencv.com, 2019.
5. Majd Latah, "Human action recognition using support vector machines and 3D convolutional neural networks," International Journal of Advances in Intelligent Informatics, Vol 3, No. 1, pp. 47–55, March 2017.
6. Dekucheng, "Skeleton based human action recognition," github, 2018.
7. Tasweer Ahmad, Huiyun Mao, Luojun Lin, Guozhi Tang, "Action Recognition using Attention-Joints Graph Convolutional Neural Networks," Chinese Scholarship Council, 2019.
8. Xu Weiyao, Wu Muqing, Zhao Min, Liu Yifeng, Lv Bo, Xia Ting, "Human Action Recognition using Multilevel depth motion maps," 111 project under Grant B17007, 2015.
9. Sijie Yan, Yuanjun Xiong, Dahua Lin, "Spatial Temporal Graph Convolutional Networks for Skeleton-based Action Recognition," Association for the Advancement of Artificial Intelligence, 2019.

23 Heartbeat-Based Failure Detector of Perfect P Class for Synchronous Hierarchical Distributed Systems

Bhavana Chaurasia and Anshul Verma
Banaras Hindu University
Varanasi, India

Pradeepika Verma
Indian Institute of Technology
Patna, India

CONTENTS

23.1 INTRODUCTION

Nowadays, distributed systems are present as an essential piece in the real-world scenario. A distributed system is a setup of interconnected devices and application software that communicate to each other for the accomplishment of a particular job.

DOI: 10.1201/9781003320340-23

293

TABLE 23.1

Classes of Failure Detectors

Completeness	Accuracy			
	Strong	**Weak**	**Eventual Strong**	**Eventual Weak**
Strong	Perfect P	Strong S	Eventually Perfect $\Diamond$P	Eventually Strong $\Diamond$S
Weak	Quasi-Perfect Q	Weak W	Eventually Quasi-Perfect $\Diamond$Q	Eventually Weak $\Diamond$W

It performs from simple to highly specific jobs for different applications, such as banking, healthcare, transportation, blockchain, air traffic control, and many more. In order to provide a reliable and fault-free environment, the concept of failure detectors in distributed systems was introduced by Chandra and Toueg in 1991 [1]. A failure detector runs at every node or process and detects the failure as well as monitors the functioning state of the process. The failure detectors are unreliable in nature so that the information regarding the operational status of a process provided by two failure detectors may vary at different processes [2]. In this scenario, the quality of failure detectors is evaluated with the help of two abstract properties: completeness and accuracy, which are briefly discussed in Table 23.1 [1].

Failure detectors are flexible and inexpensive in nature; due to this, they can be easily implemented as a module at every node or process in distributed systems. Polling and heartbeat are the two main methods used by failure detectors that observe the functional state of other processes. Polling is a pull or query/reply-based method in which each process q sends a query message "Are you alive?" to its neighbor processes p at a predefined time interval, and each process p sends a reply message "I am alive" to process q if it is working fine [3, 4], whereas heartbeat method is quite different from the polling method. In heartbeat, every process q sends a heartbeat message that "I am alive" to all its neighboring processes at a predefined time-interval. Due to this, the heartbeat method is also known as a push-based method. When a process does not receive a heartbeat message from its neighbor process within a predefined time, this neighbor process is declared as faulty [5, 6]. The information provided by failure detectors is binary in nature means that it may be trust based or suspicion based [7, 8].

Distributed systems are classified in two aspects: topology and time as shown in Figure 23.1 [9]. The topological aspect is determined by the physical organization of nodes, whereas the time aspect is determined by the event's completion time bound, which is further classified as synchronous, asynchronous, and partially synchronous systems. The time aspect is embedded in two-time attributes, the first is the message transmission time between two processes and the second is the process execution time to execute a task [2].

In synchronous systems, processes communicate as well as execute within defined lower and upper time-bound [10]. While there is no time-bound for message transmission as well as process execution in asynchronous systems [7], partially synchronous systems are the combination of synchronous and asynchronous systems; it has both systems properties [11–13].

Failure detectors for fully connected mesh topology are reviewed in the literature. These are designed for synchronous, asynchronous, or partially synchronous

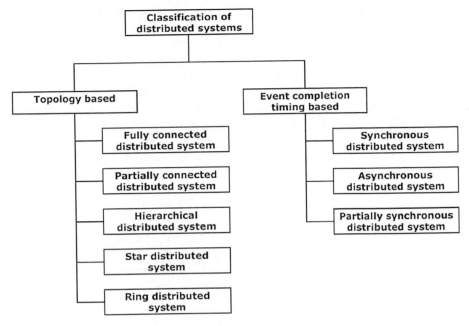

FIGURE 23.1 Taxonomy of distributed systems.

systems that provide information regarding the operational status of other processes to each process in the system. When these kinds of failure detectors are applied to hierarchical arrangement-based real-time applications, they cause unnecessary complex computation and unnecessary communication overhead. Cable TV networks, DNS (domain name server) systems, NTP (network time protocol) systems, wireless networks for military, and multi-agent-based train control systems [14–17] are examples of hierarchical arrangement-based distributed systems. In hierarchical arrangement-based systems, a parent process is only responsible to maintain the information regarding the operational status of all its children processes in the hierarchy.

The majority of available failure detectors follow the fully connected mesh topology that provides the information regarding the operational status of all processes in the network to each process. Dissemination of the operational status of all processes in the network generates message transmission overhead, and each process is not interested in knowing the status of all other processes in hierarchical networks. To overcome this scenario, a new suspicion-based failure detector algorithm was proposed in [9] for synchronous hierarchy-based systems. This Perfect P class failure detector refers to a polling approach and can detect crash failures, crash-recovery failures, omission failures, link failures, and timing failures. The authors also proposed two suspicion-based failure detector algorithms of Strong S and Perfect P classes. These algorithms were implemented for time-synchronous hierarchical arrangement-based distributed systems. The Strong S class failure detector algorithm efficiently detects a permanent crash failure, omission failure, link failure, and timing failure, whereas the Perfect P class failure detector algorithm proficiently detects crash failures, crash-recovery failures, omission failures, link failures, and timing failures for time-synchronous hierarchical arrangement-based systems [18].

The existing failure detectors for hierarchical distributed systems only detect crash failures, crash-recovery failures, omission failures, link failures, and timing failures. This chapter presents a suspicion-based failure detector algorithm that satisfies the strong completeness and strong accuracy properties of the Perfect P class. This follows the heartbeat approach for monitoring the processes in the hierarchical network and can detect crash failures, crash-recovery failures, omission failures, link failures, and timing failures. The organization of the chapter is as follows: Section 23.2 discusses the related works; Section 23.3 describes basic terminologies related to failure detectors; Section 23.4 discusses the detailed implementation of the proposed failure detector algorithm, and its correctness proof is presented in Section 23.5; Section 23.6 concludes the chapter.

23.2   RELATED WORKS

The theoretical sight of failure detectors was firstly presented by Chandra and Toueg in 1991 to solve the problems like consensus, atomic broadcast, reliable broadcast, and many more in asynchronous distributed systems [1]. In distributed systems, processes communicate and collaborate with each other through the massage passing. Therefore, synchronization and failure detection are the fundamental issues that must be resolved [19]. The implementation of failure detectors depends on the system types, topological aspects, and failure types. The non-identical distributed systems have different failure detection algorithms that are analyzed in the literature for synchronous, asynchronous, and partially synchronous systems. Majority of failure detectors work in either fully connected or partially connected environments.

The theory of unreliable failure detectors is proposed in [7] that can solve the problem of consensus with crash failure models in asynchronous systems. In this work, suspicion-based unreliable failure detectors are discussed, which deal with crash failures in asynchronous systems. This failure detector follows the polling approach for monitoring the processes. The quality and reliability of unreliable failure detectors are measured through the completeness and accuracy properties. They are classified into eight classes in terms of completeness and accuracy properties. The authors verified that unreliable failure detectors solve the problem of consensus and atomic broadcasts.

An advanced version of the failure detector algorithm presented in [7] is proposed in [4] that follows a pull-based approach for monitoring and detecting crash failures in partially synchronous systems. In this scenario, processes are arranged under a logical ring topology through which they communicate and exchange messages periodically with the most linear number of messages. It considers that most of the processes are correct, connected using reliable links and crash failures never recover, whereas such considerations are not possible in real networks.

A heartbeat failure detector is proposed in [5], which is a non-suspicion-based algorithm and achieves reliable communication with quiescent algorithms. It detects crash failures as well as link failures and also deals with the issues like consensus, k-set agreement, atomic broadcast, and atomic commitment. It represents a matrix of suspected processes as an output that shows a list of correct and faulty processes. Basically, this algorithm is compatible with asynchronous systems so it can't applicable to synchronous systems because of the unavailability of the time-out concept.

A weakest failure detector concept that solves the consensus problem in an asynchronous system environment, which is an enhancement of failure detector Ω [20], is presented in [21]. This proposed algorithm efficiently detects the crash-stop and permanent omission failures with the consideration of the majority of correct processes. This failure detector is specially designed for asynchronous systems because no time-bound is considered. So, it is inappropriate for synchronous as well as partially synchronous environments.

The conceptual view of the timed asynchronous distributed system model is proposed in [22] with a brief explanation of why problems like consensus and leader election are not implemented in a purely asynchronous environment. This model shows the large-scale calculation of actual messages, process scheduling latency, and hardware clock drifts. In [23], authors proposed the perfect failure detectors for the timed asynchronous systems that deal with the crash failures. The implementation of a perfect failure detector is discussed for the specified system with the assumptions that each system can evaluate time intervals with a known maximum error, and in each system, there is a hardware watchdog that crashes the system until the watchdog is updated in a periodic manner.

A suspicion-based partially perfect failure detector for the partitioned (partially) synchronous systems is developed in [24], which follows a polling-based monitoring approach. Some other properties like strong partition synchrony and timeliness oracle were addressed for the implementation of failure detector of Perfect P class. Since the proposed algorithm is designed for fully connected partially synchronous systems, it can't be directly applied to time-synchronous and synchronous hierarchical systems.

A failure detector of the eventual Perfect $\Diamond\neg P$ class is implemented for the general omission failure model that is communication efficient and detects crash failures and message omission failures [6]. Heartbeat process monitoring approach is used by this algorithm in fully connected topological arrangement in a partially synchronous environment. A matrix of correct and faulty processes is produced as an output. Only a linear number of links are exercised for exchanging messages, which shows the communication efficiency of this technique. This algorithm is specially developed for fully connected partially synchronous systems.

Two new failure detector classes, $H\Omega$ and $H\Sigma$, are proposed in [25] for homonymous distributed systems. These classes are equivalent to the weakest failure detector classes, Ω and Σ. Based on these classes, two trust-based failure detector algorithms have been implemented that deal with crash failure and consensus problems in homonymous systems with the consideration of majority of correct processes. These algorithms follow the pull-based approach for monitoring the processes. These algorithms are suitable for the asynchronous environment. So, it can't be easily implemented in a synchronous and partially synchronous environment as well.

To resolve the non-blocking atomic commitment problem in a crash-prone asynchronous system, a suspicion-based M* failure detector is implemented in [26]. This failure detector algorithm lies between the eventual Perfect $\Diamond P$ class and the Perfect P class. It follows the push-based (heartbeat) approach for monitoring the processes with the consideration that most processes are non-faulty. It is basically designed for asynchronous systems so that it cannot be applied in a synchronous environment.

A suspicion-based failure detector algorithm of the Perfect P class is implemented in [9] for hierarchical synchronous systems. This failure detector algorithm follows the pull-based approach for failure monitoring and deals with crash failures, crash-recovery failures, link failures, timing failures, and message omission failures. Processes are connected under the hierarchical arrangement. Parent processes are responsible to maintain the status of only their child processes so that there are no extra message overheads. This failure detection algorithm is developed for a multi-agent communication-based train control system [14–17, 27], which is basically a time-synchronous hierarchical distributed system.

Similarly, a suspicion-based failure detector of the Strong S class is developed for the timed synchronous distributed systems in [18]. The setup of the proposed system model is arranged under the hierarchical topology. The Strong S class failure detector algorithm is explored failures like permanent crash failures, omission failures, and link failures, but due to latency, it is unable to identify timing failures and crash-recovery failures. A review of various failure detection algorithms for distributed systems is given in [28].

From the literature survey, it is concluded that only a few of the above research-ers prioritized the implementation of failure detector algorithms for the hierarchical topology-based synchronous networks. However, to the best of our knowledge, none of the researchers have developed a heartbeat-based failure detection algorithm for hierarchical synchronous distributed systems.

23.3   PRELIMINARIES

23.3.1   SYSTEM MODEL

The system model is a process-oriented representation of a system with its charac-teristics, hypothesis, and limitations for which the failure detector algorithm is being developed. While developing a failure detector algorithm, it is important to define a system model with its all aspects. Every system needs its own failure detector algorithm because of the diversities in the specification and characteristics of the systems. It is difficult to develop an efficient generalized failure detector algorithm that is compatible with all types of system models, but if we make some changes in the existing algorithm, then it can be applied to other systems. An algorithm is said to be compatible with a real-life system when the characteristics of system model of the algorithm match with the properties of the real-life system. In this section, the system model is discussed for the *hierarchical synchronous distributed systems* for which the failure detection algorithm has to be developed.

23.3.2   PROCESSES

In this system, every process runs the same failure detector algorithm indepen-dently through which it monitors and maintains the operational states of all other processes. The system is composed as a finite set of n processes represented by Π, where $\Pi = \{P_1, P_2, P_3 \ldots P_n\}$. Processes are connected in a hierarchical manner and interacted through pairwise bidirectional communication channels. A parent process and its children processes are denoted by P_m and P_mC_n respectively. In this hierarchical system, processes can be considered correct or faulty as per their specifications.

Correct processes: If a process properly responds or communicates to its parent process and does not experience any failure during execution, then the process is labeled as a correct process.

Faulty processes: If a process does not respond to its parent process on time, or if there is any type of delay in exchanging messages, or a correct process that is not connected with the root process due to any type of failure between the path such as intermediate process or link failure.

23.3.3 COMMUNICATION LINKS

In this hierarchical topological network, parent and its children process are connected through a single directional unreliable link in which only children process can send their heartbeats and messages to the parent process. Parent process does not need to communicate to its children process. While transmitting messages, links can delay the transmission or can drop messages. Therefore, the links are called unreliable.

23.3.4 EVENT GENERATION

The system pursues both time-driven as well as event-driven approaches. As a time-driven approach, a process sends a heartbeat message "I-am-alive" to its parent process in a periodic manner, and a parent process monitors heartbeat messages of its children process to know their current operational state. As an event-driven approach, when a new faulty process is detected or a faulty process is recovered, all the parent processes up in the hierarchy update their list of faulty processes.

23.3.5 TIME AND TIMING MODELS

A local clock is present in each process that helps to synchronize the execution of sub-processes within the process. Message transmission as well as process execution has a time-bound in synchronous systems.

23.3.6 FAILURES MODELS

Many types of failures might occur in a distributed system like byzantine failures, crash failures, crash-recovery failures, omission failures, link failures, and timing failures (Figure 23.2) [2]. The solution of these concerning problems is divided into two classes. The first one belongs to byzantine failures, and the second one belongs to remaining failures. While dealing with byzantine failures, a component of a system may suffer with an arbitrary type of failures, i.e., the process generates

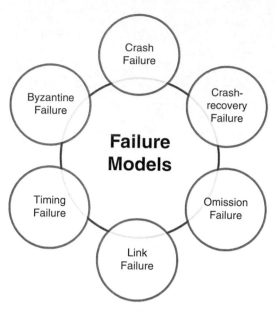

FIGURE 23.2   Failure models including different types.

inappropriate or inconsistent results. But while dealing with other types of failures in a system, a process may crash or may omit messages or may stop responding. The proposed failure detector algorithm detects the all types of failures occurred during the execution of processes in the system except byzantine failure.

- **Crash failure:** In this type of failure, a process may stop responding or may stop executing the sending and receiving the messages. Crashes are persistent and hard to recover. So that, it is also be known as crash-prone or crash-stop failures.
- **Crash-recovery failure:** In this type of failure, a process may stop executing and after sometime may recover itself.
- **Omission failure:** This kind of failure happens because of buffer overflow. Messages are dropped out in a process during the transmission, not in the communication link. These types of failures are further classified into two types: send-omission failure and receive-omission failure. If a message is sent but never reaches the outgoing link, then this type of failure is defined as send-omission; however, if the message is received but never executed at the destination, then this type of failure is known as received-omission. Crash failure, send-omission failure and received omission failure are altogether referred as general-omission failure. This proposed failure detector algorithm handles both permanent as well as transient omission failures.
- **Link failure:** This kind of failure happens due to link break-down or congestion. In this scenario, a link is not able to transmit a message between two processes.

- **Timing failure:** If an event execution or a message transmission is not performed within a time-bound period, then this failure is considered a timing failure.
- **Byzantine failure:** It is an arbitrary type of failure into which an active process seems like faulty but actually not faulty or may respond slowly or a link may transmit an arbitrary message in place of assigned message. Therefore, it is difficult to identify this type of failure.

23.4 FAILURE DETECTOR

A failure detector is capable to provide information about the operational state of other processes at each process. Every process has a copy of the same failure detector algorithm that is executed, and it creates a health monitoring tree known as HMT [9]. HMT of a process shows subtrees with all its children process. Failure detector monitors child processes and stores the information referring to their operational states. The operational states of whole system are demonstrated with the help of global HMT. The proposed failure detector algorithm of Perfect P class has strong completeness and strong accuracy properties that are described below (referring to hierarchical model):

- **Strong completeness:** In upward hierarchy, all parent processes will eventually detect all the faulty processes.
- **Strong accuracy:** Any correct process never suspects a correct process.

23.4.1 FAILURE DETECTION ALGORITHM

The proposed failure detector algorithm follows a heartbeat-based monitoring approach. In this procedure, children process continuously sends an "I-am-alive" message to parent process to inform that they are alive. The received heartbeat message contains faulty process information $F_{m,n}$ with message identity $MID_{m,n}$. Processes received faulty process information, and this information helps to create their respective HMTs. $MID_{m,n}$ refers to the message identity of the received heartbeat message within a given time period. If a heartbeat message is not received on time or received beyond the given time-bound, or if the process received an arbitrary message in place of the assigned "I-am-alive" message, then the monitored process is considered faulty and this message identity is stored in the faulty process list F_m. Table 23.2 shows the list of variables with their explanation are being used in this algorithm.

There are five functions into this failure detection algorithm (refer Algorithm 1). Algorithm starts from function 1, failure detector of child process P_mC_n periodically sends a heartbeat message "I-am-alive" to its parent process P_m (line 10). The time-bound is defined (line 9) for this corresponding transmission process. Where T( ) represents the current time of child process, OutT and InT represent the upper time-bound of incoming and outgoing links for heartbeat message transmission, and α is a safety margin that signifies the total of time taken to accomplish Function 5 and permissible clock skew between two processes. The sequence number $SID_{m,n}$ of next heartbeat message sent to parent process P_m is increased by 1 (line 11).

TABLE 23.2

Variables and Descriptions Used in the Algorithm

Variables	Description
HMT_{root}	Pointer of root process node in the hierarchy
P_m	A parent root process
$P_m C_n$	A child process of P_m
$P_p C_q$	A recovered process
$SID_{m,n}$	Sequence number of send heartbeat message to P_m
$RID_{m,n}$	Sequence number of received heartbeat message from $P_m C_n$
$MID_{m,n}$	Sequence number of heartbeat message from $P_m C_n$
$M[\ ]$	An array of heartbeat message
F_m	Faulty process list of P_m
$F_{m,n}$	Faulty process list of $P_m C_n$
f_m	A process in the list of $F_{m,n}$
$Tout_{m,n}$	Timeout of heartbeat message from $P_m C_n$
CPT	Pointer of a recovered process node in HMT
FPT	Pointer of a faulty process node in HMT

Function 2 is accomplished after receiving heartbeat message from the child process $P_m C_n$. Parent process P_m examines that if the expected heartbeat messages are received within time-bound and also investigates that the process must receive the expected message (line 15). After this, parent process P_m investigates about child process $P_m C_n$ to know whether it was earlier a faulty process or not (line 16). If this condition is true, then $P_m C_n$ is eliminated from F_m (line 17). According to the output, HMT is updated (line 19), because this process is not faulty now, a message is sent to parent process P_m that this $P_m C_n$ is a correct process and remove this process from the faulty process list (line 20). A list of faulty processes $F_{m,n}$ is sent by $P_m C_n$ to parent process P_m. P_m integrates $F_{m,n}$ with F_m (line 22) to include the faulty processes identified by $P_m C_n$. The time-bound for receiving heartbeat message from $P_m C_n$ is reset (line 23). The Sequence number $RID_{m,n}$ of next heartbeat message from $P_m C_n$ is increased by 1 (line 24). According to updated F_m, Parent P_m updates its HMT (line 25–28). If heartbeat message "I-am-alive" is received in the inappropriate sequence or after the given time-bound, then parent P_m simply ignores this message.

Function 3 is executed when the heartbeat message is not received from $P_m C_n$ within given time-bound. If $P_m C_n$ was not a faulty process and time-bound expires before receiving message (line 33, 34), P_m considers this process as a faulty and updates F_m (line 35) based on this the HMT is updated (line 37, 38). The sequence number $RID_{m,n}$ of next heartbeat message from $P_m C_n$ is also increased by 1 (line 36). If $P_m C_n$ already belongs to faulty process list, then only the sequence number of next heartbeat message is increased by 1 (line 40).

Function 4 is based on the process recovery that is mandatory to update F_m at all parent processes in the hierarchy. When P_m receives message from child process $P_m C_n$ regarding the elimination of faulty process $P_p C_q$ from faulty list F_m, P_m

eliminates P_pC_q from F_m (line 47) and updates the corresponding HMT (line 48, 49). This message is also forwarded to its parent process by P_m (line 50).

Function 5 is executed when a parent process P_m receives a heartbeat message from its child process P_mC_n (line 54). This heartbeat message is stored into an array M[] with its corresponding $MID_{m,n}$ (line 55). $MID_{m,n}$ is heartbeat message identity for the corresponding $SID_{m,n}$.

```
Algorithm: Failure detector algorithm of Perfect P class.
Initialization
 1.HMT_root = Root_Process_Address_of_HMT
 2.for ∀ P_mC_n, P_m do
 3.     SID_m,n = 1
 4.     RID_m,n = 1
 5.     M[ ]← MID_m,n
 6.end
 7.Function 1: Send heartbeat message to parent process
   periodically after a fixed time interval
 8.for ∀ P_mC_n ∈ P_m,
 9.     Tout_m,n = T( ) + OutT + InT + α
10.     Send SID_m,n + "I-am-alive" to P_m
11.     SID_m,n + +
12.end
13.Function 2: Receive heartbeat from child process
14. when MID_m,n + "I-am-alive" + F_m,n is received from P_mC_n, P_m do
15. if((Tout_m,n≥T( ))∧(MID_m,n = RID_m,n)∧(M[ ]=="I-am-alive"))
16.        if(P_mC_n ∈ F_m)
17.           F_m = F_m∩P_mC_n
18.           CPT = search(P_mC_n, HMT_root, "correct")
19.           updateHMT (CPT, "correct")
20.           sendRemoveCorrect(P_mC_n)toparentprocessof P_m
21.        endif
22.           F_m = F_mUF_m,n
23.           Tout_m,n = ∞
24.           RID_m,n + 1
25.           for ∀ f_m ∈ F_m,n do
26.              FPT = search(f_m, HMT_root, "faulty")
27.              updateHMT (FPT, "faulty")
28.           end
29.     endif
30.end
31.Function 3: Did not receive heartbeat messages from child
   process
32.when MID_m,n +"I-am-alive"+ F_m,n is not received from P_mC_n
   within Tout_m,n, P_m do
33.        if(Tout_m,n < T( ))
34.           if(P_mC_n ∉ F_m)
35.              F_m = F_m ∪ P_mC_n
36.              RID_m,n + 1
37.              FPT = search(P_mC_n, HMT_root, "faulty")
38.              updateHMT(FPT, "faulty")
```

```
39.            else
40.                RID_{m,n} + 1
41.            endif
42.        endif
43.end
44.Function 4: Received heartbeat message from child processes
   for removing correct process from faulty process list.
45.whenRemoveCorrect(P_pC_q) is received from P_mC_n, P_m do
46.        if(P_pC_q ∈ F_m)
47.            F_m = F_m ∩ P_pC_q
48.            CPT = search(P_pC_q, HMT_root, "correct")
49.            updateHMT(CPT, "correct")
50.            sendRemoveCorrect(P_pC_q)to parent process of P_m
51.        endif
52.end.
53.Function 5: Received heartbeat message form child process
54.when MID_{m,n} + "I-am-alive" is received from P_mC_n, P_m do
55.    M[ ] ← MID_{m,n} + "I-am-alive"
56.end
```

While executing functions 2, 3 and 4 each time, F_m (lines 17, 22, 35, and 47) and its corresponding HMT is updated. F_m and its corresponding HMT are always updated whenever a process became faulty or a process is recovered. Referencing Figure 23.3, if process P_m becomes faulty, then it's all child processes also became faulty for Z [9]. There are two steps to update HMT. First step, search the address of corresponding child process on HMT for which changes are required. Second step, update the

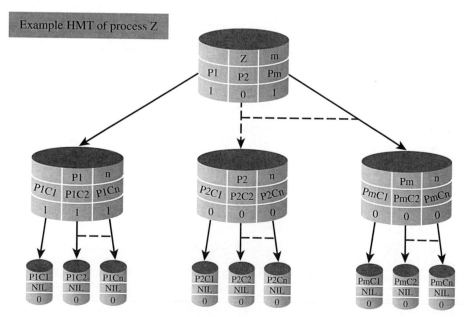

FIGURE 23.3   Example HMT of process Z.

position of all child processes including that corresponding process according to the operation performed (correct or faulty). The pseudo-code of algorithm that manages HMT is referenced from Algorithm 2 of [9]. This pseudo-code has two recursive processes: search and update HMT. In search process, it takes input like process name, HMT root address and operation then searches that specific process and gives its parent process address as an output. In update HMT process, it contains a process address and operation as input then updates the status of all its child processes according to the operation.

23.5 CORRECTNESS PROOF

In this section, the strong completeness and strong accuracy properties of the proposed failure detector algorithm of Perfect P class are examined. Additionally, the effectiveness of the algorithm is analyzed in terms of its ability to detect permanent crash failure, crash-recovery failure, omission failure, link failure, and timing failure as discussed in Section 23.3.

Theorem 1

The proposed failure detector satisfies the strong completeness property in which every faulty process (according to hierarchical system model) will eventually be detected by all its parent processes up in the hierarchy.

PROOF

A child process P_mC_n sends heartbeat message "I-am-alive" to its parent process P_m at time t (function 1). If child process P_mC_n fails, there may be two situations. First, if P_mC_n fails before sending heartbeat message "I-am-alive", then parent process P_m will detect it after time-bound (t+OutT+InT+α) due to not receiving heartbeat within the time-bound (function 3). Second, if P_mC_n fails after sending heartbeat message and message received by P_m within (t+OutT+InT+α), P_m does not have any idea regarding this failure and still considers the child process healthy. Conversely, this failure is detected in the next time slots (t'+OutT+InT+α). A parent process identified its faulty child process within almost two time slots. In subsequent time slot, P_m sends identified faulty process list F_m to its parent process (function 2). Further, information regarding faulty process is passed out to its parent processes at the next level up in the hierarchy in every time slot and the corresponding HMTs are revised accordingly. As a result, the information of all faulty children process is revised in HMT of parent processes, and this step verifies the strong completeness property. Please note that a subtree of correct processes may be disconnected in the hierarchical network due to crash of internal processes. In this case, all the correct processes of this disconnected subtree will be treated as faulty processes. Because, as per the definition of faulty process of hierarchical model, the inefficiency of communication with the root process makes a correct process as faulty.

Theorem 2

This proposed failure detector algorithm satisfies strong accuracy property. According to this property, a correct process is never suspected by any correct process.

PROOF

If a child process P_mC_n is correct, then it continuously sends heartbeat message "I-am-alive" to its parent process P_m within time-bound (t+OutT+InT+α) (function 1). Consequently, the condition of (t+OutT+InT+α) < T() is never satisfied (line 33), and parent process P_m does not suspect P_mC_n because it does not execute Function 3. The condition of $P_mC_n \in F_m$ of function 2 (line 16) would be true if P_mC_n has a faulty record in past. In this case, the process P_mC_n will be eliminated from the list of faulty process F_m by executing line 17 of function 2. Subsequently, execution of lines 18 and 19 of function 2 updates the status of this process as well as all its children process in HMT of parent process P_m. A message request RemoveCorrect (P_mC_n) is also sent to the parent processes of process P_m regarding the elimination of correct process P_mC_n from the faulty process list (line 20). After receiving this message, a faulty process P_pC_q is removed from the list by the parent process and then HMT is updated. Similarly, this message is further sent to the parent process and HMT is updated (function 4). Hence, a correct process is never suspected by any correct process eventually.

Theorem 3

The proposed failure detector algorithm identifies crash failure, crash-recovery failure, omission failure, link failure, and timing failure.

PROOF

When P_m does not receive heartbeat message "I-am-alive" from P_mC_n within the time-out (t+OutT+InT+α), it detects that the said process has been crashed (function 3).

There is a small difference between crash-recovery failure and crash failure is that a crashed process never recovers. When a crashed process recovers, it starts sending heartbeat message "I-am-alive" to its parent process. When a parent process P_m receives "I-am-alive" message from a recovered child process P_mC_n, P_m detects it by condition $P_mC_n \in F_m$ of function 2 (line 16). P_m eliminates P_mC_n from F_m and updates HMT accordingly and afterward sends this message to its parent to update F_m and HMT as described in the proof of Theorem 2.

Omission failure may occur at both parent P_m and child P_mC_n processes during message transmission between them. Due to any omission failure, whether it occurs on P_m or P_mC_n, P_m detects P_mC_n as a faulty process (function 3) because P_m did not receive heartbeat from P_mC_n. For example, in the case of send-omission at P_mC_n, P_mC_n sends heartbeat message "I-am-alive" to P_m but the message does not reach at the link, which means it does not reach at P_m; therefore, P_m is not able to receive heartbeat of P_mC_n and considers as faulty. In case of receive omission at P_m, heartbeat message "I-am-alive" reaches at P_m but it is not delivered to P_m, so that P_m considered P_mC_n as faulty.

Parent and its children process are connected through a single directional link in which only children process can send their heartbeats to the parent process. Parent process does not need to communicate to its children process. Children process periodically sends heartbeat messages to their parent processes. When the parent does not receive heartbeat message from a child process, the child process is considered faulty (function 3).

Timing failure happens when either a process execution or message transmission takes time beyond their corresponding allowable timeout. The timeout includes incoming and outgoing links' time-bound, and the event execution time-bound. A child process P_mC_n is detected as faulty when its parent process P_m does not receive its heartbeat message within the predefined time-bound (function 3).

23.6 CONCLUSION

A failure detector algorithm of Perfect P class is designed for the hierarchical synchronous distributed systems. It is a suspicion-based technique that follows the heartbeat monitoring approach to reduce the number of messages in the network. In comparison to the polling-based failure detection algorithm presented in [9] for hierarchical synchronous distributed systems, the proposed heartbeat-based algorithm reduces the number of messages sent for failure detection approximately 50% in same network scenario. The functional correctness of the algorithm is verified with the help of correctness proof with respect of strong completeness and strong accuracy that are the properties of Perfect P class. In future, such network- and application-specific failure detection algorithms can be developed for specialized mobile ad hoc networks (such as opportunistic networks and delay tolerant networks [29–34]) or IoT networks [35–37] those form a distributed system.

REFERENCES

1. Chandra, T. D., & Toueg, S. (1991, July). Unreliable failure detectors for asynchronous systems (preliminary version). In Proceedings of the Tenth Annual ACM Symposium on Principles of Distributed Computing, Montreal, Quebec, Canada, August 19–21 (pp. 325–340).
2. Rodríguez, R. C. (2011). Failure detectors and communication efficiency in the crash and general omision failure models (Doctoral dissertation, Universidad del País Vasco-Euskal Herriko Unibertsitatea).
3. Larrea, M., Arévalo, S., & Fernndez, A. (1999, September). Efficient algorithms to implement unreliable failure detectors in partially synchronous systems. In International Symposium on Distributed Computing, Berlin, Heidelberg (pp. 34–49). Springer.
4. Larrea, M., Fernández, A., & Arévalo, S. (2004). On the implementation of unreliable failure detectors in partially synchronous systems. IEEE Transactions on Computers, 53(7), 815–828.
5. Aguilera, M. K., Chen, W., & Toueg, S. (1997, September). Heartbeat: a timeout-free failure detector for quiescent reliable communication. In International Workshop on Distributed Algorithms, Berlin, Heidelberg (pp. 126–140). Springer.

6. Soraluze, I., Cortiñas, R., Lafuente, A., Larrea, M., & Freiling, F. (2011). Communication-efficient failure detection and consensus in omission environments. Information Processing Letters, 111(6), 262–268.

7. Chandra, T. D., & Toueg, S. (1996). Unreliable failure detectors for reliable distributed systems. Journal of the ACM (JACM), 43(2), 225–267.

8. Hayashibara, N., Defago, X., Yared, R., & Katayama, T. (2004, October). The/spl phi/ accrual failure detector. In Proceedings of the 23rd IEEE International Symposium on Reliable Distributed Systems, Florianopolis, Brazil (pp. 66–78). IEEE.

9. Verma, A., & Pattanaik, K. K. (2016). Failure Detector of Perfect P Class for Synchronous Hierarchical Distributed Systems. International Journal of Distributed Systems and Technologies (IJDST), 7(2), 57–74.

10. Hadzilacos, V., & Toueg, S. (1994). A Modular Approach to Fault-Tolerant Broadcasts and Related Problems. Cornell University, Ithaca, NY.

11. Dolev, D., Dwork, C., & Stockmeyer, L. (1987). On the minimal synchronism needed for distributed consensus. Journal of the ACM (JACM), 34(1), 77–97.

12. Dwork, C., Lynch, N., & Stockmeyer, L. (1988). Consensus in the presence of partial synchrony. Journal of the ACM (JACM), 35(2), 288–323.

13. Widder, J., & Schmid, U. (2009). The theta-model: achieving synchrony without clocks. Distributed Computing, 22(1), 29–47.

14. Verma, A., & Pattanaik, K. K. (2014). Mobile agent based train control system for mitigating meet conflict at turnout. Procedia Computer Science, 32, 317–324.

15. Verma, A., & Pattanaik, K. K. (2015). Multi-agent communication based train control system for Indian Railways: the structural design. Journal of Software, 10(3), 250–259.

16. Verma, A., & Pattanaik, K. K. (2015). Multi-agent communication-based train control system for Indian railways: the behavioural analysis. Journal of Modern Transportation, 23(4), 272–286.

17. Verma, A., Pattanaik, K. K., & Goel, P. P. (2014, April). Mobile agent based CBTC system with moving block signalling for Indian Railways. In Proceedings of the 2nd international conference on railway technology: Research, development and maintenance, Ajaccio, Corsica, paper, Stirlingshire, UK (Vol. 278, pp. 8–11). Civil-Comp Press.

18. Verma, A., Singh, M., & Pattanaik, K. K. (2019). Failure detectors of Strong S and Perfect P classes for time synchronous hierarchical distributed systems. In Applying Integration Techniques and Methods in Distributed Systems and Technologies (pp. 246–280). IGI Global, Hershey, PA.

19. Raynal, M. (2016, June). A look at basics of distributed computing. In 2016 IEEE 36th International Conference on Distributed Computing Systems (ICDCS), Nara, Japan (pp. 1–11). IEEE.

20. Deepak Chandra, T. (1996). The weakest failure detector for solving consensus. Journal of the ACM, 43(4), 685–722.

21. Delporte-Gallet, C., Fauconnier, H., Freiling, F. C., Penso, L. D., & Tielmann, A. (2007, September). From crash-stop to permanent omission: automatic transformation and weakest failure detectors. In International Symposium on Distributed Computing, Berlin, Heidelberg (pp. 165–178). Springer.

22. Cristian, F., & Fetzer, C. (1999). The timed asynchronous distributed system model. IEEE Transactions on Parallel and Distributed systems, 10(6), 642–657.

23. Fetzer, C. (2003). Perfect failure detection in timed asynchronous systems. IEEE Transactions on Computers, 52(2), 99–112.

24. De Araújo Macêdo, R. J., & Gorender, S. (2009, March). Perfect failure detection in the partitioned synchronous distributed system model. In 2009 International Conference on Availability, Reliability and Security, Fukuoka, Japan (pp. 273–280). IEEE.

25. Arevalo, S., Anta, A. F., Imbs, D., Jimenez, E., & Raynal, M. (2012). Failure detectors in homonymous distributed systems (with an application to consensus). In Proceedings of the 32nd International Conference on Distributed Computing Systems, Washington, DC, USA (pp. 275–284).

26. Park, S. H., Lee, J. Y., & Yu, S. C. (2013, April). Non-blocking atomic commitment algorithm in asynchronous distributed systems with unreliable failure detectors. In 2013 10th International Conference on Information Technology: New Generations, Las Vegas, NV, USA (pp. 33–38). IEEE.

27. Ghosh, C., Verma, A., & Verma, P. (2022). Real time fault detection in railway tracks using Fast Fourier Transformation and Discrete Wavelet Transformation. International Journal of Information Technology, 14(1), 31–40.

28. Chaurasia, B., & Verma, A. (2020). A comprehensive study on failure detectors of distributed systems. Journal of Scientific Research, 64(2), 250–260.

29. Verma, A., Singh, M., Pattanaik, K. K., & Singh, B. K. (2018). Future networks inspired by opportunistic networks. In Opportunistic Networks (pp. 230–246). Chapman and Hall/CRC, Boca Raton, FL.

30. Verma, A., & Pattanaik, K. K. (2017). Routing protocols in opportunistic networks. In Opportunistic Networking (pp. 123–166). CRC Press, Boca Raton, FL.

31. Verma, A., Pattanaik, K. K., & Ingavale, A. (2013). Context-based routing protocols for OppNets. In Routing in Opportunistic Networks (pp. 69–97). Springer, New York, NY.

32. Singh, M., Verma, P., & Verma, A. (2021). Security in opportunistic networks. In Opportunistic Networks (pp. 299–312). CRC Press, Boca Raton, FL.

33. Verma, A., & Srivastava, D. (2012). Integrated routing protocol for opportunistic networks. arXiv preprint arXiv:1204.1658.

34. Verma, A., Verma, P., Dhurandher, S. K., & Woungang, I. (Eds.). (2021). Opportunistic Networks: Fundamentals, Applications and Emerging Trends. CRC Press, Boca Raton, FL.

35. Verma, A., Verma, P., Farhaoui, Y., & Lv, Z. (Eds.). (2022). Emerging Real-World Applications of Internet of Things. CRC Press, Boca Raton, Florida.

36. Rudra, B., Verma, A., Verma, S., & Shrestha, B. (Eds.). (2022). Futuristic Research Trends and Applications of Internet of Things. CRC Press (Taylor and Francis), Boca Raton, FL.

37. Srivastava, S., Verma, A., & Verma, P. (2022). Fundamentals of internet of things. In Futuristic Research Trends and Applications of Internet of Things (pp. 1–30). CRC Press, Boca Raton, FL.

Index